THE POLITICS OF REFORM 1884

*Cambridge Studies in the History and
Theory of Politics*

EDITORS
MAURICE COWLING
G. R. ELTON
E. KEDOURIE
J. G. A. POCOCK
J. R. POLE
WALTER ULLMANN

For complete list of books in this series see page 282

THE POLITICS OF REFORM 1884

ANDREW JONES
Lecturer in History, University of Reading

CAMBRIDGE
AT THE UNIVERSITY PRESS
1972

Published by the Syndics of the Cambridge University Press
Bentley House, 200 Euston Road, London NW1 2DB
American Branch: 32 East 57th Street, New York, N.Y.10022

© Cambridge University Press 1972

Library of Congress Catalogue Card Number: 72–172832

ISBN: 0 521 08376 1

Printed in Great Britain
at the University Printing House, Cambridge
(Brooke Crutchley, University Printer)

CONTENTS

For the Absent and Afar

'I have always had a propensity to justify my action. Not to defend. To justify. Not to insist that I was right but simply to explain that there was no perverse intention, no secret scorn for the natural sensibilities of mankind at the bottom of my impulses. That kind of weakness is dangerous only so far that it exposes one to the risk of becoming a bore; for the world generally is not interested in the motives of any overt act but in its consequences. Man may smile and smile but he is not an investigating animal. He loves the obvious. He shrinks from explanations. Yet I will go on with mine.'

Joseph Conrad, Prefatory note (1920) to *The Secret Agent*

ACKNOWLEDGMENTS

IT WOULD be tedious to list the number of persons whom I have approached, inquiring as to the survival and whereabouts of the papers of a relative or forbear who flourished politically c. 1884; to those who replied with a sympathetic negative, I offer my thanks. Where fate has been kinder, and where I have trespassed on privacy, I gladly acknowledge the hospitality, tolerant humour and interest of Lord and Lady Ashbourne, the late Mr Randolph Churchill and Mr Andrew Kerr, the Earl of Elgin, Mrs Hubert Elliot, Viscount Harcourt, the Earl of Harrowby and Miss Pauline Adams (Archivist, Harrowby Mss. Trust), Lord St Oswald and Mr Geoffrey Beard (Archivist), Earl Spencer, and Mr and Mrs Samuel Whitbread. I am indebted to all other owners of manuscripts for permission to inspect and make quotation from collections: those not mentioned by name must not suppose me the less grateful. I have worked in a fair number of national, municipal and university libraries, public and county record offices. To the archivists and keepers, indeed to all who have carried volumes or tin boxes without complaint, I acknowledge my debt. For their patience and the trouble they have taken, I thank Mr G. E. V. Awdry (Librarian, National Liberal Club), Mrs E. A. Cooke (Librarian, Longleat), Dr L. A. Parker (Leicester County Archivist, at Belvoir), Mr Thomas Wragg (Librarian and Keeper, the Devonshire Collections), and Major T. L. Ingram (Archivist, Hickleton Mss.).

I should not have tracked down several collections had it not been for assistance provided by the secretaries and staff of the National Register of Archives, both in London and Edinburgh. Two others deserve my special gratitude: Mr S. C. McMenamin detailed all that might be of relevance in the Public Record Office of Northern Ireland, while Mr J. M. Collinson, the Leeds Archivist, directed me to the Ramsden Mss. It is pleasant also to recall that Mr A. B. Cooke, who has been working in adjacent fields, divulged the location of the Ashbourne and Churchill papers, and made available his transcript of the Charles Dalrymple diary for 1885.

ACKNOWLEDGMENTS

Research for the Ph.D. thesis from which this book emanates was supervised by Dr Henry Pelling. Doubtless had he himself tackled 1884–5, the product would have borne only the faintest resemblance to the present offering. To his catholicity this is, then, in some small way a tribute. It goes without saying that he has helped me rid the text of countless factual errors. Mr Maurice Cowling has read most chapters at first draft, the whole at a later stage, talked, encouraged and criticised freely. Had it not been for his study of 1867, the structure of the present work would have been much different. Dr Jonathan Steinberg, in a rigorous critique, did that which would strain the firmest friendship. He called for explicit prose wherever allusion made intolerable demands on a reader unversed in English politics of the 1880s; and he enjoined major revision. I have not gone perhaps more than a quarter of the way to meet him, which apology is a measure of the thanklessness of candour. I have profited too by lengthy conversation with and the comments of Dr Derek Beales, Mr Charles Crawley, Dr David Cuthbert, Professor John Vincent and Mr Allen Warren.

My final debts are corporate but far from impersonal: to the Governing Body of Trinity Hall, Cambridge (whither the dedication, had this book not been dedicated as it is); and to the University Press – *circumspice*.

ANDREW JONES

CHRONOLOGY

THERE IS about 1884 an ignorance far greater than that faced by the recent historians of earlier Reform episodes. Nor is there even a chapter of a book on the politics of Gladstone's Second Ministry which one could recommend to the reader before he enters on the intricacies of succeeding pages. This chronology of 'overt things' may be of assistance.

1883

Oct. 3 Northcote opened his Ulster campaign.
    17 National Liberal Federation Conference assembled at Leeds.
    25 First of the autumn Cabinets.
Dec. 1 *Pall Mall Gazette* sent out questionnaires to Liberal back-benchers on 'The programme of next Session'.
    11 Testimonial Fund cheque presented to Parnell in Dublin.

1884

Jan. 1 Committee on Irish Affairs published their first tract.
    11 Publication of the 1881 Census report.
    16 Lubbock's 'private conference' of Proportionalists: resolved to form an Association; provisional committee appointed.
    18 Gordon despatched to Egypt.
Feb. 5 Opening of Parliament.
    19 Commons: Vote of Censure on Government's Egyptian policy rejected by 311 to 262.
    29 Commons: Gladstone introduced Franchise bill.
Mar. 5 First General Meeting of Proportional Representation Society.
    16 Commons: motion by Labouchère on Egypt rejected by 111 to 94 (the 'dirty trick' division).
Apr. 7 Commons: Franchise bill second reading carried by 340 to 210.
    8 Commons: Harcourt introduced London Government bill.
May 1 Commons: Franchise bill into Committee.
      Gladstone announced that the proposal for a Conference on Egypt and its finances had been accepted by all the Powers except France.
    13 Commons: Vote of Censure on Government for failing to provide for Gordon's safety rejected by 303 to 275.
    16 Churchill re-elected Chairman of Conservative National Union Council.

CHRONOLOGY

CHRONOLOGY

May 11 Commons: Redistribution bill third reading.
     15 Lords: Redistribution bill second reading.
June 8 Lords: Redistribution bill through Committee.
         Commons: Government defeated on amendment to Budget by
         264 to 252.
     23 Salisbury accepted office.
     25 Royal Assent to Redistribution bill.

A NOTE ON REFERENCES

ALL REFERENCES to collections in the British Museum are to the Additional Manuscripts. Where cataloguing and foliation were in progress at the time of inspection, I have followed the injunction to give volume number alone. With quotations drawn from lengthy documents, folio reference is to the first page of that particular letter or diary entry. Where I have seen and transcribed from the original, but where the document may be printed (in full, in part, inaccurately or whatever) in a volume of 'Life & Letters', I have cited the one source only: this is solely to save time and space.

Titles of books are given in full on first reference but thereafter in abbreviated form. Place of publication is London, unless otherwise stated.

INTRODUCTION

THE REFORM ACT OF 1867 was, as Lowe had foreseen, essentially self-destructive. The very completeness of the borough franchise accentuated neglect of the counties; the very removal of anomalies between borough and borough, county and county, brought into full focus the partiality shown there to boroughs at the expense of counties. All this might have remained far longer a subject of academic banter, fit for the Commons only on a Friday afternoon, had not the Disraelian redistribution of seats been so puny, and had not population growth and movement rendered what was puny both a nuisance and a matter of fruitful political concern. The necessary assimilation of the franchises to household level may be seen, not without reason, as but a marginal constitutional amendment, the correction or completion of Disraeli's handiwork – neither a large step nor one into the unknown. Several constituencies with borough qualifications and the occupation franchise were of greater territorial extent than small counties, and possessed a wholly agricultural character. And if the peasantry had behaved well in East Retford, Cricklade, New Shoreham and Aylesbury, then why deny the vote to those no poorer, no less educated, no more susceptible to the bribes of demagogues – why use an arbitrary line? South Lancashire, the West Riding, North Lanark and Essex provided the obverse of that coin;[1] and here denial of electoral rights was made more acute by industrial migration. The Secretary of the Shipwrights' Association on the Clyde made plain the case:[2]

In the districts of Govan and Partick there were 94,000 inhabitants, the majority of whom were skilled mechanics. Of this population, 19,442 persons exercised the municipal franchise; but only 3,426 persons had a voice in the political affairs of the country. That was through no fault of their own, but was due to the shifting character of their employment, occasioned by the removal of large firms to cheaper land.

[1] Charles Seymour, *Electoral Reform in England and Wales: the Development and Operation of the Parliamentary Franchise, 1832–1885* (Yale Historical Publications: Studies III, New Haven, 1915), pp. 293 and 308.
[2] Letter to Broadhurst, read by the latter to the Commons, 3 Apr. 1884. 3 *Hansard* cclxxxvi. 1552.

THE POLITICS OF REFORM 1884

The subject of the county franchise brought forth much talk about 'Hodge the country clod', his political nature and the use he might make of his vote. There recurs in press and pamphlets a balancing of various pressures and instincts – the squire's 'screw' and the 'solid weight of county Tory organization' against a 'just sense of grievances endured', 'pure spite' towards the farmer, and 'mere contrariety'.[1] But we have already touched on this most crucial point: there was no polarity between county (i.e. landed) interest, and borough (i.e. smoke-stack) interest; and though many publicists chose to play the equalization of franchise between boroughs and counties as granting the *whole* agricultural community a voice,[2] any accompanying redistribution of seats must work against the agricultural counties and small non-industrial boroughs, against southern England, and in favour of the mining and manufacturing districts. Publication of the 1881 Census report early in 1884 opportunely provided Reform combatants with statistics of the pursuits of the people, the continued drift to the towns and the encroachment of urban upon rural. Population in English and Welsh urban sanitary districts had risen in the decade since 1871 by more than 4 million to a total of over 17 million; rural districts betrayed in that same period a net loss of 1 million to $8\frac{1}{2}$ million. Responsible, far from extreme radical, opinion suggested that exclusively rural areas in England and Wales could no longer expect more than 160 Members.[3] And Disraeli, it will be remembered, had actually granted additional representation to the agricultural counties.

Raikes, a Conservative who preferred the title of 'Constitutional reformer', was unseated at Chester in the great overthrow of 1880. Accepting defeat, he looked immediately to a future 'altogether in the hands of the democracy', when 'the views of town artisans & country bumpkins though both oscillating as violently as has been the case in these last three elections may possibly by oscillating in

---

[1] *Pall Mall Gazette*, 28 Dec. 1883, p. 4. Compare Lord Deramore to Akers-Douglas, 7 Dec. 1885: 'The present Parlt. cannot fail to be a very short one and during the interval, our county magnates must cultivate the agricultural voter & bring him to a sense of his responsibilities.' Chilston Mss., C167/1.

[2] Elliot, though impressed by Kimberley's speech in the Lords, thought he treated the bill 'far too much as if it was confined to enfranchising the agriculturing labourers, whereas this class will be surpassed in numbers by the new urban voters.' Diary, 7 July 1884. Elliot Diaries, Vol. 10.

[3] Shaw-Lefevre, 7 Apr. 1884. 3 *Hansard* cclxxxvi. 1878.

2

different directions to a certain extent neutralize one another.'[1] He may be excused his easy identification of county householder and country bumpkin; more revealing is his sense that the great battle was over, and the cynicism which registered no party or political despair.

Raikes shared a widespread belief that the grant to counties of household suffrage would follow upon Liberal success at the polls. From the early 1870s, Trevelyan had annually moved such a Commons resolution. Hartington, as party leader in opposition, openly signified approval in 1877. And in 1880, after 153 of the returned Liberals,[2] including the candidate for Midlothian, had made favourable and specific mention of the measure in their election addresses, Disraeli saw fit to sketch out Conservative tactics upon a bill whose introduction he expected forthwith,[3] while Chamberlain, newly admitted to the Cabinet, 'urged the importance of dealing immediately with the question'. These fears and hopes were premature: 'Mr. Gladstone considered that this subject, entailing as it would a new dissolution, ought to be deferred till towards the close of the Parliament just elected.'[4] And so it was. There intervened three and a half years of Irish torment; and Disraeli died.

In October 1883, the National Liberal Federation, to which Gladstone was reportedly looking to 'swell the sails'[5] for the coming Session, held a conference at Leeds. It undertook – a solecism this – to formulate the course of Westminster business, with Parliamentary Reform taking precedence over any Local or Metropolitan Government bills, and Franchise being brought forward independently of Redistribution proposals.[6] 2,500 Radical delegates behaved as Radical delegates, not particularly sure of

[1] Raikes to Elliot, 9 Apr. 1880. Elliot Mss., Bundle 21.
[2] Wemyss, 8 July 1884. 3 *Hansard* ccxcv. 438. Wemyss had obtained his figure from a 'most valuable institution, called the Universal Knowledge and Information Office, in Bloomsbury, which had been instituted by Lord Truro.' Since he was concerned to dispute that the issue had been prominently before the constituencies at the general election, this total will not be generous.
[3] Balfour to Salisbury, 8 Apr. 1880. Balfour Mss., 49688 fol. 18.
[4] C. H. D. Howard (ed.), Joseph Chamberlain, *A Political Memoir, 1880–1892* (1953), p. 4.
[5] Morley to Chamberlain, 14 Oct. 1883. Chamberlain Mss., JC5/54/511.
[6] If the Conference's function or the organizers' design was more limited – to 'settle' the priority of County Franchise over London Government – none entertained doubt as to that issue: the metropolis was sorely under-represented at the gathering. John Morley, Viscount Morley of Blackburn, *Recollections* (2 vols., 1917), Vol. I, p. 198; *Standard*, 18 Oct. 1883, p. 4.

themselves, would. There was more than an element of that class-room desire to gratify the teacher with unison chants to his angled question. Mistakes were few, if predictable. Contentious detail inevitably baffled even the most willing, as Morley found to his dismay: 'Were they to have a single residential franchise, or to accept the great principle of one man one vote? (Hear, hear.) Were the clergy to retain the four seats for the two Universities of Oxford and Cambridge? (No, yes.)'[1] There were also moments of mis-directed exuberance which threatened to cast discredit upon all the other resolutions that were passed, and indirectly to cast discredit upon the seriousness of the whole affair. Thus at Leeds, women's suffrage was carried – an emotional genuflection before the altar of Bright and Cobden, whose daughters were its advocates there. In the Commons, the cause had lately sunk to the lowest form of existence, a motion on going into Committee of Supply. But the guidance was, in general, good, and most delegates knew what they were about. Cheers were more readily accorded to an appeal that legislation proceed along the lines set by the Reform Acts of 1832 and 1867 than they were to the Jacobin alderman who would have had the question of Redistribution taken out of Parliamentary hands on the grounds of Parliamentary self-interest.[2]

The autumn Cabinet at which Gladstone first broached the possibility of a Franchise bill for the next Session followed hard on the heels of this Conference. The Government moreover, passing over the Conference's extravagances, followed the 'dictated' programme as regards essentials in allowing Parliamentary Reform pride of place for 1884 and in holding back Redistribution. In one crucial respect, though, the Cabinet went a good deal further in the direction of uniformity. A single measure encompassed the United Kingdom; the union of the kingdoms was, indeed, the very founda-tion of the bill. What had been passed over in silence at Leeds, what was passed over in silence during subsequent jamborees at Bristol, Glasgow, London and Reading, and what had hitherto been passed over in almost total silence, was the inclusion of Ireland in the measure. This question, said one discomfited Liberal, would have been felt to be a 'staggerer'.[3]

What may have been a 'staggerer' in October 1883 could not be so described four months later. Gladstone rightly allowed a limp-ness of predetermination to hang about his introduction of the

---

[1] *The Times*, 18 Oct. 1883, p. 6.   [2] *The Times*, 19 Oct. 1883, p. 4.
[3] Courtney, at Liskeard, 29 Oct. 1883. *Annual Register*, p. 177.

INTRODUCTION

Franchise bill. The major provisions were utterly simple and, by then, widely predicted – extension to the counties of the £10 occupation, the household and £10 lodger qualifications established in the boroughs in 1867, and as corollary to that uniformity, unity between the kingdoms. Henceforward in England, Wales, Scotland and Ireland, four-fifths and more of all voters, both in boroughs and in counties, would exercise their vote as occupiers. That Gladstone should have spent as long as he did on 28 February 1884 in straight exposition of the remaining details bears witness to the complexity of electoral privileges. There was no attack on property qualifications in the counties – the 40/– freehold, £5 copyhold and £50 and £5 leasehold qualifications. Conversely, except for the introduction of a service franchise which recognized the responsibility of those whose rent was deducted *per contra* from their salary, there was nothing new. Maitland found the Act 'a very clumsy document'.[1] To the extent that, where they did not lead directly to the creation of fictitious votes, existing rights and oddities were spared, he was justified in the charge; but even the constitutional and legal historian might welcome the establishment of an occupation franchise at £10 clear annual value in place of a £12 rateable value in English counties, a Scottish £14 occupation and an Irish £4 rating qualification which had been given in respect of land alone.

Complete as to area, the measure was so in no other respect. Incompleteness in regard to the apportionment of electoral power gave rise to a forceful Conservative charge – that the landed interest would be most surely swamped in county after county by the town 'overflow' vote if an election under household suffrage preceded redistribution. After 1867, variety in the Commons had been secured by a Redistribution Act which rested on quite different franchise qualifications in borough and county. With the two franchises assimilated to one another, so much more would depend on the character of Redistribution in the new bill. Gladstone immediately appealed to 'deck-loaders' 'that any friend of the Franchise Bill, who approves of it as it stands while thinking it might be made still better, & who waives attempts at improvement for fear of endangering its life, renders in my opinion a real service to the interests of the nation'.[2] The appeal to Liberal restraint enjoyed huge success. From February to July, Conservative

---

[1] F. W. Maitland, *The Constitutional History of England* (Cambridge University Press, 1950 ed.), p. 361.
[2] Gladstone to Samuel Smith, 21 Apr. 1884. Gladstone Mss., 44547 fol. 59.

amendments, designed to draw from the Prime Minister the Government's Redistribution scheme, and varying only between the demand that Franchise should not proceed without certain additions and the concession that it might proceed with those additions, were negatived in the Commons with monotonous regularity. On the Second Reading, Manners' amendment was lost by 340 votes to 210, only Goschen and Ennis of the Liberal party going against, and the Parnellites giving a solid vote for the Government. Though on Raikes' instruction to the Committee, the Liberals were caught unawares and struggled home by only 27, in Committee itself they reasserted their authority to defeat Colonel Stanley's motion by 276 to 182. A threat to Liberal unity from within was posed by Albert Grey's proposal to postpone operation of the Franchise bill until 1 January 1887. This amendment was withdrawn, in its stead the Government accepting H. H. Fowler's embodiment of Gladstone's own suggestion, 1 January 1885. On a different tack, Claud Hamilton's attempt to substitute 'Great Britain' for 'United Kingdom' not only failed to detach any of the anti-Irish elements in the Liberal ranks but secured no more than 137 Conservative supporters. Women – if they presented a Conservative threat to Liberal enfranchisement – fared no better, their cause (Woodall's amendment) being voted down by 273 to 137. Those who favoured the perfection of proportional representation were told that this was a matter pertaining to Redistribution. Others, of course, entered their protests in the order book: the gesticulations – anything from 'one man, one vote' to extension of the property qualification – had no political importance. The bill was read a third time, *nem. con.*, on 26 June, in effect unaltered since introduction.

There had for a month been too many reminders in Conservative speeches of the right of the Second Chamber to act as guardian of the popular will for doubt to remain as to the advice which the Conservative majority in the Lords would offer. The essential decision to reject the bill was taken in early May. Notice of the exact form, which is the Manners, Raikes and Stanley tack yet again, came under Cairns' signature on 1 July:

That this House, while prepared to concur in a well-considered and complete scheme for the extension of the franchise, does not think it right to assent to the Second Reading of a Bill having for its object a fundamental change in the constitution of the electoral body of the United Kingdom, but which is not accompanied by provisions for so apportioning the right to return Members as to insure a true and fair representation of the people, or by any adequate security in the proposals of the Government that the present Bill shall not come into operation except as part of an entire scheme.

Activity in the soliciting of votes was immediate and intense, for and by both Government and Opposition. Between them, Wemyss was no less active, urging his Peers first to pass the Second Reading and then to support an Instruction in Committee which might secure Redistribution before dissolution. Wemyss made no mark. Cairns' amendment (by design) divided the House on almost straight party lines, and the Government in the circumstances did well to muster 146 votes against 205 on 8 July. In the days following, Wemyss and other political adventurers or philanthropists vainly sought after an accommodation. Gladstone and Salisbury each determined in every way to emphasize the enormity of the other's action, Salisbury charging Gladstone with having steered a collision course, Gladstone announcing an Autumn Session in which Franchise would be brought forward alone once more. This total intransigence was reflected in the division on Wemyss' new resolution, the majority against being within a handful of that secured by Cairns.

To a contemporary chronicler with a sublime faith in the political worth of noise and an eye for symmetry, subsequent events were too good to be true. Just as a mandate to the Government from an orderly assemblage of Liberal delegates at Leeds in the autumn of 1883 marked for him the origin of this Reform, so now in the early autumn of 1884 did an orderly demonstration for the enlightenment of the Lords presage its successful conclusion.[1] Too good, in truth, to be true. In coarsening the flavour of a delicacy proper to politicians for the common palates, the Government found itself in a position no less delicate than that of its opponents. Conservatives, having trusted to the Lords, were now urging on an appeal to the people which might bring to the forefront of practical politics the very existence of that House; Liberals, caught somewhere between earnestness on the tired theme of Franchise first and an onslaught on the Peers, still needed to prise thirty of their number from allegiance to Salisbury.

Parliament reassembled. The Franchise bill, in its July form,

---

[1] James Murdoch, *A History of Constitutional Reform in Great Britain and Ireland: a Full Account of the Three Great Measures of 1832, 1867 and 1884* (Glasgow, 1885), p. 263.

was introduced to the Commons without discussion on 24 October, and reappeared for the Second Reading on 6 November. Colonel Stanley moved his former amendment, which was lost by 372 to 232 – and again, for good measure but to no further avail, in Committee. The Lords took up the measure without delay, 18 November being appointed for their Second Reading. The day before, however, Gladstone in the Commons and Granville in the Lords stated their willingness, if the Franchise bill was allowed to pass at an early date, to make the provisions of Redistribution the subject of friendly communication with the leaders of the Opposition. That evening, Hartington gave Balfour his private gloss upon timing: the Conservative pledge to pass the Franchise bill through the Lords that Session was not to precede agreement with regard to Redistribution.[1] Heneage, 'one of the Whig "bonnets"', added (only later troubling to check his answers with Gladstone) 'that in the event of the Government bringing in a Bill mutually agreed upon...they will stake their existence on the Bill, the same as in the alternative case of bringing in a Bill of their own.'[2] On this basis, Salisbury and Northcote entered Gladstone's drawing-room. They did not enter into or upon total darkness, since Cabinet Committee proposals had conveniently found their way to the *Standard* more than a month before, and the wide range of negotiable matter had meanwhile been revealed in 'irresponsible' conversations. Men of both parties intent on a business settlement now settled Redistribution business and, that they might not be disturbed, adjourned Parliament for the week.

The Commons was presented with a *fait accompli* on 1 December. Ninety-one boroughs with less than 15,000 population, the 6 agricultural boroughs, and Sandwich and Macclesfield (corrupt beyond all redemption) were merged into their respective counties. Thirty-five boroughs and 2 counties, with a population between 15,000 and 50,000, were docked of one Member. The City of London lost 2 of its 4. Haverfordwest and Pembroke were to be treated as one. Seats liberated by want of population went where population demanded, by application of a uniform rule – to the metropolis and to the great or new industrial and manufacturing areas, whether borough or county, English, Welsh, Scottish or Irish. Though, curiously and suspiciously, the net result was that no country

---

[1] Hartington to Gladstone, 17 Nov. 1884. Iddesleigh Mss., 50020 fol. 103.
[2] Smith to Salisbury, 17 Nov. 1884, enclosing copy by Smith of Heneage's note to Ritchie of same date. Salisbury Mss., Series E.

filched from another – Ireland maintained its Union total, and an increase of 12 in the numbers of the House met Scotland's need – this was a large-scale redistribution. Perhaps, however, greater novelty lay in adoption of the system of single-member districts, save only for Universities, the City and those 23 boroughs which were to retain their two members. Such safeguard as was afforded to the variety of separate interests present within large counties and boroughs by dividing them was reinforced by the direction given to the Boundary Commissioners – that in dividing, they should take note of variety, and in a rough manner keep like with like. Before the Commissioners even began their labours, the Commons was hustled to a Second Reading ratification of the leaders' performance. This they agreed to without division, while the Franchise bill moved from the Lords to receive the Royal Assent.

The Redistribution agreement bound both front benches to support of its terms. As to the manner in which these provisions had been arrived at – what was Liberal give, what Conservative take – secrecy reigned. Thus opposition, were it to be meaningful, demanded either a wholesale rejection by either party of its leadership on grounds of suspected treachery, or else a union of backbenchers. This was to ask much of Redistribution which affected each Member and each constituency differently; or it was to expect nothing from discipline and traditional ties. The penalty paid was, in fact, small. Courtney, Financial Secretary to the Treasury, resigned upon the failure to incorporate the principle of proportional representation; and Conservative Members' unwillingness to support each and every proposal by following Northcote into the Government lobby served to highlight the latter's thankless task, and fatally undermined his already precarious authority as party leader in the Commons. In Committee, Redistribution was never in any danger. Proportional representation found only 31 supporters. Bryce, a Fellow of Oriel urging abolition of university seats, secured 79. Arnold proposed to raise the disfranchisement level for boroughs to a 20,000 line, and was swamped by over 200 votes. The House then passed to consideration of the Schedules, and gave itself over to antiquarianism and lamentation; it was without effect, no condemned borough being granted a reprieve. On 11 May 1885, Courtney entered his last protest against single seats, and the bill passed the Commons – no amendment of importance or alteration of principle having been allowable or, in the event, allowed. Within four days and without demur, it had been read twice in the Lords. Later stages there were remarkable only for an amendment proposed by the Marquess of Lothian to lift Jedburgh from the county of Roxburghshire and add it to the Hawick Burghs. There was nothing remarkable in the suggestion, little more so in its being carried by 13 votes. But before the Liberal Commons could decline to accept the amendment or reasons for disagreeing be shunted between one Chamber and the other, the Government, defeated on a Budget resolution, had resigned. The last scene of the Third Reform Act was thus under Salisbury's direction. He played it in the appropriately low key, despatching a message that the Lords did 'not insist on their Amendments to the Bill to which this House has disagreed.'

The Third Reform bill has never been thought a dramatic episode in itself, nor is it now seen as dramatic in the development of representative government;[1] and this is explanation enough why the measure – a 'logical extension' of 1867, without any Disraelian thrills – should have attracted no historian. One would hesitate to suggest that others have positively funked the task of unearthing what it was that politicians were attempting in 1884; yet acknowledgment has often been of that variety where fame accrues and importance is ascribed in inverse proportion to informed understanding. The historian of the 'age of Disraeli and Gladstone' quite rightly takes his leave before 1884. His 'late Victorian' colleagues take their cue at the first election under the new rules. Both pay their respects, but the event itself is passed by. There is then some excuse for the present work.

Nevertheless, this book will be judged on a wrong basis unless it is accepted that it could not have appeared with any approach to honesty under the title, *The Third Reform Bill*. It is not exhaustive nor is any such claim made for it. The weight of evidence cited may initially give rise to erroneous expectation. A moment's attention to the nature of this evidence ought to dispel any such expectation. The historian who comes to late nineteenth century politics knows perfectly well that so much and such varied material is available that he can feel free to write whatever sort of history he chooses to write. He unearths an abundance of correspondence. He explains the abundance: Parliamentary recesses were still lengthy, and

[1] How much remained of the old after 1885 and how far in practice removed from universal male suffrage was the vote has been demonstrated by N. Blewett, 'The Franchise in the United Kingdom, 1885–1918', *Past & Present* No. 32 (1965), pp. 27–56.

politicians scattered far and wide for much of the year; the postal service had reached its acme, while telephones (mercifully for the historian) had yet to make their rude impact on a way of life. He knows its potential: the corpus of raw stuff permits hour-by-hour reconstruction of activity. What is perhaps less obvious is the essential attraction of the material for one whose interest lies in the nature of high politics, and who has already some impression of the nature of the political decision-making process in nineteenth century England. Near exclusive concentration upon evidence of one kind inevitably throws up a certain kind of history; what one is asking is that the kind of history presented here be accepted as self-sufficient.

Where the historian whose intention is to unravel the processes of political determination may be misguided is in devoting time to material which does not assist towards an understanding of the object of his interest. This is more than simple temptation. It is the scholar's instinctive defence against the charge of uncritical faith in unpublished documents.[1] Meekly to bow before the silly orthodoxy that truths are drawn from sources of different kinds is to mislead others in the worth of one's bloated bibliography. The conclusion emerges from discouraging experience that the return is marginal for involvement in pamphlet literature, newspapers and most especially provincial newspapers, for such a study. At best, from this wide and varied reading, the historian of 'decision-making' may derive encouragement in his belief in the irrelevance of so much. The narrowness which others detect in concentration upon Hawarden, Hatfield and Highbury is, it is contended, more apparent than real.

This is not to assert the superiority of the history presented here. But it is a distinct history – an attempt to explain the actions of politicians by relating them to the actions of other politicians – resting on the premiss that 'the people' rarely demanded a dialogue with politicians. The bluntest of messages must be this, that neither were newspapers taken by politicians in the 1880s as interpreters of

[1] One may cite Kitson Clark because he is a historian whose grounding was in the nineteenth century and because his experience is laid before each history graduate embarking on a Cambridge Ph.D.: 'It is not likely that all your most important sources will be unprinted. Those who are for the first time engaged in historical research often make the mistake of believing that what is unpublished is necessarily of greater significance than what is published.' G. Kitson Clark, *Guide for Research Students Working on Historical Subjects* (Cambridge University Press, 1965 ed.), p. 24.

'the mind of the people' nor did they radically change the minds of politicians. At various times in this story, publicists play their part. Their role is seen here as both limited and strictly controlled. Buckle, assistant to Chenery on *The Times* from 1880, effectively editor from the autumn of 1883 and officially so from February 1884, was the object of much political attention, not for what he said day by day, but because he might be of use one day, used one day and thrown away the next. It was, indeed, his fate at Churchill's hands in mid-July 1884. Dilke was grateful for the columns of the *Standard* on 9 October, and the political importance of the inspired leak is undeniable. Austin, Borthwick, Cooper, Hill, Reeve and Stead each merit a place in this study. Had their activity remained untraced because it evoked no comment in political correspondence, or had mention of it been sacrificed in the pursuit of economy, the story perhaps would have been impoverished but the structure unaffected.

What emerges is, of course, intended to be plausible. It may carry conviction. If it does carry conviction in the stress laid upon personality, personal attraction and personal repulsion, then it will contribute to understanding the subtleties of political persuasion practised by men whose life was this art. If it does carry conviction, then it can do so only to those who will recognize that the language of politics, even where it seems to obscure realities, is a reality in its own right. The historical exercise must at times simply follow the political exercise in semantics. If, for instance, deference has here a place, it is as an assumption, not for its proven or measurable existence. The deferential community is seen rather as an offshoot of Oastler's definition of the Tory ideal – 'a place for everything and everything in its place'. Its relevance is to a mentality which could see Reform as a holding action and make nuisance or necessity quite acceptable. The exercise which historians recognize was recognized for the exercise it was by participants, though only those who could not play the majority game might say so. Leatham had been reiterating the theory of 'generous confidence', the willingness of working men to be represented by their social superiors. Courtney struck at Leatham, but no less at his audience: 'That was what Members said for themselves.'[1] His was a very singular observation upon what the House thought it was doing. Offensive in his academic eccentricity, Courtney was not suffered gladly.

[1] 3 Mar. 1885. 3 *Hansard* ccxciv. 1925–6.

This collective self-persuasion is different only in kind from bullying. Both are part of the educative process. Perhaps the latter alone is accorded its due in these pages. Why? Because the author declines to join those who, having steeped themselves in its pamphlet literature, sing of the reforming spirit of this age. And because – more specifically – to the equation of National Liberal Federation pressure in the late 1870s with the demand of popular Liberalism (and further to the equation of popular Liberalism with sense), he would counter with Herbert Gladstone's bitter recollection: 'There was a structural defect in the N.L.F.; the Executive was at too great a distance from its base. The design...suited Mr. Chamberlain's purpose.'[1] Moreover, to the evidence adduced of the gathering momentum of a reform wave, the author would counter with the claim that the Corrupt Practices legislation of 1883 was, if it was anything, Gladstone's chosen herald to Reform bills proper. In rebutting the broad charge of Liberal commitment, he would cite Hartington's dismissal of all commitment.[2] His contention is that the questions which need to be asked, the testing questions of timing and detail, are political questions barely posed before the autumn of 1883, at which point the microscope is applied because that is when it needs to be applied. The historian who enjoys a right to ask what questions he will of the material under his scrutiny, has also an academic responsibility to devote his time to questions of a searching character and a duty rigorously to extract as much as is possible (more than could ever be admissible in a court of law) from that material.

Within the space of these months, there is quite sufficient material for the historian both to establish the problem of Liberal party discipline and to linger over the party leader's chosen course of correction. Was the inclusion of Ireland, as was said in October, a 'staggerer'? Not so, according to a poll conducted by the *Pall Mall Gazette* two months later. Questionnaires were sent to all 'non-Conservative' MPs not in the Government: 95 % of the 170 statements received in reply favoured 'admitting Ireland to all the rights and privileges of England.'[3] But no less weight need be (nor is) placed on the individual impression than on statistics as evidence of party opinion; for one who sees no reason *prima facie*

[1] Memorandum on Liberal Party Organization, 1923. Viscount Gladstone Mss., 46110 fol. 222.
[2] Hartington to Gladstone, 24 Oct. 1883. Gladstone Mss., 44146 fol. 222.
[3] *Pall Mall Gazette*, 3 Jan. 1884, pp. 1–2.

why party opinion even over a few weeks of the Parliamentary recess ought to remain static, it is the lapse of time which assumes importance. We should, then, look to see if in those weeks leaders made it clear that a bill, should one emerge, would encompass the United Kingdom. And, having found that they did, we might remember the moan of truculent independence that, 'so far as the rank & file of our party are concerned, they would...swallow any pill prescribed by Gladstone & declare it to be good for the Constitution.'[1] The nature of the argument, which was extraordinary, carried politicians before it; it is for the reader to decide whether or not it is worthwhile to explore personal difficulties in Cabinet, when Leeds' dictation and the *Pall Mall* concord could make for an easy historical journey.

The politically sensitive saw through to a personal core. Elgin, moving adoption of a 'not...very pretentious' annual report to the Scottish Liberal Association, in January 1884, 'need[ed] scarcely [to] remind [the meeting] that it was not the duty of the Executive Council...to frame a political manifesto.' This direct censure of Caucus impertinence led on to a sneering dismissal of journalistic 'push'. 'He did not know how they could [frame a manifesto] even if they followed the latest precedent, and sent out a catechism to the sixty Scottish members as to their political views, unless indeed they were to obtain answers from the member for Mid-Lothian.'[2] The sneer is platitudinous, and the platitude one of political insight. Gladstone it was who determined the extent of the measure, the precedence to be accorded it, and the mode of procedure. At the Cabinet on 22 November 1883, Dilke heard 'Mr. G. read a splendid memo. in favour of the views of himself, myself & Chamberlain.'[3] But Dilke and Chamberlain were for the moment and for their own purposes playing 'follow my leader'. Indeed, it is not a new generation of politicians employing new methods, but the established leaders playing an old game who leave their stamp on the events we are describing.

The real significance of the Leeds Conference lay in the recall to the stage-front of Bright, in part as reminder that it was the senior and not the junior Member for Birmingham who knew more of Gladstone's mind on the subject of Parliamentary Reform, and

[1] Rylands to Lubbock, 11 Oct. 1882. Avebury Mss., 49643 fol. 48.
[2] Annual meeting, at Edinburgh, 23 Jan. 1884. Scottish Liberal Association Minute Book, 1882–1893, fol. 46.
[3] Dilke Diary, 22 Nov. 1883. Dilke Mss., 43925 fol. 75.

further as symbol that Reform was 'not to be an instalment' for Chamberlain to complete but a 'settlement' by Gladstone for a generation.[1] A source of special satisfaction to the Prime Minister, accruing from the whole Reform crisis, was the 'disposition of the country to confide in, and defer to, old age, which (as I conceive) is entertained out of doors to excess, but which may on occasion be turned to good account.'[2] Gladstone's reflection neatly dovetails a record of the Franchise march on 21 July 1884. Each detachment of the procession, filing past Bright's house in Piccadilly, vied there with its predecessor in acclamation of the 'hero'; in Hyde Park, only Bright and Gladstone 'came in for any mark of popular favour.' The 'complete eclipse' of all younger men was both the most remarkable and, certainly for Chamberlain, 'not the most satisfactory' feature of the parade.[3] Churchill now singled out Bright for attack, and prefaced his denunciation with an apology – he had ignored Bright before, believing him to be 'out of the hunt'.[4] It was a bitter jest at Chamberlain's expense. But the phenomenon confined itself not to one party, and the jest was to rebound on Churchill himself. Above Bright, above all others, one old man continued to dominate the politics of these years. It is, in its twisted way, a powerful testimony to that dominance, and at the same time a valuable commentary upon the *politics* of Reform, that Stansfeld thought the 'tone' of Parliamentary life endangered not by any doubling of the electorate nor even by the return of 'vestrymen' in single-member constituencies: 'What we want is that Gladstone should vanish & people reassert themselves.'[5]

Gladstone, who did not vanish, may be allowed to set the historical tone. In conversation with Lionel Tollemache, he named Homer one of the three great poets of the world; with Dante and Shakespeare, Homer was able 'always to throw our sympathies on the right side.' Tollemache demurred, citing the case of Dolon. 'That', countered Gladstone, 'was a night march, and it was necessary to meet stratagem by stratagem.'[6] Parliamentary Reform legislation, the shaping of bills in Cabinet and their passage through both Houses, are seen here as a political 'night march'. But if rational, well-informed discussion upon the merits of various modes

[1] Gladstone to Shaw-Lefevre, 12 Nov. 1883. Gladstone Mss., 44546 fol. 189.
[2] Gladstone to Trevelyan, 25 Jan. 1885. Gladstone Mss., 44547 fol. 168.
[3] *Pall Mall Gazette*, 22 July 1884, p. 3.
[4] *The Times*, 1 Feb. 1884, p. 7.
[5] Stansfeld to Halifax, 19 Mar. 1885. Hickleton Mss., A4.51.
[6] L. A. Tollemache, *Talks with Mr. Gladstone* (1898), p. 76.

of procedure emerges as subordinate in Cabinet to the playing off by the Prime Minister of dissident colleagues, if a Conservative tactic of opposition was determined by the struggle for supremacy in the party after Disraeli's death, and if the Parnellites were concerned more with their market value as a Parliamentary force whose cohesion Reform threatened than with righting the palpable injustices of the Irish franchise, all this does not of itself lead to a political treatise upon Ambrose Bierce's devilish definition – 'Public, n.: The negligible factor in problems of legislation.'[1]

Reform remains the *locus classicus* for any study of the relationship and interaction of political personalities and groupings, of a political system and the political class structure. In terms of personal involvement, the Third Reform bill vitally affected the seats of a majority of Members. In separating Franchise from Redistribution, it presaged the annihilation in Parliament of a purely landed interest. As such, it filled the minds of contemporaries. In exacerbating differences within each party (along Whig–Radical, 'old identity'–Tory Democracy axes) and across the parties (upon the safeguarding, by special provision, of Ulster), it might well have occasioned that realignment which occurred in 1886 on the Irish question. And that which did not come to pass in 1884 may be, in an historical study of 1884, of as much concern as that which did.

[1] E. J. Hopkins (ed.), Ambrose Bierce, *The Enlarged Devil's Dictionary* (1968).

1

CABINET: FRANCHISE FIRST, FOREMOST, AND WITH IRELAND

They cannot help themselves but must stick together & fool each other to the top of their bent.
Stansfeld to Halifax, 20 Feb. 1884. Hickleton Mss., A4.51.

I have more than once heard Mr. Gladstone lament his own defect in not being able always to say precisely what he means; neither more nor less...
MacColl to Salisbury, 21 July 1884. G. W. E. Russell (ed.), *Malcolm MacColl: Memoirs and Correspondence* (1914), p. 98.

> 'The goal of three score years & ten
> Afar behind me lies:
> The daily voice of Nature, then,
> For rest unprompted cries.'

In Gladstone's hand, preserved among Cabinet Memoranda, n.d. (? Feb. 1884). Gladstone Mss., 44768 fol. 13.

DISRAELI AND NORTHCOTE completed their tally sheet of the 1880 elections; they counted 240 Conservatives, 237 Whigs, 113 'extreme or unclassed Radicals' and 62 'Home Rulers (of various shades)'.[1] They neither looked for, nor did they find, a Liberal party as such, arrayed against their forces. All they saw was a coalition whose purpose was office, and they rightly suspected that Members whose prime attachment was to Radicalism or to Whiggery might find the alliance irksome.

The Cabinet provided more than a concentration of such unease. Upon any issue, there was likely to be unanimity neither *in posse* at the speculative stage nor barely *in esse* at the moment of supposed fusion into immediate policy. That was not because of ideological commitment. Essentially, the Cabinet over which Gladstone presided was too distinguished in composition to be other than distinguished by disunity. Too many eligible candidates sought the prize which had yet to be offered – succession to Gladstone; one stood between another and leadership, a third (or

[1] Northcote Diary, 21 Apr. 1880. Iddesleigh Mss., 50063A fol. 321.

17

Gladstone himself) might play upon jealous antipathy. Too many sought only the right moment to strike, and meanwhile prepared their ground. The Franchise bill of 1884 – in itself (for Reform is a difficult subject), in its tenderness to Ireland, in its divorce from Redistribution or in its displacement of Local and Metropolitan Government bills – could easily be represented as objectionable. The occasion was as good as any chosen in the earlier years of the Ministry by Argyll, Forster or Bright on which to 'go out'. Yet the making of the measure was accompanied by no Cabinet resignations. Why not?

The easiest introduction to the question is to see what politicians were saying after the Home Rule bill of 1886 of what they were attempting in 1884. And a linear descent is well attested. For Morley and Bryce, the lowering of the suffrage in 1884 rendered 'inevitable' the grant of self-government to Ireland,[1] and proved itself 'one of the cardinal landmarks in our history.'[2] Gladstone's own testament upon the Irish question is equally explicit: 'We went or tried to go to the bottom of it in the Land Act of 1881, only to discover that we had not reached the core...By the Franchise Act of 1884–5 we made a long step towards the solution [enabling] virtually the whole Irish people to speak its mind. That mind was spoken plainly enough at the general election of 1885.'[3] The memoirs of these participant apologists could be more easily dismissed if they were not confirmed, as they are, by contemporary statements from politicians at either end of the political spectrum. The Tory, Brodrick's, prophecy was delivered to a packed House of Commons in May 1884: 'if this franchise [is] now given, [we shall] be forced to concede Home Rule. All that the loyal men in [this] House and in the country could do would not be sufficient to prevent it, and the responsibility would rest upon the Parliament which accepted and the Ministry which had initiated the movement.'[4] Parnell's enunciation of his party's needs was made more than two years earlier at the founding of the National League. Under the existing franchise, he calculated, a general election would increase his following to 65 or 70. 'But to get such a representation as would secure, for instance, the creation of National Self-Government for Ireland, we require to return 80 or 90 Members to the

---

[1] H. A. L. Fisher, *James Bryce (Viscount Bryce of Dechmont, O.M.)* (2 vols., 1927), Vol. I, p. 199.
[2] Morley, *Recollections*, Vol. I, p. 182.
[3] Gladstone Mss., 44790 fol. 117.
[4] 16 May 1884. 3 *Hansard* cclxxxviii. 578.

House of Commons, and we cannot hope for this until the franchise
has been lowered, at least as far as the basis of household suffrage.'[1]
We are here concerned not with the effects of franchise extension
in Ireland after 1885, but with the expectations that were entertained about them in 1883 and early 1884. The basic question –
why were there no resignations – may now be refined to encompass
interdependent political manoeuvre. How was it that Gladstone,
who had found himself isolated in Cabinet over the granting of
local government to Ireland in 1883, was able within twelve months
to bring off the notable *coup* of isolating Hartington over the
franchise? The idea of Irishmen voting in their hundreds of thousands was acceptable, while the idea of Irish control of Irish roads,
drains and pauper lunatics had been unacceptable to Gladstone's
colleagues. What lay behind this apparent inconsistency?

Powerscourt, one of the handful of Irish Liberal Peers, professed
to look forward to the introduction of Gladstonian legislation
enabling the Irish to 'manage such matters as Railways, Gas or
Water Bills etc.'[2] In early 1883, ministers did not see Irish Local
Government in this light – as a matter of fabian caution. Hartington described Gladstone's plans as a sell-out to the Fenians.[3]
Harcourt, who in any case doubted the efficacy of buying off Irish
opposition since 'there is not one of them to be trusted',[4] argued
that the Government might just as well issue revolvers to the
Dublin assassins.[5] Any share in local administration, for which *per
se* the Irish 'don't care two straws', would be used as a tool for
agitation.[6] Above all, they suspected Gladstone of attempting to
by-pass the Cabinet[7] and of pulling himself together for this as a
last 'constructive effort', which he knew they would not collectively
sanction. This suspicion was rendered all the more plausible by his
promotion to the Exchequer of Childers, 'who has got all sorts of
schemes about Irish payments in his head.'[8] As ever, the fear – a
fear not confined to the Cabinet – was that Gladstone meant 'to
propose something which will be plausible & yet violent in its

---

[1] 18 Oct. 1882. Words quoted by Plunket, 3 Apr. 1884. 3 *Hansard* cclxxxvi.
1583.
[2] Powerscourt to P. J. Smyth, 6 Mar. 1882. Smyth Mss., 8215.
[3] Hartington to Harcourt, 3 Feb. 1883. Harcourt Mss.
[4] Harcourt to Chamberlain, 22 May 1882. Harcourt Mss.
[5] Harcourt to Spencer, 29 Jan. 1883. Spencer Mss.
[6] Hartington to Spencer, 25 Dec. 1882. Spencer Mss.
[7] Hartington to Granville, 25 Jan. 1883. Devonshire Mss., 340.1315. All
Devonshire Mss. references are to the 2nd Series.
[8] Hartington to Spencer, 25 Dec. 1882. Spencer Mss.

principle and in its consequences.'[1] Northcote wondered whether or not Gladstone would 'rise to the bait that will be offered, and propose an Irish Local Govt. bill in a Home rule sense',[2] while Goschen publicly warned his party against conceding what might ultimately be construed to involve it, and drifting into Home Rule through incomprehension and despair.[3]

Hartington, making public his objections in a series of constituency speeches, effectively 'bitched'[4] Gladstone's proposals, and incidentally put paid to 'hopes of an active session.'[5] Though Gladstone, at Cannes, was reported to have assumed his 'fixed fighting look',[6] Hartington had not merely Harcourt but the Irish administration with him. Spencer, the Lord-Lieutenant, demanded a year of quiet.[7] Trevelyan, his Chief-Secretary, thinking the Gladstone era was past, despatched a note of obsequious accord to Chatsworth: 'It is really futile to hope to act with people whose bread depends on their keeping up a violent anti-English agitation. The policy seems to be, to go our own way; to appeal to the law-abiding party in the country; ... nothing but discredit can come out of making the conciliation of the rebellious party the principal object.'[8] These were the big guns. Cabinet dead weight and Chamberlain's reluctance to touch any branch of Local Government did the rest.

Hartington's line did not soften in the course of 1883. At the same time as the Leeds managers were suppressing any anti-Irish outbursts from avowedly hostile bodies like the Liverpool '900', he was rehearsing for Spencer's benefit the objection which Lord George Hamilton had urged from the Opposition front bench four months earlier – that political reform for Ireland was useless, inopportune and dangerous until social unity was restored.[9] 'If the Land Act is now to give satisfaction to anybody, it will be to the Tenant farmers or existing voters. But just as we have satisfied them, we are going to bring in a new class of voters who are pretty sure to support the most extreme Nationalist candidates.'[10]

[1] Argyll to Halifax, 14 Nov. 1881. Hickleton Mss., A4.82.
[2] Northcote to Gibson, 16 Jan. 1883. Ashbourne Mss.
[3] At Ripon, 22 Jan. 1883. *Annual Register*, p. 4.
[4] The strongest language which Gladstone allowed himself in such trying circumstances. Hamilton Diary, 1 Jan. 1885. Hamilton Mss., 48638 fol. 104.
[5] Derby to Rathbone, 28 Feb. 1883. Rathbone Mss., IX.7.83.
[6] Acton to Granville, 25 Feb. 1883. Granville Mss., PRO. 30/29/27B.
[7] Spencer to Hartington, 13 Jan. 1883. Devonshire Mss., 340.1310.
[8] Trevelyan to Hartington, 21 Jan. 1883. Devonshire Mss., 340.1312.
[9] 12 June 1883. 3 *Hansard* cclxxx. 421–2.
[10] Hartington to Spencer, 18 Oct. 1883. Spencer Mss.

Gladstone had good cause to fear that this frame of mind would still command sympathy and respect amongst Cabinet Whigs. He was equal to the occasion. If local government legislation was to be denounced as playing into Parnell's hands, he for his part would present a Franchise bill as the logical outcome of Peel's policy of 'disciplining the Irish people'.[1] Years before, Kimberley had noted Gladstone's practice of giving 'exaggerated weight in council to arguments useful perhaps in debate but more plausible than sound';[2] and, though this had endangered his control of every Cabinet over which he presided, it had brought in its wake a mass of triumphs sufficient for the day. The germ which Gladstone injected was this: 'Is not the admission of another class, the labourer, by household suffrage, *quite* as likely to establish a dual current in the constituencies, as to increase the volume of that single force which now carries all before it?'[3] That, which may appear thin and marvellous even as debating argument, was marvellously effective. Trevelyan toyed enthusiastically with the possibility of any 'counterpoise to the class of farmers who now have quite an inordinate and dangerous influence' on the Parliamentary party.[4] Spencer latched on to the idea of the labourers as a moderating influence, and repeated it to Hartington – doubtless as Gladstone intended.[5] Hartington was not thus to be won over, nor yet by Gladstone's suggestion that a £4 stopping-point (by implication the least that could be offered) might prove no more conservative than

---

[1] Compare Emil Strauss, *Irish Nationalism and British Democracy* (1951), pp. 163–4: 'Like Peel before him, Gladstone aimed chiefly at the disintegration of the all-Irish coalition confronting him.' Marxism here comes extraordinarily close to Gladstonian argument.

[2] Kimberley Journal, 2 Mar. 1870. Ethel Drus (ed.), *A Journal of Events during the Gladstone Ministry, 1868–74, by John Wodehouse, First Earl of Kimberley*, Camden Miscellany, xxi (1958), p. 12. Some would call this 'crookedness'; some will deduce that while the actual word has been avoided, the reading here of Gladstone's behaviour is unfavourable. This dilemma – between the charge of innuendo and the employment of a code which has no relevance to political conduct under pressure – reflects ill upon the language political historians perforce employ. 'Here lies Gladstone, he always did' was Smith's mock epitaph, and we have not progressed beyond that crudity. One incident, impressive because the matter (Derby's mood) is of only slight political significance, neatly illustrates the point which is of importance (Gladstone's power of instant persuasion): 'I saw the chief at 7 last night. He seemed very sanguine as to a settlement: and made me so while he talked: but afterwards, thinking of the reasons he had given, they seemed feeble.' Derby to Granville, 8 Nov. 1884. Granville Mss., PRO. 30/29/120.

[3] Gladstone to Trevelyan, 23 Oct. 1883. Gladstone Mss., 44546 fol. 180.

[4] Trevelyan to Gladstone, 26 Oct. 1883. Gladstone Mss., 44335 fol. 130.

[5] Spencer to Hartington, 21 Oct. 1883. Spencer Mss.

the household base.[1] But Carlingford, Selborne and Northbrook were.

This was not, of course, the sole reason for 'conversion'. To provoke a struggle with Ireland by refusing her the franchise granted elsewhere was, to Carlingford's mind, 'far worse than the results of household suffrage, however bad they may be.'[2] Northbrook resigned himself to the loss of a handful of 'Loyal' MPs in the hope that this 'act of justice' would win over 'a fringe of our Irish opponents.'[3] Selborne, like Granville, had been scandalised by Radical truckling to the Nationalist element in a recent Manchester by-election. He now adopted Trevelyan's thesis that the 'unnatural power' of the Irish vote in England (for the Irish were 'unnaturally' concentrated in boroughs) would be countered; and – further consolation on a broad front – the 'strong, homogeneous' party[4] of 'honest Liberals', which Reform must yield, would have no need to court the Irish.[5] Trevelyan had the reputation of always speaking on Irish politics ' as if a greater crisis was approaching than the British public had yet brought itself to face, and that it might as well come soon as late.'[6] But Trevelyan, right as he was, had no inkling of any denouement in a Home Rule sense. He held that an election 'now' would produce no less Parnellite a representation than any future one under an extended franchise.[7] To Harcourt, the only material point was whether it was possible to make the state of Ireland worse than it already was.[8] He answered that question in the negative. The true relation of the party to Parnell would be decided upon the renewal of the Crimes Act in 1885. That was to be the Liberals' 'Waterloo'. The calculation was straightforward; if Parnell was denied the franchise, he would carry with him a dangerous measure of British sympathy.[9]

But it was the prospect of dividing Parnell's ranks which caught the imagination of those who had already acknowledged intellectual and practical defeat. The Times left off thundering against franchise concessions to Ireland, having recognized or thought it recognized

1 Gladstone to Hartington, 22 Oct. 1883. Gladstone Mss., 44546 fol. 179.
2 Carlingford to Spencer, 22 Nov. 1883. Spencer Mss.
3 Spencer to Northbrook, 22 Nov. 1883. Spencer Mss.
4 Trevelyan to Gladstone, 26 Oct. 1883. Gladstone Mss., 44335 fol. 130.
5 Trevelyan to Chamberlain, 27 Dec. 1883. Chamberlain Mss., JC5/70/6.
6 Elliot Diary, 18 Sept. 1883. Diaries, Vol. 13.
7 Elliot Diary, 5 Dec. 1883. Diaries, Vol. 9.
8 Harcourt to Gladstone, 9 Nov. 1883. Gladstone Mss., 44198 fol. 131.
9 Harcourt to Gladstone, 28 Dec. 1883. Gladstone Mss., 44198 fol. 170.

a Trojan horse.[1] The *Spectator* held as a political certainty that 'large popular constituencies' would 'dissolv[e]' the Parnellite 'oligarchy'.[2] At Bradford, Forster echoed Chamberlain[3] – rare concord this, for he lavished no generosity upon either Gladstone or Ireland. Whitbread encouraged his Bedford constituents with a reminder that the strength of the separatists lay among the small landholders of Munster and Connaught; extend the franchise, 'and I am not at all sure that you would find that the labourers thought their interests identical with the farmers.'[4] Lansdowne, owner of 100,000 Irish acres, found cause for relief in the Government proposal as tending to diminish the threat of social revolution.[5]

Such party unanimity or, one might perhaps say, orthodoxy by bamboozlement may be traced to these non-altruistic motives. Indeed, altruism may be relegated to the second division if we go beyond the evidence to allow what is just as plausible – that with the inclusion of Ireland Whigs saw a greater chance of the Lords rejecting the measure altogether, and that Radicals saw inclusion as likely to provoke the crisis with the Lords on which they might fight the next election, drive out Hartington and re-define the character of the Liberal party.

George Russell's dictum that 'the veiled desire of most of the House on both sides is to prevent anything being done'[6] ought not to be dismissed as mere cynicism. When an established mode of representation and the separate vitality of constituencies are threatened, inertia is in the nature of things, and what Wells called the 'passionate resistance of the active dull' reveals itself in obstruction. Liberals had of course by 1883 not only swallowed their pride but assumed the credit for developing Disraeli's proposals from their 'original narrow and stunted proportions'[7] into the great measure of household suffrage. Yet they feared that the prize might again be snatched from their hands as it had been in 1867. The *Daily News*, anticipating that the battle would not be fought out to its end in the present Parliament, held – some meagre solace, this – that the present Administration 'will none the less

[1] 27 Nov. 1883, p. 9.
[2] 17 Nov. 1883, p. 1472.
[3] *The Times*, 14 Dec. 1883, p. 6.
[4] 31 Jan. 1884. Whitbread Mss., Press cuttings.
[5] Lansdowne to Granville, 17 Feb. 1884. Granville Mss., PRO. 30/29/28A.
[6] G. W. E. Russell, *Sir Wilfrid Lawson: a Memoir* (1909), p. 169.
[7] Gladstone, 28 Feb. 1884. 3 *Hansard* cclxxxv. 113.

THE POLITICS OF REFORM 1884

have associated its name with the final and certain victory.'[1] Ministerial reluctance to take up the 'act of happy despatch' needs no underlining. Arnold, a fervent reformist, calculated that half-a-dozen years would elapse between the raising and settling of the question.[2] Morley thought the Leeds Conference would 'give me much to think about and to do in the next two or three or four years.'[3] 'Changes of Government, general elections, interruption of business, and general discomfiture' were the common expectation.[4] An omnibus measure was doubtless a political impossibility. To be reduced to manageable proportions, Reform could be divided laterally (by separating a Franchise bill for the three kingdoms from Redistribution for the three kingdoms) or vertically (by joining Suffrage and Seats, but producing separate bills for England, Scotland and Ireland). The case against the former was that the motive power for Redistribution would be lost, and legislative success become dependent upon the generosity of opponents in 'giving what you want, when you have nothing to give, and they nothing to expect in return';[5] in Hartington's terms, a single-barrelled bill was 'a rather lazy electioneering trick.'[6] The argument in favour, reduced to its elements by Dodson, was no more than the obverse of Hartington's coin: 'If franchise only, Lords throw out because no redistn.... If Rn., Lords throw out because Rn bad (Very likely Commons will throw out if Rn.) Advantage of Franchise only, that C. will pass it & we shall not have got a Rn. scheme round our necks.'[7]

Gladstone nailed his personal position to this course. He did not state his case. In introducing the county suffrage question to his Cabinet as a conversational tail-piece, he simply pronounced himself unable in his seventy-fifth year to face the tiresome *minutiae* of Redistribution. Two months later, Harcourt felt that the substantive merits of the whole issue had been evaded,[8] while Harting-

1 27 Oct. 1883, p. 4.   2 30 Mar. 1883. 3 Hansard cclxxvii. 1131.
3 Morley to Grace Morley, 5 Nov. 1883. F. W. Hirst, *Early Life and Letters of John Morley* (2 vols., 1927), Vol. ii, p. 173.
4 *Morning Post*, 20 Oct. 1883, p. 4. See also Kimberley Memo., 16 Jan. 1883. Dilke Mss., 43891 fol. 253; and Derby Memo. of same date. Dilke Mss., 43891 fol. 255.   5 Halifax to Albert Grey, 29 Jan. 1884. Grey Mss.
6 Hartington to Spencer, 18 Oct. 1883. Spencer Mss.
7 Dodson Memo., n.d. Monk Bretton Mss., 63. Dodson employs mathematical symbols in his 'politics made easy' notes and memoranda. I have translated where appropriate to 'because', 'therefore', etc.
8 Agatha Ramm (ed.), *The Political Correspondence of Mr. Gladstone and Lord Granville, 1876–1886* (2 vols., Oxford, 1962), Vol. ii, p. 131 n. 3.

24

ton complained of 'a disposition to avoid looking the question in the face'.[1] These impressions correspond with reality. Gladstone never allowed the open throwing of views into the common stock. He could say to Hartington at Christmas 1883 that the separating of the two measures, against which Hartington belatedly entered his formal protest, 'had been decided on in ignorance of his [Hartington's] real sentiments'.[2] But Gladstone could say this because no one had been asked to express 'his real sentiments' and because in a very real sense there were Cabinet decisions neither about separation nor about the inclusion of Ireland. Gladstone baulked and forestalled opposition by forcibly equating the alternative proposition with disavowal of his leadership. The 'one smooth even forward current of opinion and feeling' in the Cabinet, which Gladstone related to his wife,[3] was simply the reluctance of colleagues to mutiny. Gladstone's action is politically quite intelligible. Defections were expected.[4] But since Hartington for one was going to cause a rumpus anyhow,[5] Gladstone needed to take the line which would cause least offence to others. That line, 'Franchise first', had the incidental advantage of cutting the ground from under several 'Irish' objections. When Carlingford and Selborne threatened to stick out for postponing Irish Reform until 1885 – advocating a complete measure, which involved not merely wholesale reduction in the number of her Members but also internal proportionate bolstering of Ulster representation – they received the sharp rejoinder from Spencer that whatever the difficulties, 'that seems to be a settled matter as...Mr G. wd. not undertake the double bill at all'.[6]

Parnellite support was the only means, as Gladstone put it, of carrying Reform through the Commons. There was to be no loss of Irish clauses, no reduction in Irish representation, nor any internal reallocation, granting Ulster the five extra seats to which she was entitled upon a population basis. Gladstone's lack of sympathy with 'an old Burke and Grattan Whig' like Rowland Blennerhassett,[7] and his unwillingness to save those who would not see 'that

[1] Hartington Memo., 25 Dec. 1883. Gladstone Mss., 44146 fol. 258.
[2] Gladstone Memo., Dec. 1883. Gladstone Mss., 44767 fol. 131.
[3] 26 Oct. 1883. A. Tilney Bassett (ed.), *Gladstone to his Wife* (1936), p. 243.
[4] Seymour to Hamilton, 19 Oct. 1883. Hamilton Mss., 48615.
[5] Granville to Spencer, 23 Nov. 1883. Spencer Mss.
[6] Spencer to Carlingford, 17 Nov. 1883. Spencer Mss.
[7] Blennerhassett to Albert Grey, 5 May 1884. Grey Mss.

practically they *must* move on ',[1] was presented to the Cabinet as the sacrifice of those who would go under 'equally if the present franchise remained.'[2] This was, if nothing more, totally at odds with the upward trend established by the Liberals in Ulster county constituencies – from 1 seat in 1868, to 3 in 1874, and 8 'posing as the party of the villager and the small farmer' in 1880.[3] What makes Gladstone's abandonment of Ulster the more conspicuous is Parnell's later offer to accept 'special arrangements for securing to the Protestant minority' a representation proportionate to their numbers.[4] The myth (a tribute to Mill's influence) that the Liberals were destined to split upon the question of minority representation may have been exercising Gladstone's mind. Ulster was the obvious stalking-horse for faddists. Trevelyan's estimates of the effect of franchise extension reinforce another consideration – that with 9 new Irish county voters to every one in the boroughs, any wholesale redistribution would work against the Conservatives whose strength was concentrated in the Ulster towns.[5] Was there anything more positive, over and beyond such calculations? Possibly this, which is dramatic, that Gladstone did not decide in mid-1883 simply to abandon Irish reform and turn to Franchise as some party-unifying device.[6] What he saw in suffrage legislation was the means of nullifying Ulster – both as the source of that ambiguity, born of tactical unwillingness to differentiate between Nationalist party and Irish people, which pervades the thinking of English politicians about Parnell's Ireland, and as the focal point of a mass of argument revolving around the political representation of property, manufacture and capital.

The 1866 Franchise bill emerged by itself 'because Gladstone had been too busy to prepare' a Redistribution scheme.[7] In 1884,

[1] B. F. C. Costelloe to Herbert Gladstone, 24 Nov. 1883. Viscount Gladstone Mss., 46017 fol. 24.
[2] Trevelyan to Gladstone, 26 Oct. 1883. Gladstone Mss., 44335 fol. 130.
[3] H. J. Hanham, *Elections and Party Management: Politics in the Time of Disraeli and Gladstone* (1959), p. 183.
[4] Katherine Parnell (Mrs. O'Shea), *Charles Stewart Parnell: his Love Story and Political Life* (2 vols., 1914), Vol. II, p. 18.
[5] Trevelyan to Hamilton, 11 Feb. 1884. Gladstone Mss., 44335 fol. 139. The Conservatives had 10 seats, the Liberals just 1.
[6] Compare J. L. Hammond, *Gladstone and the Irish Nation*, new impression (1964), p. 343.
[7] F. B. Smith, *The Making of the Second Reform Bill* (Cambridge, 1966), p. 228; but compare Maurice Cowling, *1867: Disraeli, Gladstone and Revolution. The Passing of the Second Reform Bill* (Cambridge, 1967), p. 100.

'Franchise first' was the outcome of a definite Gladstonian decision. This decision took cognizance of the impossibility of absolutely guaranteeing that the bills should be disposed of in the same Session or even by the same Parliament. This admission, by inference, all but identified uniformity of franchise as an absolute benefit – and this implication was taken to be obnoxious to the great body of Parliamentary opinion.[1] It made exact calculation of effects a fantastic dream. It raised the bogy of the destruction of a purely rural, landed or propertied interest – and this offended powerful Liberal, as well as Tory, instincts. It lent itself to dramatic representation as a surrender to the Radicals, who would sweep in on 'bastard' constituencies and settle Redistribution to their own satisfaction. It was denounced by Halifax as 'a complete specimen of the folly of Gladstone in dealing with his own measures'.[2]

The counterpoise, in its essential form, was that opposition from MPs for condemned boroughs would be inevitable once an actual Schedule was produced.[3] Shaw-Lefevre reproached Conservatives for aspiring to intrigue with 140 of the endangered, but his point was, after all, a tacit acknowledgment that the Tories might intrigue to very good purpose.[4] The logic (though this would bother no-one) was impaired by the reliance Chamberlain placed upon the enthusiasm for county franchise displayed in large urban constituencies, who 'would know that redistribution must follow.'[5] It was impaired still further by his disposition to argue that while small boroughs would react only when proscribed, large and expanding ones, in the expectation of an ultimate increase in their representation, would accept a Government scheme on trust without seeing any of the details. More to the point, the 'angular and impracticable'[6] Grey emerged to demonstrate that the disaffected would find a pretext for disaffection. While Childers reported that Grey, dreading the possibility of an election on the new franchise and old constituencies, would oppose Suffrage *without* Seats,[7] the *Economist* asserted that he would play an Adullamite role, along with Lord Colin Campbell, the Fitzwilliams and a dozen others,

---

[1] Arnold, 30 Mar. 1883. 3 *Hansard* cclxxvii. 1125–6.
[2] Halifax to Albert Grey, 29 Jan. 1884. Grey Mss.
[3] See the experience of 1866. Cowling, *1867*, pp. 99–100.
[4] *The Times*, 24 Jan. 1884, p. 9.
[5] Chamberlain to Maxse, 14 Dec. 1882. Maxse Mss., 206.
[6] Hamilton Diary, 14 Dec. 1883. Hamilton Mss., 48635 fol. 23.
[7] Childers to Gladstone, 10 Dec. 1883. Gladstone Mss., 44130 fol. 342.

'*if* the Government speaks plainly of redistribution'[1] – i.e., of the supremacy of numbers.

If the expectations of the 'big constituencies' could not be fulfilled, Chamberlain had every reason to postpone publication of the Redistribution proposals. In advocating a combination of County Franchise and dissolution,[2] he was 'simply doubting how much this Radical Government would get out of this Conservative House of Commons.'[3] He took it that a Franchise bill might be passed but that Redistribution on any other basis than that of 'a seat here for a seat there' would be impossible in Parliamentary terms. Hence his efforts after 1882 to show that there was no absolute connection between the two component parts of Reform. Hence too the birth of a new Birmingham heterodoxy – that it was impossible to project a fair Redistribution scheme until after the county electorate had been enlarged and its precise strength on the Registers assessed.[4]

If this tactic was intended to appease and dupe those practical minds which hungered after accurate forecasting of the effects of legislation, it misfired. A distribution of Members by reference to the size of an electoral roll rather than constituency population was seen to destroy all pretence at finality.[5] Chamberlain had no wish, as some mistakenly thought, 'now' to settle the question 'for ever',[6] since Redistribution could not 'now' be settled on his terms. His tactics were unexceptionable: Tory opposition to separation pointed 'conclusively to the probability that the course would be the most advantageous...to take'.[7] The confidence of his tactical assertion was exceptionable only as regards the language he employed – 'agitation on the Franchise as the *card* to play which would give the Liberals a majority at the next elections!'[8] What Chamberlain *desired* was postponement of Redistribution, not to 1885, but to the Greek Kalends or to Gladstone's retirement. Such things, such exceptionable ambition, he had to keep to himself. Even Morley knew nothing of Chamberlain's mind at the time of the Leeds Conference. Never looking beyond 1885, he was still

[1] *Pall Mall Gazette*, 12 Jan. 1884, p. 11. (My italics.)
[2] Chamberlain to George Dixon, 23 July 1883. Chamberlain Mss., JC5/27/15.
[3] Salisbury, 18 June 1883. 3 *Hansard* cclxxx. 751–2.
[4] Chamberlain, at Bristol, 26 Nov. 1883. *Annual Register*, p. 183.
[5] *The Times*, 29 Jan. 1884, p. 9.
[6] Elgin to R. P. Bruce, 29 Nov. 1883. Bruce Mss.
[7] Chamberlain to E. R. Russell, 21 Apr. 1883. Chamberlain Mss., JC5/62/6.
[8] Kate Courtney Journal, 9 Dec. 1883. Courtney Mss., 21.

mystified by and finding fault in Chamberlain's legislative timing: 'it makes against us, because we shall be settling Redistribution when the Crimes Act falls in.'[1] Morley had been one of the earliest proselytes to the programme of separation. He was long unaware of the implications of the 'plot for postponement'.[2] Hartington's fear of a plot was, of course, symptomatic of Cabinet malaise. Historically, the incident has greater interest as shedding light on the relationship and supposed identity of purpose between the Radical 'twins'. Dilke's readiness to take his orders from Birmingham[3] and to echo Chamberlain 'with the faithfulness of a parrot',[4] were more apparent than real. If Parliamentary Reform was taken in hand, he was prepared to stand firm by Chamberlain for separate dealing, though viewing the question primarily as one of sound administration. It was Chamberlain's motivation, wholly dissimilar, which gave rise to talk of the conspiracy whereby 'Franchise only' was to be substituted for 'Franchise first'. But was Reform, however dealt with, to take precedence in 1884? Northcote found it beyond belief that the Government 'should lay aside their Local Government schemes' on this count,[5] and gave warning to his party: 'We are told...as if it were gospel, that the next session...is to be devoted to a great measure of [Parliamentary] reform;...they have in reserve for us something much beyond that.'[6] Northcote's belittling of Reform sharpened the edge of Dilke's personal involvement in Local Government, which already threatened to outbalance the promotion of Radical (i.e. Chamberlain's) interests. The episode merits attention.

A few days after the Redistribution bill had been presented to the Commons, Elliot talked at length with Hartington about the legislative programme of the two previous years: 'He says [the] Country does not care a bit about reform of local government, though it *ought* to; that the Govt. attempt to whip up interest in the subject had proved a failure.'[7] Late in 1882, Hartington had 'made Mr. G. extremely cross' by suggesting that 'if we were to have the Local Govt. Bill again...some of us ought to try to get up

[1] Morley to Chamberlain, 14 Oct. 1883. Chamberlain Mss., JC5/54/511.
[2] Gladstone to Hartington, 29 Dec. 1883. Gladstone Mss., 44146 fol. 267.
[3] Dilke to Chamberlain, 3 Feb. 1883. Chamberlain Mss., JC5/24/47.
[4] Cooper to Rosebery, 16 Jan. 1885. Rosebery Mss., Box 9.
[5] Northcote to Gibson, 8 Nov. 1883. Ashbourne Mss.
[6] At Belfast. *The Times*, 4 Oct. 1883, p. 10.
[7] Elliot Diary, 14 Dec. 1884. Diaries, Vol. 10.

the subject during the vacation.'[1] Legislation had been shelved for 1883 because 'Gladstone felt he could not keep out of so big a question and felt not equal to it'[2] once his Irish scheme had been destroyed, and because, in the 'general post' of December 1882, it was by no means clear whether it would be Childers as Chancellor or Dilke – Dodson's successor at the Local Government Board – who would take charge of the measure. If the former, as one of Gladstone's secretaries drily remarked, 'perhaps Dilke will be converted' to a belief that it ought to be postponed till after the Franchise bill.[3] In any case, since Dilke found the Dodson–Fitzmaurice draft 'a poor thing which I should not like to father',[4] the old but available scheme was condemned before the new could be framed. Most of the Cabinet were, however, clear as to relative priorities. A memorandum by Lambert, advocating delay until after Franchise had been settled, brought forth short and sharp protests from Hartington, Derby, Kimberley, Granville, Spencer, Carlingford and Selborne; while Harcourt, whom Dilke congratulated as 'the only member of the Cabinet who had the sense not to write a minute',[5] made plain in private correspondence his concurrence with the majority, against the Birmingham programme.[6] Carlingford suspected Chamberlain's purpose – to procure Government acknowledgment of the inherent incapacity of the existing Parliament to deal with any part of County Government.[7] Derby, a month later, thought Chamberlain had probably succeeded in that aim: there was no hope of taking the bill now, and next year seemed booked for the Franchise measure.[8]

In understanding the Radical reaction in 1884, we must abandon the innocent belief that the Radical heart had warmed once and for all to franchise extension after the election of 1874 when the counties south of the Trent and north of Cornwall returned only four Liberals.[9] In fact, the Radical duumvirate was sorely strained over Gladstone's programme.[10]

[1] Hartington to Spencer, 25 Dec. 1882. Spencer Mss.
[2] Rathbone to his Wife, 4 Mar. 1883. Rathbone Mss., IX.4.78.
[3] Seymour to Hamilton, 11 Jan. 1883. Hamilton Mss., 48615.
[4] Stephen Gwynn and G. M. Tuckwell, *The Life of the Rt. Hon. Sir Charles W. Dilke Bart., M.P.* (2 vols., 1917), Vol. I, p. 514.
[5] Dilke to Harcourt, 3 Feb. 1883. Dilke Mss., 43890 fol. 192.
[6] Dilke to Chamberlain, 3 Feb. 1883. Chamberlain Mss., JC5/24/47.
[7] Carlingford Memo., 20 Jan. 1883. Dilke Mss., 43912 fol. 127.
[8] Derby to Rathbone, 28 Feb. 1883. Rathbone Mss., IX.7.83.
[9] G. M. Trevelyan, *The Life of John Bright* (1913), p. 438.
[10] This is not at all apparent from a reading of the Dilke Memoir. On 17 August, 'I had a long talk with Mr. Gladstone at Holland House in which I thought

Chamberlain expressed concern for London whose quota of seats might be trebled; he anticipated that 'Hodge' would record an agricultural (i.e. Conservative) and not a labouring (i.e. Liberal) vote; moreover, Yorkshire and Lancashire, certain to benefit under any Redistribution, would, so all others contended, produce more of that 'stamp of radical who ought to be in the Govt.'[1] than Caucus toadies. Nor was Chamberlain given to Radical dreaming of the promised land. Elliot, in a dinner conversation, could not discern any 'political *ends* at which he was aiming;' he did 'not throw out any light, as to what use should be made of this [democratic] power.'[2] Elliot was not deceived. Chamberlain entertained no big political ideas. He pushed for Reform in order to extend his territorial base, calculating that the 'chief advantage' would be found in the counties of Nottingham, Shropshire, Stafford, Warwick and Worcester, whose enfranchised voters would be of precisely 'the same class as that which gives us our best representatives.'[3]

Chamberlain in 1883 was a disappointed, frustrated man. Office, once accepted, had brought him little further to the forefront. The years of the Second Ministry, indeed, witnessed 'rather a diminution than an augmentation of the great authority he exercised in the ranks of the party outside, and especially in Birmingham.'[4] The office he accepted – the Presidency of the Board of Trade – was moreover one which in Disraeli's late administration had not even commanded a Cabinet seat. But where Chamberlain lacked strength was not so much in the Cabinet (where the person may count for more than his job) as on the 'Gladstonolatorous' benches of the Commons where he hoped a franchise extension would bear fruit. More immediately, though, Chamberlain's eyes were fixed on the fruits of a Franchise bill crisis – a dissolution on Reform and the powers of the Lords; when the Radical thousands marched on Hyde Park, Chamberlain saw himself at their head.[5]

that I had induced him to take the franchise in 1884 and to put it first.' A similar tale of conquest (for which it was a necessary premise that Gladstone should favour keeping Reform for 1885) was despatched to Grant Duff in India. Dilke Memoir, 17 Aug. 1883. Dilke Mss., 43937 fol. 153; Dilke to Grant Duff, 17/18 Aug. 1883. Dilke Mss., 43894 fol. 110.

1 Seymour to Hamilton, 13 Jan. 1883. Hamilton Mss., 48615.
2 Elliot Diary, 22 Nov. 1883. Diaries, Vol. 9. There was no love lost between Chamberlain and the Minto family; at one of his first Cabinets, Chamberlain had attempted to secure the recall of Sir Henry Elliot (son of the Second Earl), Ambassador in Vienna.
3 Chamberlain to Maxse, 14 Dec. 1882. Maxse Mss., 206.
4 T. P. O'Connor, *Memoirs of an Old Parliamentarian* (2 vols., 1929), Vol. i, p. 315.
5 Chamberlain to Labouchère, 18 Dec. 1883. Chamberlain Mss., JC5/50/16a.

Such things were not to Dilke's taste. His 'greater personal popularity, his higher social position, his being more a man of the world, his superior faculties of leading or influencing others'[1] suggested an alternative route. To those who knew how the political world worked, Chamberlain appeared, however unjustly, as the 'bruiser'[2] who used 'the simple power of "You shall, and you go to the devil if you don't."'[3] To a fellow member of the Melbourne, his sins were such as would destroy 'the spirit of Clubs'. He was 'loud, argumentative, laid down the law on every conceivable point, even as regards points of which...[he was] ludicrously ignorant, [and] bullied the servants'. His 'high moral rectitude', which none questioned, did not make him any the less an 'objectionable beast'.[4] To a junior Government minister with a spurious Radical reputation, he was a dirty trickster.[5] To Gladstone – and this was important – he was a man of 'no reverence'.[6] Chamberlain looms large in the letters of contemporaries; Dilke does not, precisely because he caused so much the less offence. Hence Hamilton's forecast that, though there was 'more in Chamberlain's little finger than in the whole of Dilke', the latter would win 'the political race'.[7]

But Dilke, as junior member of the Cabinet, needed to prove his administrative and legislative abilities before Reform swallowed everything else. The bill which he and Thring produced during the summer of 1883 made ridiculous Chamberlain's arguments, urged earlier in the year, for postponement of Local Government. Several Cabinet ministers objected to the draft as 'too complete'.[8] Dilke himself, never given to modesty, called it 'revolutionary: – a sort of 1789'.[9] He always looked on the introduction of a County Franchise bill as immediately preparatory to, and heralding, dissolution.[10] It was the card to play during 1882 in face of the probability of defeat on the *clôture* or of sustained Lords' opposition

1 Hamilton Diary, 25 Mar. 1883. Hamilton Mss., 48633 fol. 76.
2 William O'Brien, *Evening Memories* (Dublin, 1920), p. 2.
3 Beatrice Webb, *My Apprenticeship* (1926), p. 128.
4 A. K. Finlay to Elliot, 31 Dec. 1882. Elliot Mss., Bundle 31.
5 Mundella to Leader, 23 Jan. 1883. Mundella–Leader Mss.
6 Hamilton Diary, 1 Jan. 1884. Hamilton Mss., 48635 fol. 49.
7 Hamilton Diary, 25 Mar. 1883. Hamilton Mss., 48633 fol. 76. But see also Cooper to Lady Rosebery, 25 June 1884: 'Chamberlain has been complaining bitterly about Lord Granville, and has been whispering about changes. Oddly enough he has, it seems, let it be known, that Dilke can get no further.' Rosebery Mss., Box 9.
8 Dilke Memoir, 25 July 1883. Dilke Mss., 43937 fol. 146.
9 Dilke to Grant Duff, 29 Aug. 1883. Dilke Mss., 43894 fol. 111.
10 Dilke Memoir, 9 Feb. 1882. Dilke Mss., 43936 fol. 50.

to the Arrears bill —[1] an issue on which no right-minded Liberal would choose to go to the country. So now, in August 1883, he sketched out his campaign for the ensuing year: though all three major measures were to be announced in the Queen's Speech, Local and Metropolitan Government were to be pressed and a Franchise bill to be brought on only if either of the others came to grief.[2] The most likely explanation of Dilke's conversion is a hint from Gladstone as to Dilke's role in framing a future Redistribution bill.[3] In October, a Cabinet Committee was formed to deal with the question of Local Government; in November, it split into two camps when Carlingford, Derby, Dodson and Kimberley turned to a rival 'very timid' scheme of Fitzmaurice's in preference to Dilke's.[4] But it was not these Whig backslidings which led Dilke to tag it a 'funeral meeting' that produced the final, and from his point of view much emasculated, draft of the bill in January.[5] Rather, from the previous October, chances of *legislation* materializing had become, granted Gladstone's political survival, inversely dependent upon Franchise bill fluctuations. Reform survived the Cabinet. All else was thereby reduced to 'a great scheme of bribery and temptation'.[6]

It is abundantly clear that when Gladstone surrendered his Irish Local Government proposals, he simultaneously dissociated himself from any Liberal toying with a measure for Great Britain alone. The innocence of his language — that franchise equalization 'need not occupy, perhaps, so much as half the Session [,] and it might thus leave room for a measure or measures of Local Government, comprehending England and Scotland, though hardly Ireland too' —[7] fooled no-one. The County Government bill was put into shape not, as Gladstone asserted, 'without prejudice',[8] but

---

[1] Dilke to Grant Duff, 10 Aug. 1882. Dilke Mss., 43894 fol. 90; Dilke Diary, 2 Aug. 1882. Dilke Mss., 43925 fol. 18.

[2] Hamilton Diary, 15 Aug. 1883. Hamilton Mss., 48634 fol. 50.

[3] Dilke records an unofficial Cabinet at which were 'discussed the general lines upon which I was to privately prepare in my office a Redistribution scheme.' Memoir, 23 Nov. 1883. Dilke Mss., 43937 fol. 196.

[4] Dilke to Gladstone, 19 Nov. 1883. Gladstone Mss., 44149 fol. 186.

[5] Dilke to Gladstone, 15 Jan. 1884. Gladstone Mss., 44149 fol. 198.

[6] Northcote to Winn, 5 Jan. 1882. Nostell Mss., 1/65. All Nostell Mss. references are to the series D3.8.4. Compare Kimberley to Ripon, 10 Jan. 1884: 'There is much talk of other measures, but I believe that whatever is proposed, Parliamentary Reform, like Aaron's rod, will probably swallow them all up.' Ripon Mss., 43524 fol. 132.

[7] Gladstone to Hartington, 22 Oct. 1883. Gladstone Mss., 44546 fol. 179.

[8] Gladstone to Hartington, 7 Nov. 1883. Gladstone Mss., 44146 fol. 231.

under Gladstonian slight. Nevertheless, the Liberal record after three and a half years of office was far from comforting. Caine, Melly, Rathbone, Stansfeld and Whitbread, all more or less 'identified with Local Govt.'[1] but yet representing the 'centre' of Liberal opinion, were agreed that to go to the country 'with no more practical legislation [for] the great practical mass of the liberal party'[2] and only upon County Franchise (by implication an election cry, and non-practical) would prove disastrous. It was, therefore, Governmental calculation which determined that, while Franchise was undertaken, at least an appearance should be given that 'the rest [would] not [be] left undone.'[3] Herbert Gladstone, hot-foot from Hawarden, impressed on the Leeds delegates that a Suffrage bill did not mean dissolution. The *Manchester Guardian* sowed promising seeds of doubt, claiming it as a fact that Gladstone put Franchise behind Local and Irish Government, and Metropolitan Reform 'first in point of precedence and of obligation.'[4] Dilke, speaking at Glasgow, dwelt on the close connection between Parliamentary, Local and London Government Reform 'with an emphasis which might be intended to prepare men's minds for a different order of procedure from that recommended by the National Liberal Federation.'[5] One Member, at least, concluded 'from the official newspapers' that the Government were 'fishing as to whether they can postpone their reform bill for another session.'[6]

Gladstone intended, so he said, to 'take London in the first pause in franchise' and to send it to a Special Grand Committee;[7] the Cabinet settled on 4 January to introduce the measure after the Second Reading of the Franchise bill. Precise programming mattered the less after Gladstone's initial declaration to the Cabinet of his intentions for 1884, which were rightly interpreted to mean 'franchise I & all the rest nowhere.'[8] The important consideration was to pack as much as possible into the Queen's Speech, even though Gladstone saw as inevitable the postponement for a

---

[1] Rathbone to his Wife, 24 Feb. 1883. Rathbone Mss., IX.4.76.
[2] Rathbone to Gladstone, 23 Oct. 1883. Gladstone Mss., 44483 fol. 266; see also Rathbone to Carlingford, 29 Nov. 1883. Carlingford Mss., 322/CP3/187.
[3] *Daily News*, 24 Oct. 1883, p. 4.
[4] 16 Oct. 1883, p. 5.
[5] *The Times*, 31 Oct. 1883, p. 9.
[6] Elliot Diary, 16 Oct. 1883. Elliot Diaries, Vol. 9.
[7] Dilke Diary, 30 Nov. 1883. Dilke Mss., 43925 fol. 76.
[8] Dilke Diary, 21 Oct. 1883. Dilke Mss., 43925 fol. 71.

forty-ninth year of the London bill,[1] and feared that Radicals and the City might anyway unite to throw out legislation on the vesting of the Metropolitan police force in the Home Secretary's hands.[2] After Leeds, Chamberlain's optimism about the attraction of Franchise *tout court* was boundless,[3] but on this he stood alone. Those with first-hand knowledge and, like Dilke, with seats at stake, saw the fate of London Liberals as resting upon a Government pledge to deal, at the very least, with the more practical question of water supply.[4] In the event, because Harcourt who expected the Government to 'go smash' on Franchise[5] 'came round to leaving the police alone',[6] the shop-window contained its full measure of attractions.

In the course of a prolific speech-making tour during the autumn, Childers was able to ascertain the opinions of a considerable number 'of our party in different parts of the country (not Ireland)' and to satisfy himself that the Leeds programme 'greatly offended large bodies of Liberals'.[7] The manner in which the National Liberal Federation forced forward 'separation' probably did no more than propel the wavering towards opposition; only babes in politics believed that the Government acted on Leeds' dictates, however much political capital was made of the assertion. Childers himself, having previously 'seen the advantages of dealing with the Franchise first',[8] had moved to the opposite flank *before* the Conference pronounced one way or the other.[9] Nearly three months later, he half-heartedly vindicated Gladstone's proposal to begin by giving the Commons a preliminary outline of his redistribution

[1] Gladstone to Childers, 10 Sept. 1883. Gladstone Mss., 44546 fol. 157.
[2] Firth to Harcourt, 6 Nov. 1883. Harcourt Mss. The omens were not favourable. The Government could count on the active opposition of 15 Members out of 22 – 'a nice working majority to go to a Grand Committee', as Harcourt sneered. Harcourt to Lewis Harcourt, 16 Dec. 1883. Harcourt Mss. Moreover, on the Liberal side, 'experienced members of town-councils such as Rathbone, Fowler of Wolverhampton &c. [were] not at all enthusiastic about the bill'. Elliot Diary, 4 July 1884. Diaries, Vol. 10. And finally, the Nationalists (according to a report in *The Times*) had resolved to oppose any such legislation unless a similar measure was promised for Dublin. 6 Feb. 1884, p. 9.
[3] Chamberlain to Dilke, 28 Oct. 1883. Chamberlain Mss., JC5/24/342.
[4] Fawcett to Derby, 8 Oct. 1883. Derby Mss., Box 3.
[5] Harcourt to Lewis Harcourt, 10 Jan. 1884. Harcourt Mss.
[6] Dilke Diary, 8 Nov. 1883. Dilke Mss., 43925 fol. 73.
[7] Childers Memo., 12 Nov. 1883. Gladstone Mss., 44130 fol. 330.
[8] *Ibid.*
[9] Elliot Diary, 16 Oct. 1883. Diaries, Vol. 9.

proposals, on the ground that it was the 'only possible compromise ...Less concession than this would have been fatal. More was unattainable. I agree with you, but I belong to a very small minority.'[1] The minority may be traced quite simply to Gladstone's identification with the programme of 'Franchise first', which of course lay behind Hartington's self-pitying wail that he was led to expect 'from what had fallen from the Chancellor, and from what others had said to me in private, that there would have been at least some discussion.'[2] Note has already been taken of Carlingford's and Selborne's objection, expressed vis-à-vis Ireland, and of Spencer's inability to meet their argument except by reference to Gladstone's 'personal' statement. What others said 'in private' demonstrates clearly that Childers, while faithfully portraying Cabinet pressures, concealed – perhaps took as read – the natural reluctance of more than an insignificant few to sanction the proposed course.

Cooper, editor of the *Scotsman*, awakening to the fact that he had earlier been swindled into spreading Birmingham doctrine, now settled scores by spelling out the Chamberlain design to Northbrook.[3] Northbrook, who entertained a dislike of 'meddling with delicate matters' outside his own province at the India Office, acted promptly on Cooper's information and, while host to Gladstone in late November, ventured to suggest that at the very least 'we ought to be prepared with the main lines of the redistribution'.[4] Kimberley had long dreaded the inevitable political crisis and postponement of more practical legislation that would result from separation.[5] Dodson's position was indistinguishable from Shaw-Lefevre's, as detailed by a memorandum in favour of joint dealing: 'At best, if we carry Franchise this year we shall be upset on Rn. next.'[6] Derby was strong against providing the Lords with the 'plausible pretext... "We must see your whole plan before we will sanction it"'.[7] And Granville, though opposed to *binding* the Government to combining Franchise and Redistribution,[8] still

[1] Childers to Halifax, 7 Jan. 1884. Hickleton Mss., A4.90.
[2] Hartington to Gladstone, 31 Dec. 1883. Bernard Holland, *The Life of Spencer Compton, Eighth Duke of Devonshire* (2 vols., 1911), Vol. i, p. 401.
[3] Northbrook to Spencer, 26 Nov. 1883. Spencer Mss.
[4] Northbrook to Granville, 27 Dec. 1883. Granville Mss., PRO. 30/29/139.
[5] Kimberley Memo., 16 Jan. 1883. Dilke Mss., 43891 fol. 253.
[6] Dodson Memo., n.d. (? 12 Nov. 1883) Monk Bretton Mss., 63.
[7] Derby to Granville, 28 Oct. 1883. Granville Mss., PRO. 30/29/27A.
[8] Granville Memo., 20 Jan. 1883. Dilke Mss., 43881 fol. 106.

could 'not answer any of [Derby's] arguments'.[1] Whatever the motivation – and Whig practicability, a desire for settlement, Ulster anxieties and distrust of Chamberlain are inextricably intermingled – ten members of a Cabinet of fourteen comprised Childers' 'small minority'. But the personal inclinations of the several elements in a Cabinet, in whatever preponderance, rarely determine Cabinet policy.

The historian who makes a clear-cut division between specifically Irish objections and objections made specifically to severance, falsifies by masking the overlap in political instinct. There is, however, this political justification for the analytical course, that unease did tend to emerge as articulate antipathy on one count or the other. Gladstone indeed induced specific objection, for specific objection was the more readily met. Childers qualified his preference for joint dealing with the proviso, 'if it *can* be done hopefully';[2] Gladstone said it could not. The Cabinet of 22 November was to be crucial – Hartington was to argue for the double-barrelled bill. It was remarkable in the event for the sound of silence: 'Mr. G. read a memdm. in favour of a Franchise Bill only, and going into the question of redistribution to show its enormous magnitude & difficulty. He also repeated that *he* could not possibly undertake it. There was after this little to be said.'[3] On the Irish tack, Carlingford, Northbrook and Selborne met with a rebuff from Spencer. In many respects, his standing firm by Gladstone – in December 1882, he had doubted whether the Irish franchise could be touched at all when English Reform came up –[4] was decisive in clearing the Cabinet hurdle; Spencer was trusted where Gladstone was not.

Of the other doubters, Granville was neither inclined nor of the stuff nor at an age to divide the Cabinet; Argyll's testimony is sufficient, and all the more rare in political correspondence for

---

[1] Granville to Derby, 20 Aug. 1884. Derby Mss., Box 3.
[2] Elliot Diary, 16 Oct. 1883. Diaries, Vol. 9.
[3] Carlingford to Spencer, 22 Nov. 1883. Spencer Mss.
[4] Spencer to Hartington, 10 Dec. 1882. Devonshire Mss., 340.1287. See Chamberlain to Dilke, 28 Oct. 1883: 'Mr. G. sent for me on Friday to talk over the result of the Cabinet with which he is himself very much pleased. He thinks H. will go all right, in view of S.'s strong opinion.' Chamberlain Mss., JC5/24/342. But compare Spencer to Harcourt, 27 Dec. 1883: 'My intervention, which I did not voluntarily undertake, but which Mr. G. at last begged me to make, was utterly useless, not the least notice of my appeal having been taken by H. He may have been put out with me, or probably treated me with contempt, but we are such old friends it cannot matter, and I shall not refer to the matter again.' Harcourt Mss.

being direct: 'I have sometimes asked myself "is there any conceivable measure that Granville wd. *not* accept rather than split the party?" and I have never been able to answer this question to my own satisfaction.'[1] Derby, while appearing to express 'the life-long judgment of a Nestor', had sunk so low in political esteem that Dilke found it 'difficult even to remember the enormous weight he had possessed in the earliest part of his...career.'[2] The rat, having thrown himself 'helplessly at Gladstone's feet' by deserting the Tories,[3] could not re-rat.[4] Derby saw no future in Conservatism,[5] and it is in any case doubtful whether he would have cast in his lot with Hartington after the latter's celebrated dismissal of him, in a Cabinet discussion upon Agricultural Holdings, as the 'mere owner of Liverpool ground rents.'[6]

In several minds, the innate political propensity for self-preservation was probably foremost. The point need not be laboured. Granville's inefficiency at the Foreign Office and premature hastening towards senility were already the subject of comment. Dodson was 'an estimable and painstaking man, with a certain capacity for figures such as is in all probability enjoyed by nine out of ten clerks in the kingdom.'[7] There was Carlingford who, as Gladstone knew, added 'no strength to the Government'[8] but whose determination, when asked to make way for Rosebery, and

---

[1] Argyll to Granville, 10 July 1885. Granville Mss., PRO. 30/29/28A. Milner, as behoves a bright young man before his political guardian, was saying clever things – *viz.*, upon the distinction between the Whig and the moderate Liberal: 'The words are now used interchangeably by many people, a fatal thing for the Moderates. For a real Moderate Liberal is a man whose moderation is based on principle, as strong, maybe stronger and better digested than that of the more advanced men. But the moderation of the Whig is the result not of moderate principles but of the accident of birth and of having no principles at all...The identification of moderate Liberalism and Whiggery, and the confidence felt by Moderates when they see a Cabinet stuck full of Whigs is therefore a grave delusion'. Milner to Goschen, 21 Aug. 1884. Cited in T. J. Spinner, 'George Joachim Goschen, 1831–1907, British Statesman and Politician' (Unpublished Ph.D. thesis, University of Rochester, New York, 1963), p. 318.

[2] Dilke Memoir, n.d. Dilke Mss., 43937 fol. 163.

[3] Argyll to Halifax, 14 Nov. 1881. Hickleton Mss., A4.82. Derby's manner appeared to a fellow-guest at Hawarden in November 1883 as that of a schoolboy to Gladstone's headmaster. C. Milnes Gaskell to Halifax, 6 Nov. 1883. Hickleton Mss., A4.169.

[4] Churchill's verdict. Gwynn, *Dilke*, Vol. i, p. 445.

[5] S. J. Reid (ed.), *Memoirs of Sir Wemyss Reid, 1842–1885* (1905), p. 375.

[6] Dilke Diary, 21 Apr. 1883. Dilke Mss., 43925 fol. 58.

[7] J. H. McCarthy, *England under Gladstone, 1880–1884* (1884), p. 31.

[8] Gladstone to Granville, 4 Sept. 1884. *Correspondence*, Vol. ii, p. 244.

offered in compensation either the Berlin or the Constantinople embassy, was to 'stick to the cabinet for better, for worse'.[1] These three, along with Derby and the 72-year-old Selborne, were likely casualties in any Cabinet reshuffle consequent upon Gladstone's retirement.[2] Any member of his Cabinet might mouth before Gladstone's throne, 'You are the Party & your acts are its acts';[3] but for the ageing and ineffectual, the refrain was an injunction to total obedience. None could forget that Gladstone's acts and Gladstone's survival were co-terminous with their survival.

The singularity of Hartington's aversion, a source of strength rather than of weakness, was pinpointed by Derby, whose aid Gladstone invoked in resolving the crisis: 'the fact that he has not put his wish to retire on any very intelligible ground does not make the matter better since it seems to indicate rather a general dislike to the course of policy in which he is engaged, than a special objection, which could be dealt with by argument, to one particular measure.'[4] This is *not* to say that Hartington had not suggested 'rather seriously' to his confidant, Northbrook, before the Cabinet of 22 November, that he would yield on the single bill but would go out over extension to Ireland.[5] It *is* to say that Hartington was not the man to recede from 'almost hopeless embarrassment',[6] or 'frankly [to] abandon an untenable ground',[7] as Gladstone fondly called it, simply because he could not match the slickness of the other's debating mind. Harcourt found it impossible to tie Hartington down, precisely because he had 'no counter-arguments to produce, as he himself admits.'[8] Indeed, by gratuitous acknowledgment of his deficiencies in quick-fire discussion and by 'sham[ming] stupid',[9] he conducted and perfected a brand of 'obstruction' in the highest councils, which Dilke and Chamberlain found reminiscent of the Commons redoubtables, O'Donnell and

---

[1] Carlingford to Granville, 4 Sept. 1884. Cited in *Correspondence*, Vol. II, p. 247 n. 6.
[2] Lewis Harcourt Journal, 4 Jan. 1885. Harcourt Mss. (I have seen only a typescript copy of the Journal.)
[3] Harcourt to Gladstone, 16 June 1885. Gladstone Mss., 44198 fol. 205.
[4] Derby to Gladstone, 31 Dec. 1883. Gladstone Mss., 44142 fol. 35.
[5] Northbrook to Spencer, 26 Nov. 1883. Spencer Mss.
[6] Gladstone to Granville, 10 Dec. 1883. *Correspondence*, Vol. II, p. 123.
[7] Gladstone to Spencer, 10 Dec. 1883. Gladstone Mss., 44547 fol. 11.
[8] Hamilton to Gladstone, 30 Dec. 1883. Gladstone Mss., 44189 fol. 272.
[9] Chamberlain to Dilke, 5 Mar. 1884. Dilke Mss., 43886 fol. 128. Compare a recent assessment: Hartington 'found it hard to understand Gladstone, and towards the end of their association he gave up the attempt to do so.' Trevor Lloyd, *The General Election of 1880* (Oxford, 1968), p. 36.

Lowther.[1] 'When Harty left the last Cabt. he said to Brett, "I made a very bad fight of it", but he at once wrote to Mr. G. & said it must be understood that he had not given in.'[2] Hartington was not incapable of polemic or, *pace* Derby, point by point refutation of the Cabinet's proposed course of action. His memorandum of 25 December is a masterly piece of writing – its only defect being that it was so utterly damning in intention.[3]

Hartington, however, was not susceptible to the listing of his former votes and commitments respecting the junction of Franchise and Redistribution when these were compiled for his edification; this Dilke–Gladstone exercise had, in fact, the very opposite effect from that designed – a stiffening of sinews.[4] Above all, it needs stressing that Hartington had 'intelligible ground' for complaint. His grievances were not those of a man who simply had no right to be in Liberal ranks. The party, wrote Mundella, 'have nobody like him for sound judgment [and] common sense.'[5] But Hartington demanded materials for the forming of 'sound judgment' – Irish statistics which would substantiate Hartington's instinct. *Il n'y a rien de si brutal qu'un fait.* Hartington knew it, as did Gladstone who remembered perhaps better than anyone else the dramatic effect in 1866 on Parliamentary opinion and Liberal fortunes of Lambert's returns.[6]

On 7 February 1884, the Earl of Limerick moved for returns of population in Irish counties and boroughs, and the registered electorate, acreage, valuation of rateable property, number of lands, tenements, hereditaments, and inhabited houses, at their different ratings in each constituency. The request, he blandly suggested, would readily be met: 'the information was no doubt in their [the Government's] possession. They must, he thought, have considered the details which he asked for if they had come to the conclusion to bring in such a measure.'[7] The request met, in the first instance, with opposition from Carlingford. What mattered more than this was that the Lords' demand was for information which Trevelyan took to lie within the province of the Dublin Commissioner of Valuation, information whose non-availability

[1] Chamberlain–Dilke exchange, n.d. Dilke Mss., 43886 fols. 172–3.
[2] Dilke to Chamberlain, [1 Dec. 1883.] Chamberlain Mss., JC5/24/51.
[3] Gladstone to Hartington, Telegram, 29 Dec. 1883. Gladstone Mss., 44146 fol. 266.
[4] Gladstone to Granville, 18 Dec. 1883. *Correspondence*, Vol. II, p. 130.
[5] Mundella to Leader, 17 Feb. 1883. Mundella–Leader Mss.
[6] Cowling, *1867*, pp. 88 and 96.
[7] 3 *Hansard* cclxxxiv. 166.

would give 'a sort of excuse for throwing out the bill as far as Ireland is concerned'; he expressed regret at 'our *having not to press* Ball Greene [the Commissioner] for a new edition of the return of 1873.'[1]

Cabinet Gradgrinds were ill-served and discussion was destined to be ill-informed throughout the autumn of 1883. Symbolically, on the October day when Gladstone first brought the County Suffrage before the Cabinet, Harcourt announced that the Home Office could give no date for completion of the returns of electoral statistics ordered six months before.[2] And if any hopes were raised a fortnight later by an announcement from the London Correspondent of the *Manchester Guardian* that the report was in 'such a forward condition as to be practically at the service of the Cabinet',[3] they were doomed to eight weeks' disappointment. In January, again, no-one in the Cabinet knew whether or not there was a £5 Irish freehold franchise, let alone how many might exercise such a vote.[4] The very day before Limerick successfully divided the House, Lambert at the Local Government Board was discovering internal discrepancies in Parliamentary returns and fretting over the belated arrival of Dublin Castle homework 'in consequence of poor Hancock being *hors de combat* or in other words sent to a Lunatic Asylum.'[5] But alongside such setbacks, there was, as Trevelyan hinted, the withholding of the unpalatable under instruction from higher authority.

The numbers of lodgers, women occupiers, paupers, non-ratepayers and so forth complicated any prediction as to the effects of franchise extension.[6] Hartington recognized that the separation of the measures and the likelihood of an election forced on 'bastard' constituencies (i.e. before Redistribution) not merely made for uncertainty but rendered all forecasting suspect. Beyond this, he

---

[1] Trevelyan to Spencer, 7 Feb. 1884. Spencer Mss. (My italics.)
[2] *The Times*, 25 Oct. 1883, p. 10.
[3] 7 Nov. 1883, p. 5.
[4] Dodson Cabinet Minutes, 4 Jan. 1884. Monk Bretton Mss., 62.
[5] Lambert to Hamilton, 6 Feb. 1884. Gladstone Mss., 44235 fol. 161. As Limerick himself knew, the effective core of the return – effective in terms of arousing 'mud cabin' prejudice – was not so much in numbers as in value. The Treasury saw fit to present the additional estimate of £500 to cover expenses for such detailed inquiry before work could begin; thus, so far from the evidence being laid upon the Table before the Franchise bill's Second Reading, Radicals were still in April preparing to move the reduction of the Vote by the amount asked for.
[6] Hartington to Gladstone, 24 Oct. 1883. Gladstone Mss., 44146 fol. 222. See also *The Times*, 16 Oct. 1883, p. 7.

rightly suspected Gladstone of fighting shy over divulgence of facts.[1] When Hartington asked for simple statistics on uniform household suffrage in Ireland, Gladstone dredged up once more the pointlessness (which was not questioned) of preserving a £4 line and demanded that Hartington should list the 'heads of information' that he wanted.[2] When he asked for the memorandum Gladstone had read to the Cabinet on 22 November, Gladstone gave instructions for it to be 'written out fair' and sent, 'though the figures about Irish Provinces [were] not included.'[3] They were, indeed, too 'awful...for poor Hartington to swallow – 700,000 county householders' in Ireland.[4] The estimates that did come before the Cabinet, on a paper dated 14 December 1883, had been printed more than a fortnight later, and only after the Hartington difficulty was patched over. They were based upon the calculation that in Irish counties just 65 %, and in boroughs even 10 % fewer, of the householders 'would be found to register.'[5] Registration tends to be neglected by historians as a poor cousin to Franchise and Redistribution.[6] But Gladstone did not neglect it when it served his purpose to amend an inconvenient set of statistics by taking into account the restrictive mechanisms of voting.

The episode of itself does no more than betoken Gladstone's canny unwillingness to meet Hartington on the latter's ground. This failure of communication, as much as anything, crippled the Second Ministry. Hartington's 'general dislike to the course of policy in which he [was] engaged' – that is, his Whiggishness – naturally attained its apogee in anticipation of Reform. A thorough Whig in this respect, he 'believed that Government was a *practical thing*' and 'never confused inequalities with injustices and never desired to see administrations come and go by chance majorities or by the changing humours of millions of uninformed voters.'[7] What was more, another Reform struggle would aggravate (and not simply postpone the tackling of) the two fundamental problems of the day, as Hartington saw them – 'the restoration of order & efficiency to the House of Commons, and the government of Ireland.'[8] The closing scenes of the 'lost' Session of 1883, offending

[1] Hartington to Spencer, 18 Oct. 1883. Spencer Mss.
[2] Gladstone to Hartington, 7 Nov. 1883. Gladstone Mss., 44146 fol. 231.
[3] Gladstone to Hartington, 25 Nov. 1883. Gladstone Mss., 44546 fol. 195.
[4] Dilke to Chamberlain, 16 Nov. 1883. Gwynn, *Dilke*, Vol. II, p. 2.
[5] Ball Greene Memo. Cab. 37/12/1. [6] Compare Blewett, pp. 27–8.
[7] A. E. Pease, *Elections and Recollections* (1932), p. xiii.
[8] Hartington to Spencer, 18 Oct. 1883. Spencer Mss.

on both counts, had a notable impact upon his mind. Where others lamented the withdrawal of the Irish Constabulary bill as a retreat before the threat of obstruction,[1] Hartington saw it as 'an arrangement' entered into by Gladstone and Grosvenor with Parnell;[2] hence his urging that Trevelyan, 'dogged, semi-sulky'[3] and above suspicion, be given a Cabinet seat and the Parliamentary control of Irish affairs.[4] Reform, indeed, portended further below-board compromise with the disloyal, and here once more the impasse between leader and ex-leader was evident. When T. A. Dickson, the Tyrone Liberal, complained of the Government kowtowing to Parnell in 1883, Gladstone was not satisfied with repudiation of the charge 'except upon the merits', but questioned the right of the Irish 'moderate Liberals' to any special consideration.[5] Upon such an issue, Hartington acknowledged himself to be 'nearer the moderate Conservatives than I am to Mr. Gladstone.'[6] Borthwick's *Morning Post* instinctively echoed and consciously wooed him on behalf of the Conservative leader in the Commons: the distinction between Hartington and Northcote was 'artificial, arbitrary, personal', that between Hartington and Chamberlain (it might have substituted Gladstone) 'vital, fundamental, and essential'.[7] Hartington scanned the Irish Members returned since 1880, and preferred 'boldly' to refuse any whittling away of 'the powers which belong to...the well disposed classes.'[8] The present so-called 'sham' constituted less of a 'mockery of representation' than a 'system which will exclude...more than a million protestants... [all those] opposed to Home Rule,...the owners of landed property and the great majority of capitalists, manufacturers, merchants, men of business and professional men in Ireland...and will not only exclude them, but will misrepresent them by a body... hostile to every interest they possess and every opinion they hold.'[9]

Just as Churchill and his Fourth party cronies first assaulted

[1] Seymour to Spencer, 31 July 1883. Spencer Mss.; Forster to Spencer, 3 Aug. 1883. Spencer Mss.
[2] Brett Memo., 1 Sept. 1883. Viscount Esher, *Extracts from Journals, 1880–1895*, printed for private circulation (Cambridge, 1914), pp. 12–16.
[3] Trevelyan to his Sister, Alice, Jan. 1884. G. M. Trevelyan, *Sir George Otto Trevelyan: a Memoir* (1932), p. 115.
[4] Granville to Spencer, 23 Aug. 1883. Spencer Mss.
[5] Gladstone to Spencer, 2 Oct. 1883. Gladstone Mss., 44546 fol. 165.
[6] Brett Memo., 1 Sept. 1883. Esher, *Journals*, pp. 12–16.
[7] 4 Oct. 1883, p. 4.
[8] Hartington to Spencer, 25 Dec. 1882. Spencer Mss.
[9] Hartington Memo., 25 Dec. 1883. Gladstone Mss., 44146 fol. 258.

Smith, Cross, Dalrymple, Clarke and Robert Fowler – that is to say, those by whom Northcote was surrounded rather than Northcote himself;[1] just as Dilke and Chamberlain assaulted Goschen rather than Hartington in the long prelude to the 1885 election; so did the Conservatives, in attempting to detach Hartington from Gladstone, stress a Hartington–Chamberlain polarity.[2] So riven was the Tory leadership that wishful thinking, or hoping for 'a lucky break from some parliamentary combination'[3] in large measure replaced the backstairs derring-do of 1866–7. Salisbury's November journey to Inverary (at Smith's prompting) was not to sound out Argyll who, as anticipated, showed himself to be in 'a very Conservative frame of mind only hampered by his love for Gladstone & by a sort of fatalism.'[4] With 'no followers', Argyll's future was 'politically...a blank',[5] but he *was* a possible channel to Hartington. The whole episode is probably indicative more of Salisbury's desire to forestall Northcote in a similar move and to deprive him of all credit which might accrue in the effecting of that 'lucky break'. In the main, however, overtures were public. Henry Northcote, the 'little goat',[6] called for a banding together of moderate men. Salisbury challenged the Whigs outright to divorce themselves from imperial 'disintegration' by Gladstonian instalments.[7] Gladstone was himself struck by the ingenuity of an article in the *Standard*, which suggested that Hartington was committing political hara-kiri in allowing his name to be linked with what must be to him distasteful legislation.[8]

The die was not cast over Reform. Hartington, as Gladstone put it, behaved 'extremely well'.[9] He was unkindly treated, as any

[1] Gorst to Churchill, 15 Aug. 1883. Churchill Mss., 1/157.

[2] Stead, the editor of the *Pall Mall Gazette*, played his own game of journalistic exacerbation, inviting the Duke of Devonshire to make an open reply to Chamberlain's article in the December issue of the *Fortnightly Review*; Devonshire declined to consider himself 'in any respect a suitable representative of the London Ground Landlords.' Devonshire to Stead, 5 Dec. 1883. Milner Mss., Box 181.

[3] John Vincent, *The Times*, 24 Aug. 1968, p. 20.

[4] Salisbury to Manners, 24 Nov. 1883. Belvoir Mss.

[5] James Donaldson to Rosebery, 11 June 1884. Rosebery Mss., Box 11.

[6] Wolff to Churchill, 15 Nov. 1883. Churchill Mss., 2/213.

[7] Salisbury, 'Disintegration', *Quarterly Review*, Vol. CLVI (Oct. 1883), pp. 559–95.

[8] Hamilton Diary, 30 Nov. 1883. Hamilton Mss., 48635 fol. 7.

[9] Gladstone to Granville, 3 Jan. 1884. *Correspondence*, Vol. II, p. 143. Compare Gladstone to Granville, 9 July 1886: 'There is this difference between Hartington and Chamberlain, that the first behaves like and is a thorough gentleman. Of the other it is better not to speak.' *Ibid.*, p. 458.

chronicle must betray. Hartington demanded security, which Spencer favoured, for the Irish loyal minority.[1] Gladstone side-stepped; finding that Spencer treated minority representation as a branch of Redistribution, he made of that suggestion incontro-vertible doctrine and postponed consideration of this 'most unfortunate & annoying subject'.[2] Hartington was not impressed until Gladstone undertook to leave 'minorities' an open question in his statement to Parliament,[3] and to accord it ultimately 'a thorough and dispassionate consideration'.[4] Granville thought this 'an admirable bridge'; it was, if we recognize that Gladstone not only 'utterly disbelieve[d] in minority clauses' but 'believe[d] we sh[ould] never have [them].'[5] Hartington urged a reduction in the number of Irish Members; Gladstone acknowledged this to be 'a most grave question', and then in his Commons speech, to Hartington's disgust, 'expressed a strong and decided objection to any such proposal.'[6] Nor did Hartington fare better on other, and non-Irish counts. Here, Bright was pressed into service; his sentimentality for the 40/- freeholder 'might possibly be made the thin end of the wedge for a compromise'.[7] There was, in fact, no wedge, for all Hartington's self-consoling certainty that the class would be extinguished but for Gladstone's conservatism.[8] On the one hand, Conservatives had reasoned that a direct *non possumus* 'might and probably would be interpreted as meaning that if the 40*s.* freeholders were preserved we should not object to household suffrage in the Counties' – i.e. they foresaw objection on the basis of occupation being turned, by Government reprieve of the free-holders, to disarm their Second Reading opposition.[9] On the other, Parliamentary Radicals accepted that any attempt to slay the 40/-freeholders would unite 'all the foes of real reform...under the flag

[1] Hartington to Gladstone, 2 Dec. 1883. Gladstone Mss., 44146 fol. 235.
[2] Gladstone to Spencer, 6 Dec. 1883. (Wrongly dated, 8 Dec.) Gladstone Mss., 44310 fol. 175.
[3] Hartington to Devonshire, 14 Jan. 1884. Devonshire Mss., 340. 1401.
[4] Gladstone Memo., 3 Jan. 1884. Gladstone Mss., 44768 fol. 2.
[5] Gladstone Cabinet Minutes, 4 Jan. 1884. Gladstone Mss., 44645 fol. 9.
[6] Hartington to Gladstone, 6 Mar. 1884. Gladstone Mss., 44147 fol. 35. Compare Dilke to Chamberlain, n.d.: 'Mr. G. will fight a whole day in Cabinet to avoid telling Parlmt. something, & then after all will tell them twice as much in reply to Ashmead or Hicks.' Dilke Mss., 43886 fol. 157.
[7] Granville to Gladstone, 15 Dec. 1883. *Correspondence*, Vol. ii, p. 129.
[8] Hartington to Devonshire, 14 Jan. 1884. Devonshire Mss., 340.1401.
[9] Manners to Northcote, 4 Dec. 1883. Salisbury Mss., Series D.

of an ancient and yet democratic electoral right.'[1] 'But the matter', as all knew, turned upon 'personal questions.'[2] The Phoenix Park murders, Mrs Gladstone opined, had deprived Hartington of able counsel and 'insensibly' clouded his reading of Irish affairs.[3] The Duke of Devonshire, whether spontaneously or under his son's influence, was with him.[4] His mistress and 'Antient Egeria', the Duchess of Manchester, was, if loyal to the man, 'perpetually working against his colleagues',[5] and for years had been supposed to have prevented Hartington 'running straight' on County Franchise.[6] Derby took it that such 'social influences' could not be countered.[7] It is of course arguable that the volatility of these so-called stable (social) elements was no less than that of those that were labelled volatile; but his colleagues, working towards circumvention, concerned themselves exclusively with the latter. Harcourt and Grosvenor, 'fresh from Chatsworth & crammed with the bent of Ld. Hartington's mind',[8] convinced themselves that at bottom lay disinclination to bear the chief responsibility for Redistribution after Franchise – and Gladstone – had passed.[9] Gladstone mortgaged 'another small piece' of his 'small residue of life'.[10] Hartington graciously acknowledged the personal sacrifice, but until he knew the 'principles' for Redistribution, and until these had been 'stated by Mr. Gladstone in such a

---

[1] Henry Fowler to Morley, 26 Dec. 1883. Edith H. Fowler (Mrs. R. Hamilton), *The Life of Henry Hartley Fowler, First Viscount Wolverhampton* (1912), p. 155.

[2] Gladstone to Granville, 10 Dec. 1883. *Correspondence*, Vol. ii, p. 124.

[3] Gladstone to Granville, 3 Dec. 1883. *Ibid.*, p. 115. Compare Lady Frederick Cavendish's account of Gladstone's reaction: 'then Uncle W. came in...I saw his face, pale, sorrow-stricken, but like a prophet's in its look of faith and strength....his first words were, "Father, forgive them, for they know not what they do." Then he said to me, "Be assured it will not be in vain", and across all my agony there fell a bright ray of hope, and I saw in a vision Ireland at peace, and my darling's life-blood accepted as a sacrifice for Christ's sake, to help to bring this to pass.' John Bailey (ed.), *The Diary of Lady Frederick Cavendish* (2 vols., 1927), Vol. ii, p. 318.

[4] Granville to Gladstone, 4 Dec. 1883. *Correspondence*, Vol. ii, p. 119.

[5] Granville to Gladstone, 19 Dec. 1883. *Correspondence*, Vol. ii, p. 131. Compare Gladstone to Spencer, 30 Dec. 1883: 'Hartington is at present going all wrong....I have asked him to meet me (*from Kimbolton I am sorry to say*)'. Gladstone Mss., 44310 fol. 186 (My italics.); and Harcourt to Lewis Harcourt, 27 Dec. 1883: 'I fear the female influences are very adverse, and he is spending his Xmas at Kimbolton.' Harcourt Mss.

[6] Dilke Diary, 9 Aug. 1882. Dilke Mss., 43925 fol. 20.

[7] Derby to Gladstone, 31 Dec. 1883. Gladstone Mss., 44142 fol. 35.

[8] Hamilton Diary, 22 Dec. 1883. Hamilton Mss., 48635 fol. 35.

[9] Gladstone to Granville, 20 Dec. 1883. *Correspondence*, Vol. ii, p. 133.

[10] Gladstone to Harcourt, 26 Dec. 1883. Gladstone Mss., 44198 fol. 169.

way as to bind every member of the Cabinet',[1] difficulties would remain. 'However, no doubt it offers the possibility of an arrangement if there is any real agreement among us, as to what is to follow the Franchise Bill. If there is not, there does not seem to be much good in postponing a split which must come.'[2]

Postponement was imperative, and all that was deemed feasible. Harcourt, in a blithe moment, was heard to remark, 'if Mr. G. remains, it do'nt much matter who goes.'[3] Despondency immediately reasserted itself,[4] and for the rest gloom was unmitigated. Spencer prepared to leave Ireland 'for good'.[5] Hamilton from the first assumed that without Hartington the Government could not last out the Session[6] and that the Liberal party, thus discredited, would face disruption 'for years to come.'[7] On being shown Hartington's letter of resignation 'with a back door not absolutely shut',[8] Gladstone 'exclaimed [to Hamilton], "This is the deuce to pay... but I have never receded for a colleague. My practice has been to leave behind those who can't keep up with me." I remarked "No Hartington means no Reform Bill." Mr. G. said nothing for the moment, but after a pause remarked "I am inclined to think you are right."'[9]

Harcourt was worried by the possibility that Gladstone was not 'altogether aware' of the gravity of Hartington's retirement, 'and what a smash would ensue not only to the Govt. but to the Party.'[10] If so, Granville, 'with a refined discernment',[11] not only gave a negative answer to Gladstone's query, 'Can we go on if H. resigns?', but added more menacingly, 'even if all were ready to go on' –[12] a timely reminder of Whig unease in their Cabinet stronghold. The expectation was that, in the event of secession, Hartington might attempt to play Peel[13] with no chance of an early accession to

---

[1] Hartington Memo., 25 Dec. 1883. Gladstone Mss., 44146 fol. 258.
[2] Hartington to Harcourt, 24 Dec. 1883. Harcourt Mss.
[3] Seymour to Hamilton, 25 Dec. 1883. Hamilton Mss., 48615.
[4] Compare Carlingford Diary, 11 May 1885: 'Harcourt is an extraordinary fellow...He never attempts to excuse or reconcile his violent changes of opinion.' Carlingford Mss., DD/SH 360.
[5] Spencer to Harcourt, 27 Dec. 1883. Harcourt Mss.
[6] Hamilton Diary, 23 Nov. 1883. Hamilton Mss., 48634 fol. 134.
[7] Hamilton Diary, 3 Dec. 1883. Hamilton Mss., 48635 fol. 10.
[8] Granville to Spencer, 4 Dec. 1883. Spencer Mss.
[9] Hamilton Diary, 3 Dec. 1883. Hamilton Mss., 48635 fol. 10.
[10] Harcourt to Lewis Harcourt, 27 Dec. 1883. Harcourt Mss.
[11] Gladstone to Granville, 3 Jan. 1884. *Correspondence*, Vol. II, p. 143.
[12] Granville to Gladstone, 19 Dec. 1883. *Ibid.*, p. 132.
[13] Spencer to Granville, 6 Dec. 1883. Granville Mss., PRO. 30/29/29A.

power, but forming a party to maintain 'sound constitutional principles' and attract 'the best men'.[1] This, however, though Hartington may or may not have realized it, was thought dangerous in some quarters since 'its inevitable result [would] be to enlist on Parnell's side the radical forces in England.'[2] It was this threat of a 'Socialist' Anglo-Irish alliance[3] which a Whig with Irish estates thought 'infinitely more dangerous'[4] than any confiscatory lengths to which Gladstone's 'revolutionary temper' might carry him.[5] By the end of January 1884 – with 'good friends...kiss[ing] all round' –[6] a tendency to alarmism had given way, as ever, to wholesale complacency. In 'view of such a consensus of opinion' as to the expediency of including Ireland, mused Harcourt, where would Hartington 'have been, & how would he have felt now, had he carried out his threat?'[7] Harcourt was guilty of political naivety. Hartington's 'hounds' might have hunted as well as Chamberlain's had he only chosen to 'lift them on.'[8] He did not; and those who might have responded by forming a predominantly Whig Cave,[9] turned to Proportional Representation instead.

That an alliance of moderate men, and the abandonment 'by the Whig aristocracy of their hold upon, and leadership of, the Liberal Party',[10] would result in a deleterious imbalance of political forces,[11] and that the 'possessors of cultivation & refinement' within Liberal ranks had a 'duty...to correct the rougher ways of the time to come'[12] – these may have impressed themselves upon Hartington.

1 Earl Grey to Halifax, 7 Feb. 1884. Hickleton Mss., A4.55.16. But Grey was probably right in thinking that the moment for this – during Disraeli's last Ministry – had passed. See also Minto to Elliot, 27 Jan. 1884. Elliot Mss., Bundle 32; and Halifax to Albert Grey, 29 Jan. 1884. Grey Mss.
2 Brett Memo., 1 Sept. 1883. Esher, *Journals*, pp. 12–16. Compare Viscount Lymington, 20 Feb. 1883: 'The question of Home Rule must stand on its own merits; and he was willing to admit that if the Liberal Party, or whatever Party might be in power, were to listen to the language of panic, and to treat Ireland as a nation of traitors and criminals, and govern it without a Constitution, a Party would arise in England – the Radical Party – who would raise the question of Home Rule.' 3 *Hansard* cclxxvi. 481.
3 Bath to his Son, Weymouth, 13 July 1882. Bath Mss.
4 Bath to Weymouth, 11 July 1880. Bath Mss.
5 Fitzjames Stephen to Lady Grant Duff, 18 May 1883. Stephen Mss., 7349.13.
6 Harcourt to Lewis Harcourt, c. 4 Jan. 1884. A. G. Gardiner, *The Life of Sir William Harcourt* (2 vols., 1923), Vol. I, p. 449.
7 Hamilton Diary, 1 Feb. 1884. Hamilton Mss., 48635 fol. 79.
8 Albert Grey to Halifax, 28 Jan. 1884. Hickleton Mss., A4.84 Part 4.
9 Derby to Gladstone, 31 Dec. 1883. Gladstone Mss., 44142 fol. 35.
10 T. F. Firth to Ramsden, 11 Sept. 1882. Ramsden Mss., Box 39.
11 W. L. Guttsman, *The British Political Elite* (1963), p. 88.
12 C. S. Roundell to Selborne, 3 Oct. 1883. Selborne Mss., 1868 fol. 210.

He conceived his position in personal terms. Chamberlain, he rightly concluded, was working to a fixed plan, not simply to conquer and drag Hartington at his wheels,[1] but to make him 'go out on franchise'.[2] The theme stressed by Gladstone and Harcourt in their dealings with Hartington was that he was 'preparing the way for more dangerous measures than are likely to be passed by the present Gov.'[3] and leaving 'the game in [Chamberlain's] hand.'[4] If Harcourt's message was delivered straight from the shoulder, Gladstonian insinuation was none the less telling, with its emphasis upon that 'impracticable, incureable [sic]' and highly serviceable 'element of old age',[5] and the effects of 'your removal along with mine'.[6] Hartington's was the natural succession. The question was not as to his remaining in politics, but as to his remaining in the Liberal fold. Granville, who had at first asked sillily, 'What are you going to do if you give up politics?',[7] turned properly to query the heir apparent's timing of his fight, when Chamberlain had Gladstone, the Cabinet and the Dublin Administration with him.[8] Chamberlain's adoption of Hartington's definition of the division of labour, Whigs controlling what the Radicals pushed for,[9] was paradoxically his undoing. He forced Hartington to take shelter in Gladstone's retention of power; and Hartington who, like Harcourt, dreaded Gladstone, posthumously or out of office, 'throwing his shield over Parnell, Chamberlain, Dilke &c.',[10] committed Gladstone to the lines of Redistribution and thus deprived Chamberlain of authority for a more sweeping measure[11] 'with the help of the labourers' vote.'[12]

1 Dilke to Chamberlain, 28 Nov. 1883. Chamberlain Mss., JC5/24/50.
2 Dilke, quoting Chamberlain, to Chamberlain, 24 Jan. 1884. Dilke Mss., 43886 fol. 117.
3 Granville to Gladstone, 15 Dec. 1883. *Correspondence*, Vol. II, p. 129.
4 Lewis Harcourt Journal, 1 Feb. 1885. Harcourt Mss.; compare Hamilton Diary, 1 Jan. 1884. Hamilton Mss., 48635 fol. 49.
5 Gladstone to Granville, 14 Dec. 1883. *Correspondence*, Vol. II, p. 128.
6 Gladstone to Hartington, 3 Dec. 1883. Gladstone Mss., 44146 fol. 239.
7 Holland, *Devonshire*, Vol. I, p. 398; Granville to Spencer, 23 Nov. 1883. Spencer Mss.
8 Granville to Harcourt, 17 Dec. 1883. Gardiner, *Harcourt*, Vol. I, p. 496.
9 Chamberlain to Gladstone, 24 Dec. 1883. Gladstone Mss., 44125 fol. 229.
10 Carlingford Diary, 11 May 1885. Carlingford Mss., DD/SH 360.
11 Hartington to Devonshire, 14 Jan. 1884. Devonshire Mss., 340.1401.
12 Granville to Gladstone, 15 Dec. 1883. *Correspondence*, Vol. II, p. 129. Compare Hartington to Gladstone, 12 Nov. 1882: 'The advanced section, which forms the strength, if not the majority of the party, would require stronger measures from any successor [i.e. Hartington] than it would from you.' Gladstone Mss., 44146 fol. 101.

Derby expressed the hope in October 1883 that Gladstone would give no public hint as to his early retirement: 'It weakens his hold on the party. Nobody will put himself out of the way to serve a minister who is politically dead.'[1] What may have been pertinent to the Parliamentary following was emphatically untrue of the Cabinet. There, durability rested upon recognition of Gladstone's indispensability, which in turn rested upon Gladstone's demonstrating to all Cabalists, the dissident and the discomfited, that it was still in *their* interest to retain him.

Carlingford's record reinforces yet another, and the most critical, consideration – that Gladstone's stepping-down would prove no more than temporary, no more than the prelude to an 'unmuzzling'. Rathbone, with one eye to expediting business in the Commons (and perhaps the second to securing Hartington's succession), actually suggested another post-1874 ruse. 'Suppose...that even as early as the middle of July Dr. Andrew Clarke [*sic*] ordered you to take rest...the Tories would feel that you were recruiting your strength...to take...your leadership of the nation; while the Liberal Party would be on honour to work all the more loyally... lest any failure on their part should bring you back from your needed repose.'[2] Tory fears of an extra-Parliamentary crusade were probably less striking than the Cabinet's fear of a 'Second Coming'. In December 1884, Gladstone put it to Granville that, if the Government were 'baffled, at the threshold', he had a right 'to put upon H. the duty of accepting the Govt. with Liberal Colleagues and Reform postponed [,] we supporting his Govt.'[3] The sting lay, of course, in the tail – in Gladstone's insistence, as a direct alternative to 'your removal along with mine',[4] upon 'your succession *without* my removal from the political scene'. Granville ridiculed the scheme even before he was cajoled into relaying it to Chatsworth.[5] This was, as his colleagues by now knew, one of the constant ploys which Gladstone had used in the decade since his defeat at the election of 1874. At the close of 1882 he had once more promised to '*protect* the Govt. as Peel did Ld. J. Russell after 1846' – until Harcourt delivered his 'grand remonstrance',[6] pronounced the notion of patronage 'intolerable & impracticable', and deprecated

---

[1] Derby to Granville, 28 Oct. 1883. Granville Mss., PRO. 30/29/27A.
[2] Rathbone to Gladstone, 9 May 1883. Gladstone Mss., 44480 fol. 309.
[3] Gladstone to Granville, 18 Dec. 1883. *Correspondence*, Vol. II, p. 130.
[4] Gladstone to Hartington, 3 Dec. 1883. Gladstone Mss., 44146 fol. 239.
[5] Granville to Gladstone, 19 Dec. 1883. *Correspondence*, Vol. II, p. 132.
[6] Harcourt to Chamberlain, 10 Dec. 1882. Harcourt Mss.

Gladstone's taking a Peerage since 'the *faithful* would always be looking towards Mecca.'[1] If Gladstone's removal presaged the rupture of a sorely-strained alliance,[2] that in itself was deterrent to Hartington. But, as all recognized, the Radical section's making more din than the rest was designed to boost Radical spirits, to offset and camouflage their numerical impotence. Better for Hartington, then, that the split, when it came, 'be caused by the Radicals against the Whigs and Gladstone than by the Whigs against the Radicals and Gladstone.'[3] Chamberlain needed Gladstone's mantle, and it seemed to Hartington that this was precisely the protection which would be afforded Chamberlain by Gladstone as freelance-cum-freebooter.

His health plays so signal a role in the history of the Second Administration that it needs saying outright that Gladstone both evaded the unpalatable and made political capital out of a 'normal state of worry and nervous excitement.'[4] Of the Midlothian campaigns, perhaps the most crucial was the one that did not take place – the proposed 'dying speech & confession' scheduled for January 1883,[5] which had to be postponed until the calming of Rosebery's 'present tempestuous state of mind'.[6] And once Gladstone was convalescing at Cannes, a thousand miles from his

[1] Harcourt to Hartington, 10 Dec. 1882. Devonshire Mss., 340.1285A.
[2] Compare Hartington to Gladstone, 12 Nov. 1882. Gladstone Mss., 44146 fol. 101.
[3] Hartington to Devonshire, 14 Jan. 1884. Devonshire Mss., 340.1401.
[4] Gorst to Churchill, 14 Jan. 1883. Churchill Mss., 1/97. Note T. P. O'Connor's astute commentary on Gladstone's extraordinary performance in the immediate wake of his near-defeat over Khartoum: 'There was no special reason why he should come down this evening to the House, and yet there he was...He entered rather pale, and he carried a stick on which he leaned – even when he rose to speak. It was the first time I ever saw anything about him that brought home to the mind the undeniable, but usually forgotten fact that he is a very old man. The effect was excellent. When he entered, the cheer was not very keen, but when, towards the close of question time, he did rise – still with the ominous stick supporting him – there was a really strong and sympathetic cheer. The old man could not conceal his delight; he paused for several minutes, gave a profound bow after the manner of a prima donna, and paused again until the applause had died away with the same – shall I say – simper on his face, as if he were a member of a great operatic or theatrical corps.' *Gladstone's House of Commons* (1885), p. 502.
[5] Harcourt to Hartington, 10 Dec. 1882. Devonshire Mss., 340.1285A.
[6] Hamilton Diary, 24 Dec. 1882. Hamilton Mss., 48633 fol. 40. Gladstone, said Dilke, looked on Rosebery as no more than a 'nice, promising baby'; certainly it was hard on Rosebery to learn that the Parliamentary Under Secretary for War, Lord Morley, was thought to have a stronger claim to the much-sought Cabinet seat. Dilke to Grant Duff, 19 Mar. and 25 Mar. 1883. Dilke Mss., 43894 fols. 95 and 105.

Scottish constituents, it was palpable that there could be 'no pretence of retirement in summer if he is sent for after two days of the new Session.'[1] What is remarkable is that the periods when, to judge from Hamilton's diary, Gladstone was genuinely ill do not coincide with the official, political scares. Gladstone was neither the first nor the last statesman to fall 'ill of chagrin more than influenza'[2] nor need sensibilities be offended by such a fear as Granville's in February 1883 'that Mr. G. will at once resign (on the ground of health) if Hartington's view prevails.'[3] Gladstone's was a highly-strung nature, his 'brain and nerves' requiring, 'clear[ing]' and thriving on intellectual stimulation.[4] Homeric complexities doubtless made greater demands on his mind than did Egyptian finance, but what is important is that Gladstone's 'brain and nerves' so thrilled to *politics* that Andrew Clark, his physician, held it to be physiologically injurious if not fatal for Gladstone to be deprived of the challenge and exhilaration involved. He was 'constitutionally unfit to stand aside.'[5] The medical validity or even therapeutic vogue is of no concern. Gladstone comprehended and accepted this diagnosis. But he could invoke Clark's authority in a wholly contrary direction to serve an immediate political purpose. When, looking 'unwell & weak', he told the Cabinet 'with some emotion, that he had lost his sleep, & did not know what A. Clark might order',[6] he was hinting at a step which Clark had said could kill him.

What specifically of the second half of 1883? On 29 July, Hamilton was 'quite clear...that Mr. G. has abandoned the idea of immediate retirement', and attributed this 'mainly to his feeling in such rude health.'[7] On 10 November, Gladstone, performing a charade for his secretary and Chief Whip, 'ran into the corner of the room to illustrate' the absolute and inevitable immolation of Reform by postponement to 1885: 'with an immediate dissolution

[1] Acton (from France) to Granville, 20 Feb. 1883. Granville Mss., PRO. 30/29/29B. [2] Smith to Gibson, 22 Oct. 1881. Ashbourne Mss.
[3] Dilke to Chamberlain, 3 Feb. 1883. Chamberlain Mss., JC5/24/48.
[4] Gladstone Diary, 29 Dec. 1884. John Morley, *The Life of William Ewart Gladstone* (2 vol. ed., 1906), Vol. II, p. 410.
[5] Hamilton Diary, 12 July 1892. Cited in Peter Stansky, *Ambitions and Strategies: the Struggle for the Leadership of the Liberal Party in the 1890s* (Oxford, 1964), p. xiii. See also Brett to Wolseley, 9 Jan. 1885: 'Mr. G. is still bent on retirement, immediately after the Seats Bill is through Parliament. It is doubtful whether Andrew Clarke will permit it. He is said to hold that excitement is indispensable to an old man's health.' Esher, *Journals*, p. 69.
[6] Carlingford Diary, 2 Jan. 1885. Carlingford Mss., DD/SH 360.
[7] Hamilton Diary, 29 July 1883. Hamilton Mss., 48634 fol. 33.

confronting you, you will be fighting with your hands tied.'
Hamilton found the energetic, gambolling display irresistible.
Furthermore, 'Mr. G. is wonderfully well. He really seems to be
five years younger than he was a twelvemonth ago. He never now
talks of retiring; is never fussy; and is evidently resigned to his
fate.'[1] On Gladstone's 74th birthday, he was again 'a younger man '[2]
– and this in the midst of one of those racking personal crises. Yet
Hamilton could Boswellise the repeated declaration to Cabinet
colleagues without apparent recognition of the falsity which under-
lay the self-contradiction. 'Mr. Gladstone...says in effect: "I can
undertake a measure of principle such as that of simply giving to
counties the same electoral privileges as the Boroughs enjoy; but
...[if] the Cabinet decide to couple redistribution with the Franchise
question, which would involve herculean labour I must consider my
position....But I want the decision of the Cabinet to be taken on
its merits and without reference to myself." '[3] He did not; and he
ensured that that decision could not be so taken.

Some time before the Parliamentary recess in August 1883,
Gladstone talked 'with apparent sincerity' to Granville of the
future course. 'It amounted to this...That he thought he might
begin with extension of the Franchise without distribution of seats
& without dissolution. I asked him whether he could not leave to
younger men to frame, & to pass such measures[4] as he did not feel

---

[1] Hamilton Diary, 10 Nov. 1883. Hamilton Mss., 48634 fol. 113.
[2] Hamilton Diary, 29 Nov. 1883. Hamilton Mss., 48635 fol. 5.
[3] Hamilton Diary, 12 Dec. 1883. Hamilton Mss., 48635 fol. 17. The Hamilton
diaries are of great value for any post-1880 study of Gladstonian politics both
as a reliable factual record of the comings and goings at Downing Street at all
hours (Hamilton had a 'bachelor flat' on the second floor), and for the
gossipy chat of those coming and going. They are not a *passe-partout* to
Gladstone's mind or motivation. J. A. Godley, whom Hamilton succeeded as
principal Private Secretary, wrote: 'He was not in the first class for intellectual
gifts, but he was very industrious, painstaking, accurate and obliging.' *The
Reminiscences of Lord Kilbracken* (1931), p. 121. That, faint praise though it
was, is probably not far wide of the mark. Hamilton, if not uncritical, was
overawed by Gladstone: he 'knew his place', and his loyalty was unquestion-
ed. One cannot but feel that the son of a Gladstone-admiring Bishop of
Salisbury failed to penetrate 'that unintelligibility [which Gladstone]
himself went so far as to say...was a characteristic common to all men of
political mark.' E. W. Hamilton, *Mr. Gladstone: a Monograph* (1908), p. 42.
[4] i.e. Local Government – and perhaps simultaneous Redistribution? See also
Hartington memo. of 9 Jan. 1883: 'Why should not the questions of registration of voters and of electoral areas be dealt with and settled in the County
Govt. Bill? The County Franchise Bill would then be simplified to the extent
of reducing it to a single Clause, and it would become possible, so far as time
is concerned, to deal in the same Session with the question of re-distribution.'
Dilke Mss., 43891 fol. 53.

inclined to undertake – reserving to himself the general superintendence. He said that a Peer could do this and that Palmerston had done so, but that it was impossible for him.'[1] While cruising off Oban in September, Gladstone let drop in a letter to Childers (thereby ensuring dissemination through Childers' wife) that he could answer none of the specific points put to him on future legislation, since 'I can hardly say at this moment whether I am to regard myself as part of the Govt. for the coming year'.[2] In a letter of guidance to Herbert Gladstone at Leeds, 'you can I think safely give an opinion that...taking the suffrage at once would not be likely...to hurry my retirement...I am by no means sure that I can remain in office for the two very large and complex measures' of Local and London Government.[3] The same message, with appropriate stress upon the inadequacy of his 'mental force' for 'any very grave and constructive' bills, was despatched to Hartington.[4] At the Cabinet of 25 October, Gladstone made 'allusions to his own incapacity for dealing with a complicated bill' and suggested 'that we should begin with' the Franchise.[5] A fortnight later, he reminded Hartington that he had '*proposed* nothing to the Cabinet; but [had] merely stated hypothetically a course of main business, which would enable me – in my 75th year – at least to begin the Session with my colleagues.'[6] Harcourt had impressed upon Gladstone that Hartington's views 'shut the door to his project of retiring at the end of next Session, and of washing his hands of the redistribution question.'[7] Seymour, who was politically naive, concluded that it was not 'pleasant to Mr. G. to learn' this.[8] Childers, who recognized Gladstone's age as a political weapon, drew the right conclusion: 'Nothing would have induced our Chief to go on with redistribution this Session.'[9]

---

[1] Granville to Hartington, n.d. Devonshire Mss., 340.1372.
[2] Gladstone to Childers, 10 Sept. 1883. Gladstone Mss., 44546 fol. 157.
[3] Gladstone to Herbert Gladstone, 13 Oct. 1883. Gladstone Mss., 44546 fol. 172.
[4] Gladstone to Hartington, 22 Oct. 1883. Gladstone Mss., 44546 fol. 179.
[5] Granville to Derby, 26 Oct. 1883. Derby Mss., Box 3.
[6] Gladstone to Hartington, 7 Nov. 1883. Gladstone Mss., 44146 fol. 231.
[7] Seymour to Spencer, 23 Dec. 1883. Spencer Mss. Seymour continues: 'I expect that the Home Secretary overtalked. I told him afterwards that if he gave him another dose, he would drive Mr. G. to Cannes again – upon which Harcourt replied that it was the very best thing that could happen as the franchise question could be shelved, & an amicable session ensue.'
[8] *Ibid.*
[9] Childers to Halifax, 7 Jan. 1884. Hickleton Mss., A4.90.

2

CONSERVATIVES IN THE DARK

We now have *two* leaders. One [i.e. Salisbury] is a Statesman. The other [i.e. Northcote] is an old woman. Lord Salisbury has been *shamefully* treated by his party. Instead of rallying round him, they have given him the 'cold shoulder', discredited him, discouraged him, & restricted him.

George Bowyer to Churchill, 4 July 1882. Churchill Mss., 1/74.

The Country looks to *you* as the *coming man*. Lord Salisbury was the coming man – but he *did not come*.

George Bowyer to Churchill, 11 Nov. 1882. Churchill Mss., 1/82.

There has for a long time been a growing *Borough* Conservatism...The Working Classes in Lancashire (& I believe throughout the country) recognize in you the champion they are looking for – who will give them what is reasonable and right under the present Constitution and not tack them on to Chamberlain & Republicanism – Illingworth & Dissent – Bradlaugh & Atheism – Parnell & Home Rule – Bright & Dismemberment of the Empire – a *vigorous Conservative* Policy they want....Your *tone* towards Sir Stafford they regret – he is deeply respected & *beloved* by them...you can lead 'young Toryism' & yet do *better* work *with* him – so think your friends here.

Thomas W. Freston to Churchill, 26 Apr. 1883. Churchill Mss., 1/117.

In July 1884, when it seemed necessary to find a counter to Liberal hullabaloo against the Peers, Salisbury rejected the proposal for a Conservative party manifesto in favour of something 'less formal'. The 'dual leadership', he wrote, was 'one difficulty. Have you ever composed a document of any kind in conjunction with anyone else? & were you satisfied with the result? Such compositions have a hybrid air about them – & retain only the worst characteristics of both parents.'[1]

What was true enough of authorship was the more pertinent to party government. If the former yielded mongrel literature, there was an end to the affair; the latter brought forth claims, aspirations and internecine strivings. Salisbury–Northcote 'dual control' was no more than a euphemism for the leadership being altogether 'in suspense' and up for auction.[2] The pattern-maker, knowing who

---

[1] Salisbury to Austin, 24 July 1884. Austin Mss.

[2] Cranbrook Diary, 5 Jan. 1884. Cranbrook Mss., T501/299 fol. 156.

emerged undisputed leader, will conclude that Salisbury had simply to allow the brilliant and audacious Churchill to undermine North-cote's authority, and then wait for the impetuous and syphilitic Churchill to destroy and be destroyed.[1] Salisbury was doubtless front runner in the race to ultimate control. But quite how many others in addition to Northcote and Churchill saw themselves or were seen as contenders for 'Elijah's mantle', quite how vulnerable was Salisbury's position as leader of the *Lords* in the three years after Disraeli's death, quite how distrusted he was by those who called themselves 'moderate', and quite how out of sympathy with the Anglo-Irish landowning aristocracy and defenders of the Union are considerations which need emphasizing in any attempt to understand the Reform episode.

Readers of political correspondence become inured to Tory vilification of Gladstone. 'If he were younger', Disraeli had told Lady Chesterfield, 'the Crown would not be safe.'[2] By the 1880s, moreover, Chamberlain's daring, and supposed ascendancy in Liberal counsels, threatened the perpetuation of 'Arch-Villainism'; Cranbrook feared that his party's disunion would destroy all 'chance of checking the revolutionary race wh. Gladstone started & Chamberlain will run.'[3] Disraeli's was the half-humorous expression of profound personal loathing, Cranbrook's a species of alarmism and fatalism. 'Great questions are coming, and we must be called upon for decisions, involving principle and the destiny of the Constitution and the country. And then – I will not forecast the future, but dread it.'[4]

[1] Compare Salisbury to Akers-Douglas, 26 Dec. 1886: 'R.C.'s conduct can only be accounted for on the theory that the work has upset his nerves – & when his nerves go, his judgment goes altogether.' Chilston Mss., C18/17. Smith's verdict was perhaps more telling: 'It was really Salisbury or Churchill: and if Salisbury had gone, none of us could have remained.' Smith to Akers-Douglas, 24 Dec. 1886. Chilston Mss., C25/10.

[2] Robert Blake, *Disraeli* (1966), p. 740.

[3] Cranbrook Diary, 5 Jan. 1884. Cranbrook Mss., T501/299 fol. 156. See also a piece of contemporary doggerel, 'W.E.G. (Apologetic)':

'Friends, just help me to the box-seat, I will drive you with a will;
Easy is Avernus-driving, for it's all the way down-hill.
If I fail to reach the bottom, why, I'll fling the leader's rein
(And *they'll* do the job completely) unto Dilke and Chamberlain.'

Anonymous, *The Gladstone Rule, a Retrospective Commentary. By an Outsider* (Edinburgh, 1885), p. 64.

[4] Cranbrook Diary, 11 Aug. 1882. A. E. Gathorne Hardy (ed.), *Gathorne Hardy, First Earl of Cranbrook: a Memoir. (With Extracts from his Diary and Correspondence)*, (2 vols., 1910), Vol. II, p. 182.

At such a time the reluctance of a definable set of self-styled 'moderates' to align themselves behind Salisbury acquires some significance. His capriciousness accounts in part for the refusal of Wemyss to consider himself anything more positive than an anti-Radical.[1] By mid-1884, Bath had concluded that Gladstone was a 'madman'; yet the Conservative leader in the Lords seemed to him so 'strangely deficient in judgment as well as principle' that 'I am disposed to trust Goschen more than anyone else perhaps because we know least about him.'[2] Halifax, allowing that Hartington 'made a good fight' and carried his objections to a point beyond which he 'would have broken up the Govt.',[3] held this to have been the right course for a Whig to take in view of the consequences of Liberal collapse – Salisbury coming to power, and 'an *unwise* Conservative Govt.'[4] 'to be followed by Chamberlain.'[5]

In avowedly Liberal circles, Salisbury was looked on as 'bound to mislead his party. Despite all his intellect, he is absolutely devoid of all political *nous*'.[6] 'Reckless as to consequences'[7] and 'going the way to plunge Ireland into a state of anarchy'[8] was Mundella's verdict. With Salisbury's accession to leadership in the Upper Chamber, Chamberlain saw what he wanted to see – the enhancement of chances for 'a serious brush with the Lords',[9] preferably upon Reform. Henry Lucy regarded Salisbury's contempt for the Commons – after a vain attempt to evade the call to the Lords when his father died – as the 'animosity of a dismissed lover.'[10]

---

[1] Elcho to A. Gemmell, 12 Feb. 1882. Wemyss Mss.

[2] Bath to Weymouth, 2 July 1884. Bath Mss. Hamilton, at Longleat, was unable to ascertain whether his host's 'detestation' of Salisbury was stronger than his abhorrence of Chamberlain – and of the latter 'one will soon begin to think he is not worth all the trouble he gives.' Hamilton Diary, 10 Jan. 1884. Hamilton Mss., 48635 fol. 60.

[3] Halifax to Albert Grey, 29 Jan. 1884. Grey Mss.

[4] Earl Grey to Halifax, 7 Feb. 1884. Hickleton Mss., A4.55.16.

[5] Halifax to Albert Grey, 29 Jan. 1884. Grey Mss.

[6] Hamilton Diary, 24 Aug. 1883. Hamilton Mss., 48634 fol. 53. Compare Gladstone's judgment, c. Dec. 1876: 'he is very remarkably clever, of unsure judgment, but is above everything mean.' Morley, *Gladstone*, Vol. II, p. 168.

[7] Mundella to Leader, 14 Aug. 1882. Mundella–Leader Mss. See also Ripon to Dilke, 18 Aug. 1881: 'It will be a wonder if Salisbury does not succeed in blowing the institution [the House of Lords] to pieces before long.' Dilke Mss., 43894 fol. 32; and John Ball to Ripon, 17–18 May 1881: 'I never expected to regret the loss of Beaconsfield on political grounds as I now do for I dread the influence which Salisbury has acquired.' Ripon Mss., 43545 fol. 181.

[8] Mundella to Leader, 23 Feb. 1882. Mundella–Leader Mss.

[9] Chamberlain to William Harris, 10 Aug. 1881. Chamberlain Mss., JC5/39/14.

[10] H. W. Lucy, *Memories of Eight Parliaments* (1908), pp. 118–20.

That chimes with, and may be ascribed to, a good deal of dinner-party chatter in 1884, to the effect that Salisbury would sell his fellow Peers down the river to secure control of Redistribution. But then, if we dismiss all thought of Salisbury as the very embodiment of Unionism and Tory tradition, if we accept for the moment that he could posit as alternative to a gamble the annihilation of his party, we should ask, quite simply, was that price excessive?

Like 1906, 1880 was an electoral reverse best passed off by Conservatives in the hours of collective neurosis as occasioned by some ill-understood novel force. Robert Fowler counted the Conservative deficit in the Commons at 170, and recognized that such a majority could not readily have been turned.[1] Whipping-boys, of necessity, were brought forward. Defeated candidates' tales of woe gave rise to the fiction of the cumulative inefficiency of local agents' organization – though the absolute number of the Conservative vote was greater than that recorded in 1874.[2] Carlton Club opinion hardened against Hart Dyke as the man responsible for spurring Disraeli into dissolution when, so it was said, three months more might have witnessed trade revival and actually brought a decent harvest.[3] But if Micawberism had allowed the least unfavourable moment for dissolution to slip by in 1879, further delay might, as Mundella thought, have given the Conservative party forty years in the wilderness.[4] By the time Reform was brought forward, Tory helplessness was seen to lie less in the emptiness of their benches than in low morale and internal dissension: 'so entirely' was the Commons force 'at the mercy of Parnell and Gorst' that Manners looked 'with more interest at what may happen in your [Upper] Chamber'.[5]

Nevertheless, from the Liberal resumption of office, conflict threatened between elected and non-elected assemblies. 'A Reform Bill is looming in the distance', wrote one pamphleteer; it followed preternaturally that 'All our institutions are more or less on trial.'[6] Another prefaced his guide to its composition, 'The "House of Lords" is fast becoming one of the "burning questions" of the

---

[1] J. S. Flynn, *Sir Robert N. Fowler* (1893), p. 252.
[2] J. P. D. Dunbabin, 'Parliamentary Elections in Great Britain, 1868–1900: a Psephological Note', *English Historical Review* LXXXI (1966), p. 88.
[3] Flynn, *Robert Fowler*, p. 252.
[4] Mundella to Leader, 9 July 1882. Mundella–Leader Mss.
[5] Manners to Salisbury, 27 Dec. 1883. Belvoir Mss.
[6] Frederick Calvert, *The Representation of Minorities* (1881), p. 1.

day.'¹ A third, the professed 'crotchet-monger[ing]' advocate of life peerages, reflected that the 'whole course of public affairs' had been drawing, and would increasingly draw, attention to the propriety of Peers thwarting the popular will. Just as 1832 had brought into recognition and 1867 confirmed 'a power antagonistic to landed and hereditary pretensions', so the coming measure would necessarily 'make the Upper House tremble for its very existence.'² At Leeds Bright, plagiarising James Mill rather than anticipating 1911, proposed a check upon the power to reject any bill re-submitted by the Commons in a subsequent Session. Recognition of potential constitutional crisis was widespread. 'How to broaden and deepen the stream of radical principles, keeping meanwhile the government both alive & steady, without harassing or frightening it' was 'the question', as William Morris saw it in 1880.³ How to provide a 'solid meal' sufficient to prevent the 'liberal lions...from rending one another' was the question for Chamberlain.⁴ How best to buoy the spirits of the vast majority in the Lords, while not entering into direct conflict unless 'some substantial gain [could] be obtained thereby' was the question as Disraeli put it to Balfour.⁵

Disraeli's mildly phrased admonition went unheeded: 'escapades' ensued,⁶ objectionable not as such but because no substantial gain was seen to be obtained thereby. Over the 1881 Irish Land bill, Northcote intended to divide the Commons on the Second Reading, viewed the Government proposals as 'rooted and grounded in injustice'⁷ and held to the opinion that 'unless we can offer a successful resistance...we may say goodnight to all we value';⁸ nevertheless, he thought it possibly provided 'a framework on which to mend, and darn, and cut out, and sew in.'⁹ With the bill approaching its crisis, amendment and the prospect of further concession convinced him that effort must now be concentrated on depriving the Ministry of any opening to 'throw the responsibility for their (almost certain) failure upon the House of Lords'. But so oblivious was Salisbury deemed to be of the actual legisla-

¹ George Panton, *The House of Lords, 1882* (Manchester, 1882), p. 3.
² J. G. Delaploc, *The House of Lords* (1883), p. 3.
³ Morris to Broadhurst, 4 Apr. 1880. Broadhurst Mss., Vol. I, fol. 99.
⁴ Chamberlain to Harcourt, 10 Apr. 1880. Harcourt Mss.
⁵ Balfour to Salisbury, 8 Apr. 1880. Balfour Mss., 49688 fol. 18.
⁶ Cranbrook Diary, 5 Jan. 1884. Cranbrook Mss., T501/299 fol. 156.
⁷ Northcote to Salisbury, 15 Apr. 1881. Iddesleigh Mss., 50020 fol. 3.
⁸ Northcote to Elcho, 24 Apr. 1881. Wemyss Mss.
⁹ Northcote to Salisbury, 15 Apr. 1881. Iddesleigh Mss., 50020 fol. 3.

tive points in question – and, by implication, so spoiling for a fight, any fight – that Gibson was asked to detail the salvage operation.[1] As a dress rehearsal for the 1884 performance the politics of the Arrears bill of 1882 demand attention. The bill allowed a clearance of accounts in Ireland; it was chosen by Salisbury as a matter about which the general public did not care 'two pence'[2] but upon which he might instigate a dissolution at a time when the parties were perhaps on level terms.[3] Salisbury was clear why the issue ought to be forced. If Liberal unity survived Irish assaults and the Egyptian imbroglio, if the *clôture* could be imposed and procedural reform in the Commons effected, Gladstone would take up the County Franchise; and with 'his present majority which on such a question will be intact, he can easily so manipulate these [redistribution] arrangements as to efface our party for a generation.... [While] if a dissolution happens *now*, he must lose considerably – & we shall be in a position to make our influence really felt in the discussions on the Reform Bill.'[4] In July 1882, the Government had been narrowly beaten in Committee on a minor aspect of the Prevention of Crimes bill, whereupon Gladstone, piqued at what was recognized to be a triumph for Harcourt, had raised once more in public the question of his own position; Elliot, a few days later, still found 'Everybody [in the Commons] laughing at the absurdity of Mr. Gladstone's behaviour in *manufacturing* a sham "crisis".'[5] Salisbury's task was simply in turn to throw the Arrears crisis at Gladstone and bank on a similar loss of temper revealing 'the hands of a very rough Esau...[behind the] voice of Jacob.'[6] Smith, for one, proceeded upon the assumption that Gladstone meant 'mischief if he can do it and [that] it would be a real pleasure with him to have a fall out with the Lords.'[7]

[1] Northcote to Salisbury, 11 Aug. 1881. Salisbury Mss., Series E. Compare Pembroke to Salisbury, 15 Aug. 1881: 'I offer you my congratulations on the great concession that the Government have made tonight...Might I suggest that it would be good policy to let Mr. Gladstone down pretty easy as regards most of the rest of our amendments...[He] refrained from the smallest expression of irritation against our House, or of reluctance to make the concessions he was making. It does not seem to me that it would be our cue to alter his attitude, and throw his great weight into the agitation against the House of Lords.' Salisbury Mss., Series E.

[2] Northcote to Salisbury, 6 Aug. 1882. Salisbury Mss., Series D.

[3] Dunbabin, *EHR* LXXXI, p. 87.

[4] Salisbury to Lord George Hamilton, 6 Aug. 1882. Salisbury Mss., Series D.

[5] Elliot Diary, 10 July 1882. Diaries, Vol. 9. (My italics.)

[6] Cranbrook to Cross, 2 Mar. 1882. Cross Mss., 51267.

[7] Smith to his Wife, 1 Aug. 1882. Hambleden Mss., A/924.

There is much in the view that the two major problems of the 1880s were, if not insuperable, at least sufficient to preclude party consensus. A Conservative Ministry would doubtless have been as baffled by the chapter of accidents and as incapable as Gladstone of carrying all sections forward in execution of any policy, could one have been decided upon. But if Sandon was prepared to preface a public speech, 'Heaven forbid that at this moment the Conservatives should come into office',[1] Salisbury would never admit it to be in the interest of opposition to declare bankruptcy. Moreover, to judge by Liberal disillusionment in the Commons, he was justified in his choice of moment. The Third Reading of the Arrears bill had been marked by massive abstention on the part of both Whigs and Radicals, while all lobby talk was on the theme, ' "it's nothing but fear of a dissolution that keeps the party together." '[2] For success however, the Conservatives relied on Governmental connivance in allowing a crisis to be provoked. And here, whatever the advantages to the Liberals of a snap election – before income tax 'pinch[ed]',[3] and while the Government enjoyed the credit of actively prosecuting a war – it was Hartington's contrariness which undid Salisbury.

On 19 July 1882, at a meeting in Arlington Street, attended by members of the ex-Cabinet, with Gibson, Abercorn, Waterford and the Chief Whip in attendance (but Cairns a conspicuous absentee), Salisbury found a good measure of support from Northcote, Cross, Smith and Winn for his own suggestion, that 'if we could provoke a dissolution it would be a good thing.'[4] It was decided to recommend the party to insert two stiff amendments on the Second Reading. The first gave the landlord the option of refusing to compound for arrears of rent due to him; the second proposed that, in the event of tenant-right being sold, the tenant should repay the sum which the landlord was compelled to relinquish under the terms of the bill, i.e. the unliquidated arrears. It was decided, further, not simply to insert the amendments but to 'stick' to them.[5] A subsequent meeting of ninety-nine Peers, 'very warlike' and preponderantly young bloods, overwhelmingly endorsed this decision, Leitrim alone dissenting (incoherently), Beauchamp and Hereford on the other

---

[1] At Liverpool, 7 Aug. 1882. *Annual Register*, p. 121.
[2] Stansfeld to Halifax, 6 May 1882. Hickleton Mss., A4.51.
[3] Cairns to Salisbury, 6 Aug. 1882. Salisbury Mss., Series E.
[4] Salisbury to Cairns, 21 July 1882. Cairns Mss., PRO. 30/15/6, fol. 92.
[5] Balfour Notebook. Balfour Mss., 49962 fol. 47.

flank howling for out-and-out rejection.[1] Salisbury now went ahead, to assert his authority, to prevent such a Conservative 'skedaddl[ing]' as had sullied 1881,[2] and to fulfil the pledges which he had given 'with as much distinctness as [he] was capable of using'.[3]

Northcote had long before reminded him[4] of the commonplace that fighting on Second Reading was immeasurably easier than playing the game of 'battledore and shuttlecock' between the two Assemblies.[5] This latter game became more complex when the Queen, who understood neither of the amendments, approached Abercorn as 'an old & kind [Conservative] friend' to 'arrest what might be very serious now & do much harm to the House of Lords',[6] and when Cairns, who aimed at depriving Gladstone via Salisbury of any 'lever for a dissolution',[7] proposed a compromise retaining only the second.[8] It became impossibly complex and even unintelligible when Selborne, who was supposed to have misunderstood the amendments, let it be known that the Government were likely to concede the first,[9] and when the aid of Carnarvon and Cranbrook was sought by Richmond[10] to persuade Salisbury to accept a Liberal amendment to his amendment upon a clause which Balfour considered essential[11] and Abercorn stigmatised as 'not much regarded in Ireland even by the Landlords and agents.'[12] Once the question had thus been 'dragged...down into the grovelling rut of comparatively paltry detail', the game was lost. The 'half-hearted & "flabby"' '–[13] including Churchill –[14] threatened

---

[1] Salisbury to Cairns, 21 July 1882. Cairns Mss., PRO. 30/15/6, fol. 92. For all but the largest gatherings – at the Carlton Club – Arlington Street was a convenient headquarters. Poor Northcote had foreseen the implication: 'If our party councils were always to be held there, it would give the owner a position which might lead to embarrassment if the Chief [Disraeli] were to retire.' Northcote Diary, 28 Apr. 1880, cited in E. J. Feuchtwanger, Disraeli, Democracy and the Tory Party: Conservative Leadership and Organization after the Second Reform Bill (Oxford, 1968), p. 35.

[2] Elcho to Colonel Aitchison, 30 Apr. 1882. Wemyss Mss.

[3] Salisbury to Cairns, 7 Aug. 1882. Draft. Salisbury Mss., Series E.

[4] Northcote to Salisbury, 20 May 1882. Salisbury Mss., Series E.

[5] Northcote to Salisbury, 10 Aug. 1882. Salisbury Mss., Series E.

[6] The Queen to Abercorn, c. 7 Aug. 1882. Cairns Mss., PRO. 30/51/12, fol. 7.

[7] Cairns to Richmond, 6 Aug. 1882. Goodwood Mss., 871/D7.

[8] Carnarvon to Cranbrook, 5 Aug. 1882. Cranbrook Mss., T501/262.

[9] Salisbury to Cairns, 26 July 1882. Cairns Mss., PRO. 30/15/6, fol. 96.

[10] Cranbrook to Cairns, 7 Aug. 1882. Cairns Mss., PRO. 30/51/7, fol. 131.

[11] Balfour Notebook. Balfour Mss., 49962 fol. 47.

[12] Abercorn to Cairns, 9 Aug. 1882. Cairns Mss., PRO. 30/51/12, fol. 3.

[13] Lowther to Salisbury, 6 Aug. 1882. Salisbury Mss., Series E.

[14] Gibson to Northcote, 4 Aug. 1882. Salisbury Mss., Series E.

to allow a Government majority in the Commons of 180 and to reduce the Conservative margin of advantage in the Lords to twenty or thirty.[1] Northcote, recognizing that he was unlikely to induce more than a hundred to follow him into the lobby, thought they must now settle for 'a real compromise consistent with the honour of your House';[2] and in the Commons division on the first amendment, 'not 10 men on our side voted with enthusiasm or with the least desire or intention of prolonging the contest.'[3]

Salisbury, backed by Balfour, now attempted to rally his troops – that is to say, *after* Northcote had raised his following to 157 'with a secret confidence that it would lead to nothing further.'[4] The meeting in Arlington Street, attended by one hundred Peers, was disastrous. Waterford saw the potato blight, poor turf supply and police disaffection as now releasing Salisbury from his previous commitment. Richmond dissociated himself from belligerence. Carnarvon displayed casuistical skills, giving 'excellent reasons' for the adoption of any course. And Cranbrook advised against continued resistance 'with so desiccated a party.'[5] The tenor and bent of this discussion was reflected in the division which followed it; even in their host's drawing-room, all but thirteen 'pass[ed] to the other side.' Salisbury's subsequent speech in the Lords was, not unnaturally, 'a confession of defection and irritation such as no leader ever made before.'[6] He might well have retired from public life that day.

Though Liberals pretended to believe or even believed that the Lords had 'found [Salisbury] out',[7] such was not the case. Salisbury, with a gratuitous acknowledgment that his 'engagements' and 'idiosyncrasies' precluded his being *au fait* with what 'people in the party [were] thinking on pressing questions', had taken soundings of Lords and Commons opinion.[8] Having taken these soundings, he made clear that he would 'stand to his guns to the bitter end'; and warlike expressions had been as reassuringly and as 'enthusiastically cheered' at a Carlton Club meeting of Conservative members of the Commons[9] as by the Peers. Evidently,

[1] Cairns to Salisbury, 6 Aug. 1882. Salisbury Mss., Series E.
[2] Northcote to Salisbury, 5 Aug. 1882. Salisbury Mss., Series E.
[3] Balfour Notebook. Balfour Mss., 49962 fol. 47.
[4] Northcote to Cranbrook, 9 Aug. 1882. *Cranbrook Memoir*, Vol. II, p. 181.
[5] Richmond to Cairns, 13 Aug. 1882. Cairns Mss., PRO. 30/51/4, fol. 134.
[6] Mundella to Leader, 14 Aug. 1882. Mundella–Leader Mss.
[7] *Ibid.*
[8] Salisbury to Henry Manners, 8 July 1882. Salisbury Mss., Series D.
[9] Balfour Notebook. Balfour Mss., 49962 fol. 47.

between 18 July and 8 August, large numbers had become
'frightened'.[1] Why?

Reasons, of course, were given which *looked* as though they were
decisive. Bath, whose Irish rents were being paid only after the
serving of writs,[2] saw as the alternative to an admittedly humiliating concession by the Peers, only a general election which would be
'tantamount to something very like a revolutionary outbreak in
Ireland.'[3] Conservatives whose seats were notoriously insecure or
costly[4] said that they could not at this juncture rely on patriotic
sentiment or (more tangibly) the solid Irish vote in their constituencies.[5] Some Ulster Peers feared 'it would not be safe...to go
back and live in Ireland if the Bill was thrown out'.[6] Conversely,
but with the same effect, any Conservative amendment which gave
Gladstone a pretext for abandonment or resignation would further
allow him to lay whatever troubles might occur in Ireland at
Conservative feet.[7] But all this, and a great deal of prosy talk about
the harvest, was as relevant on 18 July as on 8 August. It is, indeed, difficult to avoid Salisbury's conclusion that 'out of a number
of convergent motives, the most important places must be assigned
to those that are purely personal – in your House as well as ours.'[8]

Gibson claimed that those who did comprehend the first amendment 'on the merits' were not impressed,[9] Cairns that the fighting
ground had become unintelligible and potentially ruinous.[10] The
crucial point is not that the ground was unintelligible but that the
anti-Salisbury forces had deliberately rendered it unintelligible, as
a means of raising 'battalions'[11] from amongst those who did not
relish the prospect of drifting into a crisis but who would otherwise
have remained inarticulate and 'lame'.[12] Gibson threw up the
sponge,[13] but Gibson was 'pos[ing] now as a sort of leader'.[14] Lord
George Hamilton who, like so many others, had never forgiven the

[1] Carnarvon to Cranbrook, 5 Aug. 1882. Cranbrook Mss., T501/262.
[2] Bath to Weymouth, 25 June 1882. Bath Mss.
[3] Bath to Weymouth, 13 July 1882. Bath Mss.
[4] Lord George Hamilton to Salisbury, 4 Aug. 1882. Salisbury Mss., Series.
[5] Salisbury to Northcote, 6 Aug. 1882. Salisbury Mss., Series D.
[6] Richmond to Cairns, 13 Aug. 1882. Cairns Mss., PRO. 30/51/4, fol. 134.
[7] Abercorn to Salisbury, 23 July 1882. Salisbury Mss., Series E.
[8] Salisbury to Cross, 10 Aug. 1882. Cross Mss., 51263.
[9] Gibson to Northcote, 4 Aug. 1882. Salisbury Mss., Series E.
[10] Cairns to Richmond, 4 Aug. 1882. Goodwood Mss., 871/D6.
[11] Salisbury to Cross, 10 Aug. 1882. Cross Mss., 51263.
[12] Richmond to Cairns, 13 Aug. 1882. Cairns Mss., PRO. 30/51/4, fol. 134.
[13] Balfour Notebook. Balfour Mss., 49962 fol. 47.
[14] Gorst to Churchill, 14 Oct. 1882. Churchill Mss., 1/80.

Whips for their waywardness in timing the 1880 election, now warned Salisbury against over-reliance upon Winn,[1] but Hamilton, as spokesman for the second and younger rank in the preceding administration, was simply professing that group's antipathy to the ex-Cabinet.[2] The Commons' revolt was in fact a revolt against the leadership of the 'old identity'. It was a move to discredit and upset it, masquerading as a complaint that Northcote, Smith and Cross were out of touch with Commons and party sentiment. The Lords' revolt constituted a direct challenge to Salisbury's leadership by Richmond and Cairns who, the year before, had proposed and seconded his nomination. All three were acting in full recognition of the likelihood of a 'split...destroy[ing] all confidence in our majority & in the use wh. we may be thought likely to make of it.'[3]

The immediate result was that the Liberals ended the Session 'stronger than we began it',[4] while the Conservatives had 'nothing to do...but sit still and chew the...bitter...cud.'[5] The 'activity of the House of Lords, for a time, must be at zero';[6] and when 'everybody is doing nothing the English language is of course inadequate to describe the negative activity of the House of Lords.'[7] The bringing forward by the Government in 1883 of predominantly non-contentious legislative matter made more bitter the loss of the 'golden opportunity' afforded by the Arrears bill 'for breaking Gladstone's dictatorship'[8] and confirmed Salisbury's fear that there would 'now be no chance of picking a quarrel with the Government before the County Franchise bill comes on – &... we...have to face the election upon that.'[9] But the Lords were not inactive through 1883, and Salisbury did not disappoint those who had come to look to him for a show of 'hanky-panky' in the summertime.[10] In the course of two August evenings, he threw out the Irish Registration and Scottish Local Government bills[11] and stood

---

[1] Lord George Hamilton to Salisbury, 4 Aug. 1882. Salisbury Mss., Series E.
[2] Balfour Notebook. Balfour Mss., 49962 fol. 47.
[3] Carnarvon to Cranbrook, 5 Aug. 1882. Cranbrook Mss., T501/262.
[4] Mundella to Leader, 14 Aug. 1882. Mundella–Leader Mss.
[5] Northcote to Gibson, 12 Aug. 1882. Ashbourne Mss.
[6] Salisbury to Manners, 10 Oct. 1882. Belvoir Mss.
[7] Salisbury to Lady John Manners, 1 Mar. 1883. Salisbury Mss., Series D.
[8] Salisbury to Cross, 10 Aug. 1882. Cross Mss., 51263.
[9] Salisbury to Manners, 30 Jan. 1883. Belvoir Mss.
[10] Hamilton Diary, 24 Aug. 1883. Hamilton Mss., 48634 fol. 53.
[11] The Corrupt Practices bill escaped: 'If the House of Commons insists on inflicting publicly this severe flagellation upon itself, it seems ungracious to interfere with so edifying a penance.' Salisbury to Cross, 12 Aug. 1883. Cross Mss., 51263.

fast on Lords' amendments to the Agricultural Holdings' bill. It was this which provided the best spectacle – a tie in the division, the Liberal Chancellor (by custom of the House) casting his vote against Government colleagues, and the subsequent appearance of an unknown Peer to carry Salisbury's substantive motion by a majority of one. The episode enhanced no reputations. Gladstone had sent a major bill to the Lords after he had announced the end of the Session.[1] (He now showed no hurry to take up cudgels but his outwardly conciliatory mood and ungrudging acceptance of several of Richmond's proposals were clearly intended to encourage the formation of a Cave.) For his part, Salisbury was held to have botched everything and to have played 'a very sorry part' in yielding to Richmond to whom 'he ought not to have yielded.'[2] Within the Conservative ranks, Wolff mourned that the Lords should make their stand on a subject in which they were too evidently self-interested, Balfour answering plausibly that it was only upon such property matters that the Peers could be persuaded to remain in Town.[3] Cairns found Salisbury's strategy incomprehensible: 'The Govt. wd., I feel sure, have been ready to let it be thrown over, & left the odium on us' –[4] incomprehensible that is to say, unless Salisbury for his own purposes was aiding and abetting Gladstone in the policy of filling the cup of misdeeds.

On the personal level, Salisbury had come out of Arrears not at all badly. To be sure, there remained after 1882 the problem as to whether it would 'ever be possible to carry Cairns & Richmond with us in resistance to a second reading'.[5] But Salisbury had not learnt the lessons that *they* would have had him learn. He had not been taught 'better [to] understand his position.'[6] Moreover, Balfour wasted no time in repairing his uncle's fortunes at Richmond's and Cairns' expense. A dinner of Scottish Peers, under Lothian's auspices and Buccleuch's chairmanship, was arranged for November, not that they might in private 'enjoy the (doubtful)

---

[1] Argyll to Granville, 17 Aug. 1883. Gladstone Mss., 44105 fol. 159.
[2] Earl Grey to Halifax, 25 Aug. 1883. Hickleton Mss., A4.55.15. Compare Halifax to Ripon, 16 Aug. 1883: 'Salisbury has been very pugnacious...and not shewn much appreciation of what was wanted to make the bill work... while the Govt. has had no notion of anything but adhering to their own proposals. I am rather disappointed at the conduct of both parties.' Ripon Mss., 43531 fol. 35.
[3] Wolff to Churchill, 28 Aug. 1883. Churchill Mss., 1/164.
[4] Cairns to Richmond, 28 Aug. 1883. Goodwood Mss., 871/D19.
[5] Salisbury to Northcote, 10 Aug. 1882. Iddesleigh Mss., 50020 fol. 38.
[6] Cranbrook Diary, 11 Aug. 1882. *Cranbrook Memoir*, Vol. II, p. 182.

pleasure of each other's society, but to express in a public manner their confidence in *you* [i.e. Salisbury].' Richmond and Cairns were, almost literally, to be made to eat the leek before their compeers, and, in order to make the affair more 'creditable' and 'politically use[ful]', a list of those present and an account in outline of their professions of loyalty was to be furnished to the press.[1] No such active campaign was called for against Northcote. What Salisbury 'learnt' was the curious political lesson that while both Conservative leaders were discredited by Arrears, he himself escaped fullest censure as having been 'badly used'.[2] Indeed, he profited by reaction, for what was initially adjudged foolhardiness came rapidly to be accepted as resolute leadership. The nervous disorder from which the Conservative party suffered during the early 1880s was manifest in its ill-temper, and that ill-temper after the summer of 1882 found vent in abuse of Northcote, the 'Goat' becoming now an almost indispensable scapegoat and all troubles being laid at his door.

Salisbury earned from Gladstone the sobriquet, 'Prince Rupert';[3] Northcote, 'half humorously, wholly pathetically', acknowledged himself, by comparison, to be a less romantic figure, somewhat 'lacking in go'.[4] Wolff would have found such disarming self-effacement inadequate: the 'Goat' was 'a loathsome creature, full of small spite & destitute of virility except in its lowest germ development, a kind of earthworm.'[5] Outbursts were, however, rare and unnecessary since Northcote in the main could safely be left to condemn himself. He was, perhaps, at his happiest and, from an academic viewpoint, his most impressive, addressing the annual *conversazione* of the Exeter Literary Society in January 1884 on 'Nothing':[6]

Masterly inactivity is the art of sitting still and not committing yourself to any action at a time when it is not convenient you should do so. It means waiting for your turn; waiting for your particular opportunity; waiting, in fact, in a manner that will embarrass your opponent and not

---

[1] Balfour to Salisbury, 28 Sept. 1882. Salisbury Mss., Series E.
[2] Cranbrook Diary, 11 Aug. 1882. *Cranbrook Memoir*, Vol. II, p. 182.
[3] Hamilton Diary, 24 Aug. 1883. Hamilton Mss., 48634 fol. 53.
[4] Lucy, *Memories of Eight Parliaments*, p. 218.
[5] Wolff to Balfour, 17 Nov. 1881. Balfour Mss., 49838 fol. 101.
[6] *The Times*, 21 Jan. 1884, p. 7. Compare Northcote's 'golden rule' for his children – 'Whatever you are going to do, Don't.' Lady Iddesleigh (ed.), Stafford H. Northcote, Earl of Iddesleigh, *Scraps, Odds and Ends*, privately printed (1888), p. 540.

commit yourself; for very often, by acting too quickly, you are giving impulse to forces which, if you leave them alone, will exhaust themselves and do no harm. Masterly inactivity is an excellent principle; but you must take care it is masterly, and that it does not arise from indolence or timidity or from not knowing your own mind.

Northcote was unfortunate in his timing, for his philosophy was indistinguishable from Disraeli's disapprobation of the airing of 'remedial theories' and the flying of 'pilot balloons' from the Conservative side when in opposition.[1] He was unfortunate in that the more vociferous elements in his Commons party thought his *modus operandi* timorous, the expression of incapacity. His Parliamentary speeches tended to be either humdrum little talks or laborious discourses – the latter, on occasion, marred by a 'somewhat unfortunate hiatus...owing to the right hon. gentleman leading up to a point he greatly desired to make, and then suddenly forgetting what it was'.[2] Raikes painted the memorable portrait of Gladstone's former secretary still, as Opposition leader, mesmerised by the power of the other's Despatch Box oratory, 'the hands of perplexity travelling up and down the sleeves of irresolution'.[3] Northcote's inadequacy was heightened by selective memory and deification of Disraeli, by Churchill's audacity and imitation of the young Disraeli and by Gladstone's tendency to follow Churchill in debate and address his argument to the corner seat below the Gangway.[4] With combative leadership at a premium, 'wriggl[ing] into office' at a discount,[5] Northcote found 'something petty' in simple denunciation of Government policy,[6] whatever the opportunities afforded by bungling abroad or in Ireland. There was always method in his apparently weak line. On the Kilmainham treaty, for instance, a Lords investigation or committee of inquiry – which the hotheads demanded – might well have resulted in a

---

[1] Disraeli to Richmond, 12 Dec. 1880. Goodwood Mss., 865/W97.
[2] *Morning Post*, 8 Apr. 1884, p. 4. See also Gorst, 28 May 1883: he 'wished to point out that the right hon. Gentleman at the head of the Government had forgotten to answer the Question which the Leader of the Opposition forgot to put.' 3 *Hansard* cclxxix. 965.
[3] Edward Clarke, *The Story of my Life* (1918), p. 206.
[4] Churchill, preferring ostentatious separation, had rejected a typically shrewd suggestion of Gorst's that the Fourth party should plant themselves immediately behind Northcote on the second bench, be seen to take their 'places in the ranks', have him under their thumb, or overhear private converse between Northcote and his satellites. Gorst to Churchill, 16 Sept. 1880. Churchill Mss., 1/12.
[5] Gorst to Churchill, 26 Sept. 1880. Churchill Mss., 1/14.
[6] Northcote to Winn, 14 Dec. 1880. Nostell Mss., 1/49.

whitewash, eliciting nothing; rather 'leave the Govt. in the[ir] hole [and]...hold up to the public suggestions & suspicions, accusations & innuendos, with Ministers professing to court investigation, & yet throwing every obstacle in the way of it'.[1] Rather than 'blackguard' the Land bill, wait for it to be shown that the 'banishment of political economy from Ireland [was not] the panacea for all its ills'.[2]

This is not to deny Northcote's failings – his inability to turn to good account 'independent action in his followers',[3] his being a 'born second-in-command'.[4] But we must enumerate the 'wheels within wheels'[5] with which he could not cope. Some months before Disraeli's death, Salisbury had given his blessing to the Fourth party; if Northcote must needs act as 'arbitrator...that attitude involves no censure or slight on any one of the sections, who are not in the least bound to adopt the same attitude.'[6] It was the knowledge that the Fourth party, while still containing Balfour, was receiving 'a little too much encouragement from quarters which I need not now mention' –[7] Hatfield certainly, and possibly Hughenden too – that so upset Northcote's reasonable expectations.

Northcote certainly had reasonable expectations (*pace* his angina) of reaching the summit: he had, after all, six years' head-start on Salisbury. And in one respect, he acted more positively than those who, with unbounded 'faith in Gladstone's power of committing follies',[8] waited supinely for him to 'ruin his party'.[9] Careful steering and discreet management of opposition, to which of course Northcote was constitutionally suited, might tempt the more conservative elements in the Liberal ranks into a Cave and ease the transference of Goschen, Hartington, Lansdowne or Argyll into a moderate-Conservative Cabinet.[10] If Northcote could not use the Fourth party (they would not be used and Northcote

---

[1] Cairns to Northcote, 28 Feb. 1883. Iddesleigh Mss., 50021 fol. 14.
[2] Smith to Winn, 26 Aug. 1881. Nostell Mss., 1/53.
[3] Balfour to Salisbury, 29 Sept. 1881. B. E. C. Dugdale (ed.), Arthur James, First Earl of Balfour, *Retrospect: an Unfinished Autobiography, 1848–1886* (Cambridge, Massachusetts, 1930); p. 151.
[4] Blake, *Disraeli*, p. 545.
[5] Lady Frances Balfour to Gerald Balfour, 8 Apr. 1883. Lady Frances Balfour, *Ne Obliviscaris* (2 vols., 1930), Vol. I, p. 381.
[6] Salisbury to Balfour, 5 Oct. 1880. Balfour Mss., 49688 fol. 33.
[7] Northcote to Cross, 29 Nov. 1880. Cross Mss., 51256.
[8] Robert Bourke to Winn, 24 Apr. 1880. Nostell Mss., 1/41.
[9] R. N. Fowler Diary, 22 Apr. 1880. Flynn, *Robert Fowler*, p. 252.
[10] Northcote Diary, 26 Apr. 1880. Andrew Lang, *Life, Letters and Diaries of Sir Stafford Northcote, First Earl of Iddesleigh* (1 vol. ed., Edinburgh, 1891), p. 314.

underrated the numbers prepared to consider 'concerted action' with Churchill),[1] he was himself capable of attracting into the Conservative lobbies 'some of those broken reeds' on the other side[2] who entertained a conviction of the 'mischievous tendencies of Gladstone's leadership, and of the utter instability he is imparting to all the fundamental principles of government as hitherto understood in all civilised countries.'[3] Northcote's Parliamentary language was the stock-in-trade of pure Whiggery, designed to appeal to those who wore the 'business of government' favour in their lapels. Occasionally it sank to unconscious parody of their mumbo jumbo; 'and a very proper proceeding it is, subject to qualifications, perhaps,...to be accepted in principle when the time comes.'[4]

We may attempt to measure the worth of leading figures to their parties but we shall make little progress. We cannot know how many Liberals Chamberlain pushed towards Conservatism, nor what proportion of the Liberal mass saw him as their leader and the *sine qua non* of their Liberalism. We cannot know how many at any level were positively reassured by Hartington's presence, nor how many turned from a Liberalism whose tone was set by Whiggery to the 'Democratic Toryism' of Churchill. What we can say of Northcote is that he would have driven nobody into the arms of the enemy, that he was thought by Salisbury to be attempting 'to lure over Whig rank & file' rather than expecting a purely Parliamentary coalition,[5] and that his death – its drama matched by pathos – was said to have produced a wave of public sympathy and mourning which took long memories back to Peel. What is more relevant to Reform is to say that Ulstermen and the Anglo-Irish landowning aristocracy had more faith in him than in Salisbury, just as they had more faith in Hartington than in Gladstone.[6] Whether they had, all told, less faith in Salisbury than in Hartington is a moot point.

Northcote's health was as fragile as his leadership. Salisbury was too clever, politically unwise, and unable ever to call a halt. Small

[1] Wolff, quoting Raikes, to Churchill, 30 Aug. 1883. Churchill Mss., 1/165.
[2] Northcote to Elcho, 27 Jan. 1882. Wemyss Mss.
[3] Argyll to Reeve, 8 May 1882. J. K. Laughton, *Memoirs of the Life and Correspondence of Henry Reeve* (2 vols., 1898), Vol. II, p. 305.
[4] On a Budget proposal, 9 Apr. 1883. 3 *Hansard* cclxxvii. 1926.
[5] Salisbury to Balfour, 5 Oct. 1880. Balfour Mss., 49688 fol. 33.
[6] Compare Campbell-Bannerman to Rosebery, 4 Aug. 1885. Rosebery Mss., Box 2.

CONSERVATIVES IN THE DARK

wonder that in such circumstances other claimants came forward
to save Conservatism (as most put it) from self-destruction. Most
pinned their hopes on a traditional 'mode of emergence'. The
approach of Churchill *via* the party organization was at least
singular, if a reflection of Chamberlain's 'great notion of using
conferences, associations, & democratic forms generally, to give
absolute power, to a few individuals (himself preferred)'.[1] From
the first, he aimed at a National Union Council on which his
henchmen would have an assured majority so that, when that was
secured, they could present the National Union as 'the representative body of the whole Conservative Party' and proceed to choose a
leader.[2] Cranbrook was stung by such impertinence. 'Northcote',
he wrote at New Year 1884, 'has done his duty in substance on all
occasions though not without some weaknesses, as Salisbury has
also not without some escapades...who are these who presume to
settle [the leadership]?'[3]

Northcote, Cranbrook's guest in mid-December, had shown him[4]
a letter from Edward Stanhope which detailed the National Union
Organization Committee's latest proceedings, and relayed the
opinion of Earl Percy, at whose expense Churchill was elected
Chairman, that an attempt to carry the leadership problem into
the constituencies was imminent.[5] The details of battle need not
detain us; what was perfectly well understood at the time was that
'a mischievous split'[6] between this Committee and the Central was
inevitable. The historian may find no easy, obvious or perhaps any
dividing line between control of party organization and the use of
party organization to promote purely Parliamentary interests;
what was again perfectly well understood at the time was Churchill's
purpose. His rapid loss of interest in the National Union confirmed
Balfour's belief: Churchill had simply recognized the inability of
that body to provide the assistance which Gorst thought it capable
of providing.[7] Gorst was clear that in order 'to upset the whole
gang on the front bench...We must have an organization & a
party at our backs.'[8] But the real change as between 1882 (when

[1] Elliot Diary, 17 Oct. 1887. Diaries, Vol. 12.
[2] Northcote to Winn, 26 Sept. 1883. Nostell Mss., 1/78.
[3] Cranbrook Diary, 5 Jan. 1884. Cranbrook Mss., T501/299 fol. 156.
[4] Cranbrook Diary, 15 Dec. 1883. Cranbrook Mss., T501/299 fol. 148.
[5] Stanhope to Northcote, 13 Dec. 1883. Iddesleigh Mss., 50042 fol. 5.
[6] Northcote to Winn, 26 Sept. 1883. Nostell Mss., 1/78.
[7] Balfour, *Retrospect*, p. 174.
[8] Gorst to Churchill, 15 Aug. 1883. Churchill Mss., 1/157.

Churchill ran Salisbury against Northcote) and 1883 was the enlargement of Churchill's ambition to encompass overall leadership. Salisbury was now looked on as a 'broken reed', tolerated 'upstairs' only because he was still thought 'best for us' in view of the alternative – Richmond who was 'too goaty & afraid',[1] who had urged Disraeli to take summary action against the Fourth party,[2] and who was to express his disgust in 1885 that Churchill should have been given a Cabinet seat.[3]

We may indeed suggest that the real crisis of Conservative organization at this time was to be found far from the National Union. It lay in Bartley's failure to prepare a 'good manual' of Reform facts and figures for the edification of front and back benchers alike.[4] It lay in the failure to circulate Disraeli's 1874 pronouncement upon franchise extension as orthodoxy before Churchill gave his lead, and in Manners' total ignorance as to who was the 'manager of such matters' in the party offices.[5] It lay, at Central Office, in Bartley's antipathy towards his party leaders, in their antipathy towards him, and in the fears they felt that he was tarred with the Churchill brush. It lay in the depressing ignorance displayed when Northcote asked Gibson whether he or 'anybody [had] worked out a scheme of redistribution which would protect the Loyal Minority in Ireland from utter annihilation'.[6] It lay in Gibson's pious undertaking to embark upon the task of collecting 'information & views' upon this complex issue, the day *after* the party leaders' conference had got under way, and the day before Gibson journeyed to Boulogne on holiday.[7]

We may suggest further that the Fourth party's personnel and the relationship between these few is of greater importance in the case we are discussing than is their involvement in any organization matter. One Liberal found the combination of capabilities perfect – diplomacy in Wolff, law in Gorst, morals and culture in Balfour, infinite cheek and a certain oratorical capacity in Churchill.[8] What is too readily overlooked is the fact that though Churchill alone was a contender in the immediate future for highest office, the

[1] Wolff to Churchill, 28 Aug. 1883. Churchill Mss., 1/164.
[2] Richmond to Disraeli, 1 Jan. 1881. Goodwood Mss., 865/W99.
[3] Richmond to Salisbury, 19 Aug. 1885. Salisbury Mss., Series E.
[4] Northcote to Smith, 27 Oct. 1883. Hambleden Mss., PS8/86.
[5] Manners to Henry Manners, 17 Sept. 1883. Belvoir Mss.
[6] Northcote to Gibson, 26 Oct. 1884. Ashbourne Mss.
[7] Gibson to Salisbury, 20 Nov. 1884. Salisbury Mss., Series E.
[8] Caine's designation. Lady Frances Balfour, *Ne Obliviscaris*, Vol. I, p. 441.

Fourth party did not rely on his right arm for its Commons' nuisance value. When it was rumoured that he was politically unwell and might miss the opening of the 1883 Session, Smith took little comfort: Wolff was 'quite himself and that means much',[1] while Manners over a longer period talked of the Commons as in the hands of the Irish and Gorst. Again, it is too easy to dismiss Gorst as 'exactly' (and thus just) 'the man to buzz unpleasantly about the ears of arch mediocrity'.[2] Time after time, his was the creative force and impetus behind a particular action or manoeuvre. There is indeed a case for taking seriously the threat to Churchill's primacy, a case for doubting whether historical recognition of his influence was sufficient for Gorst. Just as Churchill had publicly cut himself loose from Northcote in 1882 and from Salisbury a year later, so in November 1884 he sharply reminded Gorst in the House of Commons that he too was dispensable.

The struggle during 1884 in which the Fourth party was involved – a struggle more crucial than any over the National Union – was for acceptance as a serious political phenomenon. Press dismissal – a belief that the Tories would never again 'set aside age and experience...[or] names all persons honour...in favour of restless and immature ambitions'[3] – reflected powerful social aversion. Lady Dorothy Nevill told Gorst that at the dinner tables of London the Fourth party was either 'denounced or pooh-poohed', nobody speaking of them 'with respect'.[4] That was certainly so. Prejudice against Churchill ran high, not simply on the grounds of disloyalty and a palpable readiness to assist, when so inclined for his own purposes, either the Government or the 'legitimate' opposition.[5] Clarke, whose origins were less exalted, looked on Churchill as a scion betraying his lineage, one who displayed 'little knowledge of literature and none of science, no familiarity with political history, and very slight acquaintance with foreign affairs.'[6] Others were less prosy: Churchill was a 'strumpet'.[7] The value of

---

[1] Smith to Winn, 11 Feb. 1883. Nostell Mss., 1/73.
[2] H. W. Lucy, *The Diary of a Journalist* (1920), p. 24.
[3] *Standard*, 20 Dec. 1883, p. 5.
[4] Gorst to Churchill, 29 Jan. 1883. Churchill Mss., 1/105.
[5] Gorst to Wolff, 7 Feb. 1883. Churchill Mss., 1/103.
[6] Derek Walker-Smith and Edward Clarke, *The Life of Sir Edward Clarke* (1939), p. 154.
[7] Rendel to Grant Duff, 26 Mar. 1884. F. E. Hamer (ed.), *The Personal Papers of Lord Rendel, Containing his Unpublished Conversations with Mr. Gladstone, 1888–1898, and Other Famous Statesmen; Selections from Letters and Papers* (1931), pp. 225–6.

Balfour to the Fourth party was clear. He provided respectability which none of the others had and, so far as Hatfield was respectable, a measure of official approval. But Balfour's loyalty was never primarily to Churchill. The conclusion which recurs is that it was Gladstone who 'made' Churchill.

Just as we may pinpoint Churchill's weaknesses, so may we with other contenders. It remains true that their names were under consideration, and it is because they might have emerged as leaders that their actions were the object of attention in 1884. Thus it is as relevant that Cairns was found singing the praises of Churchill as 'the only person who gave the opposition any animation'[1] and was thought to be 'actuated by jealousy' of Salisbury,[2] as that he was unable to attract a single Conservative vote when attempting to throw out a Railways bill in which his brother had a heavy personal interest.[3] Richmond is remembered, quite properly, as the least distinguished man ever to lead the Conservative Peers; he *was* 'as ignorant of the real principles of legislation as any of his footmen.'[4] The historian will conclude that any expectation he entertained of a second chance was illusory, and yet he tried repeatedly to upset Salisbury.[5] Cranbrook, Disraeli's former deputy who had expected the leadership of the Commons in 1876, was ready to capitalize on Salisbury's deficiencies. Carnarvon also awaited his moment – a cross-bencher whose vexation at not being invited to join the Liberal Ministry in 1880 turned to vehement Tory partisanship,[6] a 'sanguine, emotional man...[who] thought that his own personal influence was capable of working wonders with all'[7] and of taking him to the top. A broken collar bone, bronchitis and pleurisy put paid to Pembroke's political activity in 1884; his extreme hostility to the Fourth party[8] and contempt for Salisbury had suggested an active role in the Reform play.[9]

[1] Wolff to Churchill, 13 Jan. 1883. Churchill Mss., 1/96.
[2] Oranmore to Salisbury, 19 Feb. 1884. Salisbury Mss., Series E.
[3] Sherbrooke to Halifax, 2 July 1881. Hickleton Mss., A4.181 Part 7.
[4] Earl Grey to Halifax, 25 Aug. 1883. Hickleton Mss., A4.55.15.
[5] Oranmore to Salisbury, 19 Feb. 1884. Salisbury Mss., Series E.
[6] Hamilton Diary, 3 Jan. 1883. Hamilton Mss., 48633 fol. 43.
[7] Gibson Journal, 27 Mar. 1890. Ashbourne Mss.
[8] Wolff to Churchill, 19 Dec. 1882. Churchill Mss., 1/90.
[9] It is worth noting how many other Conservatives were prevented by illness from playing the role that might have been expected of them at critical moments in the Reform episode. From February to July (when he went to Marienbad), Cranbrook led 'an invalid life'. *Cranbrook Memoir*, Vol. II, p. 196. Though returning from the Continent in better health, his sister's death kept him from the crucial shadow Cabinet and party meetings on

CONSERVATIVES IN THE DARK

Of the Commoners, Gibson was so capable and so well aware of his capability in 'tear[ing] any Irish] Bill to pieces',[1] that Northcote felt 'a little jealous & rather disposed to snub him',[2] and Churchill felt obliged to solicit his support.[3] Chaplin entertained 'other views for the supersession of the present leader, and it is well understood with him the private candidate for the reversion is his colleague, Mr. Edward Stanhope.'[4] Churchill's 'hatred' for, and recognition of the serious threat posed by Stanhope, Salisbury saw as the core of the National Union rumpus.[5] Manners may not have had the 'physical strength for a continued strain':[6] an unexceptionable record as Chief Commissioner at the Board of Works and Postmaster General marked him out as an unexceptionable stop-gap. Cross was 'naturally the next man', an appalling thought which improved the chances of a Smith–Harrowby 'dual control', whatever Smith's profession of willingness 'gladly [to] follow any one'.[7] Churchill's loud talk[8] of a clean sweep of all these from the front bench allowed the emergence of Hicks Beach – to keep the seat warm for Churchill as Churchill saw it, but as 'well liked' and likely to keep Churchill from that seat in the eyes of the 'old gang'.[9]

The Conservatives found sustenance in a belief, shared by three-quarters of the Cabinet, that outside the Radical organizations there was no very great desire for Reform. Straws in the wind were reassuring. Goschen, after a long discourse and disavowal of further lowering of the suffrage, was questioned by his Ripon constituents only about compulsory vaccination.[10] The *Scotsman* declared that the decision to make a Franchise bill the first measure of 1884 would be a 'tactical blunder' and that extension of the

17 November. Harrowby was despatched on medical orders to Schwalbach for the summer. Cairns' health was suspect throughout this last year of his life; moreover, family scandal culminated in a trial, thanks to 'the Lady's desire for a public appearance', exactly coincident with the Reform denouement. Cairns to Cranbrook, 22 Nov. 1884. Cranbrook Mss., T501/262. Churchill attended his uncle the Marquess of Londonderry's funeral in early November – thus allowing Gorst to make his celebrated unauthorised statement of Fourth party policy.
1 Elcho to Earl Grey, 25 Apr. 1881. Wemyss Mss.
2 Gorst to Churchill, 14 Oct. 1882. Churchill Mss., 1/80.
3 Gibson Journal, copy of Wolff to Gibson, 1 Sept. 1882. Ashbourne Mss.
4 *Manchester Guardian*, 10 Apr. 1884, p. 5.
5 Salisbury to Balfour, 1 May 1884. Balfour Mss., 49688 fol. 74.
6 Smith to Sandon, 17 Jan. 1883. Harrowby Mss., 2nd Ser., Vol. 54, fol. 205.
7 *Ibid.*   8 Hamilton Diary, 19 May 1884. Hamilton Mss., 48636 fol. 87.
9 Smith to Harrowby, 20 June 1884. Harrowby Mss., 2nd Ser., Vol. 54, fol. 219.
10 *The Times*, 31 Jan. 1884, p. 6.

measure to Ireland was a 'proposal bad in itself.'[1] A string of halfpenny newspapers, controlled with Carnegie money by Passmore Edwards and Samuel Storey and designed to promote the cause of Reform, were making no headway in the South.[2] Municipal elections, though hardly more than semi-political,[3] showed a move away from the Liberals. At the level of Parliamentary by-elections, the successful Conservative at Manchester had declared in favour of franchise extension, but the salient features of a second victory, at York in November, seemed to be indifference to suffrage, hankering after Protection, and a longing glance to the *ancien régime* from cabmen and publicans who registered their protests against the Liberals' Corrupt Practices Act.[4] It was sound tactics to play upon apathy – to which Chamberlain's warning that the question would grow hotter with delay merely added point. It was sound tactics also to raise other issues. Salisbury dealt summarily with 'constitutional juggling' and turned attention to social reform and housing of the poor;[5] every subsequent speech-maker perforce paid at least lip service, Liberals dubbing it 'a great non-political' issue.[6] Chaplin was 'full of his scheme for not allowing live cattle to be imported', as a means to 'give us all the Counties'.[7] The control of a foot-and-mouth epidemic whose reappearance neatly coincided with the Liberal resumption of office in 1880, and the call for slaughtering at foreign ports was a 'question on which we shall have with us *all* our friends, both landlords & tenants'[8] – and perhaps a good many agricultural Whigs.[9] When it came to the

---

1 8 Nov. 1883, p. 4.
2 Wolff to Churchill, 2 Oct. 1883. Churchill Mss., 1/173.
3 And still fought here and there on such issues as gas *versus* electric lighting, or the putting down of Salvation Army processions (which won the Conservatives a seat at Folkestone).
4 Lowther to Salisbury, 24 Nov. 1883. Salisbury Mss., Series E. Manners held Sir Frederick Milner's greatest asset (he won by just 21 votes) to have been his speaking 'habitually the Yorkshire lingo with the proper Yorkshire burr.' Manners to Salisbury, 15 Nov. 1883. Belvoir Mss.
5 Salisbury, 'Labourers' and Artizans' Dwellings', *National Review* II (Nov. 1883), pp. 301–16. T. H. Escott, who had hoped to publish Salisbury's article in the *Fortnightly Review*, immediately despatched Archibald Forbes to Hatfield with the express intention of searching out cottages on Salisbury's estate in condition worse than London slums. Dilke to Grant Duff, 7 Nov. 1883. Dilke Mss., 43894 fol. 112.
6 Childers, at Knottingley. *The Times*, 7 Dec. 1883, p. 7.
7 Wolff to Churchill, 21 Nov. 1883. Churchill Mss., 2/216.
8 Salisbury to Richmond, 21 Mar. 1883. Goodwood Mss., 871/D13.
9 Fawkes to Ramsden, 7 Apr. 1884: 'the general public in the country, especially agricultural districts...*care* a great deal that their interests should

Parliamentary arena, Bradlaugh, Parnellites and the Mahdi were fair game for obstruction; 'what with Egypt, S. Africa, China and France', the Conservatives might yet be spared all embarrassment.[1] On Reform itself, none envied the Liberals their task. Northcote was grateful to be out of it. Merely to adapt the law to an altered state of circumstances, or frame proposals based on something other than numbers and simple equalization, would be extremely difficult and 'in the long run' not 'worth the candle'. 'Certainly', he added in a telling phrase, 'I should object to bring forward such proposals myself, feeling convinced that they would be twisted into forms which would be very objectionable, or turned against us in future struggles.'[2] As if to confirm that such sympathy was not misplaced, Government difficulties and the rift between the 'slowest boy in the class' and the 'quickest',[3] were broadcast with monotonous regularity. Just as the Land Act, the government of Ireland and war-making in Egypt had 'brought to light the existence of elements too heterogeneous to be combined with the mass', so now it seemed that Hartington's apprehensions were wholly incompatible with co-operation in the production of a Reform bill.[4] Nor did Chamberlain's omission of the very name of Gladstone in public speeches (always heralded as a sign that the culprit was 'riding for a fall') pass unnoticed.[5] Carnarvon rightly suspected that Chamberlain, who outraged 'every tradition', was imposing an almost intolerable strain upon an unhappy 'political wedlock', which the 'majority of his colleagues – many of whom are gentlemen – must hate.'[6]

Public utterances were not all that the Conservatives had to go on. Gladstone had assured Hartington that he would not press the Cabinet to commit themselves in October to the next year's Reform programme: 'decision so long before action might entail inconvenience.'[7] It would, in so far as it must lend plausibility to the charge of 'Government by Conference'; and Gladstone was anxious that the legislative reverberation should be seen to be

be reasonably attended to, their flocks & Herds protected from foreign imported disease, so lightly thought of & most injudiciously handled by our...scratch pack...of Ministers.' Ramsden Mss., Box 40.
[1] Manners to Northcote, 29 Nov. 1883. Salisbury Mss., Series D.
[2] Northcote to Manners, 22 Nov. 1883. Salisbury Mss., Series D.
[3] Gladstone to Chamberlain, 2 July 1883. Gladstone Mss., 44125 fol. 188.
[4] *The Times*, 1 Dec. 1883, p. 9.
[5] Hamilton Diary, 16 Jan. 1884. Hamilton Mss., 48635 fol. 65.
[6] Carnarvon to Cross, 28 Nov. 1883. Cross Mss., 51268 fol. 133.
[7] Gladstone to Hartington, 22 Oct. 1883. Gladstone Mss., 44546 fol. 179.

'preternaturally slow in following the flash' from Leeds.[1] Even those who, like Granville, professed never to have understood Gladstone's habitual postponement of Cabinets 'to the last moment of the last day' in terms other than of economy of time,[2] recognized that any delay in decision-taking was designed to allow for adjustments outside Cabinet and for Chamberlain to be played off against Hartington. But such tactical delay, and the non-convening of the Cabinet to avoid rupture, did more than preclude the needed reassessment of Nile policies; it led to widespread surmise and 'leakages' in the political world about dissension. Harcourt, who himself had the reputation of talking too much[3] but who had 'sat upon' the *Daily News* when it threatened to let the 'cat out of the bag', thought it wonderful how well Cabinet differences were kept secret.[4] Such optimism was not wholly justified. The 'rash[-] talking' James[5] at 'Mrs. Millais t'other day' had expounded upon 'the absence of all agreement' among the Government's leading members – news which Manners passed on to a grateful Salisbury.[6] Gibson had it that Harcourt (and if Harcourt, presumably others also) would favour a substantial reduction in the number of Irish Members.[7] There is more than a hint that Erskine May passed on his gleanings to Churchill.[8] Albert Grey had seen letters of Hartington's.[9] The now politically inactive Halifax heard a great deal of Cabinet troubles from Childers;[10] always 'very gossippy'[11] and certain that Liberal differences would break out sooner or later,[12] he extended the line of information through Earl Grey to Wemyss, and from the cross-bencher Wemyss to his Conservative son-in-law, Brodrick. Salisbury in 1882 had declared himself suspicious of

---

[1] Morley hoped for an 'imposing' audience in November; Gladstone declined to meet the Conference deputation until late January. The Prime Minister's dictionary offered 'Deputation – a noun of number signifying many but not signifying much.' Mountstuart E. Grant Duff, *Notes from a Diary, Kept Chiefly in Southern India, 1881–1886* (2 vols., 1899), Vol. I, p. 132.

[2] Granville to Derby, 3 June 1885. Derby Mss., Box 2.

[3] Seymour to Spencer, 19 Dec. 1883. Spencer Mss.

[4] Harcourt to Lewis Harcourt, 10 Jan. 1884. Harcourt Mss. But who had told the *Daily News* anything?

[5] Salisbury to Manners, ?28 Dec. 1883. Belvoir Mss.

[6] Manners to Salisbury, ?27 Dec. 1883. Belvoir Mss.

[7] Gibson to Salisbury, 27 Jan. 1884. Salisbury Mss., Series E.

[8] Hamilton Diary, 22 Dec. 1883. Hamilton Mss., 48635 fol. 35.

[9] Albert Grey to Halifax, 28 Jan. 1884. Hickleton Mss., A4.84 Part 4.

[10] e.g., Childers to Halifax, 5 Jan. and 7 Jan. 1884. Hickleton Mss., A4.90.

[11] Northcote to Smith, 23 Oct. 1881. Hambleden Mss., PS7/94.

[12] Halifax to Ripon, 17 Jan. 1884. Ripon Mss., 43531 fol. 80.

hearsay tip-offs respecting Selborne's unease;[1] with the marriage of Selborne's son to Lady Maud Cecil, Salisbury's eldest daughter, it is stretching credulity to doubt that at the very least the Chancellor's despondency, aired fully at dinner conversations,[2] was conveyed to the Conservative camp.[3]

Whatever he may have heard and whatever he must have observed, Salisbury was unlikely to herald his actions by declarations of intent;[4] pilot balloons could only reveal a lack of homogeneity within the Conservative ranks. Warning against giving 'Mr. Chamberlain all he wants'[5] did not commit the party to any final course nor even preclude out-trumping. It was a facile answer to say that the Lords would be asked to reject whatever Liberal fare was offered; Smith, who spent two days at Hatfield immediately before the assembly of Parliament, left there quite uncertain of the treatment to be given to the Franchise question, while as regards London Government he was clear that 'Salisbury had not made up his mind.'[6]

Morley's belief and the Radicals' calculation was that Salisbury would make his 'bitterest fight' not over the absence of a Seats bill, but over extension of the measure to Ireland; 'and as they are quite sure to force dissolution on that, why show hands in redistribution?'[7] What was certain was that there would be no direct opposition to the assimilation of the county and borough franchises. Salisbury himself ruled out the possibility once Goschen had made it clear that at best the *non possumus* of moderate Liberals would be 'designedly couched in such a shape that it cannot be successful.'[8] For Goschen and Salisbury as for Churchill, the sum of Disraeli's legacy was that Reform was a subject 'either party [could] deal

[1] Salisbury to Cairns, 26 Aug. 1882: 'Selborne told a person who told me – the witness is an accurate one...But conversational statements of this kind are not worth much.' Cairns Mss., PRO. 30/15/6, fol. 96.

[2] Elliot Diary, 26 Nov. 1883. Diaries, Vol. 9.

[3] Of course, such links, though tending to be more injurious to a Government than the Opposition, are two-way affairs. Thus Salisbury, though inclined to 'sit down & write to Richmond to incense him to bring in a bill about the dead meat trade...reflected that his first step would be to consult Charles Peel [Clerk to the Privy Council, and Richmond's cousin] on the subject: & Charles Peel would duly inform Carlingford...& enable [the Cabinet] to trump us.' Salisbury to Manners, 11 Dec. 1883. Belvoir Mss.

[4] Lady St. Helier, *Memories of Fifty Years* (1909), p. 268.

[5] Northcote to Hay, 3 Dec. 1883. Copy. Salisbury Mss., Series E.

[6] Smith to Harrowby, 2 Feb. 1884. Harrowby Mss., 2nd Ser., Vol. 54, fol. 217.

[7] Morley to Maxse, 11 Dec. 1883. Maxse Mss., 215.

[8] Salisbury to Manners, 30 Jan. 1883. Belvoir Mss.

with.'[1] The detail was more baffling. Northcote put aside '1867' as the legislation of a minority who, in the retention of office, had accepted injurious modifications to their own scheme; Conservatives were not to be bound to spurious deductions from the 'unlucky' rejection of the dual vote and abolition of the rate-paying qualifications.[2] Manners, whose instinct was to refer the perplexed to 'Lord Chatham's views as detailed in Lecky',[3] met Lord Barrington in Bumpus' and engaged in heated conversation as to whether or not Disraeli in 1874 had declared 'that equalization ought never to be allowed by the Conservatives as a Party' or whether the objection was solely to a premature reopening of the question.[4] But it mattered little that Disraelian ambiguity had led astray 'our inexperienced younger friends'[5] on these franchise matters; he had taught the fundamental truth that no stigma of defeat would be attached to acceptance of franchise assimilation if control of the Redistribution bill was secured.

In the event, procedural principle – the demand to see how the right hand would twist what the left freely gave – marked the limit of Conservative unity. To choose Redistribution as a fighting ground had the seeming disadvantage that Gladstone would turn objection to a point of procedure, whose fundamental bearing was intelligible to all politicians, into public and constituency denunciation of the withholding of popular rights. Ireland was, by comparison, easy prey. Appeals might be made quite simply to prejudice in stressing the swamping powers in Ireland of the 'lowest stratum',[6] the 'turbid froth',[7] and the 'pauper class'.[8] In terms of higher morality, postponement was imperative until the supremacy of law had been vindicated.[9] The Conservatives' calculation was that, at the very least, 'British sympathies wd. move strongly in favour of a substantial reduction' in the number of Irish Members.[10] Salisbury himself sensed 'that Ministers would fail if they attempted to extend the Franchise in Ireland under present circumstances.'[11]

[1] Churchill, at Edinburgh. *The Times*, 21 Dec. 1883, p. 5.
[2] Northcote to Manners, 22 Nov. 1883. Salisbury Mss., Series D.
[3] Manners to Salisbury, 27 Nov. 1883. Belvoir Mss.
[4] Barrington to Northcote, 21 Nov. 1883. Iddesleigh Mss., 50042 fol. 1.
[5] Northcote to Salisbury, 7 Dec. 1883. Salisbury Mss., Series E.
[6] Mulholland, 7 Mar. 1883. 3 *Hansard* cclxxvii. 1695.
[7] Carnarvon, at Taunton. *The Times*, 21 Jan. 1884, p. 10.
[8] Limerick, 7 Feb. 1884. 3 *Hansard* cclxxxiv. 166.
[9] Smith, at the Dublin Rotunda. *The Times*, 25 Jan. 1884, p. 5.
[10] Gibson to Salisbury, 27 Jan. 1884. Salisbury Mss., Series E.
[11] Salisbury to Henry Manners, 10 Nov. 1883. Salisbury Mss., Series D.

Salisbury's unwillingness to make special provisions to meet Ulster fears was in part the price paid by Abercorn, Cairns and the Irish landowners for their 'wayward tactics' and humiliation of Salisbury over the Arrears bill in 1882. In recognizing that the Ulster Conservatives imposed a self-interested 'drag' on the whole party,[1] and that the Parnellite vote was the more attractive, Salisbury was deferring to Fourth party tenets. But his concern was not for the moment with Churchill's vagaries. As Gorst feared, the Fourth party had run Salisbury too early against Northcote, and Salisbury was in a position to determine when he wanted that particular crisis, or even to wait until Churchill put himself flagrantly in the wrong by some act of party disloyalty.[2]

The course of this story becomes unintelligible if we forget that the Conservative leadership was still unsettled three years after Disraeli's death. Salisbury's decision not to concentrate upon the Irish clauses becomes intelligible only if we understand that Northcote, by means of his Ulster tour in the late summer of 1883 was asserting, and seen by Salisbury to be asserting, his leadership claim in posing as champion of the English connexion. Though ready to exploit a firebrand like William Johnston,[3] he scrupulously discountenanced ostentatious alliance with extremism, refusing to lay the foundation stone of a Belfast Orange Lodge.[4] The raising of 'a real good protest against Home Rule' was quite sufficient for Northcote's purpose.[5] His hopes rested, and foundered, on Gladstone's producing in 1884 a strong Local Government bill for Ireland,[6] revulsion from which would set on foot the anticipated 'severe struggle between the supporters and the assailants of Order, Property, and the Unity of the Empire.'[7] On Reform, Northcote made his formal protest against the annihilation of 'the intelligence and the energy of Ireland',[8] while his underlings, Clarke and Robert Fowler, took up Proportional Representation as a cross-party bridge. Northcote knew the embarrassment of his position; once the Conservatives had admitted the applicability of household suffrage to the remainder of the United Kingdom and turned their attention to delaying its application to Ireland, there

---

[1] Gorst to Smith, 14 July 1881. Hambleden Mss., PS7/58.
[2] Balfour to Salisbury, 14 Jan. 1884. Balfour, *Retrospect*, Vol. i, p. 80.
[3] William Johnston Diary, 23 Feb. 1884. Johnston Mss., D880(2)/36.
[4] Northcote to Gibson, 5 Sept. 1883. Ashbourne Mss.
[5] Waterford to Gibson, 13 Oct. 1883. Ashbourne Mss.
[6] Northcote to Winn, 29 Oct. 1883. Nostell Mss., 1/82.
[7] Northcote to Hicks Beach, 8 Aug. 1883. St. Aldwyn Mss., PCC/77.
[8] *The Times*, 4 Oct. 1883, p. 8.

was a danger that with a change of Government, 'every man Jack of the Liberal party would join the Irish in forcing it upon us.'[1] Northcote's understandable concern throughout the years of Gladstone's Second Ministry was to 'know who are with me and who are against me'.[2] Balfour and Salisbury, it needs saying, literally did 'all they could' against him[3] – until Northcote accepted a position of political dependence upon Hatfield. Salisbury's determination to avoid summoning an ex-Cabinet in the wake of Northcote's tour emanated from recognition that Cairns, Cranbrook and Richmond, Cross, Gibson, Smith and Winn would stand behind Northcote in defending Ulster; Salisbury refused even to compare notes on Reform with his partner in the 'dual control'. That the Conservatives did not raise the Irish bogey in the autumn of 1883 was an example of the hesitation of troops, left without guidance, to compromise their generals. Reform, for Salisbury's benefit, was to be played, if it had to be played, on a Lords–Commons constitutional platform, not upon an Irish one. Hence, in large measure, the irrelevance of the Proportional Representation Society, the stifling of any moves towards party realignment, and the emergence of an undisputed Conservative leader. There was little doubt that Salisbury throughout foresaw the individual advantages that might be expected to accrue from such agitation. By the late summer of 1884, he was seen not to have missed his mark (whatever the issue of the crisis) in distancing all rivals.[4] Gladstone's cruel portrayal of the tea-time conferences in Downing Street which settled Redistribution, contained a wider truth: 'Lord Salisbury took the whole matter out of the hands of Northcote, who sat by him on the sofa like a chicken protected by the wings of the mother hen.'[5]

[1] Manners to Northcote, 4 Dec. 1883. Salisbury Mss., Series D.
[2] Northcote to Winn, 2 Apr. 1883. Nostell Mss., 1/74.
[3] Gorst to Churchill, 7 Aug. 1883. Churchill Mss., 1/149.
[4] *Manchester Guardian*, 4 Aug. 1884, p. 5, and 1 Oct. 1884, p. 5.
[5] Autobiographical Memoranda, 1897. Gladstone Mss., 44791 fol. 152.

3

MINIMISING OPPOSITION

There was no need to beat about the bush. They knew that the Irish vote was in the market.

> Churchill, 8 Feb. 1884. 3 *Hansard* cclxxxiv. 369.

...if what I have to offer be found to justify my description of it, – giving an absolutely certain (when deserved) minority representation; making a valuable approach to the strictly proportional and easily and (pardon me,) Englishly workable, shall it be worth to me from your Association £3000...To be quite frank with you, I addressed myself in some such terms as the foregoing to a leading member of the Conservative party soon after the opening of the last session of Parliament and I could by no means understand the curtness of the refusal with which my offer was declined.

> W. FitzHenry to Lubbock, 27 Jan. 1885. Proportional Representation Society Mss.

He really could not tell why the sum of £10 should be the uniform limit of occupation; it had been so fixed in boroughs in 1832...The hon. Member objected to such a sum being fixed; but he had adduced no more argument in favour of the reduced sum he proposed [£5] than could be offered in support of a proposal to reduce the qualification to £2, or even to £1. It was necessary to have a uniform limit, and the £10 limit having been decided upon, and being well understood, it was desirable to retain it...although [the Government] admitted they saw no particular charm in it.'

> James, refusing Leighton's amendment, 9 June 1884. 3 *Hansard* cclxxxviii. 1828.

BILLS FOR ENGLAND AND IRELAND, Trevelyan suggested, need not 'run on all fours; but there are points on which it would not do to adopt a different policy.'[1] It was an admirable political homily for a Reform bill where Parliamentary advantage or necessity was the prime, indeed the sole, consideration. Consistency was not a strong point in Gladstone's reasoning: were Ireland to be treated on an 'all fours' footing of absolute equality with regard to the franchise, as he dictated, then why should not

---

[1] Trevelyan to Dilke, 26 Dec. 1883. Dilke Mss., 43895 fol. 61.

the proportion of her Members to population be taken into account as in the rest of the British Isles?[1] Why the convolutions to demonstrate that Ireland was still entitled to the Union total of 103, fixed on the basis of proportionate taxation? Working *backwards* from the desired conclusion, Childers produced the right, Gladstonian premisses in terms of mathematical equation: allow – for no given reason – one Member to every 109,000 of the population in the Metropolis and one to every 50,000 in the remainder of England and Wales (considered as one); allow the same in Scotland, leave the Universities with their representation of 9, and, as if by magic, Ireland emerges unaffected.[2] The object, of course, was quite simply to secure Parnellite support, offsetting defections for English, Irish or any other reasons. Not only was Ireland to enjoy the benefits of the Franchise bill, the 'great point' was that there was to be a single enactment for the whole of the United Kingdom. Or if, as a matter of drafting, it was found relatively straightforward to assimilate Ireland to a common franchise without a series of separate, substantive clauses, then that course was to be followed, even though the idiosyncrasies of Scottish law in relation to tenure and ratepaying might involve distinct dealing for that part of the Kingdom.[3] Scotland, if need be, could stand or fall by itself. It would stand the crucial Whig test, Minto taking a shepherd's speech at the Kelso Reform demonstration 'as showing that his class of men if enfranchised [were] more likely to be a balance than a support to the radical weavers &c. in towns', who already possessed the vote.[4] There was little of such ease in respect to Ireland. Her fate was to be bound up with that of England. In point of detail, the Irish clauses, drawn originally as a separate bill,[5] were so incorporated that thirty-two amendments would have been required to remove Ireland from the Franchise bill.

What of nineteenth century Reform precedents? Lambert ferreted them out and found little to encourage faith in the 'capacity of the Imperial Parliament to legislate for the Sister Isle'. The Irish Act of 1832 distinctly and separately conferred a £10 copyhold franchise; had anyone troubled to enquire, it would have been revealed that there were no copyholders in Ireland to claim

---

[1] Carlingford to Spencer, 12 Nov. 1883. Spencer Mss.
[2] Childers Memo., 20 Nov. 1883. Gladstone Mss., 44130 fol. 334.
[3] Gladstone to James, 14 Nov. 1883. Gladstone Mss., 44546 fol. 190.
[4] Minto to his Son, Gilbert Elliot, Viscount Melgund, 12 Dec. 1883. Minto Mss., Box 171.
[5] James to Gladstone, 17 Nov. 1883. Gladstone Mss., 44219 fol. 116.

their rights.[1] Less pathetic than the detail but more characteristic as a whole, the legislation for Ireland of 1868 was carried 'with a maximum of irresponsible contempt', a 'tiresome echo' of English Reform.[2] Gladstone took it to be plausible, if not more, that in so far as the existing Irish franchise was bad, its badness could not be exaggerated.[3] Ireland's promotion in 1884 to the forefront of the Liberal Reform programme is not, however, to be understood as a mere righting of wrongs. We have already seen that Gladstone suggested to members of the Cabinet that a wider franchise would tend to detach class from class and to disintegrate the 'all-Irish' coalition. That point has been treated deliberately in isolation as an illustration of Gladstone's persuasive arts. It remains to ask how acceptable the programme was to the Nationalists.

Newman had once put it to Gavan Duffy that for English legislators, far more perplexing than deciding when to coerce and when to conciliate, was to know, even in bouts of conciliation, 'when they [were] doing what [was] acceptable to Irishmen, & when not.'[4] It was Bright's opinion that, if Parnell's forces had stuck to the Liberals from 1880 and given them a sustained general support, 'they would have got whatever they chose to ask for Ireland short of repeal of the Union'.[5] There is no reason to doubt his sincerity or the validity of his judgment, the less so in that Bright, while a guest at Hawarden, was prepared resolutely to resist every word Gladstone said in defence of the Irish.[6] It was, conversely, proclaimed by the Nationalists that they would accept 'every concession of justice by the Imperial Parliament as but an instalment of our claims' until the inalienable right of self-government should be restored.[7] What view did the Parnellites take of this particular 'instalment'? The English Conservative press had swiftly seen that a logical consequence of the Franchise bill would be to grant to Irishmen a right to choose their own forms and institutions of government.[8] Northcote, in September 1883, already

[1] Lambert to Gladstone, 7 May 1887. Gladstone Mss., 44235 fol. 223.
[2] Smith, *Second Reform Bill*, p. 201. Ireland stages a few paltry appearances in Cowling's *1867* – though it is open to question whether, on an historical basis, more thorough treatment would have been justified.
[3] Gladstone to Trevelyan, 23 Oct. 1883. Gladstone Mss., 44546 fol. 180.
[4] Newman to Duffy, 8 May 1880. Duffy Mss., 8005.
[5] Lewis Harcourt Journal, 2 Nov. 1883. Harcourt Mss.
[6] Lewis Harcourt to Harcourt, 2 Nov. 1883. Harcourt Mss.
[7] Resolutions passed by a Nationalist meeting at Maryborough, Queen's County, 7 Oct. 1883. Lalor Mss., 8574.
[8] *Standard*, 8 Nov. 1883, p. 8.

suspected that 'some fresh arrangement was on foot' between Parnell and the Government.[1] The air, said Salisbury, was thick with rumours of successful compacts; but Salisbury, more shrewdly, saw any Parnellite pledge to vote straight and solid on Reform as that which they could *offer* in return for the Government's taking up, for instance, an Irish Local Government bill. That is to say, it was not that the Parnellites wanted franchise extension; support for the Liberal Reform bill was the bargaining counter.[2]

On the evening of 6 November 1883 Dilke received a note, written out by Hill of the *Daily News* and coming from Justin McCarthy, which offered 'a new Kilmainham': the Parnellites would vote with the Government 'if Spencer [would] let them hold public meetings.' Dilke resolved to tell only Chamberlain and Gladstone of the approach, 'because otherwise' – i.e. in the event of Hartington learning about such things – 'it might damage franchise'.[3] On 9 November Gladstone was informed,[4] and also Harcourt. 'This', the latter wrote in the gibberish of excitement, 'is a very important opening up very serious considerations.'[5] On the 10th, Gladstone reported to the Queen that at the Cabinet, Spencer had explained the attitude taken by the Irish Government: he had prohibited any gatherings 'in the rare cases where they were likely to bring on a revived outburst of crime, but had allowed them in all instances where that danger did not exist.'[6] Was Spencer too in the dark? Was this a clear-cut bid for Irish support? Was McCarthy acting on his own account? And what is to be made of Harcourt writing to Gladstone next month after his visit to Kimbolton?[7]–

There is only one of Hartington's apprehensions which I fully share and that is the dread lest on this or any other question the Liberal Party should be betrayed into any thing which looks like an alliance covert or avowed with Parnell – I am as ready and eager as he can be to make the breach between us and Parnell as open...& as incurable as possible. It is on this subject that I dread the tendencies of Chamberlain who seems to me to be always hankering after a policy which would secure the Parnellite vote. I think nothing has tended more to tranquillise H.'s

[1] Northcote to Gibson, 5 Sept. 1883. Ashbourne Mss.
[2] Salisbury, 'Disintegration', *Quarterly Review* CLVI, p. 595.
[3] Dilke Diary, 7 Nov. 1883. Dilke Mss., 43925 fol. 72.
[4] Dilke Diary, 9 Nov. 1883. Dilke Mss., 43925 fol. 73.
[5] Harcourt to Gladstone, 9 Nov. 1883. Gladstone Mss., 44198 fol. 131.
[6] Cab. 41/17/23.
[7] Harcourt to Gladstone, 28 Dec. 1883. Gladstone Mss., 44198 fol. 170.

mind than the pledge I have given him that I would like an early opportunity of making a public declaration that shld. as far as possible make all tactics of this description impossible now & in the future.

Was it this – or the knowledge that this was a blatant lie to keep Hartington from precipitate resignation – which made Gladstone smile?[1] Why, above all, was a second deal necessary? On 16 January 1884, Hamilton forwarded to Gladstone a letter of Labouchère's to Grosvenor in which it was stated that the Irish required an undertaking from the Government 'that Ministers will fall or stand by the measure in its entirety.'[2] Labouchère's coquetting with O'Shea raises further imponderables: did O'Shea know Parnell's mind, and even if he did, was his account faithful or deliberately misleading? And was not Labouchère himself quite capable of adding a further twist? – which would produce by double trickery a straight line for Gladstone, and a report corresponding, so Gladstone said, with his anticipation.[3] The immediate issue was a declaration by Dilke that a redistribution based upon the numbers of electors after the registers had been made out under a uniform franchise would not diminish Irish representation in the Commons.[4] The *Scotsman* found here a 'most promising fox': Dilke's 'very big bid for the Irish vote' was worthy 'of contemptuous opposition from Englishmen & Scotchmen.'[5] Did this imply another deal? It seems unlikely. All the Cabinet 'save Mr. G. himself, who lives in a fool's paradise' assumed at this very juncture that the Irish would still oppose.[6] In any case, what security was there that even if Parnell pledged himself, he could carry his men with him? At the opening of the 1884 Session, on an Egyptian censure vote, the Nationalists were reported to have decided by a majority of one, and against Parnell's advice, to support Northcote.[7] Was Parnell losing control? In April, rumours of his impending retirement drew from Hamilton neither astonished comment nor silent dismissal: the Irish lead, he reflected, was 'generally short-lived', and 'no doubt he is not the man he was.'[8] We shall not come within a mile of

---

1 Gladstone to Granville, 29 Dec. 1883. *Correspondence*, Vol. ii, p. 142.
2 Hamilton Diary, 16 Jan. 1884. Hamilton Mss., 48635 fol. 65. See also Hamilton to Gladstone, 17 Jan. 1884. Gladstone Mss., 44190 fol. 6.
3 Gladstone to Grosvenor, 18 Jan. 1884. Gladstone Mss., 44315 fol. 144.
4 At Chelsea. *The Times*, 22 Jan. 1884, p. 7.
5 Minto to Arthur Elliot, 27 Jan. 1884. Elliot Mss., Bundle 32.
6 Hamilton Diary, 28 Jan. 1884. Hamilton Mss., 48635 fol. 76.
7 Stansfeld to Halifax, 20 Feb. 1884. Hickleton Mss., A4.51.
8 Hamilton Diary, 18 Apr. 1884. Hamilton Mss., 48636 fol. 39.

Parnell's 'true opinion'[1] (or only fortuitously so) through the media of McCarthy, Hill and Dilke, O'Shea, Labouchère and Grosvenor.

The Parnellite policy in 1880 was to put demands for a popular suffrage and the just representation of Ireland ahead of those for the 'establishment of our own people in our own soil' and the 'right to manage our own affairs.'[2] By October 1884, resolutions are to be found in the constituencies insisting upon 'self-government' and the 'total abolition of landlordism', denouncing the 'whole villianous [sic] system of the present Government, [which] ...has place and pension for the monsters, whose bestialities have shocked the world', and even advocating extension of obstructive tactics to the 'landlord pastime of fox-hunting.'[3] But by this latter date, there is never a word about the franchise or Ireland's deserts at Westminster. Indeed, the Parnellites had been responsible for counting out the House on the Franchise resolution of 1883. What the historian has to do for 1872 is to reduce the Ballot Act to meagre proportions in the advance of Irish nationalism;[4] what he has to do for 1884 is to demonstrate that Parnell viewed with alarm the introduction of a Reform bill.

English electoral considerations are evident. Spencer urged upon Hartington that the more dangerous elements in Parliament were not the Irish MPs themselves, but those 'weak kneed' English Members who fawned upon the Irish electors in their boroughs.[5] The Irish balancing trick was indeed by the summer of 1883 already rumoured to be the subject of a concordat struck with Cardinal Manning, the *quid pro quo* of which was to be Irish support to the Tories in English boroughs at the next election.[6] Parnell, in appealing for a paltry £200 grant to the Executive of the National League in England, claimed that 97 Liberal seats were under Irish control.[7]

[1] Gladstone to Grosvenor, 18 Jan. 1884. Gladstone Mss., 44315 fol. 144.
[2] Arthur O'Connor's address. Lalor Mss., 8574.
[3] 'Resolutions to be proposed at the County Meeting to be held at Maryborough on Sunday, the 5th of October, 1884'. Lalor Mss., 8574.
[4] Michael Hurst, 'Ireland and the Ballot Act of 1872', *Historical Journal*, VIII (1965), pp. 326–52.
[5] Spencer to Hartington, 21 Oct. 1883. Spencer Mss. Salisbury expressed the same view a year later: 'As to the Parnellite members – are they worse than Radicals pledged to do all the Irish want? I think they are much better. They carry with them none of the moral weight which comes with the support of a sympathetic English Radical'. Salisbury to Northcote, 4 Dec. 1884. Iddesleigh Mss., 50020 fol. 106.
[6] Mundella to Leader, 28 July 1883. Mundella–Leader Mss.
[7] Parnell to Webb, 11 Nov. 1883. Harrington Mss., 8581.

The number may be inflated, or have been chosen for its very oddity and exactness to lend credibility to an exercise in 'mere bounce';[1] but Healy, for one, expressed concern to the Central branch of the League that a large extension of the franchise might destroy such a hold on 30 or 40 constituencies.[2] Why Reform should have adversely affected the Irish vote in England is unclear. Trevelyan's thesis was that the power of the town-dwelling immigrants would be whittled away with the enfranchisement of 'a multitude of Liberal voters, who are few or none of them Irishmen' in English and Scottish counties.[3] Perhaps Healy's interest in the prospect of large towns electing a block of six or eight representatives of one colour on the basis of simple overall majority was more than offset by fear of the alternative Redistribution expedient – the creation of single-member wards, with the Irish herded into one Glasgow, Liverpool or Manchester ghetto. This latter was seen by all anti-Irish elements as the lesser of two evils; it was thought better to let them 'return members of their own than that their votes should be the subject of more or less secret negotiation with the leaders of the different parties'.[4]

Irish considerations were more immediate than English, and the Parnellite by-election triumphs in 1883 demand attention. The story of stories, O'Brien's defeat of Naish the Government candidate, has been spun by the victor himself. On the eve of his pilgrimage to Mallow, he was cheered by Archbishop Croke's '"Well, God bless your mother's son." That was the blessing that overthrew the Castle power in Mallow: it was "my mother's son", and not the son's self, who brought all the golden spells of the future Chancellor to nought.... It was one of those spontaneous outbursts of local pride and love before which all human calculations and interests go down.' In fact, neither mother worship nor local pride bears any responsibility. Parnell had seen what won an election in Mallow; indeed, his 'brutally candid observations' as to the venality of the borough after the defeat there of his candidate at the general election precluded the party leader's intervention in this fray.[5] What was true in 1880 was equally true three years later. The blessing of the Archbishop mattered to the extent that Mallow was

[1] Gorst to Churchill, 31 Aug. 1883. Churchill Mss., 1/166.
[2] *The Times*, 24 Jan. 1884, p. 10.
[3] Trevelyan to Gladstone, 26 Oct. 1883. Gladstone Mss., 44335 fol. 130.
[4] Proportional Representation Society Circular, Feb. 1884. P.R.S. Mss.
[5] William O'Brien, *Recollections*, pp. 483–8.

in Croke's pocket, and Croke now in Parnell's. In 1883, venality was simply turned to the Nationalist advantage. Mallow showed not so much that Government policy had failed to arrest the progress of Home Rule as that the Parnellites knew the game of electoral influence as well as anyone else and could, by employing the threat of boycott, just as effectively as any other party coerce a small electorate of shopkeepers in a desired direction.[1] Moreover, after Healy's victory in Monaghan, this seemed to be as true of Northern Ireland as of the South.

Though the next century's history was to confirm a prophecy of 1881 that the '*religious* thing [would] probably hold out longer in Ireland than elsewhere',[2] Parnellite interest in the autumn of 1883 dictated that the religious 'thing' should be played down and the 'inevitable coalition' of North and South be stressed.[3] The party were to assert that the fostering and encouragement of Ulster manufactures would be of prime concern to an Irish Parliament.[4] The policy was 'generous toleration and consideration for all sections of the Irish nation,...[and] self-restraint and moderation ...with every possible regard...for the susceptibilities of our Orange fellow countrymen.'[5] The message to Ulster was 'one of peace' whatever the provocation.[6] But, in any event, there was no simple Protestant–Catholic dichotomy. Presbyterians and 'the younger Methodists' as well as Romanists had 'go[ne] in the "whole length of the unclean animal" with the land league.'[7] What their by-election successes in 1883 also demonstrated to the Parnellites was that sectarian bigotry need prove no match, under restricted suffrage, for the bond of social and economic self-interest.[8] It was in the counties of Armagh and Londonderry, and in boroughs like Downpatrick, where the Catholic population was only narrowly in a minority, that further gains might be looked to on this count; Donegal, Fermanagh and Tyrone, and the towns of Enniskillen,

---

[1] Gorst to Churchill, 29 Jan. 1883. Churchill Mss., 1/105.
[2] R. B. Close to Jonathan Pim, 25 Apr. 1881. Pim Mss., 8669.
[3] *Freeman's Journal*, 24 Sept. 1883, p. 4.
[4] *Freeman's Journal*, 28 Sept. 1883, p. 4.
[5] Parnell to Harrington, 9 June 1884. Harrington Mss., 8581.
[6] *Freeman's Journal*, 28 Sept. 1883, p. 4.
[7] Rev. D. C. Abbott (rector of Fivemiletown) to H. de F. Montgomery, 19 Dec. 1880. Montgomery Mss., T1089 fol. 2.
[8] Compare Halifax to Ripon, 6 July 1883, on the 'disagreeable' matter of Healy's Monaghan victory: 'It does not look well in loyal Ulster & I am afraid that the Irish tenants' greed for plundering his landlord has not been satisfied – but only stimulated.' Ripon Mss., 43531 fol. 23.

Londonderry and Newry, with their substantial Catholic predominance, were further possibilities. Parnell himself was reported to be ready to challenge the Marquess of Londonderry for County Down. All these constituencies needed to be 'worked on'. When McCarthy made his overtures, offering Irish support for the Government's Franchise bill, he knew which half of the bargain was the more vital for his party – the chance to campaign in Ulster. And if, after Nationalist attention had been turned to registration, 'all the Irish counties [would be] theirs' in any case,[1] with or without a couple of the Northern boroughs, their numbers would exceed the 85 Parnell needed, and for the attainment of which in 1882 the aid of suffrage had been invoked.

The great hope was for a general election upon the existing suffrage. In a country where, following the Lords' rejection of the Irish Registration bill in August 1883, the placing of a name on the electoral roll was still very much a matter of opting-in through self-exertion, the Parnellites devoted time and resources to the Revision Courts. T. D. Sullivan spoke to an Irish National League branch of the neglect of revision quite simply as 'for years...the cause of misrepresentation of the City & County of Dublin'.[2] Lalor and Arthur O'Connor appealed to their constituents to thwart in the Courts the attempts of the 'landlord faction...to deprive you of the franchise by serving frivolous objections wholesale.'[3] The National–popular cause, said the *Freeman's Journal*, depended for its success upon the proving of claims before Revising barristers.[4] A party which hired wagonettes to bring the men of Rathcoole a distance of twenty miles to the Revision Sessions,[5] and which placed on the register an additional 483 lodger votes in the six

---

[1] Gorst to Churchill, 31 Aug. 1883. Churchill Mss., 1/166.

[2] 28 Oct. 1883. St James Branch, Dublin, of the Irish National League, Minute Book, 12786. See Hanham, *Elections*, pp. 399–403; and Moisei Ostrogorski: 'Every year the Registration Societies started thousands of objections to the claims lodged by the electors. They calculated, and rightly, that many of those who were opposed would not or could not appear in the registration court to uphold their right to vote, or even that they would receive no notice of opposition owing to removal, etc.; and the legal consequence of the non-disallowance of an objection was that the name was struck off the list....At the same time they started unfounded claims, which had to be allowed if no one objected to them; the overseers had not the means or the wish to check them, and the Revising Barristers had no right to do so if an appeal was not made to them.' *Democracy and the Organization of Political Parties*, trans. F. Clarke (2 vols., 1902), Vol. I, pp. 156–7.

[3] Circular, Sept. 1883. Lalor Mss., 8574.

[4] 10 Sept. 1883, p. 4.

[5] *Freeman's Journal*, 12 Oct. 1883, p. 4.

North Dublin wards while the Conservatives added 9,[1] had no wish to see such efforts wasted.

Franchise extension was not openly to be resisted. A month before the Leeds Conference, the *Freeman's Journal* had noted that 'Ireland, with its far greater electoral wrongs and hardships' found no place on the agenda.[2] The concern of the Parnellites was not, however, to ensure that Ireland should not be left out in the cold – another moral outrage against her to augment Parnell's moral stature – but that if she was included in legislation, there should be no reduction in Irish representation nor any 'cunningly contrived' increase in the size of the House of Commons while Irish representation remained static.[3] Parnell could always justify a seemingly anti-popular Commons vote as impressing on both Government and Opposition the power at his command. Further, he could always talk of seeing 'what fruits [could] be snatched out of the hurly-burly' of British party strife,[4] and of the paramount need to 'lay bare the infamy of English misrule' rather than facilitate the passage of a Reform bill if that was 'the Business of the Government'.[5] Quite how far he was fighting for his own hand needs stressing. The great Parliamentary lure of the Parnellite force was its discipline and its closed ranks; it was these which an extended franchise, and concomitant expenditure, threatened. O'Brien's denunciation of the 1883 Corrupt Practices Act as legislation which Ireland 'did not want, and which would simply unsettle'[6] precisely expressed Parnell's objection to Reform.

There are but two observations to be made in conclusion. The first is that the Irish Parliamentary party needed not a franchise concession but money for 'litigious dexterity and registration jockeyship'[7] to follow up the 1883 by-election successes which had themselves cost some £1,200.[8] The electoral game was known, the technique for victory under the old rules mastered, and the appeal went out from the National League: 'England pays her members some two, three, five, seven, ten, and up to twenty thousand per annum; others she pays by social distinctions and the hospitality of the drawing-room, and Ireland, although impoverished and

---

[1] *Freeman's Journal*, 11 Oct. 1883, p. 5.   [2] 22 Sept. 1883, p. 4.
[3] *Freeman's Journal*, 5 Dec. 1883, p. 4.
[4] *Freeman's Journal*, 26 Sept. 1883, p. 4.
[5] Parnell, 10 July 1884. 3 *Hansard* ccxc. 740.
[6] 7 June 1883. 3 *Hansard* cclxxix. 1969.
[7] J. A. Thomas, 'The System of Registration and the Development of Party Organization, 1832–1870', *History*, New Series, xxxv (1950), p. 97.
[8] Hanham, *Elections*, p. 384.

crushed by unjust taxation and felonious Landlordism, must recognise the principle and act on it if she wishes for a National representation in the Senate House of the Saxon.'[1] When money was forthcoming and the Testimonial Fund cheque for £38,000 handed over to the party leader in December 1883, English politicians took solace in the expectation that Parnell might pocket the lot and decamp to America.[2]

The second, which is more personal, is perhaps a surmise rather than observation. Parnell's command was threatened by none of his immediate Parliamentary lieutenants. Healy, not yet thirty, could bide his time. T. P. O'Connor's ambition was fulfilled in entering the Commons, McCarthy was too loyal, Dillon at this juncture too ill. The threat from colleagues came less from supersession than from exposure – by O'Shea or by Callan who possessed and was waiting to use a telegram to Parnell which read: 'The Captain is away. Please come. Don't fail. – Kate.' There was another who threatened, and he, Davitt, who had yet to enter Parliament, stood to gain by the events of 1884 and what he would label the democratic implications of Reform agitation. Parnellites were not generous in their assessment of Davitt. His land nationalization scheme, said Biggar, was the 'dream of a lunatic'. Worse, for dreams are harmless, it was a 'deliberate breach of faith' after his declaration of willingness to toe the Parnellite 'occupiers' proprietary' line. Worse still, it reflected his readiness to let 'a great Cause go to destruction [rather] than see any one but [himself]... get the credit of success.'[3] Though the bitterness was mutual, Davitt in his turn made no accusation which lacked plausibility. Indeed, he touched on the essential nature of the Parnellite party when he complained of Irish Members' blindness to democratic forces and their hindering him in his efforts to direct and assist the great social-revolutionary movement.[4] Healy made light of all this: 'If the labourers will not be Parnellite', he wrote, 'they will be something worse, and much comfort that will be to English politicians.'[5] Such bravado was of little comfort to Parnell.

Trevelyan suggested to Gladstone that the aid of the Parnellites

1 Queen's County Circular, 24 Nov. 1882. Lalor Mss., 8574.
2 Grosvenor to Spencer, 7 Dec. 1883. Spencer Mss.
3 Biggar to John Miskelly, 7 Nov. 1884. Miskelly Mss., T1160/1.
4 T. W. Moody, 'Michael Davitt and the British Labour Movement, 1882–1906', *Transactions of the Royal Historical Society*, 5th Series, III (1953), pp. 62–3.
5 'The Irish and the Government', *Fortnightly Review*, Nov. 1884, p. 650.

was the only means of carrying Reform through the Commons, short of raising 'an amount of revolutionary excitement which would be a very great disaster'[1] and which might well recoil upon itself. An assumption was made that Parnell would not dare proclaim his 'heart of hearts' dislike of the Franchise bill;[2] and attempts were made to bolt exits and guard against any sort of Nationalist defection. The Ulstermen and Irish Liberals were treated less 'indulgently', the Member for Armagh even being singled out for the dubious honour of moving the Address to a Queen's Speech which promised such legislation as would wipe him and his fellows off the political map.[3] They were, in fact, given the choice of moving on or moving out – their survival depending on the adoption of a programme drawn up and published by Bryce, B. F. C. Costelloe and T. A. Dickson banded together as the Committee on Irish Affairs. A name deliberately omitted from the published list of the Committee was that of Herbert Gladstone, already under a cloud as prepared to go 'all lengths with the Irish party.'[4] His, however, was the driving force. Anything and everything 'compatible with the maintenance of the Empire' was to be bestowed[5] – equal franchise, full county government, reform of the Castle administration, leasehold amendment and a widening of purchase facilities in the Land Act. It was, indeed, a 'stick at nothing' bid against Parnell. The failure of the escapade and the historical oblivion into which the Committee has fallen need little explanation: Charles Russell, upon whose vigour much was supposed to depend, proved himself 'slack [and] disheartened',[6] the Liberal Irish had 'no pith',[7] and Dickson, who was 'prepared to risk something in order to lead or drive them up', could never convince anyone – was perhaps never convinced himself – that the

[1] Trevelyan to Gladstone, 26 Oct. 1883. Gladstone Mss., 44335 fol. 130.
[2] Hamilton Diary, 16 Jan. 1884. Hamilton Mss., 48635 fol. 65; *ibid.*, 28 Jan. 1884. Hamilton Mss., 48635 fol. 76.
[3] Richardson declined on account of illness. Hamilton Mss., 48635 fol. 75.
[4] Derby to G. H. C. Powell, of the South-West Lancashire Liberal Association, 18 July 1883. Derby Mss., Box 3. Powell had suggested that Herbert Gladstone might be asked to stand for a Liverpool constituency; Derby pooh-poohed the idea in view of the unacceptability to a section of the local party of such views – adding, for good measure, that Herbert Gladstone's Parliamentary work was not highly regarded.
[5] James Bryce, and others, 'England and Ireland: an Introductory Statement', *Committee on Irish Affairs* Paper No. 1, 1884, p. 5.
[6] Costelloe to Herbert Gladstone, 24 Nov. 1883. Viscount Gladstone Mss., 46017 fol. 24.
[7] Caine to Herbert Gladstone, 20 Nov. 1883. Viscount Gladstone Mss., 46050 fol. 148.

next election would be fought on a reduced franchise. Rather than take up under such constraint a 'forward' programme,[1] the great majority took refuge in the Proportional Representation Society.

Salisbury (as Cranborne) had castigated the Commons of 1867 for their customary inattention and ill-mannered laughter while the advocates of Proportional Representation held forth: '*any* plan proposed and entertained by such a great thinker as Mr. Mill deserved respect.' But if Mill did believe that the idea 'was taking hold of one after another of the thinking men',[2] he would have been sorely disappointed at the minimal advance made in its propagation during the years between the Second and Third Reform bills and would have lamented the failure to knock 'into the thick skull of Demos the truths which lie at the bottom of our position.'[3] Had there been an ever-ready organization supplying literature, lecturers and explanation of voting procedure – as was suggested in 1888[4] – there might have been less need for the publication in 1884 of such indigestible matter as *An Amendment of Mr. Hare's Quota*, or of titles so apologetic as *Is Proportional Representation a Puzzle?* Was it? Commons punsters readily answered that it was a Hare-brained scheme. Was there such an organization serving as an information centre? When Lubbock got matters under way in January 1884 – forming a society, appointing a provisional executive committee, advertising in the press and circularising MPs – he received a somewhat pained note from George Howell to the effect that there already was a Proportional Representation Association, with Thomas Hare as President and Howell himself as Secretary, though it would now regard itself, *de facto* if not ungrudgingly, as defunct. It was a poor excuse that 'illness and domestic trouble prevented my doing anything for some months [and]...re-opening the matter early last year.'[5] The fact was, as a prebendary of Chichester put it to Courtney, that 'the friends of scientific voting [had] taken it too easy' for many a year;[6] the question had never been made an election cry nor ever given the semblance of determining a single contest. Courtney's proposal that electoral reform be postponed to

[1] Costelloe to Herbert Gladstone, 24 Nov. 1883. Viscount Gladstone Mss., 46017 fol. 24.
[2] See Cowling, *1867*, p. 22. (My italics.)
[3] Albert Grey to Lubbock, 8 Oct. 1884. Avebury Mss., 49644 fol. 74.
[4] Second Report for 1885–8, p. 9. P.R.S. Mss.
[5] Howell to Lubbock, 9 Jan. 1884. P.R.S. Mss.
[6] A. M. Deane to Courtney, n.d. P.R.S. Mss.

the sixth Session of Parliament was a tacit admission that the crusade still needed time to work.[1]

Nor did 1884 see any momentous extra-Parliamentary leap forward: none was perhaps to be expected when so little was spent on printing and public meetings.[2] One branch at Manchester prospered reasonably, thanks to C. P. Scott's financial assistance, though even here, members of the local committee admitted to having 'cut a very small figure',[3] 'been rather timid' and 'rest[ed] for the last few months.'[4] The Society's correspondence is shot through with resignation, fatalism and bewilderment, with supine criticism of supineness, and time and time again with the fear that 'steps have been taken too late.'[5] An earnest Anglesey Liberal scoured newspapers for any notice of gatherings, any advertising of Society pamphlets, 'but beyond occasional letters bearing on the subject could find nothing.'[6] Warnings had been given in the first years of the Liberal Ministry that proselytising must be effected, in Parliamentary and popular terms, while the reform controversy was still at a distance, since once the struggle had begun, 'prejudices and misrepresentation, and personal hostility or favouritism [would] in great measure take the place of reason and argument.'[7]

A 'case history' in 1884 fully bears this out. Public airing then of Proportional Representation brought a sharp rebuke from Ramsden's constituency chairman: 'I am told you occupied a whole speech at Birstal with some possible difference which may or may not arise between your views and Mr. Gladstone's. . . . It is . . . better to enlarge on the points on which we agree with the government, and argue the others if they arise in parliament, but not beforehand at popular meetings.'[8] The note arrived 'opportunely'; Ramsden suppressed another 'rather elaborate sermon on the merits' of Proportional Representation and upon 'the excessive number of Irish members'. Though 'their patience under its endless repetition [was] really amazing', he determined to tell his audience the 'old story [which] pleases them best'.[9] The autumn

[1] *Pall Mall Gazette*, 30 Oct. 1883, p. 1.
[2] £112 and £145 respectively. First Annual Report for 1884–5, Balance sheet. P.R.S. Mss.
[3] L. Broderick to Cromwell White, 29 Aug. 1884. P.R.S. Mss.
[4] C. Corbett to Cromwell White, 17 Oct. 1884. P.R.S. Mss.
[5] Limerick to Emly, 12 Jan. 1885. P.R.S. Mss.
[6] Hugh B. Price to Cromwell White, 3 Nov. 1884. P.R.S. Mss.
[7] Calvert, *Representation of Minorities*, p. 1.
[8] J. M. Dent to Ramsden, 9 Apr. 1884. Ramsden Mss., Box 40.
[9] Ramsden to Dent, 10 Apr. 1884. Ramsden Mss., Box 40.

campaign, fifteen hundred times over, was to stand powerful witness to his judgment. While the 'Peers *versus* People' battle raged, the Society's leaders 'fold[ed] their arms & [said] that nothing [could] be done until public affairs [took] a turn'.[1] More significantly for the present, Ramsden abandoned his commitment without bitterness: 'it don't really advance the questions I have at heart.' If 'moderate men need[ed] no convincing'[2] of its worth and drifted into support, so too did they, as moderate politicians, drift away from it, without undue pressure.

What *was* the value of Richard Chamberlain's attendance at a Society lecture in 1885?[3] or of the Manchester Radical Association carrying a resolution in favour of election by single transferable vote,[4] while the country 'settl[ed] down to a ratification of the Parlour Treaty'?[5] or of Grey's discovery that he could, 'with the aid of a blackboard & a bit of chalk',[6] 'bring about a *spontaneous* desire for P. R. among the Pitmen of Northumberland'?[7] It was December 1884 before he and his mining apostle, Neil, rented offices in Newcastle, their lecturing success serving only to show what might have been effected. Proportional Representation *was* received 'in a very different spirit' in Glasgow when presented as a scheme favoured by 'working men' and endorsed by the Miners' Association and the *North British Daily Mail*;[8] but, at the critical time in early 1884, it was taken by those same Northumbrian miners as worse than a crotchet. They equated it with 'mistrust of the people',[9] and in 'making a dead set against you [i.e. Albert Grey] on account of your going against the present Government with regard to the people's rights' they reduced to nil his chances of retaining the seat.[10] A correspondent wrote to Lubbock: 'My

1 F. A. Ford to S. Insull, 16 Jan. 1885. P.R.S. Mss.
2 Ramsden to Dent, 10 Apr. 1884. Ramsden Mss., Box 40.
3 S. Neil to Cromwell White, 29 Nov. 1884. P.R.S. Mss.
4 C. Corbett to Cromwell White, 4 Feb. 1885. P.R.S. Mss. This is the system associated with the names of J. S. Mill and Thomas Hare. The elector may indicate not only his first, but also his second or subsequent choices. The total of voting-papers, divided by the number of members to be elected, gives a quota; once a candidate obtains that magic number, he is declared elected. Any surplus votes for him are now transferred (following the order of preferences indicated) to those who on the first count have fallen below the mark. And so on.
5 W. FitzHenry to Lubbock, 27 Jan. 1885. P.R.S. Mss.
6 Albert Grey to Lubbock, 10 Dec. 1884. P.R.S. Mss.
7 Albert Grey to Cromwell White, 14 Aug. 1884. P.R.S. Mss.
8 J. P. Smith to Albert Grey, 2 Sept. 1884. Grey Mss.
9 S. Neil to Albert Grey, 22 May 1884. Grey Mss.
10 M. Wright to Albert Grey, 5 May 1884. Grey Mss.

mind is much exercised as to your private Meetings upon Proportional representation – that is the same as a redistribution of Seats isn't it?'[1] In similar vein, Courtney's resignation, upon the failure to incorporate or take cognizance of the scheme in the Redistribution settlement, provoked 'many kind & cheering letters [and] very little unfair criticism, though very few think the cause sufficient to leave a Government on.'[2] These experiences of Grey, Lubbock and Courtney, however various, were a measure of the propaganda failure in the years since 1867.

If Grey, albeit tardily, showed that the theory could be made popular, others bear responsibility for the fact that public ignorance gave way only to public confusion. After lengthy justification and, as he thought, sufficient practical exposition, Broderick, of the Manchester branch, invited the Newton Heath Liberal Club to conduct a mock election, and choose 7 of 14 familiar political names. Amongst those not selected was Lubbock, who by 'right' as President of the Society ought surely to have topped the poll. This, however, was not the root cause of dismay among the organizers: the victor, ahead of Harcourt, Morley, Bradlaugh and Forster, let alone Lubbock, was Joseph Arch, who absorbed more than one-third of the first votes.

Of course he could only use the quota of $\frac{1}{8}$th but it seemed to us scarcely likely that in an audience chiefly composed of mechanics he would really be the first favourite of such a large proportion. We therefore came to the conclusion that some had given him their No. 1 simply because he was first on the [alphabetical] list.[3]

Even Grey's successes were tarnished; the overwhelming victory of 'General Gordon' as a candidate upset all calculation, adding fuel to the criticism that Proportional Representation unduly favoured independents.[4]

The difficulties of simulating elections were minor pitfalls; but even the best-staged exhibitions resulted in scepticism or in a belief that whether the voters had been diddled or not, many of them might think that they had been. 'There would be a want of confidence in the result if it could not be proved to demonstration & become a matter of common knowledge, that any vote & its preferences could be checked with absolute certainty.'[5] In that

---

1 ? to Lubbock, 18 Jan. 1884. Avebury Mss., 49644 fol. 60.
2 Kate Courtney Journal, 1 Dec. 1884. Courtney Mss., Vol. 21.
3 C. Corbett to Cromwell White, 30 Mar. 1884. P.R.S. Mss.
4 Lubbock to Albert Grey, 15 Dec. 1884. Grey Mss.
5 H. G. Fordham to Cromwell White, 5 May 1884. P.R.S. Mss.

case, then, the question was, was this insurance compatible with Ballot Act secrecy? The Executive never faced it: there was, perhaps by design, no literature for the guidance of returning officers.[1] And here the Society was peculiarly vulnerable. The jape of the year was perpetrated by the *Standard* with a report that an experiment with the single transferable system carried on in the House of Commons had resulted in every Member spoiling his voting paper. This, doubtless, was legitimate journalistic fun; what was pathetic was that it was taken as serious and damaging by one who was to address his Liberal Association in favour of Hare's proposals the next week.[2]

The *Pall Mall Gazette* asked specifically, 'Should Redistribution tend towards – (a.) Equal Electoral Districts? or, (b.) Proportional Representation?'[3] Their mutual exclusiveness was questioned by Goschen, who jibbed at the Society's very name: 'Does it not carry us even further than most of us would go? Does it not involve equal electoral districts, if construed strictly?'[4] It was, in fact, of the essence of the organization that nothing was 'construed strictly'. A handful of MPs (the *Pall Mall* listed eight) declared themselves in favour of Proportional Representation and allowed their names to be divulged; ten more supporters marked their communications 'private'; a 'great number' wrote opposite the question, 'Answer postponed for further consideration.' Charles Acland preferred 'the latter at present if it means anything short of minority members, which I object to.' Lubbock added, 'If we do not have single seats, I think we must have proportional representation.'[5] There was no attempt to impose any degree of uniformity from above upon the subject; members were never tied to any detailed programme. The negative behaviour and latitudinarianism of the Society was, indeed, its only hope and strength. Once it became active, its inherent disunity became embarrassingly obvious. How many were attracted, like the Regius Professor of Civil Law at Cambridge, by 'proportionate' representation not as an object in itself but as a means of agitating for the 'great extension of direct minority representation... of the long-headed men', who would see through 'alternate sensational policies from the so called Conservative and Liberal parties', and would counterbalance 'the *impulsive* element

[1] A. Frisby to Cromwell White, 19 Jan. 1885. P.R.S. Mss.
[2] Leslie Clode to Cromwell White, 6 Dec. 1884. P.R.S. Mss.
[3] 21 Dec. 1883, p. 6.
[4] Goschen to Lubbock, 19 Oct. 1884. Avebury Mss., 48944 fol. 75.
[5] *Pall Mall Gazette*, 15 Jan. 1884, pp. 1–2.

4-2

[which] will greatly predominate...in the future constituencies'?[1] There is no knowing, no weighing the scraps of evidence. What can be done is to show how fundamentally at variance with one another the Society's members were.

Clarke had no faith in the viability of the single transferable system, believing that if anything ever was done it would be in the direction of extending three-cornered constituencies with the limited vote;[2] that is to say, just what Acland would not stomach. William FitzHenry took 'minority representation', distinct from (and almost opposed to) 'proportional', as the 'main object of desire with your Association';[3] the Proportionalist, G. J. Holyoake, removed his name from the 'list of approvers', having detected 'minority' designs in Courtney's speech.[4] Lubbock objected to Seebohm's joint-candidature scheme as putting more power than did single transferable voting 'into the hands of agents & Committees which is just what we wish to avoid';[5] and yet Shaw-Lefevre objected to the single transferable plan precisely because it involved 'the caucus & organised voting...as much as the cumulative vote system of the School Boards.'[6] The Society was labelled a 'rallying point' of objection to *scrutin de liste*;[7] and yet Northcote's 'rather strong' dislike was based expressly upon the belief that adoption of proportional representation in any form would lead directly to '*scrutin de liste*, the great object of my detestation.'[8]

F. A. Ford, after addressing several meetings in London, found the Liberal Associations 'of no use because they simply "nod their

---

[1] E. C. Clark to Cromwell White, 2 Dec. 1884. P.R.S. Mss.

[2] Clarke to Lubbock, 26 Dec. 1884. Avebury Mss., 49644 fol. 70. The 'limited' system allows each voter less votes than there are seats to be filled – e.g., where 3 members are to be returned, the elector will have just 2 votes. Compare *Pall Mall Gazette*, 9 Nov. 1883, p. 1: 'The principle of minority representation has been badly compromised by the three-cornered constituencies, which, without in any way affecting the balance of parties, have made the very name of proportional representation to stink in the nostrils of keen politicians on both sides of the House.'

[3] W. FitzHenry to Lubbock, 27 Jan. 1885. P.R.S. Mss.

[4] Holyoake to Cromwell White, 26 Jan. 1885. P.R.S. Mss.

[5] Lubbock to Cromwell White, 10 May 1884. P.R.S. Mss.

[6] Shaw-Lefevre to Albert Grey, 29 Apr. 1884. Grey Mss. The cumulative vote: each elector has as many votes as there are members to be returned, but (which distinguishes the system from *scrutin de liste*) may divide them in any manner he chooses – e.g. 6 votes all for one candidate, or 3 for one, 2 for another and 1 for a third.

[7] First Annual Report for 1884–85, p. 8. P.R.S. Mss.

[8] Northcote to Albert Grey, 30 Dec. 1884. Grey Mss.

heads to order"'[1] – an order from above which was explicit in its hostility. But the same advocate had earlier taken the view that if the Society attested to its non-partisan character by listing Commons supporters drawn almost equally from both parties, the measure of Conservative support would tend immediately to alienate Workmen's Clubs: 'Take a warning from that spectacle the Liberty & Property Defence. Mr. Donisthorpe never intended his League to be the emasculate appendage it has become... regarded as simply a piece of Conservative Electioneering Machinery.'[2] Ford had lighted, quite unconsciously, on the divorce between Parliamentary and extra-Parliamentary aims, the lack of co-ordination and complete insensitivity of Parliamentarians to activities outside Westminster. As leaders of a crusade, Lubbock, Courtney and Grey each cut an absurd figure. Family, cricket, fives, and teaching dogs to read – Lubbock put them all before the calls of public speaking. Politically – the judgment is not cruel – he was a 'poor weak' thing.[3] Courtney's outlandish dress and dropping of aspirates, distractions in the Commons, *might* have endeared him to other audiences, but he never came to terms with 'speechifying & demonstrating'.[4] (There was no point anyway when those parts of his public utterances which related to proportional representation were cut by the press.)[5] Grey's epitaph was composed by a doting admirer who could not bring himself to censure the 'eagle...for lack of farmyard complaisance.' Such is the nature of genius, and such was Grey's nature, that he could not 'bridle his inspiration to the needs of what we call practical politics.' The meaning and painful result were plain to all: he never 'in any degree swayed even a fraction of the multitude'.[6] It redounds to their credit that such men yet recognized their incapacity and made attempts to secure Fawcett and Forster[7] as champions who might 'guarantee' Proportional Representation to the 'radical' masses. It is also indicative of some slight political *nous* that they determined to 'save [their] breath for something better' than Hare's scheme.[8] But this deliberate snub to Hare and George Howell, neither of whom

---

[1] F. A. Ford to S. Insull, 29 Dec. 1884. P.R.S. Mss.
[2] Ford to Cromwell White, 28 Feb. 1884. P.R.S. Mss.
[3] Earl Grey to Halifax, 20 Dec. 1884. Hickleton Mss., A4.55.16.
[4] Kate Courtney Journal, 26 Sept. 1884. Courtney Mss., Vol. 21.
[5] Kate Courtney Journal, 24 Oct. 1883. Courtney Mss., Vol. 21.
[6] Harold Begbie, *Albert, Fourth Earl Grey: a Last Word* (1917), pp. 20 and 34.
[7] Forster to Lubbock, 6 Jan. 1884; Fawcett to Lubbock, 6 Jan. 1884. P.R.S. Mss.
[8] Ebrington to Albert Grey, 1 Jan. 1884. Grey Mss.

THE POLITICS OF REFORM 1884

received an invitation to the inaugural meeting, was of deeper significance. Proportional Representation, as a Parliamentary phenomenon, was to be uncluttered by the paraphernalia of organization, soft-headed devotees and, above all, the mathematical millstone. Lubbock, Courtney and Grey never effected clear-cut separation; it was in the interest of their opponents to ensure that they should not be able to do so. But the threat to Reform from Proportional Representation came from a purely Parliamentary coalition.

Note has been taken of Gladstone's antipathy towards Ulster and his seizing both the chance offered by Reform to rid the Irish question of the Ulster difficulty, and the chance to rid Reform of the focus of the property difficulty. However they saw it, protesters within the Liberal ranks rallied to Ulster's defence. Their medium was the Proportional Representation Society, and their aim fair shares for the North and/or the docking of Irish representation. Grey talked of a uniform franchise and dead-level, levelled-down democratisation as spelling the doom of variety, hitherto 'always thought to be of the 1st importance'. Ulster, representing the interests of Protestantism, the Union and a landed aristocracy, did more than give point to the argument. It was the 'state of Ireland' that attracted adherents.[1] There can be, of course, in dealing with Parliament as in dealing with the 'popular' organization, no easy assignation or separation of motive. The 'great unwashed'[2] in their mud huts were obvious targets for anti-democratic volleys, so that essentially Ireland was the mode of expressing in 1884 the sentiment of 1867. But certainly, more would obey Courtney's injunction – 'Whenever you are about to make a proposition, first mutter to yourselves the word "Ireland"'[3] – than would think of the Society as a rallying point of objection to *scrutin de liste*. A letter of resignation from an erstwhile supporter is instructive: 'I object *now* to your scheme *not* because it is puzzling but because it is only too palpable [what are] the ulterior views of these gentlemen...Sir John Lubbock, Mr. Courtney & Mr. Grey [with their] constant references to what they are pleased to term "the loyal minority in Ireland".'[4]

A solid core of the 73 Liberal supporters claimed by the Society

---

[1] Albert Grey to Halifax, 27 Feb. 1884. Hickleton Mss., A4.84 Part 4.
[2] *The Times*, 25 Jan. 1884, p. 5.
[3] *The Times*, 28 Nov. 1883, p. 7.
[4] Clifton to Cromwell White, 15 Dec. 1884. P.R.S. Mss.

in February 1884 was provided by 17 MPs who represented Irish constituencies and sat on the Government side of the House. The Society's circular painted a macabre picture of Ireland under an extended franchise, where 'those who hold moderate and loyal opinions, although numbering more than one third of the whole electorate, may be everywhere outvoted and reduced to silence.'[1] That household suffrage would eliminate their own forces, surrender the three southern provinces to the Nationalists and leave Ulster to be fought out between Orange Conservatives and Home Rulers, had preyed on the minds of Irish Liberals before the Parnellites captured Mallow and Monaghan. Of all the Ulster candidates, only one (and he was defeated in Belfast) ever made mention of Reform in his 1880 election address.[2] To such minds, the Proportional Representation Society, by stolidly refusing to be committed to particular mathematical schemes, appeared to have kept complete liberty of action about the actual means of establishing safeguards against 'mere numbers'.[3]

This Irish bent of the Society is confirmed by the events of subsequent years. Twenty-three Liberal adherents remained in the Commons to vote on Home Rule in 1886, of whom 15, including the President, Secretary and Treasurer, deserted Gladstone. Furthermore, of the remaining 50 who were ousted or who did not stand in November 1885, 15 later re-emerged – no less than 12 as Liberal Unionists, 2 as Gladstonians, and one (T. A. Dickson) perversely enough as a Nationalist. It was, not surprisingly, the Irish Loyal and Patriotic Union which in 1888 provided the spur to revivifying the Society, and again, not surprisingly, Proportional Representation which, so its supporters claimed in 1917, alone might effectively have blocked the Sinn Fein monopoly of South and West Ireland. As regards the Third Reform bill, the inference is surely that these avowedly Unionist elements within the Liberal ranks were potential defectors to a Northcote-style Conservative party. They used the language of high morality to confess their faith, but it was perfectly clear to Gladstone that the premium so innocently placed on independence of mind in fact foreshadowed a destructive independence.

Their immediate undoing arose from delusions of grandeur. The Society had, as Grey wrote on the eve of Gladstone's introduction

---

[1] Circular, Feb. 1884. P.R.S. Mss.
[2] Lewis, 21 Feb. 1884. 3 *Hansard* cclxxxiv. 1635.
[3] Northcote, at Belfast. *The Times*, 4 Oct. 1883, p. 8.

of the Franchise bill, 'been successful beyond our most sanguine expectations.'[1] The scent of power, with declarations of adhesion by some 180 MPs in the six weeks prior to introduction, upset all earlier Whig calculations. At the New Year, Grey had heard from Dundas that he viewed the bringing forward of the Franchise bill unaccompanied by Redistribution as 'a very unsatisfactory and hardly an honest way of dealing with Reform.'[2] Precisely the same message, with an explicit threat of defection, was conveyed by Kingscote to Hartington.[3] Widespread Whig unease, to which all the evidence points, was heightened now by a speech on political absurdity from Gibson: 'Imagine [the Parnellite] party made more numerous and more strong by a separate Franchise Bill and then asked to accept a Redistribution Bill which would lessen their numbers and their strength.'[4]

With Commons membership of the Society swelling daily, Grey was side-tracked from the 'Whiggery' of indivisible Reform and an all-inclusive measure, to the necessity of ensuring simply that Franchise should not *come into effect* without its indispensable corollary. Proportional Representation was gaining ground but wanted time; postponement of Redistribution until the theory had impressed itself on the majority of both parties became all-important – so long as there was no risk of an election on the old constituencies with the new voters. Where hitherto Grey's friends had accepted defeat as inevitable, they now saw the chance of success. They were thus ready to take Gladstone's statement about minority representation as meaning far more than it meant. There was in fact no reason why, as Gladstone put it to them, the mode of voting should have been regarded as more germane to Redistribution than to the Franchise question; it fell, and for Gladstone fell conveniently, between two stools. The crux is not that the Proportional Representation men were fobbed off – and in the event were cheated by Gladstone's promise that Proportional Representation would be considered fully and dispassionately 'in connection with the redistribution of seats'[5] – but that they were willing to be fobbed off, indeed connived in the exercise for their own purposes.

[1] Albert Grey to Halifax, 27 Feb. 1884. Hickleton Mss., A4.84 Part 4.
[2] Dundas to Albert Grey, 31 Dec. 1883. Grey Mss.
[3] Kingscote to Hartington, 14 Jan. 1884. Devonshire Mss., 340.1400.
[4] At Exeter. *The Times*, 17 Jan. 1884, p. 6.
[5] Gladstone Memo., 3 Jan. 1884. Gladstone Mss., 44768, fol. 2.

MINIMISING OPPOSITION

The euphoria of victory in 1880 can be readily documented. It is at its most sublime in Chamberlain's legislative calculation, that Reform need not be limited to a radical Franchise bill but might also incorporate a radical Redistribution.[1] It is at its most piquant in the prediction made by Harcourt to Hartington, that the majority, far exceeding his most 'lunatic' forecast, would be such 'as you will not know what to do with.'[2] Just so; quantity and quality were taken by Gladstone to preclude anything other than Gladstonian leadership. With 'grief in his stupid face', Adam, the Liberal Whip, revealed that Granville had expected both the Queen *and* *Gladstone* to ask *him* to take the highest office.[3] Gladstone later (indignantly and not without bitterness) vindicated his conduct against the charge of stealing Hartington's reward for the labours of opposition: 'Hartington might have been leading the Opposition till now, and what whit nearer victory would the Liberals have been?'[4]

The Radical euphoria, the 'necessity' for a Radical reform programme and of Radical/Gladstonian control, were neatly offset by Shaftesbury's simultaneous report that a great number of Liberals were opposed to any renewal of the Ballot Act.[5] It was Barttelot who recalled nostalgically the days when an elector could speak out his mind freely instead of having to record a 'sneaking' vote, and who censured the 'hole and corner' measure of 1872 as having *widened* the gulf between Parliament and people, cut politicians from ready access to 'the current of public feeling', and prevented their observing 'in what way persons of different classes, different creeds, and, in a certain sense, persons of different nationalities exercised the franchise.'[6] This may have been rhetorical clap-trap, but it was in spirit the consensual clap-trap the House of Commons understood even when it was expressed by a Sussex arch-Tory who had voted against the Third Reading of the Land bill. It was indistinguishable from the language of the Huddersfield 'Reformer', Leatham, who, in answer to the charge that 'the existing system has broken down, because...under it

---

[1] Chamberlain to Harcourt, 10 Apr. 1880. Harcourt Mss.
[2] Harcourt to Hartington, Apr. 1880. Harcourt Mss.
[3] Bourke to Winn, 24 Apr. 1880. Nostell Mss., 1/41.
[4] *Rendel Papers*, p. 85.
[5] Richmond to Cairns, 25 May 1880. Cairns Mss., PRO. 30/51/4, fol. 80. The 1872 Ballot Act was introduced on an experimental or probationary basis only; like income tax, secret voting has somehow survived.
[6] 6 Apr. 1883. 3 *Hansard* cclxxvii. 1724–5.

only one mechanic and one working man have been returned to this House', replied that,

I should have accepted this circumstance as a triumphant proof of its success. The working classes have shown a rare discretion. . . . It is by this process that we have arrived at the vigour of Democracy, without experiencing what I may term the shock of its brute force. . . . This is the very meaning of election. We elect, not the random elements, which in their infinite variety are to be found scattered everywhere upon the surface, but what is best and soundest; and it is only on this grand hypothesis that this House is honourable, or that it is any honour to sit in it.[1]

We may call this an anti-democratic sentiment; more precisely, it was sociocratic, though the terminology is immaterial.[2] The existence of this sentiment within the Liberal party and deference to it from the Government determined (and historically explains) the shaping of the Reform measures. Whigs were quite willing to tie themselves to the American-style coalition so long as they could persuade themselves that they were determining its direction and were being neither 'humbugged' nor 'ruled by the. . .Chamberlain party, who are really at heart no better than Home Rulers & Land Leaguers.'[3] The sentiment is part of a broader Commons susceptibility – a fundamental objection to 'must-do-something legislation'.[4] Bills so brought in were brought in 'under the worst possible auspices. . . .When legislation was undertaken in that spirit, it generally turned out very bad legislation.'[5] But then, were not 'good Liberal measures' the *raison d'être* of Liberalism, and was not the party doomed by over-reliance on the Russell maxim, that we should 'rest and be thankful'?[6] The solution lay in taking care over the form and presentation of the measure and in the public scotching of Chamberlain.

In June 1883, Salisbury executed a fine, impromptu dissection of Granville's defence of ministerial freedom of speech:[7]

[1] 2 Mar. 1885. 3 *Hansard* ccxciv. 1825–7.
[2] Certainly, to argue here from clause trivia is a wearisome exercise giving of no solution. Balance, who dare, in the scales of democracy the concession of a vote to the sub-tenant of a house let in single rooms by a non-resident owner without stipulation as to rent, against the continued disfranchisement of the tenant of several rooms to which he held the latch-key, but whose landlord resided on the premises. Ostrogorski, *Democracy*, Vol. i, p. 373; Henry Pelling, *The Social Geography of British Elections, 1885–1910* (1967), p. 7.
[3] Fawkes to Ramsden, 22 June 1882. Ramsden Mss., Box 39.
[4] Albert Grey to Elliot, 24 Aug. 1880. Elliot Mss., Bundle 21.
[5] Lewis, 4 June 1883. 3 *Hansard* cclxxix. 1653.
[6] Ripon to Dilke, 18 Aug. 1881. Dilke Mss., 43894 fol. 32.
[7] 18 June 1883. 3 *Hansard* cclxxx. 753–5.

My Lords, as far as I understand the noble Earl, Her Majesty's Government do not themselves believe in manhood suffrage, equal electoral districts, and payment of Members; but Mr. Chamberlain believes in them...at least in Birmingham....If it should happen in the future that manhood is carried it will be carried by the splendid exertions which Mr. Chamberlain, speaking as an agitator in Birmingham, has made. If it is not carried it will be repelled by the prudent Government of which Mr. Chamberlain, as President of the Board of Trade, forms a part.

If ever there was a Parliamentary ace up Gladstone's sleeve, it was Chamberlain and the Chamberlain backlash. What made worthwhile the almost daily chore of reassuring the Queen about his Birmingham harangues was the fact that Gladstone could turn them to his Parliamentary advantage. Allow Chamberlain rein to dot his *i*s and cross his *t*s, allow him the appearance of dictating policy to the Cabinet, and then produce an appendage upon well-established lines to the legislation of the last half-century. Allow him to air revolutionary notions, allow an outcry to be raised against such vocabulary with its continental, socialist or communistic overtones, allow the fear of what might be in store to take hold of alarmist minds, and then reassure one and all with the language to which they had for long become accustomed. Dilke noted sourly that their not getting 'one man, one vote', let alone 'one vote, one value', was entirely 'Mr. Gladstone's fault, for the Cabinet expected & would have taken it[,] Hartington alone opposing, as he opposed everything all through.'[1] In fact, Dilke was wrong: if blame is to be laid at all, it must be laid on Chamberlain for 'over advocacy'.

But is blame to be laid anywhere? Gladstone was still one move ahead of his critics. Writing to Granville, he made light of the Queen's latest remonstrance: 'Evidently H. M. is still bewitched by Disraeli's minimizing statements to her on Household Suffrage and believes it to be something infinitely different from manhood suffrage.'[2] The implication is surely this – that Gladstone did not himself take 'household' and 'manhood' to be 'infinitely different'. If synonymous in his mind, they were not however presented to the Commons as even similar. The terms were never confused, never interchanged. When Beresford Hope characterized the bill, 'whether we like it or not' as 'self-evident[ly]...a very long stride towards manhood suffrage', *Hansard* records that 'Mr. Gladstone

[1] Dilke Memoir, 28 Nov. 1883. Dilke Mss., 43937 fol. 199.
[2] Gladstone to Granville, 12 Dec. 1883. *Correspondence*, Vol. II, p. 125.

dissented.'[1] In all this, indeed, something resembling a Whig manner was integral to success. Gladstone knew this, Salisbury knew it, and Salisbury, had he thought for a moment, would never have repeated the silly adage that Gladstone's 'eloquent indistinctness of expression' broke down when translated by the draftsman into clauses.[2]

Whether seen as structural flaws or as indispensable conditions of Gladstone remaining at the head of a reforming Government, the separation of Franchise from Redistribution and the extension of household franchise to Ireland were taken, rightly, to be vulnerable points. The Conservatives might choose to launch their attack on either count or both. But, in the face of so manifestly divided an Opposition, no attempt to accommodate their wishes was warranted. The Conservatives might even be relied upon effectually to minimize themselves by internal dissension. Gladstone's sole concern was with likely defaulters, and his objective to send the bill to the Lords backed by weighty majorities. He offered the Irish Liberals an alternative to annihilation. He was tender in his dealing with the Nationalists. He was fortunate in the self-interestedly warm reception given to his appeals by the supporters of Proportional Representation. Of course the bellicose Conservatives would demand nothing less than a black-and-white Redistribution *Act* before they would willingly assent to franchise extension.[3] But Gladstone's humble substitute in introducing the Franchise bill, a 'little sketch' of his redistribution predilections, was directed neither to Cranbrook, nor to Lowther with his proposal for an augmentation of plural voting, nor even to Raikes who advocated assigning agricultural labourers to Parliamentary boroughs so as to leave the counties representative of property.

Gladstone's 'little sketch' was designed to soothe other qualms than Hartington's. Dilke was idle in supposing that if 'H. is not squared, Mr. G. would probably go back'.[4] Why should he? It is difficult to conceive how the Radicals could have revolted or been detached on the franchise question, short of democratic fusion with Churchill. Gladstone's eyes were fixed more realistically on those who might be tempted to subsume their separate Whig identity in a

[1] 12 June 1884. 3 *Hansard* cclxxxix. 134. Beresford Hope never intended to imply 'that it was so in the intention of my right hon. Friend', but threw in for good measure that 'bystanders may often see further than the actors.'

[2] Salisbury to Balfour, 15 Jan. 1881. Balfour Mss., 49688 fol. 37.

[3] Cranbrook, at Huddersfield. *The Times*, 30 Jan. 1884, p. 6.

[4] Dilke to Chamberlain, 24 Jan. 1884. Dilke Mss., 43886 fol. 117.

moderate Conservative alliance. The 'sketch' certainly fore-shadowed 'a large measure of redistribution', but this measure was to be one of 'relative finality', which maintained, as 'expedient, becoming and useful', the distinction between borough and shire, and recognized their separate 'pursuits...associations, and... social circumstances'.

If one lesson was learnt from 1867, it was that Redistribution was the very heart of Reform: hence the faith put in Gladstone's belittling of the unpalatable Irish concession, the heinous mode of procedure and the levelling down to uniformity; hence too, the Prime Minister's ability to direct Commons attention to the future bill. 'Although our franchise is nearly identical, that is not the question.'[1] It was many months before a first voice disturbed the peace of conviction, questioning the confidence placed in the relevance to 1884 of the 'practices which prevailed upon the last occasion' and doubting 'very much whether redistribution would have the effect that was commonly supposed.'[2]

In preserving the freehold franchise in its bill, the Government was doing something more than meet Proportional Representation Society demands. It is true that this was what Grey wanted as safeguard against pure majority rule if Redistribution was not to be based on the latter.[3] But sacrosanctity was no mere Whig cry. Henry Fowler had achieved notoriety at Leeds in declaring that Radicals could expect no more in the way of reforming measures from the present Parliament, yet he believed minimal disturbance, involving retention of the forty-shilling vote, to be essential.[4] Bright too (a 'really splendid fellow; – so rounded off by mature old age')[5] earned Gladstone's gratitude by recalling in public what help he had had from the freeholder in his greatest battle in the 1840s. But if the freeholder could not be done away with, nor could the franchise in respect of property owned in a borough be transferred to the borough register for fear of enraging the borough Members. Nor, as regards assimilation between the three countries, could it be introduced into Scotland or Ireland, without risking the creation of fictitious votes. Such considerations militated against the great Radical proposal of identic legislation *tout court* and a three-lined bill to establish household suffrage in all four countries.

[1] 28 Feb. 1884. 3 *Hansard* cclxxxv. 129.
[2] Lord Waveney, 11 Aug. 1884. 3 *Hansard* ccxcii. 409.
[3] Albert Grey, at Hexham, 5 Jan. 1884. *Annual Register*, p. 5.
[4] Fowler to Morley, 26 Dec. 1883. *Life of Henry Fowler*, p. 155.
[5] From one septuagenarian to another! Hamilton Diary, 27 Apr. 1884. Hamilton Mss., 48635 fol. 53.

It was because uniformity and equality were not accepted as self-evident benefits, because they threatened local or national characteristics, and because those regional idiosyncrasies were still held to be powerful influences on the actions of MPs, that the maxim, 'If in doubt, touch not', was adopted. Gladstone admitted to 'sweating' over the bill[1] and to finding it as much as he could manage to cram the detail and refinements into his head before addressing Parliament.[2] Why? Because the burden of his speech and his object in framing legislation was to provide *existing* franchises, where possible, with an intelligible and secure base, and never to disfranchise for the sake of Radical neatness. This was pure conservatism – the lopping off of those rotten branches which threatened wholesale contamination.

What calls for comment is not that a Liberal Government put paid to the rent-charge sham, but that it needed a good deal of pressure from Dilke, and specific evidence that Raikes, Wolff and Lowther controlled enough paper votes materially to affect the result of an election in Hertfordshire, before Gladstone would do away with this most fertile source of faggots.[3] What calls for further comment is that in restraining abuses, 'one person, one property, one vote' still exempted any claim derived by succession, marriage, marriage settlement or demise and still exempted joint inhabitancy and occupation by trade or business partner. Such minor additions as were made were also presented as positively conservative, even Conservative – the extension of the lodger vote to the counties as the enfranchisement of so many curates, and the service franchise[4] as that of the deferential shepherd, hind, farm labourer and lodge-keeper whose 'tied dwellings' would not appear on the Scottish valuation roll. A blind eye was turned to the untidy state of the franchise where it was no worse than untidy or where legislation was not worth the candle.

The significance of relics, in numerical terms, was negligible, but they were a symbolic refutation of the assumption that 'now we

---

[1] Morley to Spence Watson, 24 Feb. 1884. Hirst, *Morley*, Vol. II, p. 193.
[2] Gladstone to Granville, 27 Feb. 1884. *Correspondence*, Vol. II, p. 161.
[3] W. H. Winterbotham, of the Hertfordshire Liberal Association, to Dilke, 14 Nov. 1883. Gladstone Mss., 44149 fol. 157.
[4] 'Note the unfairness of WEG's language about the Service franchise. He would have you believe it was for the relief of gamekeepers &c; but it is in truth intended to enfranchise those labourers, miners and others who live in cottages for which they pay no rent. This is another step towards manhood suffrage, for it goes beyond the householder.' Northcote Notebook labelled 'Reform Bill', p. 8. Iddesleigh Mss., 50060.

are running amuck against anomalies.'[1] Four Taunton potwallopers survived. The liverymen of the City of London and the freemen in Stafford comprised in 1885 a quarter of their respective electorates, while in Coventry ancient right voters numbered almost half. The plural-voting freehold and ownership franchise was claimed by more than a third of those registered in 25 of the recast divisions. At Pudsey, Shipley, Stretford and Bootle, outvoters could well-nigh hold their own against all comers.[2] This was, *in its detail*, just what Chamberlain called it – the most moderate Reform bill a Liberal Government could offer,[3] so framed as to disarm opposition under the flag of established rights. Issue was to be joined upon the completeness of legislation in regard to area and its incompleteness in regard to Redistribution, 'Ireland' and 'dates' superseding the rating and rental wrangles of 1867.

[1] Minto to Arthur Elliot, 29 Jan. 1884. Elliot Mss., Bundle 32.
[2] Seymour, *Electoral Reform*, pp. 478–9.
[3] Chamberlain, at Birmingham. *The Times*, 29 Jan. 1884, p. 10.

4

ABILITY AND INTENT:
FRANCHISE IN THE COMMONS

There is a general impression here [in Dublin] that the Mahdi is a Tory.
Gibson to Salisbury, 27 Jan. 1884. Salisbury Mss., Series E.

What can be more pitiable than John Morley's conduct?...He is not
fit for Parliament and the sooner he goes back to his books the better.
Chamberlain to Maxse, 19 Mar. 1884. Maxse Mss., 206.

I am asked whether I was correct in saying 'the 1st of January, 1886.'
I think I was; but the House will well understand that under these words
what would accrue on the 1st of January, 1886, would be a right to be
registered, and the right to vote would become living and effective only
on the 1st of January, 1887....I wish I could understand the cause of the
right hon. Gentleman's complaint.
Gladstone, 11 July 1884. 3 *Hansard* ccxc. 835–6.

PARLIAMENTARY SESSIONS are untidy phenomena. In this
they are like press headlines, which may develop the previous day's
instalment or jump abruptly to another item of news before
returning to the former. The historian who recites the passage of a
particular measure, catching the drift of debate, the impact of
particular argument and the subtlety of amendments pressed or
withdrawn, may do so tidily. The political historian might be better
advised to illuminate disorder. This is to say more than that
Parliamentary attention in 1884 tacked from successive Egyptian
censure motions to the fortunes of the Franchise bill. It is to posit
a political connection between the two, missed by the *Annual
Register* and by all who in straight exposition would accord
separate chapters to Reform and to Egypt. Such an exasperated
lament as Morley's – 'When Ireland is completely content, and the
last soldier is out of Egypt, I see no reason why we should not
resume our old habits of rational discussion'[1] – is the lament of
political innocence and the invocation of cloudcuckooland. There
will always be extraneous pressures to pervert rationality. How
complex and pervasive was the interdependence in Parliament and

[1] Morley to Maxse, 17 Jan. 1885. Maxse Mss., 215.

in political minds of subjects so disparate, it is the object of the following pages to show.

Granted the Government's ability to survive (i.e. to survive 'Egypt'), the questions that have to be asked of the Session of 1884 and of the unadventurous passage of the Franchise bill through the Commons during that Session, revolve around Government intention, the revelation of that intention and the modification of purpose to the pressures of party and Parliament. Even when stripped of Egyptian surrounds, Franchise was never 'for Franchise's sake', but was talked of and even more *thought* of in relation to its legislative brothers, Redistribution and Registration. In an understandable compression of these obscure connections, one historian has raised the settlement of January to a peak of significance: 'Hartington had contrived that there should be no election between Franchise and Redistribution.'[1] Were that summary warranted and were it not in its simplicity simply untrue, the latter half of the chapter would be an irrelevance. But then, so too would have been the great bulk of the politics of 1884.

The Liberal Ministry of 1880 might have foundered upon Reform, Egypt or Ireland. It fell, as all know, on a side issue. The Liberal coalition fractured only when Gladstone chose Ireland as the base on which to define anew the purpose, content and direction of his party, when he successfully drove from his party the two men most likely to define this purpose in ways unpalatable to him, and when in defeating Chamberlain and Hartington, he chose a wrong base for the long-term survival of his party. Though students of Victorian imperialism have set the 1886 split firmly in the context of imperial crisis, Egypt, like Reform, has been overshadowed. Two questions are thus left to those who can afford to dabble in the historical fancy of a past conditional tense. First, could any party positively have identified itself as simply against meddling with the Constitution without risk of immediate effacement as an 'All centre and no circumference' Parliamentary fusion?[2] Secondly, was there sufficient centrifugal and centripetal force in the distinct imperial poses of expansion, non-Jingo consolidation, or abandonment? This latter was answered by Labouchère. He looked with pleasure upon the 'growing...dissatisfaction against your Egyptian policy'

[1] Donald Southgate, *The Passing of the Whigs, 1832–1886* (1962), p. 380.
[2] Harcourt's *mot* applied to Churchill's projected 'moderate alliance' three years later. R. R. James, *Lord Randolph Churchill* (1959), p. 323.

and eagerly anticipated the time when the Government, *after* passing a Franchise bill, should be 'sent about their business, and the country divided between Conservatives and Radicals.'[1] Certainly, the immoderate pushing for a democratic peace party was what made Labouchère such a thorn in Chamberlain's side during these months. More immediately, Egypt and Reform are bound by Conservative tactical considerations. What was abundantly clear was that, if the Tories decided on a flank march as a viable means of securing control of Reform, Egypt rather than Ireland afforded the better opportunity. If needs be, they might still have recourse to enlisting anti-Irish prejudices in 1885, connecting the fate of Redistribution with the question of renewing the Coercion bill for Ireland. But in 1884, there was no need to alienate. There was need simply to attract, to drive a wedge between the Government and both supporting wings, or to intensify strain between Whigs and Radicals to a point at which both would opt simultaneously for breakage; and there were Nationalists to be courted if Liberal disaffection was to be converted into Government defeat. Self-interest demanded a coalition between all the forces which were dissatisfied with Gladstone. If Parnell desired a dissolution more earnestly than all else, he was right in voting with the Opposition on Egyptian votes of censure and tactically to be commended if he put the Government in a hole by letting it be supposed that he would support it and then inducing weak-kneed Liberals to take themselves off before the Irish ratted at the last moment. If the Conservatives, taking encouragement from by-election successes during the early months of 1884 and reckoning on 'a great gain from the general alienation of the country gentlemen & land-owners'[2] promised themselves a dissolution, then they too were right in seeking to effect such an alliance, the more so if it was purely temporary. If there was a price to pay for such 'dirty tricks' – 'several of the old, respectable Tories were so ashamed of was being done that they walked away, and would not vote'[3] – it was not exorbitant for the reward of office. One immediate and striking consequence was that a 'feverish desire to please the Irish

---

[1] Labouchère to Dilke, 10 Oct. 1882. A. L. Thorold, *The Life of Henry Labouchère* (1913), p. 180.
[2] Halifax to Ripon, 17 Jan. 1884. Ripon Mss., 43531 fol. 80.
[3] Mundella to Leader, 16 Mar. 1884. Mundella–Leader Mss. 'So this dirty trick has not succeeded', Harcourt had stage-whispered at the announcement of the Ministry's escape by 17 votes; the epithet was subsequently bandied about, an 1884 catch-phrase, whenever Parnellites joined the Tories.

members' was seen to mark Ministerial temper and action;[1] another, that the Parnellites escaped, as they would not have done twelve months before, the stigma of complicity in Fenian attempts to dynamite Nelson's Column, the Junior Carlton Club, Scotland Yard and Paddington, Victoria, Charing Cross and Ludgate Hill stations. The monthly punctuation of outrages was allowed to by-pass the stage of political controversy. One Whig called for the hanging of an Irish Member for each outrage committed, but his was a voice which cried in the wilderness.[2]

Yet the merest mention of dissolution is at odds with Trevelyan's New Year elation: 'As long as we keep the Franchise Bill driving on we are in the best position, in or out, that a party ever was in, in our time.'[3] How likely was an election? Certainly the Ministerial programme as outlined by Gladstone in introducing his Franchise measure involved two more Sessions. Programmes are, however, no more than programmes, vulnerable to the malice of time and chance, where not misleading by design. '*L'homme propose, mais...*' was Mundella's seasoned verdict, apprised though he was of a resolve on the part of several Cabinet members 'not to be forced into a Dissolution, but to fight Reform *again and again*.'[4] The theme is constant at all levels amongst all sections of the Liberal party throughout the months under consideration. Bright curtly told Hartington at the convening of Parliament that 'the Egyptian blunder [would] destroy the Govt. and break up the Party.'[5] Harcourt linked the fortunes of the Ministry with those of the Scriptural imbecile despatched to the Nile.[6] Morley knew that an election – because of Egypt 'certainly not remote'[7] – would go harder with him at Newcastle than with most, the Merchant Shipping bill having raised such 'a perfect tornado' on Tyneside as to involve sure disruption of his Parliamentary career.[8] Lobby talk by mid-April turned simply upon timing, everyone accepting that the Government required 'only a gentle push out of office.'[9] Hartington

[1] O'Connor, *Gladstone's House of Commons*, p. 368.
[2] Pease, *Elections and Recollections*, p. 72.
[3] Trevelyan to Chamberlain, 16 Jan. 1884. J. L. Garvin and Julian Amery, *The Life of Joseph Chamberlain* (6 vols., 1932–69), Vol. I, p. 460.
[4] Mundella to Leader, 6 Apr. 1884. Mundella–Leader Mss.
[5] Bright Diary, 5 Feb. 1884. R. A. J. Walling (ed.), *The Diaries of John Bright* (1930), p. 508.
[6] Harcourt to Lewis Harcourt, 8 Feb. 1884. Harcourt Mss.
[7] Morley to Spence Watson, 12 Mar. 1884. Hirst, *Morley*, Vol. II, p. 194.
[8] Morley to Grace Morley, 12 Mar. 1884. *Ibid.*
[9] Chamberlain to J. T. Bunce, 16 Apr. 1884. Chamberlain Mss., JC5/8/73.

pronounced an Egyptian Censure defeat almost inevitable by the end of May;[1] Harcourt concurred, Chamberlain quoted 'even betting' and Granville was prepared to ride for a fall: 'If we are to be defeated on a subject of Foreign Policy, I cannot say that I object to this being the one selected.'[2] Rosebery was advised to maintain his aloof independence, even should a Cabinet seat be offered him by Gladstone since he 'would have [nothing] to gain by being in evidence as a possible member of the present government [when]...a break-down [was] impending'.[3] A large body of market borough and county Liberal Members saw fit in April to desert the Government upon Lords' stiffening amendments to the Cattle Diseases bill – an indication that they expected to appeal still to an electorate of farmers. The message to local party organizations was uniform: 'everything ought to be ready to a turn'.[4] The state of alert found one Member already assembling the 'Omnibus, Break,...Dogcart [and] commoner conveyances [from] about my farm or gardens' to provide for the carriage of voters.[5]

If these were in fact no more than grim precautions and exaggerated forebodings, they were not so interpreted by opponents. Rumours of an early dissolution – more in circulation than ever Hicks Beach could recollect – sprang from a Government plot to saddle the Conservatives with an intolerable burden and insoluble 'mess'.[6] It was a temptation to which Granville, Spencer and Selborne succumbed: dissolve in July, they thought, with 'the Egyptian question...not stand[ing] badly at present', with Khartoum 'in suspense' while the Mahdi observed Ramadan,[7] and secure in the knowledge that Dilke could produce his Local Government bill from out of the conjuror's hat, whenever 'it shall appear that we are forced by Lord Salisbury to go to the country.'[8]

The historian would be hard pressed to find in any archive a line in exculpation of the Government's handling of the Nile problems or even a sympathetic acknowledgment of besetting difficulties. Were success to attend armed intervention, as in 1882, it could but arouse the charge of being at variance with the fundamental ethics

[1] Carlingford to Spencer, 30 May 1884. Spencer Mss.
[2] Granville to Gladstone, 6 June 1884. *Correspondence*, Vol. II, p. 201.
[3] Cooper to Rosebery, 13 Mar. 1884. Rosebery Mss., Box 9.
[4] Mundella to Leader, 21 June 1884. Mundella–Leader Mss.
[5] Ramsden to Mark Stanisby, 21 Apr. 1884. Ramsden Mss., Box 40.
[6] Hicks Beach to his Wife, 10 June 1884. St. Aldwyn Mss., PPC/17.
[7] Dodson Cabinet Minutes, 9 July 1884. Monk Bretton Mss., 62.
[8] Dilke to Gladstone, 3 Apr. 1884. Gladstone Mss., 44149 fol. 207.

taken to underlie Liberal and Midlothian foreign policy.[1] Again, there can be no denying the crude electoral worth, after the singular disaster at Khartoum, of the charge of blood guilt. The Tories' prize tableau was of a weeping Britannia[2] –

> Who killed General Gordon
> I said Mr. Gladstone...
> Who saw him die
> Not William at the Cri'
> With his laughing eye.

That which needs emphasizing – in absolute terms, and as of greater pertinence to Reform – is the apparent paradox that neither in 1882 nor in 1885 did the Egyptian crises coincide with crises in the Liberal party. The forthright pursuance of war, though it cost the Government Bright's services, brought its own momentum of 'hang consistency' support, and even an (at that juncture) almost true, almost endearing, boast 'that the Liberals had killed more people in less time, and done it cheaper than ever the Tories had.'[3] Three years later in 1885 complete misfortune tended rather to rally the Parliamentary Liberal party or at least reminded the 'peace' wing of their need still for Gladstone's protection. Morley's censure motion in the wake of Gordon's death was innocent by intent – 'to call the radical & dissenting conscience, & save their position for the future'; its purpose was *not* to bring down the Government.[4] The peculiar Parliamentary danger of the intermediate years was that both forward imperialists and abandonment men would simultaneously interpret governmental inaction as a mark of deliberate betrayal. The Morley of March 1884, refusing to go a step further on the road which the Government were pursuing until he knew where that road led, was an infinitely greater affliction than the Morley of 1885, because his doubts could as easily have been the doubts of Goschen or Forster.

What is undeniable is that Egypt did not receive 'the Gladstone treatment of maximum scrutiny before decision, maximum execution after decision'.[5] Indeed, Egypt was writ small on his agenda. He despatched Northbrook thither as a sort of High Commissioner but took no interest in his subsequent report on its

[1] Roundell Palmer, Earl of Selborne, *Memorials, Part II: Personal and Political, 1865–1895* (2 vols., 1898), Vol. II, p. 64.
[2] De Ricci and Barttelot election poster, 1885. Whitbread Mss
[3] Russell, *Lawson*, p. 168.
[4] Stansfeld to Halifax, 22 Feb. 1885. Hickleton Mss., A4.51.
[5] J. R. Vincent, *Cambridge Review*, 19 Jan. 1963, p. 192.

finances.[1] Within weeks of the fall of Khartoum, he advised Hartington – 'if he must resign' – against resignation over an Egyptian question on the ground of its being a matter for which 'no one cared a button'.[2] In the House, he displayed eloquent ill-temper, declaring that the constant renewal of debates was out of all proportion to the pressure or urgency of the question.[3] The evidence is all of one kind; Mary Gladstone's report in April 1884 was a fitting epitaph to a long period of time: 'Everything peaceful save Egypt, and even that does not seem to disturb the even flow of Downing St.'[4] A touch of Nemesis is added to this blithe minimization by Hamilton's summary of a report by the editor of the *Nineteenth Century*: 'He says that the feeling on the Soudan business has reached boiling point; that those whose feeling is of the strongest are Liberals. He believes it to be not so much Jingoish as sentimentalist – similar to that which was stirred up by you in Bulgarian Days.'[5] Thus, the striking feature of the situation was not that Gladstone fought shy of taking direct and immediate responsibility from Granville, but that he chose to ignore the opportunity to do for Egypt what he had already done for Bulgaria.

Of the existence of 'Egyptian' malcontents among backbenchers whose support constituted the lifeblood of a Liberal Ministry, Gladstone was fully aware, and was constantly reminded. The size of such groupings is less easily established. It is hardly sufficient to list those 'Tuesday and Friday' adherents whose adherence to particular crotchets never encompassed the possibility of a Governmental defeat. Nor does it help to count those who skulked around the doors at a critical division 'to see whether they could safely vote against their party.'[6] What has to be considered is Morley's action which was of a quite different order. Morley was aiming deliberately to cut loose from Gladstone, Chamberlain and Dilke, who 'must all take care of themselves', to seize the chance which 'does not come twice to a man' and to form with Courtney a party on the single platform, 'No reconquest of

[1] Bernard Mallet, *Thomas George, Earl of Northbrook, G.C.S.I.: a Memoir* (1908), p. 193.
[2] Hamilton Memo., 9 Feb. 1884. Hamilton Mss., 48618.
[3] 3 Apr. 1884.
[4] Lucy Masterman (ed.), Mary Gladstone (Mrs. Harry Drew), *Her Diaries and Letters* (1930), p. 312.
[5] Hamilton Memo., 9 Feb. 1884. Hamilton Mss., 48618.
[6] O'Connor, *Gladstone's House of Commons*, p. 424.

the Soudan'. At least fifty, 'the bulk of the men of 1880', he thought, could be relied on.[1]

'Lawson & Co.',[2] Labouchère, Lyulph Stanley, Buxton and Sir George Campbell would form the nucleus; Fawcett, the Postmaster-General, who threatened a noisy retirement to the back-benches were he not given a Cabinet seat,[3] was doubtless prepared to risk the taunt of 'always wanting to hunt with the Radical hare and run with the Tory hounds'.[4] What was needed perhaps was the active leadership and moral aegis of Bright. But even Bright's failure to give public expression to his strongly felt criticism of Gladstone's conduct[5] did not remove Chamberlain's impression that 'unless our friends show more backbone you will see a dissolution in the autumn'.[6]

While Radical unease undermined the party's self-confidence, Goschen and Forster openly assailed the Government. Theirs was a double act in the best traditions of Lowe and Elcho, the furore they stirred recalling (though of course within an Egyptian context) the fierceness of 1867.[7] Their joint purpose was understood by contemporaries: 'knowing that Granville cannot last & that Hartington will not be leader long, if at all, [they] are bidding for the lead'.[8] Granville's acquiescence in any Gladstonian proposition was accepted without wonder, but Hartington's never – and it was the Goschen/Forster ploy to diverge as little as possible from the supposed opinions of the latter, while making his path as difficult as possible by probing the rumoured, 'leaked' or patent sources of friction between him and Gladstone. Thus the bitterness, and significance, of Goschen and Forster's intervention in the Gordon

---

[1] Harrison to Morley, 12 Feb. 1884. Harrison Mss., A(5). It is an estimate whose approach to accuracy was confirmed by Childers. Childers to Northbrook, 28 May 1884. E. Spencer Childers, *The Life and Correspondence of the Right Hon. Hugh C. E. Childers, 1827–1896* (2 vols., 1901), Vol. II, p. 183.

[2] Mundella to Leader, 21 June 1884. Mundella–Leader Mss.

[3] Dilke Diary, 3 Nov. 1882. Dilke Mss., 43925 fol. 28. Gladstone and he played cat and mouse. When Fawcett walked out of the House on the 'dirty trick' division, Gladstone feigned ignorance in order that Fawcett might not so easily escape the restrictions of office. On women's franchise, Fawcett had the last word, even if the 'cause' was lost. Guilty of breach of discipline, and wallowing in Gladstone's leniency, he declined to 'go through the form of withdrawing a resignation which he had never tendered.' Millicent Fawcett, *What I Remember* (1924), p. 113.

[4] Hamilton Diary, 17 July 1884. Hamilton Mss., 48637 fol. 21.

[5] Stansfeld to Halifax, 20 Feb. 1884. Hickleton Mss., A4.51.

[6] Chamberlain to J. T. Bunce, 16 Apr. 1884. Chamberlain Mss., JC5/8/73.

[7] Dilke to Grant Duff, 13 May 1884. Dilke Mss., 43894 fol. 28.

[8] James Donaldson to Rosebery, 11 June 1884. Rosebery Mss., Box 11.

debate of 12 May arose directly from Hartington's refusal to speak until Gladstone ordered him to do so.[1] That Goschen was ready to accept a sufficiently attractive Cabinet seat under Hartington and to swallow a County Franchise bill is well attested.[2] Vulnerable to the charge of raising objections which 'ought to have applied to the last reform bill rather than this one'[3] and subject to Harcourt's memorable scorn as 'pissing against the wind',[4] Goschen yet knew that 'seriously [to] oppose' a further lowering of the franchise might well entail the risk of political isolation.[5] What Goschen had done in 1880 under the pretext of such opposition, was simply to dissociate himself from Gladstone. While never renouncing his party, he used the years of the Second Ministry to exacerbate differences, to promulgate his own 'unauthorised programme' of government in conformity with the principles of orthodox political economy and to offer a style of leadership which he believed would prove attractive to moderate Parliamentary opinion – a style which others took to be attractive to the country.[6] Thus it was in Gladstone's interest to minimize personal antagonism. He tried to gag Goschen by offering him the Speakership. He tried to involve him in complicity by offering the War Office. Goschen refused both since it was in his interest, remaining free as a 'candid friend', yet to assert both his power and disinclination (as representative of the responsible nation) to hand *Salisbury* a blank cheque.

While Goschen held out the hope of sound government once the existing party lines had been destroyed, Forster set about the work of destroying them. For the 'best stage Yorkshireman' of his generation,[7] it was a natural performance. His masterly retort to Nationalist rowdies at a Bradford speechmaking – 'you did not manage to kill me in Ireland, you will have to hear me in England'[8] – embodies the essence of his appeal. His need, as he saw it, was 'to assert himself' whenever and wherever opportunity arose.[9]

[1] Dilke to Grant Duff, 13 May 1884. Dilke Mss., 43894 fol. 28.
[2] Rendel to Grant Duff, 10 Nov. 1882. *Rendel Papers*, p. 220.
[3] Elgin to R. P. Bruce, 1 Nov. 1883. Bruce Mss.
[4] Dilke Diary, 7 Apr. 1884. Dilke Mss., 43926 fol. 7.
[5] A. R. D. Elliot, *The Life of George Joachim Goschen, First Viscount Goschen, 1831–1907* (2 vols., 1911), Vol. i, p. 277.
[6] Smith to Northcote, 22 Feb. 1885. H. E. Maxwell, *Life and Times of the Right Honourable William Henry Smith* (2 vols., Edinburgh, 1893), Vol. ii, p. 151.
[7] Frank Hill's description. Lucy, *Memories of Eight Parliaments*, p. 171.
[8] *The Times*, 14 Dec. 1883, p. 6.
Stansfeld to Halifax, 20 Feb. 1884. Hickleton Mss., A4.51.

The backhander, delivered with an 'apologetic dastardliness', was his weapon,[1] 'astute personal ambition' the driving force.[2] Students of comparative meanness in the Commons of 1884 waited expectantly for Forster to repay the debt of hatred he owed Gladstone and Chamberlain for getting rid of him in 1882.[3] It needs stressing, as an illustration of the extent to which his Reform interests were subordinated to the alliance with Goschen, that Forster had previously been thought not only, in Gladstone's phrase, a 'decided friend' of Reform[4] but also an advocate of an extensive extension of the franchise. Gladstone rightly looked back on Forster rather than Goschen as the man who, by way of the Nile, had posed the greater threat to the Government's legislative programme in 1884. When warned by the Radical Rylands that 'evil will befall you if you compromise the advantages which...you have acquired' by the occupation of Egypt, Gladstone was right to see in that pragmatic doctrine the contamination of 'Forsterism'.[5]

There is one last subtlety to this 'forward realism' of which Milner's speeches in searching for a constituency serve as the epitome. Milner made perfectly clear his belief that a halt should be called to imperial expansion not because he wanted to limit the sphere of British action abroad but in order to intensify 'power, dignity and influence' within a practicable sphere: 'To try to escape from responsibilities once assumed (under whatever specious phrases the retreat may be effected) can only increase, not lessen our difficulties.'[6] Such a condition of mind, he was advised, 'though it makes York impossible for you, and...any other Northern Constituency' would prove a positive help in 'many of the small boroughs in the South',[7] if the Brighton by-election was anything to judge by.[8] This is to say, in advocating a British protectorate, Goschen and Forster had lighted on the trump card

[1] *Freeman's Journal*, 14 May 1884, p. 4.
[2] C. S. Roundell to Spencer, 14 Feb. 1875. Cited in Spinner, 'Goschen', p. 201.
[3] O'Connor, *Gladstone's House of Commons*, p. 417.
[4] Autobiographical Memoranda, 1897. Gladstone Mss., 44791 fol. 152.
[5] Gladstone to Bright, 28 May 1884. Gladstone Mss., 44547 fol. 67.
[6] Address to the Oxford Liberal Association, 4 July 1884. Milner Mss., Box 181.
[7] Caine to Milner, 16 May 1884. Milner Mss., Box 181.
[8] W. T. 'Iscariot' Marriott, having voted against the Government on an Egyptian censure motion, resigned his seat in late February and reappeared before the Brighton electors as a Conservative; he polled 559 votes more than he had there in 1880, while the new Gladstonian Liberal – 'in every respect', according to the *Annual Register*, 'an eligible candidate and a powerful speaker' – received 711 less than had Marriott at the general election.

to play before those very boroughs whose separate existence, at the very least, was threatened by any Liberal redistribution.

The construction of political histories, like the construction of a Jamesian novel, ought surely to be divided into 'the parts that prepare, that tend in fact to over-prepare, for scenes, and the parts...that justify and crown...[this] discriminated preparation.'[1] In terms of artistic fulfilment, the Parliamentary scene of 1884, so far from justifying and crowning this 'Egyptian' preparation, is a disappointment. The Liberal party held together. We may reasonably ask why?

Such reasons as were brought forward by contemporaries pass muster as standard facts, and standard explanations of the facts of political life. Bright, struck by the novelty, attributed straight voting to constituency pressures: 'You will have seen what the Bradford people have said [about Forster], & what the Constituencies, or important sections of them, at Malton & Tiverton & Kirkcaldy have done in regard to their Members. There is a watchful eye kept on Liberal Members such as I have not observed before.'[2] The reasoning here is of linear simplicity: an election on points of Egyptian policy would be embarrassing for the Party on all calculations, the more so if the Tories boldly and in unison went in for the establishment of a protectorate, and unwillingness to face a general election at an unpropitious moment or on divisive issues was quite sufficient to induce Members to 'vote black, white'.[3] Some MPs, however offended their sensibilities, refused to believe 'that the Prime Minister's heart is in this mischievous business', and in the obstinacy of faith waited for Gladstone to assert himself over and against a supposedly Whig Cabinet dominance.[4] In addition, others may have been influenced by Gladstone's express promise that the Commons should be allowed the opportunity of pronouncing upon the terms of any arrangement with France prior to consultation with the Powers.

It yet remains true that, while Parliamentary disaster did not occur (averted perhaps by these considerations) the *expectation* of imminent disaster alone explains Gladstone's handling of the Parliamentary Session. The text which Gladstone took for the

[1] Preface to *The Ambassadors*.
[2] i.e. Charles Fitzwilliam, Viscount Ebrington and Sir George Campbell. Bright to Gladstone, 5 June 1884. Gladstone Mss., 44113 fol. 204.
[3] Smith to Harrowby, 20 June 1884. Harrowby Mss., 2nd Ser., Vol. 54, fol. 219.
[4] See, e.g., James Gozney to Herbert Gladstone, 28 Feb. 1885. Viscount Gladstone Mss., 46040 fol. 123.

Session was provided by Peel: 'avoid...beatings at all costs'[1] and, where possible, take the initiative on the issue most likely to produce rewards. Salisbury was almost certainly right when he saw that the Government were 'pushing on [their] Franchise Bill very hard – & delaying Egyptian resolutions. May it not be that they expect a defeat – & wish to have the defeat on Franchise Bill in the Lords first – & dissolve on that: so as to escape dissolving on Egypt?...this is their game'.[2]

This is not to deny that the Government would have been less vulnerable had there been no Egyptian bankruptcy, no Gordon in Khartoum, no Mahdi and no suggestion either that the military were being betrayed by politicians or that Granville was being made the dupe of French and German diplomacy. But in relation to the total antecedent situation, the playing off of Egypt against Franchise and of Franchise against Egypt does assume the proportions of sophisticated management. Thus when Dilke, Courtney and Fawcett 'went wrong' on the Female Franchise amendment, Gladstone sought Cabinet authority to request 'that they will do us the favour to retain their respective offices' since it would be 'most unfortunate', with the Ministry approaching an Egyptian crisis, 'were the minds of men...to be disturbed' by resignations on a question relating 'mainly to the internal discipline and management of the official corps.'[3]

Harcourt ventured to doubt that 'our Party can allow us to be beaten with the Franchise Bill in view' while 'the fear of a dissolution will make even the most unwilling come up to the scratch.'[4] Yet if Salisbury and Northcote had carried their party in allowing the bill to be sent to the Lords in May so that the Government might be obliged – as alternative to a dissolution – to continue the Session under the shadow of the Lords' rejection, it is at least arguable that Gladstone could have lost control of his party. That his Franchise bill 'stuck' in the Commons till late June was not an unmitigated affliction. Gladstone's reluctance in mid-March to accept his Chief Whip's proposal to take every night *de die in diem* for the debate on the Second Reading surely involved a great deal more than an over-sentimental regard for the rights of private Members.[5]

[1] Hamilton Diary, 7 Mar. 1884. Hamilton Mss., 48635 fol. 123.
[2] Salisbury to Balfour, 15 June 1884. Balfour Mss., 49688 fol. 76.
[3] Gladstone Memo., 13 June 1884. Cab. 37/12/31.
[4] Harcourt to Lewis Harcourt, 8 Feb. 1884. Harcourt Mss.
[5] Hamilton Diary, 20 Mar. 1884. Hamilton Mss., 48636 fol. 4; Gladstone to Grosvenor, 20 Mar. 1884. Gladstone Mss., 44547 fol. 49.

Two incidents may be detailed. Grey, when compelled to withdraw a date clause he had inserted in the Franchise bill, had little doubt that he had been a victim of Gladstone's astute control of the Parliamentary time-table. 'I am afraid that the Division on Stanley's amendt. & on mine may be affected by the vote of Censure.... my doubt is whether these men after refusing to support the Govt. on one critical division will have pluck enough to do it again.'[1] Gladstone displayed similar dexterity in late June. While Hartington told Cowen, and Cowen duly told the Conservative Chief Whip, that Parliament could never be expected to accept French terms for taking part in the Egypt Conference,[2] the Opposition's immediate Vote of Censure served only to publicize their own divisions. It was a general, and right, opinion 'that the old man ha[d] put [the Conservatives] in a hole'.[3] By bringing up the Anglo-French agreement without the financial proposals to be submitted to the Powers, and before it could be known what course the Powers might take, he compromised subsequent judgment upon the entire scheme (should it survive) and threatened (should it fail) to attribute the failure of the Conference wholly to Conservative action.[4]

Hamilton's commentary is fair, if a dilution of complexities: the Tories 'would have preferred postponing their attack.... Doubtless the Franchise Bill has materially influenced the decision of the Opposition. They want to have a fight before the Lords have to make up their minds about the Bill; and they can't do this if they stay action till after the Conference.'[5] Conservative unity, and the saving of all 'bother', Beach concluded, was dependent upon Governmental defeat 'on Egypt before the Lords get to the Franchise Bill'.[6] In personal terms, Churchill would 'explode if nothing [was] done' to ensure the former.[7] By the same token, it was a Downing Street platitude that the bill's chances were dependent upon the alienation of Churchill from Salisbury. Between the day when T. C. Bruce gave notice of the Opposition's Censure resolution and the day set aside for the vote, Franchise was given its Third Reading in the Commons. When the Censure motion was reached, it

[1] Albert Grey to Halifax, 5 May 1884. Hickleton Mss., A4.84 Part 4.
[2] Smith to Harrowby, 20 June 1884. Harrowby Mss., 2nd Ser., Vol. 54, fol. 219.
[3] Hicks Beach to his Wife, 24 June 1884. St. Aldwyn Mss., PPC/7.
[4] Cairns to Salisbury, 30 June 1884. Salisbury Mss., Series E.
[5] Hamilton Diary, 25 June 1884. Hamilton Mss., 48636 fol. 134.
[6] Hicks Beach to his Wife, 12 June 1884. St. Aldwyn Mss., PPC/7.
[7] Hicks Beach to his Wife, 24 June 1884. St. Aldwyn Mss., PPC/7.

did not get beyond a vote to postpone the Orders of the Day. Egypt, in other words, could no longer serve a political purpose.

As the bill approached its Third Reading in the Commons, Gladstone commended the Liberal rank and file for having 'shewn great firmness of purpose. All evil predictions ha[d] been falsified. There ha[d] been no caves; no small or critical divisions; all crotchets ha[d] vanished.'[1] Amendments to extend the scope of the Franchise measure by the admission of women householders and of £5 occupation voters, or to qualify its breadth by excluding Ireland, illiterates or the plural voting freeholder in boroughs met with a uniformly depressing fate.

This happened because the important few in each party decided that it should, and because the unimportant many assumed the role of 'poor dummies'.[2] Gladstone deprecated anything that might provide 'the admirable patent, nay the fair argument' to Salisbury for 'hanging up' the bill.[3] Northcote did not see how his party could keep up a Franchise debate on Gladstone's introduction of the measure even for 'a couple of nights'[4] and 'trust[ed] to the H. L. throwing out the bill on 2nd Reading'.[5] To enough Radicals who saw the fulfilment of the Leeds programme and the possibilities in a battle between Peers and People it seemed desirable to 'register ...a vow...to vote against every single Amendment put forward either on that or the other side of the House'.[6] Enough Whigs saw a Reform bill so 'exceedingly moderate...that it will be [in] the interest [even] of the Tories to pass it'[7] and considered it their 'duty...to support the Govt., & endeavour to get the whole question of Reform settled while Gladstone & *Hartington* still continue to be the controlling powers in the House of Commons'.[8] Tories who could see no prospect of 'improving the House' by a franchise extension could yet suggest Redistribution proposals to disfranchise all boroughs of less than 40,000 inhabitants.[9] For all

---

[1] Hamilton Diary, 20 June 1884. Hamilton Mss., 48636 fol. 128.
[2] Lawson, 12 June 1884. 3 *Hansard* cclxxxix. 182.
[3] Gladstone to Dilke, 13 May 1884. Gladstone Mss., 44149 fol. 214.
[4] Northcote to Winn, 25 Feb. 1884. Nostell Mss., 1/114.
[5] Northcote to Salisbury, 23 Apr. 1884. Salisbury Mss., Series E.
[6] Labouchère, 16 May 1884. 3 *Hansard* cclxxxviii. 561.
[7] Albert Grey to Halifax, 4 Feb. 1884. Hickleton Mss., A4.84 Part 4.
[8] Ramsden docket on Fawkes's letter, 22 Apr. 1884. Ramsden Mss., Box 40. (My italics.)
[9] T. Collins, 28 Apr. 1884. 3 *Hansard* cclxxxvii. 817; 16 May 1884. 3 *Hansard* cclxxxviii. 564.

these various groups, Redistribution was the alpha and omega of Reform, and the Franchise bill, like any other, in terms of power, 'a trumpery little Bill'[1] whose principles might be rendered 'null and void' by the subsequent measure.[2] Thus, in the last resort, each and every Member 'held himself free to act exactly as he thought right when the question of redistribution came forward.'[3]

Particular crotchet amendments merit notice as illustrating the Government's handling of particular difficulties and the crotchet-mongers' difficulties in promoting each cause. Their acquiescence during the early stages of the Session and the ease with which Franchise was carried on its Second Reading may in large part be attributable to a hope (perhaps even a tacit assurance) that the more substantial the majority achieved there, the safer would it be for the Government to make concessions in Committee. Subsequent disillusionment was cruel and total. Thus, at the Committee stage, when Gladstone bade his party waste no time debating amendments, Stansfeld complained not only of having 'failed to be enlightened [by Gladstone]...as to the specific nature of the danger to his measure' afforded by women's suffrage but also of 'an unfairness in the position in which the right hon. Gentleman has placed us.'[4] What McLaren said in pressing to a division his amendment for the immediate eradication of faggot voting was bitter, pathetic and probably sound in tactical perception – 'that Bills which were adopted without any amendment, or attempt at amendment... very often [met] with an untoward fate in "another place"'...[Had not a bill] a very much better chance of passing if it was found that a large number of persons were anxious to make it stronger and more drastic[?]'[5] The tactical antithesis, to which Gladstone subscribed – turning even the shadow of nuisance into an issue vital to the Government – was that, if the bill was destined to meet with 'an untoward fate in "another place"', at least he would afford Conservatives in both Commons and Lords minimal excuse on side issues for such opposition. As in the initial shaping, so in the passage of the bill, he made sure that if conflict was unavoidable it would at least be direct. (And as regards the prospect of conflict, Gladstone was reported to be 'in high spirits'.)[6]

[1] Churchill, 20 May 1884. 3 *Hansard* cclxxxviii. 853.
[2] Dunraven, 7 July 1884. 3 *Hansard* ccxc. 169.
[3] Sellar, 31 Mar. 1884. 3 *Hansard* cclxxxvi. 1214.
[4] 12 June 1884. 3 *Hansard* cclxxxix. 107.
[5] 26 May 1884. 3 *Hansard* cclxxxviii. 1407.
[6] *Manchester Guardian*, 20 May 1884, p. 5.

Three crotchets – the exclusion of Ireland from the measure, the inter-related cause of Proportional Representation, and Women's Suffrage – demand separate attention.

In late 1883, Conservative Central Office had noted the Government's dilemma over Ireland: 'if they grant the franchise to the Irish [it] will be used merely to emphasize the demand for Home Rule & Separation. If they refuse they will work a revolutionary agitation on the pretext that their rights are refused – & thus produce a conflict. It is obvious that the lesser evil is to refuse the means of increasing the power of the Rebels.'[1] Gladstone had then perversely upset Central Office calculations by including Ireland in his measure and by proposing retention of an inflated total of Members without special provision for the Loyalist North. This course opened the way not only to a Tory or avowedly Whig onslaught but also to a Scottish 'bloc' revolt: 'When generosity to one part of the country inflicted, or threatened to inflict, injustice on another part, its Representatives could not hold their peace.'[2]

It was Hartington, uniquely equipped as having himself urged every counter-argument three months earlier, who now eased the Government's path. His Commons' speech of 24 March was more than a timely declaration of faith in the essential unity of Franchise and Redistribution even if, for practical convenience, two measures were being brought forward separately. It was an assertion of an Anglo-Saxon right to thwart what might henceforward be termed the democratic expression of the Irish will, or to secure by *indirect* representation the interests of those whose voices would be stilled by legislation. 'Do what you may to protect the loyal minority of Ireland, it cannot, under existing circumstances, I am afraid, possess a large representation in this House.... The real protection and the real safety of the minority...will be found in the English and Scottish representation.' Moreover, Gladstone's declaration that he would not cut the Irish representation, Hartington reminded his audience, should be seen as contingent upon acceptance of two further proposals – the enlargement of the House of Commons and the 'centrifugal' plan of increased representation in inverse proportion to proximity to London (the more Celt, the more seats). Were either of these rejected, Ireland's quota would once more become an open question.[3] Childers was even blunter:

[1] Philip H. Bagenal to Smith, n.d. Hambleden Mss., PS8/135.
[2] Sellar, 31 Mar. 1884. 3 *Hansard* cclxxxvi. 1214.
[3] Hartington, 24 Mar. 1884. 3 *Hansard* cclxxxvi. 711-12.

'Mr. Gladstone took care to say (with truth) that his language...
was his own. As I do not think there is much prospect of *his* having
to introduce a redistribution Bill, it will not affect us then;
although undoubtedly it will influence the debate on the Franchise
Bill.'[1]
Because Redistribution was settled by the party leaders behind
the back of the House of Commons, there is no knowing to what
limit opposition (from within) on such issues as these might have
been carried. The Proportional Representationists certainly chose
to defer their stroke. They were lulled by Gladstone's reminder that
the minority provision had found its way by accident into the
so-called enfranchising clauses of the 1867 bill, 'and that the
Amendment by which it obtained its accidental insertion in that
Bill was due to a freak of a clerk of the House of Lords'.[2] They were
hoping beyond hope that by 1885 they might have settled 'what
their views really [were].' A challenge for such exposition in May
1884, on Cameron's amendment, was met by silence from Lubbock,
and cries of 'No!' from his supporters.[3] When Lubbock did rise, a
month later on Collins' amendment (that in double-membered
constituencies, every elector should be 'entitled to give a single
vote for one Candidate, and no more'), it was simply to ask Collins
to withdraw his clause, leaving the House to consider the question
when they came to Redistribution since 'in discussing the question
of proportional representation in connection with dual seats, [his]
supporters did so at a disadvantage'.[4]

If any still expected to be rescued by mass Conservative opposition to the inclusion of Ireland, they were disappointed. Conservative leaders were determined not to offend Irish opinion.[5] Moreover,
at the very point at which the Carlton Club meeting was being held
to discuss Beach's Egyptian Censure motion and amendments to
the Franchise bill, Churchill was entering into a deal with Healy to
secure Parnellite co-operation on the former. It was, indeed, an

---

[1] Childers to Halifax, 17 Mar. 1884. Hickleton Mss., A4.90.
[2] Lowther, 17 June 1884. 3 *Hansard* cclxxxix. 614.
[3] Lowther, 26 May 1884. 3 *Hansard* cclxxxviii. 1333.
[4] 17 June 1884. 3 *Hansard* cclxxxix. 617.
[5] Quite how determined was the Conservative leadership not to risk alienating
any potential support – in this instance, the likely small borough victims of
Redistribution – may be judged from Raikes' removal from his Instruction
to the Committee (that provision be made at this stage for Redistribution)
his naming of the means to be employed, a transfer of seats from 'the less
populous borough constituencies' to 'populous urban sanitary districts at
present unrepresented'.

FRANCHISE IN THE COMMONS

inopportune moment for Chaplin to raise the flag of Orangeism.
'R. Churchill made a conciliatory, modest, and reasonable speech,
...urging complete union in the party. Barttelot was effusive in
his thanks for Churchill's speech, and "all went merry as a marriage
bell."'[1] Hence, what had claim to recognition as 'the largest majority
ever recorded in favour of an extension of popular liberties.'[2]
The summit of feminist achievement in 1884 was the admission
of women to certain degree examinations at Oxford. The Parliamentary achievement for effort was negligible. More had seemed
distinctly possible. In March the *Daily News* hinted that the Tories
might to their advantage as a party take up female suffrage,[3] as
being 'conservative in principle &...a set off against the proposed
new electorate'.[4] Bryce gloomily anticipated its success once
Northcote advocated it, 'there being all the Parnellites for it as
well as many Liberals'.[5] Grosvenor in fact listed 250 known 'friends'
of equality, and Woodall secured 76 Liberal signatures to a petition
urging that Women's Suffrage be an open question, as in 1867. In
the event, as many Conservatives and Home Rulers voted with the
Government as Liberals defected to the feminist cause. What lay
behind so poor a showing? Certainly it is not to be attributed to
rational pleading from the Treasury benches; to the Gladstonian
charge of haste, Manners asked pertinently for how many years the
question of enfranchising Irish cottiers had been before the House
or the public.[6] It may be attributed to the fact that some Liberals
declined to be made the instruments of a 'dirty trick'[7] – some of
these developing an ideological case for this natural political
disinclination: for every Conservative heard to declare his intention
of casting a vote 'for this time only',[8] there was a Radical counter-
part who was said to base his opposition to female *household*
suffrage on the ground that it endorsed existing conceptions of
voting rights and by its relative finality would halt movement

[1] Manners to Henry Manners, 9 May 1884. Belvoir Mss.
[2] T. P. O'Connor, *The Parnell Movement, with a Sketch of Irish Parties from 1843* (1886), p. 527.
[3] 12 Mar. 1884, p. 5.
[4] Hamilton Diary, 10 June 1884. Hamilton Mss., 48636 fol. 115. This same point of Conservative attraction (women landowners as a counterpoise to men labourers) was made in a letter from Lydia Becker to Mrs. Ashworth Hallett, 2 Apr. 1880. Cited in Constance Rover, *Women's Suffrage and Party Politics in Britain, 1866–1914* (1967), pp. 58–9.
[5] Bryce to Goldwin Smith, 15 Mar. 1884. Bryce Mss., Vol. 17, fol. 175.
[6] 12 June 1884. 3 *Hansard* cclxxxix. 94.
[7] *Manchester Guardian*, 22 Apr. 1884, p. 5.
[8] *Manchester Guardian*, 12 June 1884, p. 5.

129   J T P

towards 'one man, one vote' and the 'flesh and blood' franchise.[1] Though Woodall was not prevented from moving his amendment, the decisive fact in swelling abstentions among Liberal faddists was a cheap assurance given by the Government that 'apart from this Bill it is & may be open.'[2] Beyond this, there lay in official opposition a personal complication – that Gladstone had to balance the misogynist Attorney-General against Courtney and Fawcett. As Raikes suggested, he did well to retain James's services even though that involved risking the two latter (who might resign at any moment and on any other issue).[3] Raikes might have added the retention of Harcourt.

To explain the failure of the Opposition to oust the Government on Egypt or the failure of crotchets to win the favour of the House takes us but part of the way to an understanding of the complexities of 1884. It simply encompasses the ability of the Government to survive, thereafter to introduce, and ultimately to carry, their Redistribution measure. What remains is to examine the *intent* of the Government. That this should present an historical problem of greater magnitude than that of 'explaining away' potentially imminent schism upon Egypt, Ireland, Women's Suffrage, Proportional Representation or whatever, of itself demands explanation, for in this connection many who criticized the Government's policy did not doubt its *bona fides*. Sclater-Booth, setting himself up as Tory spokesman for the agricultural interest, declared that they 'did not dispute the intention of the right hon. Gentleman... to continue the distinction between the county and borough representation...but what they doubted was his power.'[4] Goschen foresaw that no satisfactory Redistribution was likely to be passed in the course of the next Session 'unless the two Parties lay their heads together'[5] – a suggestion which was tinged with the promise that Goschen himself might emerge as the mediator who would enable the two parties to 'lay their heads together' free from Parnellite pressure. Lord George Hamilton dismissed all guarantees and pledges, not because of disbelief in Gladstone's word, but 'because it is not in the power of the Government' to honour any such pledges.[6] Beresford Hope spoke colourfully of the Government

---

[1] *Pall Mall Gazette*, 13 June 1884, p. 1.
[2] Dodson Cabinet Minutes, 10 June 1884. Monk Bretton Mss., 62.
[3] 12 June 1884. 3 *Hansard* cclxxxix. 202–3.
[4] 6 May 1884. 3 *Hansard* cclxxxvii. 1496.
[5] 7 Apr. 1884. 3 *Hansard* cclxxxvi. 1877.
[6] 13 June 1884. 3 *Hansard* cclxxxix. 263.

'playing fast and loose with politics' by proposing 'indiscriminate enfranchisement, in view of a dark Bill for redistribution which may be passed in this Parliament or in the next Parliament by the Liberals, by the Tories, or by the Mahdi.'[1] Salisbury stripped the issue to the bone: 'Promises are mere counters. They are perfectly idle in this matter.'[2]

Nor was this empty word-play. The extraordinary scene on the collapse of the Third Vote of Censure for which Lucy could find no parallel since the Repeal of the Corn Laws[3] seemed to substantiate Salisbury's claim:[4]

Mr. Gladstone had promised to give a day for debate upon the Egyptian Policy of his Government, and when the day came, his own supporters... opposed the motion that the 'orders of the day' should be postponed in order to allow the Egyptian debate to take place, and defeated that motion – his own son and personal friends and nearly all the rank and file of the Liberal Party voting against it. Of course it was pretty well understood that [the] Government did not wish the debate to take place, and in the same manner, their wishes being one way and their pledge the other, it might happen their Party could gently oblige them to obtain the former at the expense of the latter. Then, with a new Radical Parliament re-distribution might be settled as the Radicals pleased.

Yet the problem of *intent* exists, and brings into the foreground the amendments proposed by Grey and Stanley. It brings out of the shadows, too, the question of Registration. Gladstone's initial statement upon the latter was brief to a fault – and not revealing. The Franchise bill was 'framed with the intention of preparing a state of things in which the whole occupation franchise...shall be a self-acting franchise, and the labour, anxiety, and expense connected with proof of title...will, I trust, be got rid of. But, at the same time, our Bill is not a complete Bill in that vital respect, and we look to the introduction of another Bill for the purpose, with which we shall be prepared immediately when the House has supplied us with the basis on which it wishes us to proceed.'[5] Virtually on the eve of this speech the Manchester Conservative Association had claimed to have reduced and 'purified' the register of more than 8,000 (presumably Liberal) names in the last three years, breaking through, as the *Guardian* saw it, an age-

[1] 1 Apr. 1884. 3 *Hansard* cclxxxvi. 1345.
[2] 17 July 1884. 3 *Hansard* ccxc. 1371.
[3] H. W. Lucy, *A Diary of Two Parliaments* (2 vols., 1885–86), Vol. II: *The Gladstone Parliament, 1880–1885*, p. 424.
[4] Brabourne Diary, 16 Oct. 1884. Brabourne Mss., F27/9 fol. 65.
[5] 28 Feb. 1884. 3 *Hansard* cclxxxv. 124.

hallowed mutual understanding.[1] It was only to be expected, therefore, that Gladstone's 'purely mechanical' measure should have
been seen as the eradication of an abuse by taking registration out
of local party hands. No one at the time asked for guidance in
translating the clause, 'when the House has supplied us with the
basis on which it wishes us to proceed.'
Detail and dates *were* difficult to master; unequivocal elucida-
tion *was* called for. Dodson's Cabinet minute on the subject trails
off unhappily into bewildered nothingness: 'James & Grosvenor
come in – James proposes clause to Reform bill to provide that new
voters shall not be registered till Jan/86 so as to secure that next
dissoln any how shall take place upon present franchise unless
[*sic*]'.[2] *Hansard* likewise made a complete nonsense of H. H.
Fowler's authoritative statement upon the same subject – unless
Fowler himself was guilty of a *lapsus linguae* or inversion of
meaning: he explained that even were the bill to receive the Royal
Assent prior to the end of July 1884, in the absence of any legislation to the contrary, the new franchises would not come into
operation until 1 January 1886; and therefore – so runs the
'official' conclusion – 'that question would be decided, not by the
existing constituencies, but by the new constituencies.'[3] Tokens
certainly, but perhaps no more. Most telling, though, was Selborne's
advice that Granville should explain to the Lords why the Government rejected Cairns' proposed insertion of the date, 1 January
1886, into the Franchise bill:[4]

I am not sure, that I ever fully mastered this myself: but my impression
is, that it was this:– that, if that date were fixed, the new voters could
not be on the Register, or are to vote earlier than 1887, in the spring of
which year the present Parliament would naturally expire: so that, if
(from the rejection of one or more Redistribution Bills, or any other
cause,) a dissolution in the interval should become necessary, 2,000,000
voters, admitted by Statute in 1884, would be excluded from voting at
any Election during that & the two following years. I am not sure,
whether this was a *sufficient* reason: at all events, I know of no other.

The very least we can say of a situation in which '1885' could
be said and '1886' subsequently be taken to have been meant, and

---

[1] 25 Feb. 1884, p. 5.
[2] Dodson Cabinet Minutes, 28 Apr. 1884. Monk Bretton Mss., 62.
[3] 23 May 1884. 3 *Hansard* cclxxxviii. 1192. *The Times* managed to give a more
intelligible record in its report of Parliamentary proceedings: 'not by the new
constituencies, but by the existing constituencies.'
[4] Selborne to Granville, 11 July 1884. Granville Mss., PRO. 30/29/141.

in which Grey's amendment to defer operation to 'January 1st 1887' could be discussed as if 'January 1st 1886' was intended, is that an intolerable strain was being laid upon the mental resources of back-benchers. Yet perhaps dates were easier to understand than the language of hypothesis: 'If the principle of the enlarged franchise were affirmed conditionally on the passing of such a scheme of redistribution as might be agreeable to the Conservative party, the Government could not ensure the fulfilment of the condition, of which (if they had consented to it) they would have acknowledged the reasonableness.'[1]

The process of registration which allowed of this double-talk entailed a six months' executive routine. In July of every year, the overseers prepared a list of persons qualified to vote. This list was closed on 31 July, and published on 1 August. Between 20 September and 31 October, it was revised by the Revising Barrister, but the list did not become the official electoral register for the ensuing year until 31 December, nor come into force until 1 January. What made this process so important, even when MPs did not fully understand it, was that the 1832 and 1867 Acts provided for enfranchisement and redistribution to be brought into operation simultaneously but guarded against the possibility of newly enfranchised electors voting for areas from which they might afterwards be dissociated.[2] What specifically brought Registration and dates into such prominence in 1884 was a belief that immediately after the passing of the Franchise bill the new electors would be qualified and would elect a new Parliament to settle Redistribution, or that Gladstone would press immediate legislation to ensure that they were qualified in time to do so.

'See what difference', Henry James exulted in accepting 1885 as

---

[1] Selborne, *Memorials*, Vol. II, p. 113.

[2] Lambert Memo., 7 May 1884. Gladstone Mss., 44235 fols. 177–81. On First Reform, in case of a dissolution after the passing of a Boundary Act but before Registration, the new franchises (with polling extended in counties for 15 days and in boroughs for 8) were to take effect without Registration; and, although the Act provided that the new franchises were to become operative immediately with or without previous Registration, they were to be exercised not in conformity with existing areas but with the new Redistribution scheme. The 1867 franchises were not to take practical effect until 1 January 1869, the first Registration being in the autumn of 1868. Any intermediate dissolution would result in an election on old franchise qualifications and for old areas, except that disfranchised boroughs were denied the opportunity of returning Members. In the event, the Boundary Commissioners having reported in 1868 and the Boundary Act having passed, Registration was accelerated.

the date for the coming into operation of the Franchise bill: 'Parliament has now a positive assurance...that there can be... no right of voting until the 1st of January 1886.'[1] It was a self-denial whose nature and bearing were lost on no corner of the House. In so far as the Radical benches had been deliberately misled by indistinctness, Collings was justifiably aggrieved at what he took to be, in the light of James's speech, 'a retrograde step on the part of the Government.'[2] Northcote rightly felt that, while a very considerable advantage had been derived from the discussion, it was yet 'rather hard on us to find that, after all, we have escaped the great danger of having this incomplete scheme brought into operation at once without any time being allowed for redistribution.'[3] Hicks Beach characterized this as 'a very remarkable speech...throw[ing] a new and strange light upon the intention and spirit with which Her Majesty's Government have approached this question of Reform'.[4] It may indeed be claimed that the willingness of such moderates as Dodson to threaten malcontents with enfranchisement without *any* Redistribution as an alternative to their acceptance of whatever Redistribution the Government proposed, marked the greatest break in the whole course of 1884 with the accepted orthodoxies of nineteenth century Parliamentary Reform, though it is a separate matter whether Dodson, Harcourt, Spencer or Childers drew this conclusion from the assertion that 'we ought to propose to enfranchise soon the men we say ought to be enfranchise[d]'.[5]

Radicals all along – and more particularly after Gladstone had apparently held out such a prospect on 7 April[6] – expected the Government to make provision, either in a separate Registration bill or by a clause in the Franchise bill, to place the county house-holders on the electoral roll at once. Chamberlain's calculations were quite specific: 'We should win on appeal to *present* Consty on franchise bill, or on rejection (by Lords) of our intended Registration bill to bring in new men in Jan/85 but should[/]might not win ...because defeated on redistribution bill or some o[the]r question.'[7] And for those who would attach little weight to his electoral

1 13 June 1884. 3 *Hansard* cclxxxix. 270.
2 17 June 1884. 3 *Hansard* cclxxxix. 640.
3 13 June 1884. 3 *Hansard* cclxxxix. 282.
4 13 June 1884. 3 *Hansard* cclxxxix. 271–2.
5 Dodson Cabinet Minutes, 28 Apr. 1884. Monk Bretton Mss., 62.
6 7 Apr. 1884. 3 *Hansard* cclxxxvi. 1897.
7 Dodson Cabinet Minutes, 28 Apr. 1884. Monk Bretton Mss., 62.

estimates, he added the stay of political rumour: Richmond would refuse to follow Salisbury in rejecting the major bill, preferring rather to throw out Registration – and could not Richmond, having served his purpose in ditching Salisbury, then himself be ditched by the Government's insertion of 'something' to prevent such subsequent rejection of a Registration bill?[1]

Chamberlain, however, needed to whistle in the dark to keep his spirits up. Dogmatism was a screen for anxiety rather than a measure of assurance, and Chamberlain's strident tone[2] indicated a fear that Gladstone, while refusing to allow Reform to be 'hung up' by the Lords till Kingdom come, would insert a date as an earnest of his determination not to dissolve without making attempt to carry Redistribution. From the horse's mouth had come the teaching that while defeat on the Franchise bill involved a 'crisis', on Redistribution it did not.[3]

More peculiarly wounding to Chamberlain's pride was the vision of Gladstone led astray (as it seemed to Chamberlain) by the notion that it was worth his while to pander to Churchill, and to risk the anger of Broadhurst or Collings in the attempt to achieve an accommodation with 'Tory Democracy'. And it was all the more painful at a time when Dilke was refusing to follow him in pressing for immediate dissolution in the event of the Lords carrying a date clause.[4] Churchill's date proposal came to the Cabinet as the proposal of the Liberal Attorney-General, but few doubted its source. In the telegraphese of Dilke and Chamberlain, 'James is Churchill' – an assertion which drew from Gladstone, who could not afford to build up Churchill in front of Chamberlain, the comment that 'it cd. not be as he shd. not consider that this wd. justify James' statement that [a] very "influential Conservt." wd. vote for the Bill as amended.'[5] Whether Churchill had any intention

---

[1] Dilke Diary, 28 Apr. 1884. Dilke Mss., 43926 fol. 8; Chamberlain to Dilke, n.d. Dilke Mss., 43886 fol. 189.

[2] He spoke of 'our intended Registration' as a matter of accepted fact and policy; he wrote to Gladstone, 'I know this is untrue', upon the *Daily News*'s kite that the Prime Minister intended to fix such a date for the operation of Franchise as would leave 'ample margin' for the passage of a Redistribution bill. Chamberlain to Gladstone, 26 May 1884. Gladstone Mss., 44126 fol. 34; *Daily News*, 26 May 1884, p. 5.

[3] Dodson Cabinet Minutes, 28 Apr. 1884. Monk Bretton Mss., 62.

[4] Dilke to Chamberlain, 28 Apr. 1884. Dilke Mss., 43886 fols. 143–4.

[5] Dilke–Chamberlain exchange of notes in Cabinet, 28 Apr. 1884. Dilke Mss., 43886 fol. 145. It ought surely to have been established in a work of serious political biography – Rhodes James's *Lord Randolph Churchill* – that Henry James was more than Churchill's travelling companion, more indeed than

beyond creating further nuisance may be doubted, but certainly he had lighted on an aspect of James's unease which he was to exploit fully over Home Rule eighteen months later. 'I see', he wrote then, 'that you and I will have to make another great arrangement as we did over the Reform Bill.... There is one object you and I have in common, which from its importance smothers all other differences viz. resistance to the extreme Radicals & extreme Irish. For this we should be prepared to pay a very high price.'[1]

Quite apart from his National Union exploits,[2] Churchill, by his conduct in the Commons during the early months of 1884, had not endeared himself to either of his leaders. He made common cause with Labouchère upon Egypt, attempted to outbid the Radicals on Leaseholders' Enfranchisement and Compulsory Sale of Lands in Mortmain, voted against the agricultural interest on the Cattle bill,

the medium of social reconciliation between Churchill and the Prince of Wales (pp. 111 and 171). Mr Rhodes James acknowledges the considerable debt he owes Sir Henry Lucy, commending the tomes as 'standard reading' to all 'students of the House of Commons in the 1880s and 1890s' (p. 378). This is not advice to be followed. Lucy does, indeed, serve to portray backbench moods at particular points in time, which is the gold for which historians must sift tons of ore. Lucy's mindless twaddle is in itself harmless; dully repeated mindless twaddle becomes pernicious. Mr Rhodes James would have served history well had he directed those same students to private political correspondence and to *Hansard*.

[1] Churchill to James, 30 Nov. 1885. James of Hereford Mss.
[2] Conservative internal dissension first became common knowledge with Churchill's resignation of the National Union chairmanship on 3 May and the simultaneous publication in the *Standard* of his letter to Salisbury of 3 April. It may be convenient to record here Cabinet 'intelligence' about the Churchill–Salisbury split. The conflict, Granville informed his colleagues, centred on 'an assurance alleged to have been given & then withdrawn or denied by Salisbury.' Dodson Cabinet Minutes, 5 May 1884. Monk Bretton Mss., 62. There is no knowing whether or not Granville had then elaborated, as he did to Hartington, on the detail and sources of his information: 'Bath told me that...Salisbury...had given R. an assurance, & two hours afterwards gave another assurance in writing to a third person in exactly the opposite direction. Nat Rothschild told me today...that Randolph had written to Salisbury [laying out]...the policy for the Conservative party – that Salisbury had [answered] civilly, saying he was always glad to have the opinions of a clever though younger man, and intimating that his claims would be acknowledged on the formation of a conservative Govt. – that a correspondence ensued, which was broken off by Randolph....Gladstone was told that Randolph had submitted an ultimatum to Salisbury, requiring a weeding out of the front bench.' Granville note, headed 'Gossip', n.d. Devonshire Mss., 340.1560. This latter was subsequently 'confirmed' by Churchill himself at a dinner party attended by Harcourt: 'men like Sir R. Cross on the Front Bench are to be thrown over on the formation of *his* (R. Churchill's) Govt.' Hamilton Diary, 19 May 1884. Hamilton Mss., 48636 fol. 87.

and walked out on the Deceased Wife's Sister question. 'How near does Randolph Churchill mean to come to your platform?', Chamberlain was asked;[1] this, according to Chamberlain, Churchill had himself answered by inquiring whether in the event of his secession from the Conservatives, the Birmingham Liberals would support him as an independent.[2] Churchill was not the first politician to make himself impossible to his party so that he might thereafter be accepted as indispensable; and his action upon the Franchise bill – all the more so after Salisbury on 10 May secured from the Peers a demand for its rejection – was not that of a statesman whose foresight (*pace* the ambition of a politician) made him promote the Democratic Toryism which the future 'demanded' of the party. Northcote, it may be said, favoured a 'Democratic' (*pace* Fourth party) reading of such a resolution as that favoured by the Edinburgh City Conservative Association, which called for a meeting of the party 'to express approval of extension of the Household Franchise to the Counties, coupled with a proper scheme of redistribution of seats'.[3] But Northcote favoured this reading because 'a *rapprochement* between the Tory Democrats and the Radical Democrats' would assuredly, as he reminded Salisbury, 'affect our relations with the Whigs,...the line of cleavage may alter, and some new adjustment of party forces take place.'[4] As the man who missed the prize which lay within his grasp in the early summer of 1884, Northcote's was the most signal political failure of those months. The undesirability of alienating Whigs and timid Liberals, and the desirability of a fusion from which Chamberlain, Churchill and Parnell would be excluded, were always on Northcote's mind. But this was a reading which lacked imagination, since it failed to envisage Churchill's move towards a 'centre' comprehensive enough to accommodate not only Goschen, Hartington and Henry James, but also Bryce, Forster and H. H. Fowler.

What freedom of movement Churchill enjoyed depended, so contemporaries thought, on the relationship between the two elements in Gladstone's Reform programme. If a Franchise bill was

[1] R. W. Dale to Chamberlain, 14 Mar. 1884. Chamberlain Mss., JC5/20/5.
[2] Dilke to Grant Duff, 13 May 1884. Dilke Mss., 43894 fol. 28.
[3] Northcote to Winn, 3 June 1884. Nostell Mss., 1/115.
[4] Northcote to Salisbury, 3 June 1884. Salisbury Mss., Series E. Northcote's hope that Churchill could be kept 'straight by a little consultation beforehand' makes for sad reading in the light of the 1884 Session's history. Northcote to Winn, 21 Jan. 1884. Nostell Mss., 1/99.

allowed to pass, they thought, the Government could surely be upset by a coalition of 'scheduled' Liberals, Conservatives and Irish, with the settlement of Redistribution falling to a Conservative Ministry, while if the Lords rejected it, they would be allowing a Radical Government to fight a general election on its chosen battle-ground. The flaw in reasoning lay in the danger that Gladstone might still make an intermediate appeal to bastard constituencies who would return a more strongly Radical House of Commons as the counties were swamped with a non-rural element. Indeed, Churchill's promotion of '1886' – either as such or as 1887 posing beneath the Registration mask as '1886' – could not overcome the objection that 'it would be so very easy for [the Government] either to find excuse in the condition of public affairs for no bill at all, or to introduce such a bill as would not be accepted by the various parties and interests in the House of Commons.'[1] It was a risk Churchill had to entertain if he was to counter Salisbury's attempt to turn Reform into a constitutional issue in which he would champion the established order while Gladstone attacked it.

Grey tacked on yet another year – 1887. His amendment was framed in the light of Gladstone's refusal to deliver Franchise as an escrow (its operation dependent upon a future enactment) or to acknowledge any *'sine qua non* as to the provisions of the Bill'.[2] Halifax took it that Grey wanted the operation of the Franchise bill to be delayed until Redistribution had been sanctioned – and, as self-appointed mentor, criticised his amendment as being widely at variance with his intention.[3] Grey, without mentioning Proportional Representation, replied that the amendment would unite in support of a Seats bill all those who were anxious to avoid an election on bastard constituencies – i.e. 'all the Tories & the great majority of Liberals.' Yet when the proposer of an amendment himself sees major faults in the wording and working of that amendment, its Parliamentary life-span is likely to be short; and Grey was not insensitive to the existence of flaws. 'It may be answered...that if this argument is worth anything[,] why not change the date in my amendt. from Jan. 1 1887 to Jan. 1 1886 – & to this argument I confess I have no answer'[4] – at any rate, one

[1] Thomas Salt to Churchill, 24 May 1884. Churchill Mss., 3/397.
[2] Gladstone, 6 May 1884. 3 *Hansard* cclxxxvii. 1491.
[3] Halifax to Albert Grey, 24 Mar. 1884. Grey Mss.
[4] Albert Grey to Halifax, 23 Mar. 1884. Hickleton Mss., A4.84 Part 4.

may say, none which could be stated publicly in the existing Parliament. Imperfections were more blatant. Even if both measures were to pass in 1884, no election could take place under the amended law until 1887, dates becoming in that event restrictive rather than definitive. Conversely, a decision to postpone the operation of the Franchise bill for two-and-a-half years offered no guarantee that Redistribution would then be on the Statute Book. And would not the prospect of two more Sessions encourage malcontents to obstruct, or, so the malcontents might reply, encourage the Government to abstain as long as possible from introducing their Redistribution bill?

Recognition of such defects stirred Grey to shift his ground. He neatly anticipated one of Gladstone's objections with the contention that 'should a Redistribution Bill be passed next year nothing could be more natural than that it should...contain a clause altering the date...from the 1st of January, 1887, to the 1st of November, 1885, or any other date Parliament might think fit.'[1] He was more willing[2] – and this is of greater relevance in establishing motive – to shift his ground in Stanley's direction. A second of Gladstone's objections Grey never did, nor ever could, meet – that his proposal was pregnant with a constitutional nicety, the sitting of Parliament for seven full Sessions. He did not meet that objection because his whole preference for 1887 over and against 1886 was that 'we are *independent* of the Govt. in the one case & not in the other.'[3] He approached Stanley in the hope of finding a date which would unite all who subscribed to the theory and stood by the practical imperative of indivisible Reform. He was met by courteous but complete rebuff: 'I have spoken to Northcote and to some of our friends, and we think on the whole that it is best to stick to my amendment as it stands.'[4] True Whig as he was, having been denied the right and credit of leading, Grey declined to accept the necessity of Tory protection. Perhaps recollection of the treatment accorded to Lowe acted as an awful deterrent.

The breakdown of Grey's effort (he divided against Stanley and withdrew his own amendment on 13 June without putting it to a vote) need detain us little. As has been noted before, potential defaulters to the cause were expending their limited nerve and

[1] 13 June 1884. 3 *Hansard* cclxxxix. 252.
[2] Minto to Gilbert Elliot, 9 June 1884. Minto Mss., Box 172.
[3] Albert Grey to Halifax, 23 Mar. 1884. Hickleton Mss., A4.84 Part 4.
[4] Stanley to Albert Grey, 22 May 1884. Grey Mss.

energy upon Egypt. As regards dates, Stanley had stolen a march on Grey. That he would fatally damage Grey's chance of going to a division had been foreseen by Churchill, Gorst, Goschen and Raikes who all urged Stanley not to do so. His insistence on going ahead notwithstanding marked a deliberate decision by Salisbury (joined perforce by Northcote) to avoid Churchill's unwelcome company – in effect, to deny themselves the possibility of a 'Cave'. It needs stressing that, for his part, Northcote had been as ready to make the main Conservative stand on Grey's as on Stanley's amendment, not on its abstract merits but as being more *politic*,[1] and that Salisbury was constrained, after the Government's acceptance of Fowler's proposal, to demand that Northcote should make it 'unmistakeably clear' that he (Northcote) and the Commons' Conservatives were 'in no degree reconciled to the bill by Gladstone's recent declarations – or the so-called concession about the date.'[2] It also needs stressing that Gladstone needed to decry the amendment on the ground that it would fail to embody what the majority of the House desired to see effected or would be inadequate to avert what they deemed intolerable. Finally it must be stressed that Goschen, in mid-June, saw that the greatest chance of securing the 'general object' of moderation would occur only at a later juncture when the extreme courses pursued by Salisbury and Gladstone would have been seen to be unproductive. Hence too his advice that Grey should withdraw his amendment.[3]

[1] Northcote to Salisbury, 23 Apr. 1884. Salisbury Mss., Series E.
[2] Salisbury to Northcote, 15 June 1884. Iddesleigh Mss., 50020 fol. 73.
[3] 13 June 1884. 3 *Hansard* cclxxxix. 276.

5

FRANCHISE IN THE LORDS: REJECTION

The Conservative side of the House... quite understood the alternative offered to them, to have this Franchise Bill passed without redistribution, so that when redistribution was proposed it could be handed to them, as it were, with a pistol at their heads. That was a question of tactics, and...he must say there was only one method of meeting such tactics. They held the trump card; and, with all respect to 'another place' he trusted that that card would be played.

C. N. Warton, 17 June 1884. 3 *Hansard* cclxxxix. 655.

If 'insulting' prophecies were deemed intolerable by the leader of the Commons, the leader of the Lords resented the Government's attempt to compel the Upper House to pass beneath the 'Caudine Forks'. Doubtless in both cases deeper calculations guided policy.

Balfour, *Retrospect*, p. 185.

IN THE SUMMER OF 1884 Dilke and Morley produced a serviceable Liberal handbook of Conservative pronouncements against franchise extension. In like manner and for the same purpose, the party press, scouring their columns of 'Parliamentary Proceedings', found many explicit squirearchical pronouncements that the more numerous a class was, the more perilous and unconstitutional it was to give it a representation in proportion to its numbers. Anyone who has the time to ferret diligently through *Hansard* may assemble his own clippings, may hold them up to the ridicule of minds numbed by the platitudes of democratic power. He will find, as contemporary Radical politicians and publicists found to their delight, Churchill's shrill denunciation of the agricultural labourer as 'absolutely unfitted for the exercise of the franchise'.[1] He will seize upon a 'class' philosophy and on 'class' amendments; Biddell's proposal to allow a second vote to householders rated above £8 was, after all, a crude, practical deduction from the platitude that 'when political power is given to those with whom physical power rests,...the minority will be placed in a position [against] which they can have no possible appeal'.[2]

[1] 28 Feb. 1884. 3 *Hansard* cclxxxv. 175.
[2] 1 Apr. 1884. 3 *Hansard* cclxxxvi. 1308.

What is of greater moment is not that such sentiments found expression, nor that the example of Ireland and the Conservative identification with Unionism heightened them. Nor is it that county Members who were returned by a propertied, farming electorate, or whose claim to leadership depended on Conservative identification with the landed, agricultural interest, asserted themselves and their claims at this juncture. It is that Conservatives refrained as much as they did in Reform debates from mentioning the franchise itself. It was not until a month after the bill's introduction that Hartington found in Lowther 'the first speaker... who had entered a direct objection to the principle of the extension of the franchise in the Counties';[1] while, on the opposite tack, Hamilton attributed to the dates wrangle in May the great advantage that it drew from several Conservatives acceptance of the principle of equalization between town and county.[2] Simple protests in successive Conservative amendments, against 'Franchise alone' made for dull repetitive debating in the face of Liberal silence, and on the night of 28 April, Conservative inventiveness was exhausted. But again – and here there is no paradox – the important point is that so one-sided a debate should have collapsed on only a single occasion in the course of four months. When dates threatened once more to befuddle and dupe Tories into *believing* in Gladstone's concession, Salisbury was prepared with the strong simplicity of his Plymouth manifesto to reiterate demands for a complete measure and assert the right of the Lords to demand the nation's verdict. In the wake of this entreaty, remaining Opposition 'bridging' amendments were withdrawn or disposed of with commendable haste.

It is true that Disraeli's Ministry during its last days of office in 1880 had been tempted to give franchise extension the go-by and to introduce a Seats bill of meagre, avowedly biased proportions. They would have granted a third (and, under the 1867 minority clause, Conservative) Member to Bradford, Bristol, Newcastle and Sheffield, and to County Cork, Dublin and Kingstown; moreover, they would have created a borough of Accrington so that its Liberal folk might less readily contaminate the whole of North-East Lancashire.[3] But once the 1884 bill was under way, this was (as Salisbury realised, and as Gladstone expressed it in accounting for the languor of debate) 'a *res judicata* – a settled question not to-day

[1] Hartington, 24 Mar. 1884. 3 *Hansard* cclxxxvi. 698.
[2] Hamilton Diary, 24 May 1884. Hamilton Mss., 48636 fol. 93.
[3] Lloyd, *General Election of 1880*, p. 15.

and not to-morrow, perhaps by this Government, perhaps by the next Government before it is six months old – but the question is no less a settled question'.[1]

This needs saying if we are to give a sympathetic consideration both to Salisbury's position (that is to say, to the difficulties of his position) and to his determination to reject the Government measure in the Lords. It needs saying all the more because, even in Cecil family memoirs, there are discreditable cartoons of a mind temporarily crazed: 'Personally, I was entirely with the Liberals', recalled Lady Frances Balfour, of 1884. 'The Tory party have always lost their heads whenever enfranchisement has had to be faced, and have again and again stultified themselves for naught.'[2] It needs saying finally because *The Times*, which Gladstone labelled 'really an anti-reforming paper',[3] conceived of Lords' rejection as possible only in view of the impossibility of forecasting Salisbury's action 'by reference to the considerations that weigh with other men.'[4]

The considerations will, in fact, be seen to have been both politic and politically intelligible, once it is understood that the Conservative leaders had to remain uncommitted to opinions which might divide the party and had to take special pains to avoid unnecessary, specific or ambiguous pledges, if they were to enable a united party both to pass and to keep control of the redistribution question. The stages by which he should lead the Commons' back-benchers to depend upon the Second Chamber were clear to Salisbury: play upon the alternative of effacement for a generation; assure them that the Franchise bill, allowed to take effect without checks and balances, would produce so anomalous an electoral machinery as to deprive Tories of 47 seats upon which they might reasonably depend if 'voting values' were more fairly distributed;[5] hold out the certainty that, thanks to Cabinet dithering in Egypt and over Gordon, the Conservatives might be expected to improve their standing in the House at a dissolution; call in the meantime to the

[1] 7 Apr. 1884. 3 *Hansard* cclxxxvi. 1843.
[2] *Ne Obliviscaris*, Vol. I, p. 407.
[3] Gladstone to Granville, 15 Feb. 1883. *Correspondence*, Vol. II, p. 25.
[4] *The Times*, 19 May 1884, p. 11.
[5] Lady Gwendolen Cecil, *Life of Robert, Marquis of Salisbury* (4 vols., 1921–32), Vol. III, pp. 105–6. Cowen had told Winn that the Parliamentary Liberals were convinced the Lords would give way in November. 'He went on to say, "*I can tell you* if the Lords stand firm *you will get a dissolution* but if they don't your party is done for"'. Winn to Salisbury, 1 Sept. 1884. Salisbury Mss., Series E.

present electorate for a 'thorough and far-reaching' measure of redistribution which might protect 'the conservative classes' and 'the conservative school of thought all through the country';[1] finally, remind likely defaulters – those who had shied before a crisis on Arrears – that it was absolutely 'vital...to the party that a question of such supreme importance to its future welfare shall be referred to a more equitable tribunal' than the present Commons.[2]

And was not the Queen 'prepared to play her part boldly'?[3] She had required a 'little forewarning, so as to be fortified to a certain extent when the Crisis arrives'. This, as an 'old and experienced friend', Manners had provided. Unable 'to contemplate without apprehension and deep sympathy the position of the Sovereign under such a Polity' as would follow from the Lords' now yielding, he was explicit in his prognosis: the Queen would find herself face to face with a Commons swayed by 'some one clever orator', while constitutional Government itself would be rendered impossible 'except by sufferance of Mr. Parnell'. The Queen, of course, having listened to this depressing sermon, 'quite comprehend[ed] now the condition of affairs,...wh. is as much as to say, there is life in the old hound yet.'[4] The Government's decision to ask for a prorogation and an autumn Session instead of dissolving in the event of the Lords rejecting the bill was thus highly unpalatable to her. It might be added that (independently even of the Franchise question) the Queen was passing through a particularly dyspeptic phase. 'Egyptian tummy', a trying and Liberal affliction, was at its worst. Gladstone's proposal to make Malcolm MacColl a Canon of Ripon

[1] Salisbury, at Plymouth. *The Times*, 6 June 1884, p. 12.
[2] Salisbury to Cairns, 4 July 1884. Cairns Mss., PRO. 30/15/6, fol. 148.
[3] Manners to Salisbury, 14 July 1884. Belvoir Mss.
[4] Colonel Charles Lindsay (from Balmoral) to Manners, 15 June 1884; Manners to Lindsay, 17 June 1884; Lindsay to Manners, 19 June 1884. Belvoir Mss. Lindsay was Groom in Waiting to the Queen and former Conservative MP for Abingdon. Both sides in their dealings with the Queen adopted an identical tone. See, e.g., Gladstone's Memo. of 25 August, deprecating Salisbury's having brought the hereditary principle into direct conflict (which it could not afford) with the representative power: 'Separable as the subject of the Monarchy may be in argument from that of the Peerage, it is a momentous practical inquiry whether the Monarchy isolated and laid bare will have the same securities, as the Monarchy associated with a gradation of kindred institutions, has hitherto enjoyed'. Gladstone Mss., 44768 fol. 109. From which premise there could, in Carlyle's parody of the Prime Minister's manner, be only one practical deduction – 'Madam, I find that popular opinion is so matured against the continuance of an hereditary monarchy, that it becomes my painful duty to cut off yr. M.'s head.' Hamilton Diary, 3 Oct. 1884. Hamilton Mss., 48637 fol. 107.

was extremely irritating.[1] Harcourt, who rarely came in for special disfavour, found himself under royal pressure to hang a sixteen-year-old for the murder of her illegitimate child – an act of official barbarity which, so he had to point out, would spell the doom of capital punishment.[2] And when the Queen was subjected to hissing at Paddington Station – which confirmed her worst fears about the logical outcome of a Gladstone-provoked 'constitutional crisis' agitation – Harcourt was left to explain that the hissing occurred because of police rigour in holding back the excited crowd.[3]

An 'early dissolution, by hook or by crook'[4] was comprehensible policy – particularly in view of the feeling among local Liberal associations that it would be better to avoid an election until 'Egypt' had been purged from the popular mind.[5] Given the Queen's feelings, it was on the cards. Even the Nile promised a simultaneous climacteric: the *Daily Telegraph*, on the morning of 7 July, splashed an (unsubstantiated) 'Fall of Khartoum' headline.[6] The 8th, the day of the Lords' division, saw the revived circulation of rumours that Parliament would be dissolved immediately the Peers rejected the bill.[7]

'Will it get through the House of Commons? It ought not *alone* to pass the Lords.'[8] The ease with which Cranbrook moved from idle speculation upon a matter beyond Conservative control to confidence that Conservatives could determine the bill's fate is the best proof of the bicameral nature of the Reform crisis. Two further points need be made before the historian joins the chorus of 'moderate' contemporaries who were only too ready to condemn Salisbury's collision course. The first is this – that, in May, whatever the pressures known to be working to his advantage (i.e. the threat of disorder arising from Churchill's challenge *via* the National Union), Salisbury afforded his ex-Cabinet and the front-benchers in both Houses the opportunity of *proposing* action. The Commoners proposed Lords' rejection, to which 'all the Peers present, Cairns, Richmond, Northumberland, Carnarvon, Cadogan &c. assented, Beauchamp alone suggesting as an alternative postponing the 2nd reading for a month to give [the] Government time to bring in a

---

[1] Hamilton Diary, 7 July 1884. Hamilton Mss., 48637 fol. 9.
[2] Lewis Harcourt Journal, 25 June 1884. Harcourt Mss.
[3] Dodson Cabinet Minutes, 14 July 1884. Monk Bretton Mss., 62.
[4] Salisbury to Richmond, 14 July 1884. Goodwood Mss., 872/P18.
[5] *Pall Mall Gazette*, 2 July 1884, p. 1; 8 July 1884, p. 3.
[6] 7 July 1884, p. 5.   [7] *Pall Mall Gazette*, 8 July 1884, p. 3.
[8] Cranbrook Diary, 29 Feb. 1884. Cranbrook Mss., T501/299 fol. 176.

Redistribution Bill if they were so minded.'[1] (And who, it might not irreverently be asked, was Beauchamp among so many?) Further, the vital question of the mode of rejection was left open for close on two months – which was long enough for the development of a 'moderate' revulsion against the collision course if one was going to develop. But unity was never disturbed – again, one may guess, because 'moderation' was seen to be Churchill's game. 'As to the House of Lords and the Franchise Bill', Smith reported to Harrowby in the second half of June, 'there is but one opinion on *our* bench and that is that they should carry out the policy embodied in Lord John Manners' amendment on the[ir] second reading.'[2] Northumberland, Abercorn, Bury, Cadogan, Cairns and Cranbrook met to settle the details.[3] Immediately after that conference, Balfour sent Austin 'notes...represent[ing] accurately and in detail the action ...which the leaders desire should be followed by the Lords', requesting that Austin 'press this advice' in the *Standard*:[4]

1. The Lords should be recommended to avoid the mistake of amendments in Committee and to deal with the Bill on the second reading.

2. But they should avoid with great care the mistake of offering a blank resistance to the bill – or resistance which can be mistaken for resistance to the extension of the franchise.

3. They should object to the second reading by moving a counter resolution: a course for which many precedents could be found. It was in this way that Lord J. Russell turned out Mr. Disraeli's reform Bill in 1859.

4. The resolution should bear on the forefront a statement that the Lords are favourable to a great and full measure for the extension of the franchise; But they should make it clear that an incomplete measure; – a measure which while giving large enfranchisement makes no provision for a just redistribution; takes no security that the result shall be an accurate representation of the nation, and does not even offer the moderate, and perhaps doubtful, safeguard which would have been provided by such an amendmt. as that of Colonel Stanley; – cannot be assented to by them.

At the full meeting of Conservative Peers on 1 July, the Second Reading 'wrecking' amendment bore Cairns' signature. Richmond defended himself against the allegation of willingness to pass a simple Franchise bill, and such 'feeble remonstrance' as was heard

---

[1] Manners to Henry Manners, 11 May 1884. Belvoir Mss.
[2] Smith to Harrowby, 20 June 1884. Harrowby Mss., 2nd Ser., Vol. 54, fol. 219.
[3] Salisbury to Henry Manners, 16 June 1884. Salisbury Mss., Series D.
[4] Balfour to Austin, 22 June 1884. Austin Mss.

came from Jersey, Ravensworth, Wemyss and Norton – the latter by proxy since a Railway Committee, clashing with the Arlington Street meeting, was thought more important.[1] Again, regard must be had to pressures: Halifax, echoing Balfour's lament of 1883, singled out the belief that Peers could not be relied upon in August to attend, vote and insist on the reinsertion of a 'simultaneous operation' amendment should the Commons have thrown out the Lords' Committee clause.[2] But what Salisbury had done between May and July was to anticipate charges, sound out opinion, declare his intentions in deference to opinion and see whether *la nuit porte conseil* – a form of insurance which is intelligible when viewed in the light of the events of the three previous summers.

The second comment to be made is that although Conservatives followed Salisbury, neither he nor they believed that they were rushing headlong to destruction. In November 1883, Hartington publicly ridiculed the naivety of the Leeds Conference's electoral calculations: 'Do you suppose that there does not exist in this old and still highly Conservative country a great affection and a great respect for an ancient institution such as the House of Lords'?[3] Or, as another Whig put it eight months later, 'there is certainly no revolutionary spirit in the country at present, nor a state of things in the least resembling that of 1832, to which the Lords for the sake of peace & order would be forced to bow'.[4] If Whigs thought thus, it is hardly surprising to find a Tory rural Member neither sorry nor afraid to accept Bright's challenge and fight the next election upon 'House of Lords, or no House of Lords'. Manners estimated that once clear proof had been given that the Peers 'don't mean to yield the point in dispute in the Autumn', *The Times* might be induced to 'execute a *demi-volte*, and appeal to the Government not to be too stiff.'[5] Harrowby, whose sense of conservatism merits the utmost respect, went further still. He dreaded the constitutional question being allowed to 'drag on' or 'a new generation of Peers growing up, without what you may call a fresh mandate from the Country, cowed & avoiding public life, & only occasionally showing their power by foolish votes on petty questions like that of pigeon shooting'; and if, as seemed beyond doubt, the 'position of the

---

[1] *The Times*, 2 July 1884, p. 9; Norton to Wemyss, 1 July 1884. Salisbury Mss., Series E.
[2] Earl Grey to Richmond, 5 July 1884. Goodwood Mss., 872/P5.
[3] Hartington, at Manchester. *The Times*, 28 Nov. 1883, p. 7.
[4] Elliot Diary, 8 July 1884. Diaries, Vol. 10.
[5] Manners to Salisbury, 25 July 1884. Belvoir Mss.

H. of L. must be settled soon, after Gladstone's persistent endeavours to reduce it to nothing...it is well that the country's opinion should be taken respecting that position, on a great Constitutional question.'[1] Salisbury had asked of the Commons Conservatives that they should 'not forget to give the Franchise Bill a good parting kick' on Third Reading, 'especially dwelling on the utter worthlessness of the change of date as any security.'[2] Northcote, in the event, muffed his lines. The Opposition benches emptied and Gladstone seized the moment to place on record that the bill had passed its final stage *nemine contradicente*, dissentient mumblings from Pell and C. S. Read never reaching the Speaker's ear. Even Hamilton found Gladstone's manner in 'speed[ing] farewell' to the measure 'more rattling perhaps than judicious'[3] and likely 'to put the backs up of the proud Tory Peers'.[4] There ought to be no doubt as to Gladstone's mood. More than a month before, he had warned privately that if the Lords 'do carry out their threats they will not hear the end of it in a hurry.'[5] Buckle excused Gladstone to Churchill: in view of Salisbury's stumping the country and of the Commons' speeches by Balfour, Cross and Lowther, it would have been 'affectation' on Gladstone's part to have ignored the bill's probable fate in the Upper House;[6] while Gladstone excused himself to the Queen as having spoken 'with a view to the peaceful maintenance of our Parliamentary Constitution.'[7] Members of his own party were less responsive to the semantic distinction between candid warning and prophetic menace. They would have accepted the historian's verdict that 'the most revolutionary aspect' of 1832 was 'not the Reform Bill...but the coercion of the House of Lords.'[8] Thus when Gladstone, pleading for the Archbishop of Canterbury's vote, proposed to refer to this aspect of the 1832

[1] Harrowby to Smith, 13 June 1884. Harrowby Mss., 3rd Ser., Vol. 65, fol. 417.
[2] Salisbury to Northcote, 25 June 1884. Iddesleigh Mss., 50020 fol. 75.
[3] Hamilton Diary, 27 June 1884. Hamilton Mss., 48636 fol. 136. Small wonder that a Tory partisan should conclude that 'if ever there was a speech less calculated than another to obtain the end which it seemed to have in view, it was the speech which the Prime Minister had delivered that evening.' Barttelot, 26 June 1884. 3 *Hansard* cclxxxix. 1448.
[4] Hamilton Diary, 30 June 1884. Hamilton Mss., 48637 fol. 2.
[5] Hamilton Diary, 19 May 1884. Hamilton Mss., 48636 fol. 87.
[6] Buckle to Churchill, 27 June 1884. Churchill Mss., 3/417.
[7] Gladstone to the Queen, 30 June 1884. Philip Guedalla (ed.), *The Queen and Mr. Gladstone, 1880–98* (1933), p. 279.
[8] Norman Gash, *Reaction and Reconstruction in English Politics, 1832–52* (Oxford, 1965), p. 30.

story,[1] Granville urged that he remove from the draft what could only be construed as 'a distinct threat coming from so powerful a prime minister as yourself.'[2] Gladstone's talk of a dissolution forced by the Lords as creating a precedent against Liberty 'worse than anything since [the] beginning of reign of Geo. III',[3] and his open characterization of Salisbury as a 'learn nothing & forget everything' Bourbon,[4] could only convey to the intelligent mind that 'he was not easily to be kept back by the Lords from getting his way, & that they must look out for the consequences.'[5]

The existence of an unreformed and irresponsible Second Chamber, where the Liberal party could rarely count on the support of more than 30 Peers apart from Government members, explacemen or recipients of favours,[6] always had advantages for a Liberal Ministry. In the context of 1884, the only objection Acland heard amongst fellow Liberals to Rathbone's pamphlet on Parliamentary efficiency was that 'it would make the Upper House too powerful.'[7] Rosebery's tentative attempt to 'galvanise the House of Lords into usefulness'[8] – by moving for a Select Committee to alter its constitution and composition – though warmly greeted by a number of Tories, provoked Granville's hostility. It was, indeed, not Salisbury alone who had 'the bit between his teeth'.[9] When the Lords acted, there was only the slightest Cabinet hesitation before '*throw[ing] overboard everything in the way of legislation*', so as to 'emphasize the mischievous action...in the most distinct manner before the country', and deprive opponents of 'every opportunity to harry us on miscellaneous subjects and distract attention from the main point on which we wish to fix the [public] mind.'[10]

In the House of Lords at five o'clock on the afternoon of 1 July, Cairns gave notice of the Conservative amendment. As advised by

[1] Gladstone to Benson, 2 July 1884. Gladstone Mss., 44109 fol. 95.
[2] Granville to Gladstone, 4 July 1884. *Correspondence*, Vol. II, p. 209.
[3] Dodson Cabinet Minutes, 9 July 1884. Monk Bretton Mss., 62.
[4] Gladstone Notes for Foreign Office Speech, 10 July 1884. Gladstone Mss., 44768 fol. 72.
[5] Elliot Diary, 10 July 1884. Diaries, Vol. 10.
[6] Hamilton Diary, 16 Feb. 1884. Hamilton Mss., 48635 fol. 96.
[7] Acland to Rathbone, 22 July 1884. Printed as Preface to William Rathbone, *Reform in Parliamentary Business: House of Lords* (1884). The article was reprinted from the *Fortnightly Review* of October 1881.
[8] Cooper to Rosebery, 19 May 1884. Rosebery Mss., Box 9.
[9] Hamilton Diary, 8 July 1884. Hamilton Mss., 48637 fol. 11.
[10] Harcourt to Gladstone, 9 July 1884. Gladstone Mss., 44199 fol. 75.

Brand, his former Chief Whip,[1] Gladstone immediately set about reducing the Tory majority and securing the episcopate: he sent an appraisal of the situation to Canterbury and circulated it to all the Bishops together with personal covering notes. These, if they said 'exactly the right thing to everybody',[2] said nothing of the point at issue: Redistribution was not mentioned. The portrait painted was in essence that presented to the Commons in February, of 'a Bill large indeed but studiously moderate, which in Great Britain enfranchises classes in the counties that have already been beneficially enfranchised in the towns, and only adds, by what is called the service franchise, a class which of all others is most likely to be swayed by the influence of property'; while of Ireland, in the light of more recent events, 'I say nothing, because the assailants in the Lords do not venture to say that she could be excluded.'[3] But if, in soliciting their votes, Gladstone refrained judiciously from dwelling on the advantage which the Bishops would derive from ranging themselves 'on the side of the people',[4] that message was implicit. Ely acknowledged the worth to the Church of a popular alliance.[5] Manchester, echoing Gladstone, was filled with apprehension at the Lords' 'infatuation' and their setting themselves 'practically against a measure which is demanded not only by popular feeling, but by the equities of the situation.'[6] Durham promised to record his first political vote – as an advertisement that 'I for one do not distrust the people'.[7] Truro acknowledged receipt of a £20 cheque and entered Gladstone's name on the list of subscribers to the Cathedral fund.[8]

As the favourable responses came in, his secretary could never recall having seen Gladstone 'more pleased about anything.'[9] Even before the Lords' division, he was using the likely adhesion of 'various conservative bishops...in great dismay at this wild proceeding of Lord Salisbury's' as a stick with which to goad other waverers back into the fold.[10] In the division, only Gloucester

---

[1] Hampden to Gladstone, 4 July 1884. Gladstone Mss., 44195 fol. 177. Brand had taken the customary Peerage upon his retirement as Speaker earlier in 1884.   [2] Hamilton Diary, 2 July 1884. Hamilton Mss., 48637 fol. 5.
[3] Gladstone to Benson, 2 July 1884. Draft. Gladstone Mss., 44109 fol. 95.
[4] Hamilton Diary, 2 July 1884. Hamilton Mss., 48637 fol. 5.
[5] Ely to Gladstone, 3 July 1884. Gladstone Mss., 44487 fol. 28.
[6] Manchester to Gladstone, 2 July 1884. Gladstone Mss., 44487 fol. 11.
[7] Durham to Gladstone, 5 July 1884. Gladstone Mss., 44487 fol. 47.
[8] Truro to Hamilton, 3 July 1884. Gladstone Mss., 44487 fol. 35.
[9] Hamilton Diary, 3 July 1884. Hamilton Mss., 48637 fol. 6.
[10] Gladstone to Tennyson, 6 July 1884. Gladstone Mss., 44547 fol. 80.

(reputed to favour the ducking of Joseph Arch in a horse-pond)[1] stood behind Cairns – a 'very unusual preponderance [being] given by the Church to the Liberal side', as the innocent by-stander commented.[2] This outcome, wholly unexpected by Salisbury,[3] was particularly galling in the light of his instruction to Richmond to 'keep the Bishops as straight as you can',[4] and is doubly ironical when one remembers that on 21 March a Liberal private Member's motion to deprive the Bishops of their seats in the Upper House had been defeated by only 11 votes in a House of 285.

As to the Parliamentary proceedings of July, Cowen was of course absolutely right in concluding that 'this is the secret of all the controversy. The two parties are manoeuvring for the best ground of battle.'[5] The crisis was created by political pressures within both parties. Dilke wrote indeed not of a 'crisis' but of 'what was called the crisis',[6] and Argyll of a situation where 'reasonable methods of Procedure [were] sacrificed to the need – *real or supposed* – of dexterous tactics, in the management of opposing factions.'[7] That said, it remains misleading to distinguish between crisis, manufactured crisis and the illusion of crisis. All three are merged when there is sufficient weight of opinion to make a crisis out of what need never have become critical at all, and the lines are blurred even when the momentum is supplied by an illusion. Just as in 1867 a bill emerged which the majority of the House had not desired, so in the summer of 1884 no method was found of effecting what the majority on both sides wished to see effected. It did not need 'a student, & a completely sequestered one' to see that 'the controversy...is one over party tactics almost exclusively',[8] but it was 'one of those speculations left to philosophers remote from the busy scene...whether some middle course might not have been hit upon had both parties been really anxious to settle the question on a mutually satisfactory basis'.[9] Speculation would be idle – that is to say historically meaningless as not advancing political understanding – for neither Salisbury nor Gladstone strove in July after that 'middle course'. For the latter,

[1] Shane Leslie, *Henry Edward Manning: his Life and Labours* (1921), p. 80.
[2] Elliot Diary, 8 July 1884. Diaries. Vol. 10.
[3] Salisbury to Manners, 12 July 1884. Belvoir Mss.
[4] Salisbury to Richmond, 7 July 1884. Goodwood Mss., 872/P10.
[5] Cowen to J. P. Taylor, 22 July 1884. Cowen Mss., F50.20.
[6] Dilke Memoir, 5 July 1884. Dilke Mss., 43938 fol. 194.
[7] Argyll to Gladstone, 11 July 1884. Gladstone Mss., 44105 fol. 170. (My italics.)
[8] Sir G. Birdwood to Salisbury, 17 July 1884. Salisbury Mss., Series E.
[9] *Annual Register*, p. 144.

a major victory was secured when he was in a position to ask rhetorically of the more troublesome 'bridge-builders' whether a Second Reading majority of 130 in the Commons was to count for less than that of 59 Peers.

Gladstone's keynote was crystal clear: the duty of preventing conflict between the Houses by all reasonable means was 'the most sacred duty incumbent upon us on this occasion, *next to* the great business of enfranchising a vast mass of the population.'[1] Granted such a table of priority, his action during the last stages of the bill in the Commons and during July becomes comprehensible. Several incidents may be detailed. Gladstone graciously accepted Churchill's suggestion that provision should immediately be made for the appointment of a Boundary Commission, while admitting that the Cabinet had not 'actually arrived at a conclusion upon that point.' It is less material that the subject had never been raised there than that the attempt, by such a commitment to detach Churchill, his friends and any 'weak kneed' Peers, rested upon a delusion as to procedural sequences, since the Redistribution scheme was an essential prerequisite to any examination of the borough boundaries affected by it.[2] In Cabinet, Gladstone pursued a line of unmistakeable intransigence. At the Report stage, Raikes and Smith had asked how the Government could expect the House to believe that there would be time for Redistribution, a Boundary Commission and a new Registration in accordance with the new constituencies before 1 January 1886: in Dodson's shorthand, 'Answer is, let them pass Redn. promptly – or let there be a Regn Bill ad hoc.' Again, left to choose between 'Rejection on 2nd Reading & cry agst. Lords' on the one hand and, on the other, 'failure of Cairns' amendment & a vicious clause in Commee', Gladstone plumped unhesitatingly for the former, though the result of the second would 'somehow be a compromise mainly in our favour, *& the passing of the Bill.*'[3] When Jersey and Brownlow approached Derby

---

[1] Gladstone, 26 June 1884. 3 *Hansard* cclxxxix. 1438. (My italics.)

[2] Churchill–Gladstone–Northcote exchange, 17 June 1884. 3 *Hansard* cclxxxix. 644–6. Lambert was again at hand belatedly to correct Gladstone by reference to the precedent of 1831–2: Commissioners concerned themselves solely with matters of detail arising in separate localities from the Government's predetermined proposal; their role was not to supply materials, principles or particulars from which the Cabinet might readily deduce a Redistribution schedule. Lambert Memo., 'Redistribution. Inquiries in relation to the Reform Bills of 1831–32', 19 July 1884. Gladstone Mss., 44629 fol. 97.

[3] Dodson Cabinet Minutes, 5 July 1884. Monk Bretton Mss., 62. (My italics.)

on 7 July with a view to resurrecting something akin to 'Albert Grey', Derby was right in judging that it was 'too late for anything of the sort' as far as Gladstone was concerned.[1] On the 8th, Gladstone agreed to Granville proposing an identical resolution in both Houses '*provided* you find any encouragement'. He did this not because such a resolution (confirmed by a joint address to the Crown) did in fact strengthen security for the passage of Redistribution before the Franchise bill should take effect, but because 'there can be no harm in your making the offer'.[2] The same day, he declined to accept Cairns' offer to be satisfied if the Government admitted an amendment to bring the bill into operation on 1 January 1886 or such earlier date as might be named in an Act to be passed in the next Session.[3] Cairns was offending against Salisbury's dictum that it was for the Government to propose whatever terms they might and for the Opposition simply to accept or reject.[4] He was holding out a compromise which some confused MPs and Peers might think the Government had already adopted in accepting Fowler's 1885 clause. He was known to be working with Richmond 'behind Ld. Salisbury's back, [having] begged that nothing might on any account be said to Lord S.';[5] Gladstone spurned them. The intransigence became ever more marked: after the Lords' division, Gladstone reported to the Queen that 'the present posture of the affair does not allow of any opening for a proceeding which would imply going back from the late vote',[6] and to Ponsonby that, having favoured the plan of giving 'all possible solemnity to our pledge [, the Cabinet] do not see what just claim there is to more.'[7] The calculation behind this intransigence was that, without the Government having to yield an inch, rank and file Tory Peers would desert Salisbury even if he decided to treat the bill as summarily in November.[8]

There is every reason to infer that in subsequently taking up

[1] Derby to Granville, 7 July 1884. Granville Mss., PRO. 30/29/120.
[2] Gladstone to Granville, 8 July 1884. *Correspondence*, Vol. II, p. 211. (My italics.)
[3] Granville Memo. of conversation with Cairns, 8 July 1884. Granville Mss., PRO. 30/29/149; Cairns to Salisbury, 11 July 1884. Salisbury Mss., Series E.
[4] Salisbury to Cairns, 4 July 1884. Cairns Mss., PRO. 30/15/6, fol. 148.
[5] Hamilton Diary, 8 July 1884. Hamilton Mss., 48637 fol. 11.
[6] Gladstone to the Queen, 9 July 1884. Cab. 41/18/37.
[7] Gladstone Cabinet Minutes, 9 July 1884. Gladstone Mss., 44645 fol. 146. Ponsonby had arrived at Downing Street while the Cabinet was in session.
[8] Dodson Cabinet Minutes, 9 July 1884. Monk Bretton Mss., 62.

Wemyss' resolution,[1] the Cabinet saw themselves as surrendering nothing. They agreed to 'anticipate' the Session of 1885 by a meeting of Parliament in November (Wemyss had originally proposed October) when Redistribution would be introduced immediately, but such agreement was dependent upon the prior passage of the Franchise bill. Their acceptance – and this was the attraction – put Salisbury in the unenviable position of having to explain why he refused to agree that the present Parliament should be allowed to continue for two further Sessions which, on the most unfavourable reading, Cairns had eight days before held to be adequate security. Salisbury was indeed driven by Cairns' 'unfortunate' lapse[2] into issuing a seven-line Whip against the proposal and into spending the evening of 16 July in an attempt to persuade Erskine May that Wemyss' motion was out of order.[3] 'But he would not have it.'[4] Nor was this surprising: May's *Constitutional History* headed Gladstone's list of manuals which proselytised towards sober, moderate Liberalism.[5] By 17 July, however, Gladstone was reduced to devil's advocacy in face of a similar compromise from Winmarleigh: 'You might take conscientious objection to parts of a diversified & complicated scheme – or you might say, this is all very well, but may not the House of Commons alter it? If you are, on the simple production of a Redistribution Bill, to be tied to go on with the Franchise Bill, that is rather like slavery indeed.'[6]

The proposals which filled these days were not all made in the interests of accommodation. Henry Northcote's was designed not for Government acceptance but to buttress and define the Conservative position by offering co-operation in an autumn Session whose two months might be devoted entirely to Redistribution.[7] Carnarvon's was put forward in the hope that Gladstone would reject it as inconveniently prolonging a Session over two years – a rejection

---

[1] Wemyss gave notice of his resolution in the Lords on 14 July: 'That this House is prepared to proceed with the consideration of the Representation of the People Bill, on the understanding that an humble Address shall be presented to Her Majesty, humbly praying that Her Majesty to summon Parliament to assemble in the early part of the autumn for the purpose of considering the Redistribution Bill...' 3 *Hansard* ccxc. 873.

[2] Northcote to Salisbury, 16 July 1884. Salisbury Mss., Series E.

[3] i.e. on the ground that it related to a bill awaiting its Second Reading, still alive and to be kept alive until joined by Redistribution.

[4] Salisbury to Cairns, 17 July 1884. Cairns Mss., PRO. 30/15/6, fol. 154.

[5] Gladstone to MacColl, 30 Jan. 1884. Gladstone Mss., 44547 fol. 35.

[6] Gladstone to Winmarleigh, 17 July 1884. Gladstone Mss., 44547 fol. 84.

[7] Henry Northcote to Salisbury, 14 July 1884. Salisbury Mss., Series E.

which, Carnarvon assumed, 'wd. greatly strengthen our position with the country'.[1] In a situation where, for the leaders on both sides, 'concession' amendments had no other purpose than to 'read well at all events',[2] it is not surprising that back-benchers, some of whom could read, tried to do what the leaders left the impression of wanting. Nor is it surprising that they failed in their attempts. The movements of some of the would-be mediators are readily traced. In the case of others, documentation is fragmentary or confused. Still more backstairs conversations were presumably never committed to paper, and here even limited conjecture is rarely justified. Before the Lords' vote, Wolff, as Churchill's emissary, had (so he subsequently recorded) 'held more than one interview with Mr. Goschen & Lord Hartington in the hope of striking out some method of compromise or conciliation. On one of these occasions Lord Hartington', who certainly did not relish the prospect of an autumn of protracted antagonism, 'had expressed a cordial wish for cooperation with Lord R.C. & ourselves.'[3] There are corroborative hints in the *Standard* and *Manchester Guardian*;[4] in the Commons Goschen had advertised his services. Wolff's tale is plausible but we know nothing about the substance of such exchanges, nor who was involved in them. Was James? Were Granville, Derby and Selborne? Was Forster? Political diplomacy involving an ever-widening circle inevitably poses more questions than the surviving evidence can possibly answer.

The roll-call of those who may have been involved impresses by weight both of name and of number. What must always be borne in mind is that many were fumbling (to the annoyance of their leaders) and that many who, like Rosebery,[5] seized the opportunity for self-advancement, were disinclined to concert efforts or were oblivious of the efforts of others. What came to be regarded as the most notorious bridging project of the Recess – Cowper's – was the product of idle, politically innocent reflection. The former Irish viceroy, so far from plotting anything, disliked the 'idea of compromises behind the scenes', was 'quite out of the way of hearing what goes on' in Switzerland, and had indeed to ask whether similar attempts were being made.[6]

[1] Carnarvon to Richmond, 15 July 1884. Goodwood Mss., 872/P19.
[2] Northcote to Salisbury, 16 July 1884. Salisbury Mss., Series E. (My italics.)
[3] Wolff Memo., 13 Nov. 1884. Churchill Mss., 4/492.
[4] *Standard*, 8 July 1884, p. 5; *Manchester Guardian*, 9 July 1884, p. 5.
[5] Reay to Rosebery, 12 July 1884. Rosebery Mss., Box 34.
[6] Cowper to Elliot, 23 Aug. 1884. Elliot Mss., Bundle 32.

155

THE POLITICS OF REFORM 1884

Activity before the vote of 8 July reflected the opinion that Salisbury's proposed mode of rejection was needlessly estranging potential allies. Whig support was self-evidently, to Hicks Beach, a 'good thing',[1] and Whigs were there for the asking. Wemyss, who 'hate[d] Gladstone & all his works not excepting his last revolutionary Reform Bill',[2] Halifax, who invoked 'God's...help to save us from an agitation all summoned against our House',[3] Bath, Fitzwilliam, Grey, Shaftesbury and Somerset – all betrayed the same perturbation. All preferred an Instruction (equivalent to Stanley's amendment) on going into Committee; none anticipated 'the least danger that peers enough wd not attend to support it';[4] all backed their fears with the promise that Wemyss' Instruction 'would place the Govt. in a great[er] difficulty'[5] than a wrecking amendment to the Franchise bill on its Second Reading. But the sense that Salisbury was in error was not confined to these Whigs who doubted the possibility of controlling an agitation and who saw 'the dethronement of the House of Lords [as] fraught with incalculable evils.'[6]

Salisbury's post was heavy with warnings of popular stupidity and the need for impossibly speedy public enlightenment if Redistribution was to be taken to mean something more than that conservative politicians wished to cage the voting millions for their own advantage. 'Even at an ordinary London dinner', it was Harrowby's observation, 'you will find half the guests perfectly unconscious of the reasons why [it] is matter of the gravest importance....The vocabulary of the mass of [electors] is so limited that half of *our* best speeches are absolutely Greek to them. Not so those of Bright & his kin.'[7] It was for Conservatives to explain and, so ran the doleful refrain of platform experience, 'the party which has to explain something is lost.'[8] Churchill put it to Edward Cook of the *Pall Mall Gazette* that Salisbury's course threatened to obliterate from the public mind much of the mud which had been thrown at the Government over the previous four years; but if he was 'downright afraid of fighting on [this] issue',

[1] Beach to Salisbury, 19 June 1884. St. Aldwyn Mss., PCC/30.
[2] Wemyss to Salisbury, 1 July 1884. Salisbury Mss., Series E.
[3] Halifax to Richmond, 1 July 1884. Goodwood Mss., 872/P13.
[4] Grey to Richmond, 5 July 1884. Goodwood Mss., 872/P5.
[5] Hamilton Diary, 1 July 1884. Hamilton Mss., 48637 fol. 4.
[6] Lady Sophia Palmer to Elliot, 23 July 1884. Elliot Mss., Bundle 32.
[7] Harrowby to Smith, 13 June 1884. Harrowby Mss., 2nd Ser., Vol. 65, fol. 417.
[8] Sir G. Birdwood to Salisbury, 17 July 1884. Salisbury Mss., Series E.

156

it was from fear not (as with the Whigs) of social convulsion, so much as of the first fruits of such action – the aggrieved hostility towards the Conservatives of newly enfranchised voters.[1] What ushered in a new phase was neither Salisbury's decision to fight on the Second Reading nor the Conservative majority there, but Gladstone's subsequent revelation that there had been inter-party negotiations on the night of the division. He told a Liberal party meeting at the Foreign Office on 10 July that the Government had offered to present a joint Lords/Commons resolution to the Queen, pledging the Government to introduce a Redistribution bill next Session, and to make every effort to pass it. He laid 'great stress on the "lever" argument. . .considering what a field for talk [Redistribution] would offer, unless there [was] some real induce-ment to the House to pass such a measure.' Salisbury, however, he claimed, had refused to negotiate 'with a rope round his neck'.[2]

Granville was taken aback; Cairns and Salisbury would retort, as they did, that 'you have not only made public private com-munications, but you have represented yourselves as the only conciliatory people, making a proposal in imaginary words, and supplying our counter proposals.'[3] But what was more significant than Salisbury's indignant declaration that the contravention of political etiquette made 'all such communications impossible for the future',[4] was the belated awareness on the part of Argyll, Grey, Halifax and Richmond that the disjunction of measures was a matter of deliberate policy. If Gladstone's was an attempt to create commotion among rank and file Conservative Peers, who might complain that they ought to have been consulted about the joint address proposal,[5] it misfired. Minto saw 'gross mismanagement on the part of the Govt. people'.[6] Lord Grey was more positive. Having previously accepted Gladstone's argument as to the impossibility of an omnibus measure on the ground that Gladstone himself believed 'Franchise alone' to be in practice 'very wrong',[7] he now concluded that 'the real object of keeping back the redistri-butn bill was to place the H. of Lords under duress when it comes to be passed'. Though still sore that the Lords had failed to take

[1] Milner to Goschen, 21 July 1884. Milner Mss., Box 182.
[2] Hamilton Diary, 10 July 1884. Hamilton Mss., 48637 fol. 14.
[3] Granville to Selborne, 11 July 1884. Granville Mss., PRO. 30/29/141.
[4] Salisbury to Carnarvon, 11 July 1884. Salisbury Mss., Series D.
[5] The Times, 11 July 1884, p. 9.
[6] Minto to Gilbert Elliot, 13 July 1884. Minto Mss., Box 172.
[7] Earl Grey to Richmond, 5 July 1884. Goodwood Mss., 872/P5.

up his suspending clause, he advised Richmond to 'enter into no negotiations or communications with them whatever' since what 'has just happened proves that they are not to be trusted.'[1] Before the Lords' vote, the *Pall Mall Gazette* had forecast the likelihood of a settlement either by means of an autumn Session as suggested by Churchill, or as a result of a Government decision to accept Albert Grey's '1887';[2] immediately afterwards, and in view of the 'astonishingly small' Conservative majority, the *Manchester Guardian* predicted Government acceptance of Stanley's clause.[3] Such hopes were falsified. Gladstone's Foreign Office address and his subsequent Commons' announcement that the autumn Session would be devoted to the Franchise bill alone, aroused in such moderates as Whitbread the sense that action had to be taken against Salisbury *and* Gladstone. Hence his intimation to Churchill, who reported it to Smith, who in turn passed on the news to Northcote, 'that it was probable or at least possible that a compromise might be made on Albert Grey's lines.'[4] Hence too Grey's letter to *The Times*, pleading for the revival of his amendment.[5]

Argyll was assured by Lady Salisbury that her husband *simply* required to be 'satisfied on the Redistribution question.'[6] MacColl, likewise, trotted between Arlington Street and 'Number 10', declaring to Salisbury and Gladstone in turn that each misunderstood the other. Such irrelevancies apart, the subsequent history of the Session revolved around Wemyss' resolution and Rosebery's promotion of it; their object was to induce thirty of Salisbury's supporters to defect to the other side or otherwise to reverse the 59 majority secured on Cairns' division. Rosebery worked fast, proposing, after consultation with Wemyss, that the joint address be expanded so as to encompass the introduction of a Redistribution bill when Parliament reassembled in October. Gladstone raised no immediate objection, while declining finally to bind himself 'by an opinion given at the first blush.'[7] Reay undertook the thankless role of 'itinerant collector of notes', and approached key figures. Goschen was found to be 'very keen about the compromise and [added] that Hartington was favorable'. Shaw-Lefevre, deprecating the futility of an autumn Session designed solely to reintroduce a

---

[1] Earl Grey to Richmond, 14 July 1884. Goodwood Mss., 872/P14.
[2] 8 July 1884, p. 1. [3] 9 July 1884, p. 5.
[4] Northcote to Salisbury, 16 July 1884. Salisbury Mss., Series E.
[5] 15 July 1884, p. 9.
[6] Argyll to Gladstone, 18 July 1884. Gladstone Mss., 44105 fol. 174.
[7] Gladstone to Granville, 12 July 1884. *Correspondence*, Vol. II, p. 213.

Franchise bill, threw in his support for early introduction of a Seats bill. Pembroke had a 'very clear appreciation of the crisis'. Lothian agreed, promisingly, to an interview.[1] After a rendezvous with Churchill at Blenheim, Wemyss journeyed post haste on the Saturday evening to make sure of Richmond. Churchill had dinner that night at the Reform Club with Buckle: Monday's *Times* commended the resolution as 'very well worthy of the serious consideration of the Conservative party.'[2] To the Cabinet, Rosebery forecast the probability of success[3] which was rendered even more likely by Wemyss' decision to delay the motion for two days in order to give time for it to 'soak' in. Optimism for the moment was boundless, and quite without foundation. Nor did Wemyss or Rosebery come subsequently to terms with defeat; they took shelter in the inconsequential reflection that 'the majority of the Peers was with us in heart';[4] or deluded themselves that failure was to be explained by their forgetting to consult Lord Fitzwilliam.[5]

The causes went deeper. Such support as they received was given with resignation since theirs was the only motion which had the slightest chance of being carried – a melancholy admission, somehow, for an advocate to make in debate.[6] That said, all else is debit. Wemyss' resolution asked the Peers, 'upon no grounds that [any] could make out to reverse the vote [they] had come to in the week before'.[7] It contained no provision for the simultaneous enactment of the two parts of the measure. Shaftesbury himself recognised that Salisbury had an 'unanswerable argument' – that the Government 'could not prepare an *adequate* Bill for redistribution, between this time, & the opening of an Autumn Session.'[8] Nor was Wemyss 'the man' to accomplish an impossibility.[9] While Sherbrooke absented himself from the Lords on 8 July, Wemyss attempted to make his mark on the history of 1884 just as he had on that of 1867. What he failed to realize was that all the defects which had been apparent in 1867 were even more apparent now.[10]

[1] Reay to Rosebery, 12 July 1884. Rosebery Mss., Box 60.
[2] 14 July 1884, p. 9.
[3] Dodson Cabinet Minutes, 14 July 1884. Monk Bretton Mss., 62.
[4] Wemyss to Rosebery, 18 July 1884. Rosebery Mss., Box 60.
[5] Reay to Rosebery, 17 July 1884. Rosebery Mss., Box 34.
[6] Shaftesbury, 17 July 1884. 3 *Hansard* ccxc. 1342.
[7] Richmond to Halifax, 20 July 1884. Hickleton Mss., A4.181 Part 7.
[8] Shaftesbury to Rosebery, 14 July 1884. Rosebery Mss., Box 60.
[9] Cranbrook Diary, 15 July 1884. Cranbrook Mss., T501/299 fol. 233.
[10] Salisbury to Richmond, 7 July 1884. Goodwood Mss., 872/P10.

Cranbrook loathed his 'airing his eccentric independence with his usual self-conceit';[1] Manners found it difficult to take seriously the threat posed by someone so 'impossible to act with';[2] Salisbury took his personal following to be limited to half-a-dozen.[3] Wemyss had his cronies – the 'extraordinarily stupid' Norton[4] (Disraeli's President of the Board of Trade), Frederick Greenwood of the *St. James's Gazette*, and Dunraven of the National Free Contract and Property Defence Association; less securely, he had Lord Grey. If Churchill thought Wemyss a worthwhile ally in July 1884 he was mistaken. Their partnership compounded antipathy and rendered Wemyss' resolution doubly obnoxious. Even if Wemyss was tolerable to Richmond, alliance with Churchill (albeit at one remove) most certainly was not.

It was presumably brought home to the Conservative Peers at the Carlton Club meeting of 15 July that if they gave way now, it would prove 'worse than any former collapse';[5] it was assumed in Downing Street that many were 'not unnaturally...deterred... knowing full well that desertion now would mean their losing their leader.'[6] What is perhaps of equal significance is that suspicion of Gladstone's real motive now impelled the waverers to retreat. If Salisbury's disposition had appeared regrettable, Gladstone's was not all that might have been hoped. Jersey, whose name had headed Rosebery's canvassing list, was being reclaimed for orthodox Conservatism by Henry Northcote.[7] Cadogan, with whom Rosebery conferred, raised his own amendment, which then received Salisbury's blessing. After 'much discussion with several friends', the attitude of Pembroke and Winmarleigh visibly stiffened against the Government, issuing in demands for 'some knowledge of the mode in which redistribution is to be carried [and for] some assurance that the whole scheme will be complete before a general election.'[8] Wemyss assisted on neither count.

[1] Cranbrook Diary, 15 July 1884. Cranbrook Mss., T501/299 fol. 233.
[2] Manners to Henry Manners, 8 July 1884. Belvoir Mss.
[3] Salisbury to Richmond, 7 July 1884. Goodwood Mss., 872/P10.
[4] Dilke Memoir, 25 Aug. 1883. Dilke Mss., 43937 fol. 155.
[5] Northcote to Salisbury, 12 July 1884. Salisbury Mss., Series E.
[6] Hamilton Diary, 15 July 1884. Hamilton Mss., 48637 fol. 20.
[7] Henry Northcote to Salisbury, 17 July 1884. Salisbury Mss., Series E.
[8] Winmarleigh to Gladstone, 16 July 1884. Gladstone Mss., 44487 fol. 88.

6

'SOME MAY BE IMPRESSED BY NUMBERS'[1]

It is all the Queen can do to bear the dreadful state of things! The Government, after ruining everything, may be turned out and not suffer a bit for all the mischief and misery they have caused (principally Mr. Gladstone), but the poor Queen *must remain* and look on at it in silent, helpless despair!

The Queen to Ponsonby, 22 Aug. 1884. Sir Frederick Ponsonby, *Sidelights on Queen Victoria* (1930), p. 191.

I know Mr. G. well enough to be sure that he . . . would never do anything which would seem to acknowledge the right of the House of Lords to force a dissolution. . .

Rosebery to Labouchère, 20 Nov. 1885. Rosebery Mss., Box 32.

They wanted to come to business, and they wanted to come to figures, and he was quite sure that if they did so their unanimity would be wonderful.

Charles Elton, 6 Nov. 1884. 3 *Hansard* ccxciii. 1163.

THE SILLY SEASON enjoyed in 1884 its fair quota of bizarre and macabre *divertissements*. A carriage, drawn by ten Pickford horses, removed the frightful Wellington statue from Hyde Park Corner to Aldershot; the Tichborne Claimant was released from Pentonville, weighed and found to have shed eight of his twenty-six stone during a decade of imprisonment; the body of an Indian rajah was cremated on the Normandy beach of Etretat. There were balloon ascents by the score, prize fights, nitroglycerine outrages, earth tremors and a Metropolitan heatwave. Reports came in of a general rising along the Zambesi. At the Oval there was an approach to riot, incensed spectators invading the pitch, hurling stumps in all directions and occupying the wicket. From Falmouth police court emerged by instalments a lurid tale of cannibalism on the high seas – as the survivors of the *Mignonette* were charged with the murder, for nutriment, of their ship's-boy after nineteen days drifting on a life-raft. In the courts again, theatre and aristocracy

[1] Cranbrook Diary, 9 Apr. 1884. Cranbrook Mss., T501/299 fol. 193.

provided the *cause célèbre* of the year, a Miss Finney whose weekly wage at the Savoy never exceeded £6 obtaining damages of £10,000 for breach of promise against Cairns' eldest son. But in satisfying the popular appetite for participation – as distinct from ghoulish interest in the affairs of others – political demonstration, as a form of active entertainment, was in a class all on its own.

And entertainment there most certainly was. Gladstone called for demonstrations of 'dignity and weight...in the old and regular forms of town and country meetings...[as] at the time of the first Reform Bill.'[1] Before Parliament reassembled in the autumn, that call was answered (though not always with 'dignity and weight') 1,277 times – according to Stead who kept a running total. The very number explains the character of the agitation and its progress and regress over a period of twelve weeks. Everything that was conceivably worth saying about the Franchise bill and the Lords' action had been said in the first few days, every variation had been played, every catchword and catch-phrase coined and repeated for the national delectation in column upon column of the daily press. At the outset novelty was sufficient to command attention, which grew into sympathy for the hundred thousand working men of the Home Counties who sacrificed a day's wages in order to march through London on 21 July.[2] It was, all accounts were agreed, 'wonderfully well managed, well conducted and orderly',[3] the crowd 'in good health & apparently good spirits'[4] and – what must have added the requisite 'dignity and weight' – careful not to bruise a single flower or shrub in Hyde Park.[5] What was lacking, thought Milner who watched from the windows of the Reform Club, was imagination: 'They do these things better abroad.'[6]

The difficulty was that few Liberal speakers – and not even Bright[7] – could make a familiar message sound interesting. Lawson

[1] Gladstone to Rosebery, 22 July 1884. Gladstone Mss., 44547 fol. 86.
[2] *The Times*, 5 Aug. 1884, p. 9.
[3] Elliot Diaries, 24 July 1884. Diaries, Vol. 10.
[4] Milner Memo., 4 p.m. [21 July 1884.] Milner Mss., Box 182.
[5] *Pall Mall Gazette*, 23 July 1884, p. 3. One would have anticipated greater discrepancies as regards numbers in the party press than were in fact displayed. What was accepted by both sides was that the procession took three hours to pass any given point, and that the rear did not enter the Park until some time after the conclusion of formal proceedings, passing of resolutions, etc. There was some delay outside the Carlton Club, where members of the brass band were stopped '& made to exchange their merry tunes for the Death March in Saul.' Milner Memo., *op. cit.*
[6] Milner Memo., *op. cit.*
[7] Milner to Goschen, 30 July 1884. Milner Mss., Box 182.

tried smutty humour. One or two went in for the purple brilliance of platform rhapsody. The academic Radical, Thorold Rogers, likened the Upper House 'to Sodom and Gomorrah, and to the collective abominate of an Egyptian temple'.[1] But the political main-course was predictable and uninspiring; it was only with the trimmings that entertainment began. Glaswegians were perhaps more fortunate than most in the enterprise of their party workers; the march there was

a sight worth seeing, not so much for the numbers though they were very great as for the loveliness and originality of the whole thing, & its great rarity. There was of course a little of commercial puffing of their own goods by the employers but the workmen had taken the matter up heartily & joined thoroughly in the spirit of it. It was more like a Carnival than anything else I have seen, animals led in procession all decorated, horses donkeys, pigs even &c., men with masks and men in armour, stuffed figures, marionettes, banners & pictures & mottoes innumerable, a few good jokes and many very bad ones. The streets were lined with a good humoured crowd and as long as the procession lasted a sober crowd. . . . even in the poorest houses they hung a bit of tartan shawl or a red handkerchief out of the window.[2]

Such audiences might understand that the Tory leaders were bad while their followers were merely misguided. What they *wanted*, and ever more so as the evening drew on or sobriety waned, was the cue to raise the chorus of 'Jeers at the Peers'. Soon, speakers themselves, ceasing to worry about the details of resolutions, measured success against the yardstick of 'burlesque & fun'.[3] Trevelyan had no time for the over-sensitive, for Whig stuffiness, or for the complaint that sentiments, 'framed to run in a uniform groove', were then passed off as '*spontaneous* ebullitions' of popular conscience.[4] The prime concern was a display of party unity, all but the most 'outrageous' resolutions being accepted as sufficient expression of the 'general direction' of the assembly. At such a crisis, Trevelyan thought, a man must take sides; 'having taken one's side, one goes and says one's say, and nobody distinguishes very much the exact words.'[5] Certainly, attempts to amend resolutions met with scant favour in any Drill Hall.[6] What could

---

[1] For which language he was taken to task in the Commons by Stanhope, 6 Nov. 1884. 3 *Hansard* ccxciii. 1164.
[2] Buchanan to Elliot, 19 Sept. 1884. Elliot Mss., Bundle 32.
[3] Elliot Diary, 20 Sept. 1884. Diaries, Vol. 10.
[4] Minto to Elliot, 9 Aug. 1884. Elliot Mss., Bundle 32.
[5] Trevelyan to Elliot, 26 Aug. 1884. Elliot Mss., Bundle 32.
[6] *The Times*, 10 Sept. 1884, p. 6.

not be expected when matters of dispute were so crudely broadcast, was that on the Reform issue any mind should get 'more "forrader"';[1] nor that any audience should understand Redistribution so long as politicians said of it 'that it [was] a complicated administrative measure but not really of political magnitude'.[2] For those who were generically titled 'the Sir Lucius O'Triggers of politics', the quarrel was a 'very pretty quarrel which explanation would only spoil.'[3]

It may be that the 'blowing off [of] a great deal of steam' served a 'useful purpose' in releasing energy and boosting Liberal self-confidence.[4] But who, specifically, profited? Morley did, as author of that ever-misquoted line whose easy prediction foundered on the course of subsequent history – that 'no power on earth can separate henceforth the question of mending the House of Commons from the question of mending, or ending, the House of Lords.'[5] Harcourt profited, increasing in stature as a hard-hitter, after years of departmental frustration at the Home Office and disappointed hankering after the Exchequer. So did Trevelyan, though on the point of breakdown under the stresses of the Irish Secretaryship. So too did Rosebery, once he had determined not to allow Gladstone to 'trade' on him in Midlothian. Host to Gladstone he might be, but 'appendage' never again;[6] he recognized as well as others his own territorial strength. 'So far as the popular voice of the North goes if Gladstone were out of the way we should have a Trevelyan–Rosebery Government tomorrow, or more probably Rosebery–Trevelyan.'[7]

Above all, Gladstone – virtually silent outside Westminster since his accession to power – stood to gain. It was 'understood', *The Times* wrote in July, 'that he regards the present occasion as one calling for a renewal of the oratorical activity which served *his* party so well in 1880.'[8] Certainly, Gladstone's hold over the country was very different from that which any Conservative could boast.[9] The Edinburgh histrionics in late August were, indeed, a timely reminder that he was still a Titan in his party[10] and understood the

[1] Sellar to Elliot, 22 Aug. 1884. Elliot Mss., Bundle 32.
[2] Reay to Rosebery, 20 Sept. 1884. Rosebery Mss., Box 34.
[3] Ormathwaite to Richmond, 16 Nov. 1884. Goodwood Mss., 872/P83.
[4] Kimberley to Ripon, 21 Aug. 1884. Ripon Mss., 43235 fol. 152.
[5] 30 July 1884. *Annual Register*, p. 156.
[6] Cooper to Rosebery, 11 Aug. 1884. Rosebery Mss., Box 9.
[7] Buchanan to Elliot, 19 Sept. 1884. Elliot Mss., Bundle 32.
[8] 19 July 1884, p. 11. (My italics.)
[9] Granville to Derby, 20 Aug. 1884. Derby Mss., Box 3.
[10] Lady Sophia Palmer to Elliot, 2 Sept. 1884. Elliot Mss., Bundle 32.

sources of his power. If it is crude to talk of a campaign engineered for Gladstone's benefit, it remains true that, within the space of a few months, Reform afforded him the opportunity to show that his control of Cabinet, Parliament and country was more complete than anyone could have supposed a year before.

What, though, in party terms was expected of agitation? What was *not* anticipated by Gladstone was Conservative counter-demonstration. Even Salisbury seems not to have thought such disruption worthwhile. He did not expect the Liberal campaign to be of 'much account – such stuff as frightens Peers, but nothing more'.[1] Older Tories were at first content to draw upon the similarity of the Hyde Park demonstration to the Chartist fiasco of 1848, to demand that 'equal firmness' be shown now, to invoke the policy of 'Thorough', and to let the violence of the Caucus 'beget an angry spirit' in which their own party might stand 'shoulder to shoulder'.[2] Such 'reaction' meetings, a week or so after the initial Liberal rally, were indeed fairly common, especially in the South of England, throughout the autumn.[3] There was, in these early days, little more positive than the ungenerous reflection that the Government would gain nothing by 'descend[ing] into the streets' and attempting to 'legislat[e] by picnic'.[4] The shape of things to come was, however, shortly apparent.

On the eve of the Conservative National Union Conference, Salisbury had enjoyed a tumultuous welcome at Sheffield; the Conference proved itself the last which Churchill threatened – or chose to threaten, for he himself now called a halt to this peculiarly tangential meander across unmapped terrain. Was there any connection between Salisbury's bold incursion into 'enemy territory' (which both surprised and angered Chamberlain)[5] and the Salisbury–Churchill armistice which followed so hard on its heels? Carnarvon had, some days previously, put it to Salisbury that the only alternative to swift compromise upon Redistribution would be an active plan of campaign involving counter-agitation in the large urban centres, 'with a view to which it was necessary, in his opinion, to come to terms with Lord Randolph Churchill.' Salisbury, with no show of good grace, declined to entertain the

1 Salisbury to Manners, 12 July 1884. Belvoir Mss.
2 Manners to Henry Manners, 18 July 1884; Manners to Salisbury, 14 July 1884. Belvoir Mss.
3 Reeve to Elliot, 18 Aug. 1884. Elliot Mss., Bundle 32.
4 Salisbury, at Sheffield, 22 July 1884. *Annual Register*, p. 154.
5 Mundella to Leader, 23 July 1884. Mundella–Leader Mss.

proposal;[1] nor did Austin fare better with Churchill in encouraging him to defend the Lords. 'He began and ended with a flat refusal, trying meanwhile to convince me that I was wrong, on the ground that there were no men on our side capable of appealing with any effect to popular audiences.'[2] More remarkable, though, than the post-Sheffield vindication of Carnarvon's foresight was the spur given to the Conservatives by Winn and the party Whips. The portrait left of Winn by contemporaries is neither attractive nor impressive. He sought a Peerage (to gratify his wife) in 1880, and was (to her dismay) appointed instead successor to Hart Dyke. It was a task to which he was temperamentally unsuited and a labour in which he never enjoyed wifely sympathy. Conservatives who adjudged Winn's own Commons' attendance less than exemplary (that woman again) were not slow to label theirs the worst-whipped party in the world. Yet it was from this highly improbable quarter that the impetus to activity came, combatting the fear and inertia of those who entertained suspicion of what had 'never been done before'.[3] Central Office advocated 'indignation meetings', for the purpose of protesting against the Government's Egyptian policy, supporting the Lords' action and urging dissolution.[4] Winn himself summoned the Metropolitan and Home Counties Tory Members to arrange something akin to the Liberals' Hyde Park procession. It could be done 'in London as easily as Manchester or Sheffield &c....if gone to work with in a proper manner.'[5] The demonstration – indubitably one of the highlights of the Recess – at Winn's own seat, Nostell Priory, testified magnificently to what might be achieved by organized effort: numbers in attendance, and this, be it noted, in a rural setting some miles out of Wakefield, certainly equalled the most generous estimates for Hyde Park or Manchester's Pomona Gardens. If the commotion was not simply the Radical din which Radicals had envisaged, so much the better for the spectacle. Both camps employed the same tactics, both betrayed the same bellicose spirit. Cooper's clarion call – 'Let it be fought out....the Bill will be endangered [only] if there be any appearance of wavering on our side'[6] – was precisely echoed by

[1] Sir Arthur Hardinge, *The Life of Henry Howard Molyneux Herbert, Fourth Earl of Carnarvon, 1831–1890* (3 vols., Oxford, 1925), Vol. III, p. 103.
[2] *Autobiography of Alfred Austin, Poet Laureate, 1835–1910* (2 vols., 1911), Vol. II, p. 242.   [3] Winn to Salisbury, 22 July 1884. Salisbury Mss., Series E.
[4] *The Times*, 18 July 1884, p. 10.
[5] Winn to Salisbury, 22 July 1884. Salisbury Mss., Series E.
[6] Cooper to Minto, 11 Sept. 1884. Minto Mss., Box 172.

Churchill, in his savage reminder to 'My hon. and learned Friend [Gorst], with his purely legal mind,...that in political controversy ...the Party which makes abject surrender is not the Party likely to attain its aim, or anything like its aim.'[1] In this contest of abuse and obduracy, Tories enjoyed sole right to the utterance of *appello Caesarem*; it was a contention of strength that the Government were determined to switch the jury before asking the electorate for a verdict of acquittal.[2] We may accept the *Pall Mall Gazette* tally of only 184 Conservative counter-demonstrations, one to every seven Liberal gatherings. But what mattered was not so much the number as the impression made by the campaigns upon politicians and the effect they had upon high political activity. The correlation between outside noise, pre-ponderantly Liberal, and Conservative defection, was extremely tenuous. If Churchill continued to recall the Lords' rejection as 'a blunder too enormous to be described' but for which 'we should have been on velvet',[3] and if Bartley at Central Office reported the party to be steadily losing ground because still open to the charge of not wanting franchise extension, they were simply preparing the way for publication of their joint Redistribution scheme and lamenting the Government's escape from censure over its 'bungling in all parts of the world.'[4] Northcote might conclude gloomily from his platform experience in Edinburgh that the cry against the Lords was 'doing us harm, even with some of the middle-class Liberals who are alarmed at the Franchise bill'; but his deduction, that 'social jealousy tells very strongly',[5] was one of no immediate political comfort to the Liberals. To Trevelyan, his party appeared, from the South Warwickshire by-election, to have been hoist with their own petard: 'we must expect great disasters, for I am satisfied that the *real* cause of these county defeats, and borough victories,

---

1 Churchill, 7 Nov. 1884. 3 *Hansard* ccxciii. 1249. Manners concurred: 'I don't know which party is more alarmed at the prospect, but am convinced that the party which shows itself least afraid is most likely to succeed.' Manners to the Duke of Rutland, 12 Nov. 1884. Charles Whibley, *Lord John Manners and his Friends* (2 vols., Edinburgh, 1925), Vol. II, p. 227.
2 *The Times*, 4 Oct. 1884, p. 9.
3 Churchill to Borthwick, 5 Sept. 1884. Reginald Lucas, *Lord Glenesk and the 'Morning Post'* (1910), p. 303.
4 Bartley to Winn, 1 Oct. 1884. Nostell Mss., 2/9; Bartley Memo., 25 Oct. 1884. Salisbury Mss., Series E; Bartley to Northcote, and copy to Salisbury, 8 Nov. 1884. Salisbury Mss., Series E. This last was an offer of resignation, which nuisance was deferred to the New Year.
Northcote to Winn, 29 Sept. 1884. Nostell Mss., 2/8.

is that in the constituencies the question has become a class question; and the privileged voters *will not* give up except by force.'[1] There was confidence in the ultimate success of Radicalism on this 'class question', a conviction that Radicals had time on their side, and a belief that all reform had resulted from the persistence of their pressure. Even Radicals recognized, however, that 'Gladstone's success in his duel with Salisbury [was] a different thing'.[2] That is the importance of Trevelyan's reflection – that the Government had gained nothing and could hope by their present conduct to gain nothing beyond 'something like a general certainty' that a Franchise bill would pass 'within a moderate term of years.'[3]

If all had inevitably to come to the political card-table, Manners thought the cards were in Tory hands, if only 'we know how to play them';[4] but even as regards these outside pressures, the Government had seemingly failed to make 'much of their agitation', the Opposition making a great deal more and taking encouragement from their exploits.[5] Consider the fate of Chamberlain in a setting almost of his choice. For more than a year he had written and talked enthusiastically about a direct confrontation with the Upper House. In August 1884 he found, to his delight, a Birmingham audience 'thirsting for the blood of the Lords', and shouting 'You're too lenient with them' at Bright's suggestion of a suspensive veto. But if it was then 'impossible to choose a better time for a dissolution',[6] both opportunity and prospects slipped. His own effort to inject 'a little more *devil*' into the agitation[7] was disastrous and a godsend to the Opposition. The Aston Park riots, where Birmingham Liberals invaded an all-ticket Tory meeting and smashed and threw chairs about (Lowther terming this a 'redistribution of seats'), exposed Chamberlain to the charge of moral complicity in disorder and violence. This simply was not Chamber-

---

[1] Trevelyan to Spencer, 8 Nov. 1884. Spencer Mss.
[2] Harrison to Morley, 6 Nov. 1884. Harrison Mss., A(5).
[3] Gladstone to Argyll, 21 Sept. 1884. Gladstone Mss., 44547 fol. 111.
[4] Manners to Salisbury, 15 Aug. 1884. Belvoir Mss. In conversation and correspondence, the suggestive parallel provided by the mutual bluff and suspicion of poker (a novelty from across the Atlantic) superseded the classic 'chessboard of politics'.
[5] Richmond to Cranbrook, 24 Aug. 1884. Cranbrook Mss., T501/257; Albert Grey to Halifax, 24 Oct. 1884. Hickleton Mss., A4.84 Part 4.
[6] Chamberlain to Dilke, c. 5 Aug. 1884. Dilke Mss., 43886 fol. 192. See *Pall Mall Gazette*, 20 Oct. 1884, p. 1: 'But if there is one thing more than another which Mr. Chamberlain objects to it is a dissolution.'
[7] Morley to Chamberlain, 29 Sept. 1884. Chamberlain Mss., JC5/54/572.

lain's year.[1] Though there was disparaging talk of Salisbury requiring 'broken heads, and arson' to convince him that the country was sincere in its desire for Reform,[2] it was perfectly clear that the people of Newcastle, Sunderland and Hartlepool would not 'bestir themselves' on the question of the Lords: indeed,

> if the men of Tyneside ever march on London, it will be to put Chamberlain out of the Board of Trade, as the popular idea up here is that he has caused the bad business. The greater part of the people is seriously concerned with questions of trade, big loaf, anti vaccination & so forth & cares only in a go-to-meeting way about the high things which trouble you & me.[3]

To those whose eyes were fixed upon local realities, Chamberlain's assumptions seemed peculiarly naive and Liberal strategists at Westminster seemed to have fixed upon a conception of Toryism as bucolic stupidity. Liverpool Conservatives, they needed to be reminded, had 'no dread of working men, little liking for the clergy, not much objection to school boards, no great fancy for game laws, a very moderate idea of the value of peers, a strong disposition to Liberalize land tenure.' The whole county of Lancashire was one which quite evidently could not be 'swept off its feet by any question of organic change' in the constitution, and where a Franchise agitation would be nugatory.[4] Talk of Franchise pure and simple could never be counted on to take a Liberal assembly by storm; yet in cluttering their legislative programme, in turning to denunciation of the Upper House as an institution (to stir an audience from apathy), the Liberal party placed itself in a dilemma from which there was no egress compatible with an approach to

---

[1] Not only was he exonerated from any blameworthy act by the narrowest of Commons' divisions but summonses for libel were immediately applied for against those upon whose depositions and affidavits Chamberlain's self-defence was based.

[2] Hamilton Diary, 6 Nov. 1884. Hamilton Mss., 48638 fol. 35.

[3] Harrison to Morley, 3 Nov. 1884. Harrison Mss., A(5). The shipowners who, on Chamberlain's appointment to the Board of Trade, had vowed that they would 'never go cap in hand to a fellow like that' (Northcote Diary, 29 Apr. 1880. Iddesleigh Mss., 50063A fol. 328), certainly carried on an effective smear campaign, accusing Chamberlain 'and his friends' of buying up shipping shares 'which he, and he alone, has driven to their present low'. William Duncan to Chamberlain, enclosing report of an address delivered to the Durham Constitutional Association, 12 Apr. 1884. Chamberlain Mss., JC2/14/80. The distress during late 1884 was, of course, of wider significance, with ships laid up for want of freight, and yards closed. See Caine to Gladstone, 6 Nov. 1884, for a Radical's view of the opposition stirred up by Chamberlain's legislation and legislative proposals. Gladstone Mss., 44488 fol. 32.   [4] E. R. Russell, in *Pall Mall Gazette*, 16 Sept. 1884, p. 2.

unity. 'What is the good', Frederic Harrison pertinently asked Morley, 'of trying to frighten a reckless fellow by levelling at him a gun, which it is understood is not *loaded*, & which if it were loaded, you & yours (or rather yours, for *you* are in a hopeless minority in "the party") would not fire off'?[1]

As the colours of the rainbow are in the eyes of the beholder, so were menace and threat in Governmental utterance. It is more profitable to view the question thus than to rely upon the feeling of opponents (ignorant of, or ignoring, Cabinet complications) that 'Gladstone would give his eyes to go to the country on the constitutional issue'.[2] At the time of the party meeting at the Foreign Office, the Prime Minister had given a written undertaking to the Queen that, though 'his conviction, his painful conviction' was that the fulfilment of Balfour's prophecies (a second Lords' rejection of the Franchise bill) would precipitate 'a new point of departure', he himself would use 'no language of this kind in public.' He obtained similar assurances from Chamberlain and Dilke against discussion of the character and composition, activity and prospects of the Upper House.[3] He scrupulously expunged from a draft letter of Herbert Gladstone's a paragraph which crossed the boundary, to the effect that the blocking of the Franchise bill in November must absolutely (and however reluctantly) commit the Liberal party 'to a second & a far more serious agitation.'[4]

Two comments need to be made: first, that the 'political world' had greater dread of Gladstone's 'restrained moderation' than of his 'unbridled vehemence';[5] second, as corollary, that it was of no use for Gladstone or ministers to pretend that Franchise and not the Lords was the issue before the country when this same 'political world' took it as read that 'they only say this because they do not wish to be ostensibly at the head of a movement to which they have given both origin and direction.'[6] The various clues Gladstone presented himself. Adverse written argument was anathema to the Queen and more likely to provoke her stubborn resistance than to impress by weight of reason; for her, he was ready to take 'common

---

[1] Harrison to Morley, 3 Nov. 1884. Harrison Mss., A(5).
[2] Portarlington to Churchill, early Nov. 1884. Churchill Mss., 4/486.
[3] Gladstone to the Queen, 11 July 1884. Guedalla, *Queen and Gladstone*, p. 283.
[4] Herbert Gladstone to R. Collier, 9 Aug. 1884. Viscount Gladstone Mss., 46050 fol. 282. See also Buchanan to Elliot, 26 Aug. 1884. Elliot Mss., Bundle 32.
[5] Hamilton-Gordon to Selborne, 18 Sept. 1884. Stanmore Mss., 49218 fol. 226.
[6] Hugh Elliot to Gilbert Elliot, 8 Sept. 1884. Minto Mss., Box 172.

ground...and *pose* as the defender of the hereditary principle.'[1] In Midlothian, he was ready to break his original self-denying ordinance with a far from innocent reflection upon the legislative action of the Peers since 1832 as neither 'a benefit [n]or a blessing to the country'.[2] His audience immediately made the logical deduction, while Morley felt obliged to counter the misapprehension under which he took Gladstone to be labouring, that he (Morley) had deprecated converting the Franchise agitation into 'a move against the Lords.'[3] Although he brought no legislative proposals before the Cabinet, the lesson Gladstone determined to draw from the public meetings was that Government manoeuvrability, in the direction of conciliation, was limited by the decisive, anti-Lords tone so manifest there.[4]

It is not surprising that many Liberals, dimly perceiving what it was that they might be aiming at, jibbed at connivance; that many more, with no idea what they were doing and less liking for it, plodded dutifully onward they knew not where (except that they were moving away from the Egyptian quicksands); and that many, whatever their outward actions, saw no solution to the difficulties in which the party was involved. There is a danger here that the historian may become hyper-fastidious or too easily sidetracked towards cynicism in lighting upon palpable flaws which matter in rational but not in political debate; he may, like Stead, have 'to write about what [he] cannot understand or to speak of the conduct of statesmen whose attitude is intellectually almost inconceivable.'[5] Yet the fact remains that the Government were in a political as much as in a theoretical *cul-de-sac*. Selborne's anxiety *was* too logical. The Liberals, it was his premise, had justified their refusal to deal with Redistribution and Franchise concurrently from fear of being frustrated on both; how then could 'men who have acted on this principle justify its total reversal by complicating both or either of these measures with a third [as to the Lords], much more dangerous and difficult...when the opposite course [of allowing the constituencies the opportunity to declare in favour of an unaccompanied Franchise bill] would ensure their passing safely?'[6]

But to the practical question – would the Lords again reject the

[1] Gladstone to Granville, 16 Aug. 1884. *Correspondence*, Vol. ii, p. 228.
[2] 30 Aug. 1884. *Annual Register*, p. 204.
[3] Morley to Gladstone, 13 Oct. 1884. Gladstone Mss., 44255 fol. 49.
[4] Gladstone to Ponsonby, 7 Aug. 1884. Guedalla, *Queen and Gladstone*, p. 294.
[5] Stead to Salisbury, 13 Nov. 1884. Salisbury Mss., Series E.
[6] Selborne to Gladstone, 28 Sept. 1884. Gladstone Mss., 44298 fol. 136.

Franchise bill in November? – there was only one answer. They must, and the great majority on both sides and in both Houses thought they would. When the Government stumped the country and claimed the right to legislate without regard to Conservative susceptibilities, when they loudly and repeatedly challenged the Lords' very existence, would not surrender now be looked on as tantamount to extinction as a political power? Such was the reasoning which led Pembroke to the conclusion that the Lords could lose no more by a '*duel à l'outrance*'.[1] And this left the Government, in the first instance, with the options enumerated by Bryce: to dissolve (which Salisbury wanted), to bring in the Seats bill (which Salisbury again wanted), or to reintroduce Franchise alone, 'wh. will look weak, & seem inexcusable with a whole new Session for Redistribution.'[2]

Dissolution was inconceivable; but would it be possible to mount a continued agitation against the Lords, 'based mainly on the ground that *they* want a dissolution'? Party agents were doubtful whether the supposed magnitude of the Lords' offence could be conveyed to the electorate.[3] Derby formulated a line of argument which Granville found impeccable in its morbidity. What would be the consequence of a repeat of the July vote? 'Can we make peers in sufficient numbers? Would the Queen consent? If we cannot do that, what follows except defeat for us? The opposition continue their demand for a dissolution on the old constituencies: and how can we prevent them from getting it? They will beat us by mere lapse of time.'[4] Granville could not answer because, as he readily admitted, he not only regretted but had 'never understood our plan of action.' In fairness to Granville it must be said that the plan of action could not stand up to analysis. In fairness to Gladstone it might be added that Granville did not think Salisbury's game worth the candle, for if the Government could not stave off dissolution, Salisbury would come to power on Parnell's back: '*et puis*'?[5]

[1] Pembroke to Hamilton, 13 Nov. 1884. Hamilton Mss., 48621. See also Hugh Elliot to Gilbert Elliot, 8 Sept. 1884. Minto Mss., Box 172; and Richmond to Cairns, 16 Sept. 1884. Cairns Mss., PRO. 30/51/4, fol. 183.
[2] Bryce to Sidgwick, 22 Aug. 1884. Bryce Mss., Vol. 15, fol. 115.
[3] Derby to Granville, 28 Sept. 1884. Granville Mss., PRO. 30/29/28A. (My italics.)   [4] Derby to Granville, 18 Aug. 1884. Derby Mss., Box 3.
[5] Granville to Derby, 20 Aug. 1884. Derby Mss., Box 3. Kimberley shared Granville's view: a dissolution would be unavoidable before the end of the year, and the Liberals would find themselves after the election in a minority against Conservatives and Irish Nationalists combined. Kimberley to Ripon, 30 July 1884. Ripon Mss., 43525 fol. 133. See also Sellar to Elliot, 22 Aug. 1884. Elliot Mss., Bundle 32.

Gladstone might flood the Upper House; at least one eligible colonial governor, tiring of severance from intellectual society and bored by the company of his officials, thrilled to the prospect of a title.[1] But *could* Gladstone do so after another rejection, even 'on the principle of the Archbishop promising to muffle his knocker'?[2] 'When are we to begin the creation of Peers?', asked Harcourt in Cabinet. 'Not till after my resignation', replied Selborne – and he would take Hartington with him.[3] Could Gladstone advance to abolition of the Lords? Henry Fowler, 'an excellent middle-aged, middle-class middling style of business man'[4] and a Radical realist, was clear that abolition was electorally a bad card to play as well as being likely to split both Cabinet and Parliamentary party. And what was the purpose of destroying the working coalition and putting 'the clock back ten degrees...in order to convince posterity that Labouchère and Storey and others are not the successors of Fox and Burke – of Cobden and Gladstone!'[5]

The other side of the coin was equally depressing: Radical feeling against life peerages and moderate reform left the present constitution face to face with a French-style senate, and that was taken to lie outside the realm of practical politics.[6] The Liberals would not countenance dissolution. They could not go forward on the Lords. Could they safely recede from the policy of 'Franchise alone'? Nothing had been secured on this score in eight months and there was nothing to alter the opinion that the personal interests affected by Redistribution would make opponents out of some backbenchers who now lent support.[7] Grey and his cronies simply waited

---

[1] Hamilton-Gordon to Selborne, 18 Sept. 1884. Stanmore Mss., 49218 fol. 226.
[2] Granville to Derby, 9 Sept. 1884. Derby Mss., Box 3.
[3] Lewis Harcourt Journal, 15 Nov. 1884. Harcourt Mss. It may be noted, further, that the expedient of resignation was suggested by Harcourt on the assumption that the Queen would refuse, thus allowing a dignified mode of escape from office. Granville to Harcourt, 9 Sept. 1884. Harcourt Mss.; Lewis Harcourt Journal, 8 Oct. 1884. Harcourt Mss.; Harcourt to Granville, 14 Sept. 1884. Gardiner, *Harcourt*, Vol. I, p. 500.
[4] Rendel to Grant Duff, 10 Nov. 1882. *Rendel Papers*, p. 220.
[5] Fowler to Morley, Aug. 1884. *Life of Henry Fowler*, pp. 161–3. See also F. W. Buxton to Elliot, 24 Aug. 1884. Elliot Mss., Bundle 32.
[6] Childers to Halifax, 12 Sept. 1884. Hickleton Mss., A4.90.
[7] Seymour to Gladstone, 28 Sept. 1884. Granville Mss., PRO. 30/29/28A; Seymour to Broadhurst, 23 Aug. 1884. Broadhurst Mss., Vol. 2, fol. 46; Gladstone to Argyll, 21 Sept. 1884. Gladstone Mss., 44547 fol. 111. See also Gladstone to Tennyson, 15 Nov. 1884: 'I have...toiled in the circuitous method; but unfortunately with this issue that, working round the labyrinth, I find myself at the end where I was at the beginning.' Gladstone Mss., 44488 fol. 78.

for the Tories to 'dish' Gladstone by going in for 'honest & thorough Proportional Repn. – & I cannot help thinking that Salisbury is aiming at this game.'[1]

In examining the various well-meant or glory-seeking[2] gestures towards a compact which were made throughout the autumn, we find the same sterility as we found with those that blossomed and died in the days immediately following upon the Lords' rejection and Gladstone's Foreign Office invective. The political historian might well heed the Prime Minister's laconic dismissal of one and apply it to all – that they were a 'Waste of breath'.[3] It is, indeed, the most signal comment upon agitation as a political weapon that this should have been so. The greatest danger to Salisbury lay, perhaps, in an attitude of mind which was neither alarmed nor impressed by the strength of logical argument and reasoning, and which neither viewed the complex timing solutions with enthusiasm nor was deluded by any of Gladstone's 'gimcrack' compromises – the attitude of Lord Feversham, who 'said he intended to support the Govt. this time as he thought the whole thing had become a great bore & as the Govt. did not intend to give way there was no good letting it hang on.'[4]

Such a solution as that suggested by the politically independent, and therefore irresponsible, Cowper meant next to nothing: couched in the language of generalities,[5] it was open to whatever interpretation party leaders might choose to impose upon it. Gladstone's reading was that the Lords should pass the Franchise bill when the Government had given sufficient indication of its

[1] Albert Grey to Halifax, 14 Oct. 1884. Hickleton Mss., A4.84 Part 4.
[2] The epithet may appear too strong; but any reader of several hundred volumes of nineteenth century political biography or memoir has his fill, and the number of participants whose 'singular initiative' was decisive in settling the 1884 brawl is almost beyond computation. Alfred Austin and Malcolm MacColl take consolation prizes behind Norton and his biographer. Students of conceit, pomposity and delusions of grandeur are directed to W. S. Childe-Pemberton, *Life of Lord Norton (Right Hon. Sir Charles Adderley), 1814–1905, Statesman and Philanthropist* (1909), p. 262.
[3] Gladstone to Granville, 15 Sept. 1884. *Correspondence*, Vol. II, p. 256.
[4] Winn to Salisbury, 21 Oct. 1884. Salisbury Mss., Series E.
[5] Cowper wrote to *The Times*: 'By the simple expedient of bringing in a Redistribution Bill in the autumn the whole aspect of things will be changed. I take for granted, what I do not think anybody ever seriously doubted, that the Bill will be a fair one. The moment it is printed all pretence for further opposition to the Franchise Bill on the part of the House of Lords will disappear'. 18 Aug. 1884, p. 8.

bona fides by introducing a Redistribution bill.[1] The mischief which these 'gush[es] of political philanthropy'[2] might effect was that, while credit could redound to Gladstone for accepting such a compromise (even if there was a comfortable certainty that no right-minded Conservative could accept it), the attempt to define its contents in terms of Parliamentary business would give the enemy two months in which to pull it to pieces. On the other hand, so Granville reminded Gladstone, 'If you leave it open, they will put their own construction on the offer, and accuse you of bad faith when the moment comes.'[3] But this was not by any means the only plausible translation. Elliot supplied a gloss on Cowper, suggesting that the Government announce their intention to introduce Redistribution into the Commons as soon as the Lords had read the Franchise bill a second time; and while Elliot's initiative was censured even by the Scottish Whig establishment as 'rather a surrender than a concession',[4] Elliot himself thought Cowper had given away 'far too much'.[5] For his part, Gladstone was clear that acceptance of Cowper in no way committed the Government to simultaneous treatment of the two subjects;[6] *if* so considered, it became an 'absurd suggestion' to which only 'd–d asses' would give a moment's thought.[7] This matters even less when one finds Salisbury and Northcote perfectly reflecting the Government's misgivings. Whatever his meaning, Cowper gave no greater security than before for concurrent operation. The project was 'quite foolish' in itself,[8] was possibly 'useful' (in Northcote's eyes) so far as it indicated unease among Whig Peers,[9] but, when it came to controlling the Tory Lords, would be troublesome should anyone with pretension to authority hint that the Conservative leaders entertained this or any similar proposition.[10] Selborne, who approved of Cowper and thoroughly endorsed Elliot's tightening modification, 'said that he feared it was hopeless & that nothing would be done. *Don't quote this.* The fact is, it is not so much a solution that is lacking as the will to use it! & that be it owned not

---

[1] Gladstone to Granville, 18 Aug. 1884. *Correspondence*, Vol. II, p. 231.
[2] Hartington to Granville, 20 Sept. 1884. Granville Mss., PRO. 30/29/134.
[3] Granville to Gladstone, 20 Aug. 1884. *Correspondence*, Vol. II, p. 232.
[4] R. P. Bruce to Elliot, 28 Aug. 1884. Elliot Mss., Bundle 32.
[5] Elliot to R. P. Bruce, early Sept. 1884. Bruce Mss.
[6] Gladstone to J. B. Potter, 22 Aug. 1884. Gladstone Mss., 44547 fol. 99.
[7] Chamberlain to Dilke, 12 Sept. 1884. Chamberlain Mss., JC5/24/357.
[8] Salisbury to Winn, 14 Sept. 1884. Nostell Mss., 2/7.
[9] Northcote to Salisbury, 21 Sept. 1884. Salisbury Mss., Series E.
[10] Salisbury to Northcote, 10 Sept. 1884. Iddesleigh Mss., 50020 fol. 83.

all on one side.'[1] Selborne's was the very true and quite inescapable conclusion of a man with access to Downing Street and Hatfield. A Gladstone–Hartington conflict over the propriety of issuing offers towards a settlement illustrates the same points. All Gladstone's letters to Ponsonby and Argyll during the Recess were written in the knowledge that both, under direct or indirect commission from the Queen, were attempting to establish contact through Conservative independents with the party leaders. Hence the stern message that the Government would be moved only by reasonable assurances that any further bid would be favourably entertained. But the Gladstonian justification, that all 'such bidding [without encouragement] is really bidding *down* the value of yr. own article',[2] Hartington would not accept; it was, he countered, a delusion to suppose that the Lords would pass the Franchise bill either by itself or when they had had a peep at Redistribution, '*whatever it may be*'.[3] 'Whether Salisbury is likely to accept a compromise or not, it is equally desirable to offer one, if it can be found.'[4] And Hartington suited action to word, public to private utterance, at Rawtenstall on 4 October.

The word 'compromise' had never passed Gladstone's lips;[5] under whatever name bids might pass, he warned Hartington of the 'extremely damaging nature of any debate on the *merits*'.[6] Hartington still spoke. 'If Lord Salisbury had said that upon seeing our Redistribution Bill, and satisfying themselves that it was founded upon fair principles...which could be made the foundation of a settlement, they would proceed to take up and dispose of the Franchise Bill...there would...in such a proposition as that have been some of the elements of a compromise.'[7] This was not so much 'looking upon a hypothetical future which is a hotch pot of contingencies'[8] as reflection upon a missed opportunity, yet, in that convoluted past tense, it was persuasive to the same political end. The unauthorised speech provoked a 'tremendous row' in Cabinet, where Hartington was 'sat on.'[9] It 'disgusted' Harcourt, as a 'stupid mistake' which 'practically concede[d]

---

[1] Lady Sophia Palmer to Elliot, 2 Sept. 1884. Elliot Mss., Bundle 32.
[2] Gladstone to Ponsonby, 2 Sept. 1884. Gladstone Mss., 44547 fol. 103.
[3] Hartington to Granville, 20 Sept. 1884. Granville Mss., PRO. 30/29/134.
[4] Hartington to Granville, 23 Sept. 1884. Granville Mss., PRO. 30/29/134.
[5] Gladstone to Chamberlain, 8 Oct. 1884. Gladstone Mss., 44547 fol. 121.
[6] Gladstone to Hartington, 1 Oct. 1884. Gladstone Mss., 44547 fol. 117.
[7] *Annual Register*, p. 219.
[8] Gladstone to Heneage, 1 Oct. 1884. Gladstone Mss., 44547 fol. 118.
[9] Dilke Diary, 4–6 Oct. 1884. Dilke Mss., 43926 fol. 32.

more than even the Tories asked' and by which the Cabinet 'entirely refuse[d] to be bound.'[1] It meant, of course, that, by accepting, Salisbury must at the very least have prised Hartington out of the Government. And yet what did Salisbury advise in comment and reply? No more than that the amicable tone be praised, no hint be given of any desire to close with the offer, 'because, in the first place, he has hardly made one, in the second, what he has sketched out is not acceptable.'[2]

Finally, we must examine that most fanciful proposal of all, the conjuring up out of retirement of a junta of righteous men, whose function would be to lay to rest what ought to be laid to rest, by settling Redistribution without allowing the settlement to be damaged or impaired by the democratic nonsense which younger men felt obliged to dangle before their constituents. For Argyll, Cottesloe, Devon, Eversley, Grey, Halifax, Hampden, Jersey, Norton, Stanhope, Wemyss and Winmarleigh this was the chance to determine the shaping of a major piece of legislation and the bases of power in supra-party terms for the next three decades. It was the only chance likely to come the way of men in the fourth and fifth political ranks, and the last for 'octogenarians in their second childhood'.[3] Such hopes were still-born or confined to those who might play a prominent part in the exercise. In the minds of others there was neither alarm nor revulsion strong enough to make it seem desirable that party should be superseded, and no sense that the present lot were genuinely unable to extricate themselves.

Nor was there the sort of panic on which an Argyll depended. Perceiving clearly, as the Parnellite press boasted, that the next house to his own was on fire and that his own countrymen were 'canny enough to steal...from Irish agitation...any hints on their rights as tenants',[4] Argyll certainly talked of civil war as a present possibility in the Highlands. His conviction did not carry. He summoned an inaugural open meeting of his Landowners' Truth Defence Association 'to contradict the continual lies as to fact told by the various new Land Leagues...But *none came*. It was an unlucky day – from Races &c.'[5] The excuse was hardly sufficient, or,

---

[1] Lewis Harcourt Journal, 7 Oct. 1884. Harcourt Mss.
[2] Salisbury to Northcote, 9 Oct. 1884. Iddesleigh Mss., 50020 fol. 86.
[3] Salisbury's wicked dismissal. Ponsonby, *Sidelights on Queen Victoria*, p. 202.
[4] *Freeman's Journal*, 17 June 1884, p. 4.
[5] Argyll to Balfour, 27 Oct. 1884. Balfour Mss., 49800 fol. 3. A Cabinet fixed for 7 October clashed with the Cesarewitch; Hartington objected, and the Cesarewitch was granted priority.

if it was, showed how little interest Argyll had been able to arouse. Throughout the autumn, as one pamphleteer put it, sensible Englishmen may have been astounded or puzzled by the political circus but, 'shrugging their shoulders, each of them is inclined to say, with Henri Mürger's Schaunard, "*Telle est la vie, passez-moi le tabac.*"'[1] The particular scheme mooted in late October by Carnarvon, Erskine May, Norton, Reay and Lefevre (on behalf of his uncle) – that perhaps eight 'men of weight' drawn from both parties apply themselves to finding a solution – was never allowed to progress beyond infancy. Northcote suspected Norton, who was simply a ham actor, of double-dealing: 'it was obvious that Mr. Gladstone expected him, for we were all three in the Chapel Royal, and I observed some significant glances as he saw Norton come up to speak to me.'[2] Details, terms of reference and intention were far from clear and distrust was thereby engendered. Were these intermediaries to bind both parties? were their outpourings to be taken merely as a basis for discussion? was theirs to be the major role in establishing principle or were they to test particular details by principle agreed elsewhere? would their existence be kept secret? or, if leakage were inevitable, how could one overcome the consequent outrage of the House (which might, so Northcote anticipated from experience of the unfairness of politics, be directed against him)?[3]

Gladstone's outward enthusiasm for the plan and his willingness to encourage Carnarvon, so long as the latter seemed to be working behind Salisbury's back, concealed a total unwillingness to allow any degree of authority to devolve upon the miniature sanhedrin: it was to meet without commission and without authoritative communication from either side. How the referees might be brought into existence, heaven alone knew; even if this hurdle was crossed, 'such questions as that of the order of procedure and the differences between the two Houses' were expressly excluded from consideration.[4] Carnarvon came to Town to press the suggestion, heard this and gave the matter up.[5] Like Selborne, he apportioned blame not

---

[1] F. B. (ed.), *The Lords and the Franchise Bill, Containing the Debates in the House of Lords, and the Ministerial Statement and Subsequent Discussion in the House of Commons* (1884), Preface.
[2] Northcote Memo., 26 Oct. 1884. Lang, *Northcote*, p. 353.
[3] Northcote to Norton, 27 Oct. 1884. Iddesleigh Mss., 50042 fol. 64.
[4] Northcote Memo., 'Substance of Conversation with May', 28 Oct. 1884. Iddesleigh Mss., 50042 fol. 69.
[5] Salisbury to Cairns, 28 Oct. 1884. Cairns Mss., PRO. 30/15/6, fol. 160.

unevenly: 'There is a certain "shiftiness" on the Govt. side, due I think to the fears wh. they entertain of their Radical supporters; they make proposals; & then when one tries to come to business, they water them down by modifications which alter their whole character. On the other hand there is a section & an influential one of our own party...opposed to any & every arrangement.'[1]

On 9 October, the *Standard* 'sprang a mine',[2] publishing draft Redistribution proposals and *minutiae* and statistics of the Cabinet Committee. As a scoop, it matched Mudford's earlier successes, *qua* receiver of stolen goods, in securing the 1880 Irish Land bill while it was still in the Government printers' hands and an abstract of Disraeli's *Endymion* a week before first review copies were despatched.[3] In immediate political terms, it solved nothing – witness still such silly escapades as Norton's, or Ponsonby's immovable belief that all might yet rest upon the simple insertion of a date clause. But the leak had the effect of producing more extensive discussion of such pressing topics as the just apportionment between urban, suburban and rural interests. It baulked those who, like Labouchère, hoped by howling for blue blood to drive nervous Whigs into political exile,[4] and it made yet more impossible an autumn Session on the well-trod lines of 'Franchise alone'. It changed the 'current of people's interest from Franchise and Lords; and there', Radicals acknowledged, was 'the mischief of it.'[5] A fortnight before, when the *Pall Mall Gazette* got wind of the Redistribution Cabinet Committee meetings, Gladstone was advised to circulate a stern memorandum to its members enjoining absolute secrecy as 'otherwise we shall have the scheme, or its details in the paper before the house meets.'[6]

There was a certain amount of melodramatic consternation; one Minister suspected for a moment that a dismissed man-servant had taken swift revenge by rifling his private papers.[7] And there was a good deal of chaff; the scheme was unmistakably 'the child of Lefevre – down to *40,000* limit for 2 which saves Reading!!!'[8] In

---

[1] Carnarvon to Richmond, 3 Nov. 1884. Goodwood Mss., 872/P64.
[2] Hamilton Diary, 9 Oct. 1884. Hamilton Mss., 48637 fol. 122; *Standard*, 9 Oct. 1884, p. 5. [3] T. H. S. Escott, *Masters of English Journalism* (1911), p. 203.
[4] Wolff Memo., 13 Nov. 1884. Churchill Mss., 4/492.
[5] Morley to Spence Watson, 11 Oct. 1884. Hirst, *Morley*, Vol. II, p. 201; H. H. Fowler to Morley, Oct. 1884. Chamberlain Mss., JC5/24/70a.
[6] Seymour to Hamilton, 28 Sept. 1884. Hamilton Mss., 48615.
[7] Mundella to Hartington, 9 Oct. 1884. Devonshire Mss., 340.1547.
[8] H. H. Fowler to Morley, Oct. 1884. Chamberlain Mss., JC5/24/70a.

fact, because the *Standard* scheme contained corrections known only to Dilke, Lambert and Howel Thomas (Lambert's secretary at the Local Government Board), all other members of the Cabinet Committee were cleared. There is no doubt that the actual sale of material was effected by the Eyre & Spottiswoode master-foreman, who had previously offered the article to Levy Lawson of the *Telegraph* for £10. Such low-level surreptitious dealing does not, of course, exclude the possibility of direction from above; it may indeed have served as a cover. And it certainly does not matter that Howel Thomas 'for months, if not years...went about armed with these documents [incriminating the printing officers] ready against attack.'[1] Playing a fine semantic game, the Government *communiqué* promptly denied authenticity (on the tenuous ground that, though palpably 'the scheme' and bearing Dilke and Lambert's signatures, it was not final because it had not been submitted to the full Cabinet);[2] but the denial made absurd reading since it was simultaneously asserted that the material had been obtained by breach of *official* trust. There must be further doubt about the detailed refinement which was offered by Dilke – that the *Standard*, given the document on the day of a Cabinet, deduced that the marginal alterations had been made there and then published the article on the day fixed for its next meeting.[3] The fact remains that despite Childers' advice to act through the Treasury Solicitor and the police, no prosecution followed; and Spottiswoode had a cast-iron defence in the sense that the parcelling out of confidential papers ensured that no employee ever had access to the whole.[4]

The 'knowing ones' on either side of St. James's Street 'knew' the leak was no happy accident and that the Government's indignation concealed considerable relief that it had managed to surrender information without an appearance of submission.[5] Those who asked who had been responsible plumped for Dilke[6] – and the culprit's hat fitted.[7] What Hartington's Rawtenstall speech

---

[1] Dilke Memoir, 9 Oct. 1884. Dilke Mss., 43938 fol. 262.
[2] Mundella to Leader, 9 Oct. 1884. Mundella–Leader Mss.
[3] Dodson Cabinet Minutes, 22 Oct. 1884. Monk Bretton Mss., 62.
[4] Clarke, *Life*, p. 231; Childers to Dilke, 10 Oct. 1884. Dilke Mss., 43891 fol. 221.
[5] *Life of Raikes*, p. 220; Mundella to Hartington, 9 Oct. 1884. Devonshire Mss., 340.1547.
[6] Morley to Chamberlain, 11 Oct. 1884. Chamberlain Mss., JC5/54/579.
[7] If anything ought to arouse suspicion in collections of political correspondence, it is not what is not there (the Dilke Diary excisions raise no problems) but what is in super-abundance. Dilke was almost obsessed by the most

had shown Dilke was that he would gain nothing, and could only lose, from the continuance of offers (which Hartington would assuredly continue to make) about the timing of the bills' stages. Publication served to draw opposition into the open and to enable Dilke to fight on his home ground.

Dilke was a natural autocrat who suffered no fool gladly. He wanted control of the details of Redistribution, with Lambert as guarantor that legislation would follow the precedents of 1832. Gladstone imposed a Committee upon him. Dilke agreed to Hartington, Kimberley and Shaw-Lefevre;[1] and ultimately found himself surrounded by Chamberlain, Childers, Derby and James in addition. They drove him 'wild with piddling points',[2] when given the chance to speak, Childers being concerned only with the fate of Pontefract, Kimberley with the re-enfranchisement of Great Yarmouth, and Hartington with the conversion of Clitheroe's 'sham borough' into a county division.[3] But for the most part Dilke could rely upon natural indolence (Derby served Liverpool interests ill by non-attendance) and the prior claims of social engagements during the Recess.[4] He made little attempt to keep others informed of developments: Hartington – in a scene which epitomised the whole – poignantly requested that papers be circulated *before* the Committee should meet again, but later admitted to Granville that he had given the first full draft little consideration and could lay no claim to have mastered its detail.[5]

Dilke's *Memoir* characteristically paints a picture of 'Dilke first

harmless intrigue. He revealed the observer's fascination but, where others would simply have maintained silence about their own activities, Dilke, rather than cover tracks, pronounced them Gladstone's, Horace Seymour's or Brett's. His protestations and denunciations are always too shrill, too full, too widely broadcast and, perhaps above all, too well preserved in their multiplicity to carry conviction. See, e.g., the Dunraven blackballing incident at Grillions; Dilke Diary, 3 May 1884. Dilke Mss., 43926 fol. 10. Or, of greater moment, the *Daily News* kite on Cowper's suggested compromise. Dilke Diary, 21, 22 and 25 Aug. 1884. Dilke Mss., 43926 fol. 29; Memoir, 25 Aug. 1884. Dilke Mss., 43938 fol. 230; Dilke to Grant Duff, 29 Aug. 1884. Dilke Mss., 43894 fol. 141; Dilke to Chamberlain, n.d. Chamberlain Mss., JC5/24/56.
[1] Dilke to Gladstone, 8 Aug. 1884. Gladstone Mss., 44149 fol. 223.
[2] Dilke to Chamberlain, 8 Oct. 1884. Dilke Mss., 43886 fol. 227.
[3] Dilke to James, 19 Aug. 1884. Dilke Mss., 43892 fol. 39; Dilke Memoir, 13 Sept. 1884. Dilke Mss., 43938 fol. 234; Dilke, 'Notes to Accompany Explanatory Memorandum', 19 Sept. 1884. Dilke Mss., 43923 fol. 179.
[4] Kimberley to Dilke, 2 Sept. 1884. Dilke Mss., 43891 fol. 264; Dilke to Gladstone, 13 Sept. 1884. Gladstone Mss., 44149 fol. 229.
[5] Hartington to Dilke, 4 Sept. 1884. Dilke Mss., 43891 fol. 72; Hartington to Granville, 20 Sept. 1884. Granville Mss., PRO. 30/29/134.

and the rest nowhere'. On 14 July, Gladstone broached his Redistribution views '& we practically hatched the Bill'. A month later no-one demurred at the general lines; the Committee sanctioned Dilke and Lambert's 'go[ing] on with our scheme', with the result that he came thereafter to expect that others would 'fall in with whatever we propose' and, satisfying his expectations time and time again, 'got my own way in everything.'[1]

This was true of detail, and why it should have been so is clear once we remember that the Redistribution scheme had much in common with a set of accounts, the smallest amendment demanding counter-balances, which themselves called for further amendment to a third equation. Reduction in the number of Irish Members from 103 would (as Gladstone so wearily reminded Hartington of the endless, repercussive process) 'entail reduction for Wales: and this would I suppose entail County amalgamation: and this would run into Scotland.'[2] Once a plausible scheme was produced, the onus would be upon others to keep the ledger straight by proposing an additional seat here or the throwing of a market town into a county constituency there; and Dilke, who had command of the relevant figures, rarely assisted by providing the complement to such suggestions. This was the essence of his control. Its limit was marked by Gladstone's insistence that Irish representation should remain constant, which Dilke himself would never have suggested.

That this was so, there can be no doubt. But why so? No ready answer is to be found in the correspondence of those immediately involved, and testimony after action is for the most part quite valueless in establishing aim and motive. James, however, reflected on the Redistribution legislation of 1884 some sixteen years later for the benefit of the Liberal Union Club. His reflection has peculiar force. It was a speech provoked by English constituency pressure to reduce Irish representation to some 70, and delivered by a Liberal Unionist defector who had been closely involved in the shaping of Gladstone's measure. It was, James contended, 'the very essence and kernel of our [Unionist] faith...that the three countries form the United Kingdom', so that equal electoral representation for Ireland as against Great Britain must mean equalisation within Ireland, within England, and within Scotland.

<hr />

[1] Dilke Memoir, 14 July 1884. Dilke Mss., 43938 fol. 199; Dilke to Gladstone, 14 Aug. 1884. Gladstone Mss., 44149 fol. 225; Dilke to James, 19 Aug. 1884. Dilke Mss., 43892 fol. 39; Dilke to Gladstone, 13 Sept. 1884. Gladstone Mss., 44149 fol. 229; Dilke Diary, 25 Oct. 1884. Dilke Mss., 43926 fol. 35.

[2] Gladstone to Hartington, 29 Oct. 1884. Gladstone Mss., 44147 fol. 166.

Thus, 'when we take 30 members from Ireland and appropriate them to the representation of England we shall have to see that justice is done in carrying out the principle that we have applied in Ireland.' But 'if you do this[,] you will see a result great and startling coming into existence. We shall have to accept equal electoral districts' which would be incompatible with the preservation of 'the representation of different interests.' The reasoning is so Gladstonian in quality that we may probably accept as historically valid what James was anxious to impress on his audience. This want of equality (i.e. equality on the basis of total populations) between the three kingdoms so as to *obviate* the creation for voting purposes of 'artificial' electoral divisions with uniform populations was 'advisedly' and 'intentionally' the creation of 1884.[1]

Not surprisingly, this disdain of mathematical precision and of the rule of numbers at the expense of community interests found no reflection in tables and schedules.[2] It would be harsh to say that Dilke chose his statistics simply in order to prove Gladstone's case about Irish representation: the 1881 Census *was* the standard reference. Yet three years' obsolescence suited Gladstone's purpose. Ireland's one Member to each 50,250 of population was defensible as very much on a par with England and Scotland, while reports by the three Registrars-General of estimated populations at 1 January 1886, when legislation after all might be expected to take effect, did not suit it so well. Ireland's quota then looked 'very different & very bad', with such areas as Glamorgan, North Lanark and Middlesex 'rapidly increasing, whereas the whole of the Irish counties, with the single exception of the county of Dublin, are decreasing, & most of them decreasing very fast.' Hence the decision not only to ignore but also to suppress the estimates as 'probably any report on Redistribution which we print may one day come into the hands of our successors.'[3]

The logic of parity may have been specious and the correlation not politically assured, but the course issuing from it was, nevertheless, extremely tortuous. Just as attainment of the mathematical

---

[1] Henry James, Lord James of Hereford, *The Question of Redistribution: Speech at the Annual Meeting of the Liberal Union Club, April 6th 1900* (1900), pp. 3–8.

[2] Bright, sensing that the excess of even 3 Members would be resented by not a few Liberals, took 100 to be unassailable – better this Act of Union buttress than any fancy figures. Bright to James, 16 Oct. 1884. James of Hereford Mss.

[3] Dilke to Gladstone, 18 Sept. 1884. Gladstone Mss., 44149 fol. 231.

norm and recommended ratio between Member and head of constituent population could at any time be ignored if the area was not homogeneous enough in terms of 'interest', so did the preservation of existing 'interests' depend upon a mathematical minimum. Whitby, enfranchised in 1832 as 'the seat of a peculiar industry in England – the whale fishery', now went under because it had fewer than 15,000 inhabitants. It was a melancholy indication to Halifax of the way things were going; there never would be 'such a highly educated class of members as were sent up by the rotten boroughs.'[1] The casual observer of the Government's decimation of Irish boroughs by application of the English rules of merger might suppose that the Liberal Government had attempted to do what James had maintained they had striven to avoid. From one light, this would simply be to mistake the packaging for the essence of the bill. From another, it would be a perfectly sensible observation, since packaging was of the essence if the Government proposals were to withstand attack, including the charge of mathematical imprecision. There was really no paradox here; the approach to equality (one vote, one value) was the very surest means, when the term was anathema to the bulk of the Commons, of avoiding equal electoral districts.

In his sardonic comment upon a *Morning Post* Redistribution kite, Chamberlain agreed with others in thinking that Salisbury had inspired it: 'Minority repn. in urban districts. Single member constituencies in Counties – i.e. Tory minority represented in towns & Liberal minority extinguished in Country.'[2] His easy assignation of party advantage has historical importance since such statements about Redistribution proposals – ascribing motive and predicting effects – are so rare that, when found, they call for comment.

In 1883, Hay had introduced a complete Redistribution bill whose core was an extension of the minority vote. Prior to this Walter Morrison had detailed a measure to provide for the abolition of all existing sub-divisions of counties and the introduction of cumulative voting by county. These schemes, said Dilke, though they might readily be drawn up, 'the Cabinet would not look at.'[3] Why not? The first answer must be that no Cabinet minister could gainsay Dilke's assurance that 'grouping with cumulative vote is

---

[1] Halifax to Albert Grey, 4 Nov. 1884. Grey Mss.
[2] Chamberlain note on letter from Dilke, 28 Oct. 1884. Dilke Mss., 43886 fol. 247.
[3] Dilke to Spencer, 26 Sept. 1884. Spencer Mss.

the Tory game.'[1] But ought it to have been? Gladstone, inviting Edward Russell's opinion upon the working of the ward system in municipal Liverpool, recalled that this mode of division was regarded by the Conservative Opposition of 1835 as the most powerful protection to their interests.[2] With Conservative votes and voters traditionally more evenly diffused and the Liberal unduly concentrated, any parcelling out of the borough electoral areas into small districts would, it was thought, benefit the former.[3] The very mention of grouping was sufficient to raise traditional Radical hackles: Tories, they believed, wished to gut the counties by erecting clusters of boroughs and wanted 'Country gentlemen & Farmers & the manageable Laborers to be kept separate in County Constituencies.'[4] But was the cumulative vote certain to produce Tory gains, and was this why Tories proposed it? Those who thought at all about the cumulative vote found a personal, rather than an electoral, explanation of Tory involvement. Salisbury, they suspected, was humouring Churchill in the 'radical' extravagance of his bidding; he was 'abandon[ing] all *impedimenta*' and would 'stick at nothing', if only for the moment. Staid Liberals consoled themselves that there must surely be 'some *arrière pensée*, some scheme of Fancy Franchises...for neutralizing the new County householders, in reserve for us'[5] – and for Churchill. Would, then, the Liberals be better advised to propose the division of 'urban counties' (the West Riding, Glamorgan, North Lanark, Middlesex, and virtually all Lancashire) into single-member districts?

Akers-Douglas, finding himself sharing a railway carriage with Chamberlain, discovered that the Government would merge a number of smaller boroughs into the counties and give some of the seats thus gained to the urban centres – proposals seemingly innocent and inevitable enough, yet to the Conservative Chief Whip

[1] Dilke to Chamberlain, 2 Oct. 1884. Chamberlain Mss., JC5/24/62.
[2] Gladstone to E. R. Russell, 23 July 1884. Gladstone Mss., 44547 fol. 87.
[3] Albert Grey to Halifax, 8 Nov. 1884. Hickleton Mss., A4.84 Part 4.
[4] Bright to James, 16 Oct. 1884. James of Hereford Mss. And if 'so palpable a dodge' might be effected in 'the wee laird interest', why, ran the querulous Radical refrain, was there 'nobody especially [appointed] to care for the Cotton or Woollen interests or for Iron & Coal.' See T. G. Rigg, *Political Parties, their Present Position and Prospects* (1881), p. 31.
[5] Mundella to Leader, 17 Sept. 1884. Mundella–Leader Mss. See also Dodson Cabinet Minutes, 22 Oct. 1884: 'Forwood's article *is* the Conserve. scheme says Harcourt – (they would use it to upset us – & then drop it & take to Salisbury's minority dodges.' Monk Bretton Mss., 62.

'as bad an arrangement for us as it would be possible to devise.'[1] Chamberlain certainly thought it would be popular to create new boroughs if the materials were available;[2] but if the Parliamentary boundaries had to be extended beyond the municipal ones in order to get the requisite population, possibly the inhabitants of 'urban districts outside of them would object to inclusion for fear city or municipal boundaries and *rates* should also be extended'.[3] And was not the game of uniting towns so as to save representation likely to meet with an even greater degree of local opposition which would be overridden only, as at Warwick and Leamington, where the two were indistinguishable rather than merely adjacent? The instances where boundary adjustment might be made were not plentiful, and on the broader scale, Dilke refused to sanction new anomalies (as unlikely to conciliate anyone) by the creation of boroughs of less than average size. The maxim that 'anomalies tell against the Liberal party'[4] was sufficiently powerful to withstand the tests of experience or reason, but if the uniform establishment of single-member seats in boroughs would make it impossible in future to harness a more with a less advanced Liberal, and if it might result even in open competition between Whig and Radical candidates, what was the real value of Chamberlain's counter-demand 'not [to] give up 2 member seats unless you get a great concession say [a] limit of 25000'?[5] Rural constituencies might on these arrangements be contaminated with an urban population, but would it not be likely to founder on MPs' reluctance to see any borough seats abolished? So argued Gladstone and Lambert against the total merger line being hoisted from 10,000 to 15,000.

The benefits to one party or the other which might be expected to stem from minority representation, single-member constituencies in town or county, the cumulative vote, equal electoral districts, new boroughs and the raising or lowering of the merger limit – these are as expectations politically comprehensible, even if they are unconvincing where they rest upon myth. Intelligible too in view of the inviolability of Ireland was Gladstone's preference for increasing the size of the Commons to accommodate twelve more Members for Scotland (his nearest approach to a Midlothian

[1] Winn to Salisbury, 16 Sept. 1884. Salisbury Mss., Series E.
[2] Chamberlain to Dilke, 1 Oct. 1884. Chamberlain Mss., JC5/24/361.
[3] Dilke, 'Notes to Accompany Explanatory Memorandum', 19 Sept. 1884. Dilke Mss., 43923 fol. 179. (My italics.)
[4] *Ibid.*
[5] Chamberlain to Dilke, 22 Oct. 1884. Dilke Mss., 43886 fol. 243.

election promise)[1] instead of making England pay for this extra representation.[2] One cannot, however, even divine what lay behind the Cabinet Committee's determination to reject the Dilke–Lambert proposal for large boroughs (by which two Members would be allotted for the first 100,000 of population, and one additional one for each 100,000 over and above that) in favour of another to give six Members to boroughs with populations over 400,000, four to those over 300,000 and two for the 100,000 to 300,000 group. In this way, Tower Hamlets, Birmingham, Hackney and Manchester each gained a Member, provided at the expense of Bristol, Greenwich, Southwark and Westminster. Did this reflect a Whig desire to fix some ceiling to the representation of industrial centres? or was it, as Lambert suggested, that uneven numbers provoked the question of minority voting, which the Committee simply shirked?[3]

The historian must confirm Dilke's boast that the majority of his colleagues on the Redistribution Committee did not know what they were doing nor why they were doing it. Amendments were offered and accepted, but the basis of Dilke's proposals was never assailed. In sharp contrast, Carnarvon demanded of the Opposition that they be prepared for all contingencies:[4]

disfranchisement of all small boros & appropriation of seats according to population

disfranchisement carried still higher so as to include towns of 40,000

districts of 50,000 *electors*...unified

some attempt to distribute according to numbers but a grouping of towns in order to maintain the difference of town & country

---

[1] 'Broken pledges' provided Tory propagandists with endless copy. It was put about in 1882 that the unavailability of the printed Midlothian speeches had a sinister explanation: Gladstone had called in all remaining stocks to save himself further embarrassment. Morley to Hamilton, 25 Oct. 1882. Hamilton Mss., 48619. See also 'Amende Déshonorable':

> I said in my haste, O Karolyi! what now I've forgotten I uttered –
> I wish not a soul to remember the eight-thousand-odd words I
>   spluttered.
> It's really not fair that a Premier should answer for gibes he
>   out-flung
> When he was but a soldier of fortune, and his sword was his
>   venemous tongue.

in 'An Outsider', *The Gladstone Rule: a Retrospective Commentary* (Edinburgh, 1885), pp. 22–3.

[2] Gladstone to Dilke, 29 Sept. 1884. Gladstone Mss., 44547 fol. 116.

[3] Lambert Memo., 27 Sept. 1884. Gladstone Mss., 44235 fol. 184.

[4] Carnarvon to Winn, 29 Aug. 1884. Nostell Mss., 1/117. (My italics.)

This may be taken as indicative of nothing more than Opposition diligence. But it does incidentally raise the question whether the Committee's thinking ever encompassed such a mass of basic options. It gave Lancashire twelve more Members, the West Riding eleven, Middlesex five, Glamorgan and Durham four, and approved a net increase of county Members (53 on the first draft) which brought county representation up to borough level.[1] Did they know that every statistic which buttressed the borough/county ratio of their first draft would have fallen to the ground if the Boundary Commissioners had added suburban populations to the towns?

Quite independently – and as such ominously presaging an alliance of Radicalism and Tory Democracy – Stead and Forwood examined this 'twopenny-halfpenny' measure when it appeared in the *Standard*. They found there some three million county voters in excess of the known rural population, and 'large centres of manufacturing industries, contiguous to large Boroughs, left in the County'.[2] They could have been far more devastating in their criticism if they had known that Dilke and Lambert, at this point, relied heavily upon the Boundary Commission Report and maps of 1868. Forwood could certainly produce figures to show that by equal electoral districts of 54,000 and the rigorous separation of 'interests', urban constituencies in England and Wales might expect 280 seats (against their present 295) and the counties 200 (against 187).[3] It was not simply a question of discussion in the dark: politicians with intimate knowledge of local idiosyncrasies boasted their ability to guarantee the return of a Member of their particular colour if given the chance to settle the boundaries in a vast complex like Manchester and South-East Lancashire.[4] So much for those who argued that, once the same franchise was established in borough, county and suburb, it would not matter where or under what circumstance the individual exercised his right to vote. Shaw-Lefevre's sublime hope 'that we might well give a

---

[1] Memo. as to the *Standard* scheme, unidentified hand (possibly A. B. Forwood's). Churchill Mss., 4/478. The attraction was abundantly clear: 'Under Equal Electoral districts (Urban & suburban separate) Liverpool would have 12 or 13 single members & I am within the mark in saying that 8 would fall to us 2 to Home Rulers & 2 to Liberals. To my mind ensuring a perfect system of representation of all interests.'
[2] *Pall Mall Gazette*, 10 Oct. 1884, p. 1.
[3] A. B. Forwood, 'Redistribution: Electoral Districts', *Contemporary Review*, Vol. XLVI (Oct. 1884), pp. 580–4.
[4] Arnold to Dilke, 10 Oct. 1884. Chamberlain Mss., JC5/24/68a.

few more seats to English agricultural counties' was the nearest any Committee member came to discussion of fundamentals.[1]

It was, quite naturally, on to this facer for the agricultural interest that Salisbury seized: 'The vice of the scheme [as given by the *Standard*] is that it does nothing to take urban patches out of counties.'[2] This was unexceptionable comment and, as such, in keeping with his rapidly maturing style of leadership. In 1867, though right in judgment and reading of the Parliamentary scene, he had lost by taking the risk of resignation. In 1884 he made no tactical error as leader – or only a minor one in suggesting to the Queen that there was no danger in prolongation of the (sham) public agitation, when to the Queen, Republican agitation in Brussels seemed uncomfortably close; though this probably did no more than surrender the advantage gained by Gladstone's effrontery in agitating 'under her nose' at Aberdeen and Perth while she was in residence at Balmoral.[3]

Salisbury succeeded throughout the autumn of 1884 in satisfying the great majority that he was their man – and this was no mean achievement when the party was charged with chaotic 'running up and down... between the two standards of class government and democratic Toryism.'[4] It was a singular achievement at a time when any serious airing of fundamental issues must have betrayed that clash of interest between the Tory borough Members and their 'Southern County' colleagues – the first with seats jeopardised by dissolution, the second fearful of any Redistribution proposed and secure in the farming community's support against change.[5] Dilke was asked by a correspondent, what was 'the game of the Lords'. He would have nothing of it: it was 'the game of Salisbury' – to make himself 'undisputed leader of his party...[while] he also scores for the Lords by appearing to win on *their* issues', and by appearing to save them from absolute ineffectiveness.[6] Even those

---

[1] Dilke, 'Notes to Accompany Explanatory Memorandum', 19 Sept. 1884. Dilke Mss., 43923 fol. 179.
[2] Salisbury to Northcote, 11 Oct. 1884. Iddesleigh Mss., 50020 fol. 88.
[3] It was always said that the Queen objected to the priority given in the press to Gladstone's whistle-stop travels over any Royal progress, and to the size of print accorded to a Court Circular beneath the verbatim report of a two-hour Midlothian oration.
[4] Beatrice Webb Diary, 24 Oct. 1884. Typescript Copy. Passfield Mss., Vol. 7, fol. 9.
[5] Childers to Halifax, 13 Nov. 1884. Hickleton Mss., A4.90. See also James Cornford, 'The Transformation of Conservatism in the Late Nineteenth Century', *Victorian Studies* Vol. vii (1963), pp. 35–66.
Dilke to Grant Duff, 18 Aug. 1884. Dilke Mss., 43894 fol. 39.

Whigs who recognized that 'the time seems to be really come...
when some change neither can nor ought to be long avoided' in the
composition and powers of the Upper House, still regretted
Gladstone's forcing forward of the question in so crude a manner.[1]
Concentration upon the constitutional issue had, however, this
drawback for Salisbury – that 'the obtuser Lords', forgetting what
it was that they were contending for upon Reform, might be
deluded into 'sav[ing] their dignity' by 'some cunning half measure'
of Gladstone's upon the latter.[2] Speculation upon the exact nature
of that 'cunning half measure' leads naturally to consideration of
Salisbury's thoughts about the principles and details of Redistribution, about the possibility of a settlement with Gladstone and
about the tactics he ought to adopt for the autumn Session. And
to ask what it was that Salisbury was contending for, raises the
question whether this standard academic approach is one that is
always the most revealing.

The course sketched out in July at the Carlton Club – by which
the Lords would defer until, say, 1 May 1885 the Second Reading of
the Franchise bill if it was re-submitted alone – had much to
commend it. The Government might be induced thereby to yield,
producing and proceeding with Redistribution, or to kill their own
bill by a second Prorogation. Furthermore, if such a date was fixed,
the vote was irrevocable and sufficient to stymie 'all attempts at
compromises, bridges, open doors, & the rest – which Wemyss or
R. Churchill, or Jersey, may be inclined to try.'[3] This range of
possibilities was never a decided policy. It was submitted for what
it was before the antics of the Recess and before the *Standard*'s
divulgation. It may indeed have been no more than a gesture of
determination to secure the support of the Tory press during the
extra-Parliamentary campaign[4] or 'a lever for obtaining a settlement, reasonably satisfactory, of the danger we...apprehended.'[5]
There is, in fact, no reason to think that any part of it was immut-
able. Time passed and circumstance altered. Northcote 'fished' but
Salisbury kept his own counsel.

During the early autumn Northcote thought a great deal and
made a good many tentative suggestions. He proposed that the
Lords might advance beyond the Second Reading before fixing the

---

[1] Earl Grey to Halifax, 2 Sept. 1884. Hickleton Mss., A4.55.16.
[2] Salisbury to Winn, 4 Sept. 1884. Nostell Mss., 2/1.
[3] *Ibid.*
[4] Austin, *Autobiography*, Vol. II, p. 243.
[5] Cairns to Richmond, 6 Nov. 1884. Goodwood Mss., 872/P68.

date for the later stages.[1] He proposed to Winn that they meet the introduction of the Franchise bill with a motion involving an Address for a Dissolution;[2] he then passed off the suggestion to Salisbury as Winn's so that Salisbury might pronounce more freely upon the efficacy of bidding for the Parnellite vote on the Franchise bill's Second Reading in an attempt to induce the Government to resign. He heard it rumoured that Gorst went about 'saying he considers the row over and a compromise certain'[3] and inquired whether Winn knew 'what Randolph thinks.'[4] He wanted, of course, to learn how things stood between Salisbury and Churchill. The *Standard*'s 'abolition' of minority voting provoked a direct inquiry of Salisbury whether this might be made a vital issue,[5] though this question was secondary in Northcote's mind since he was much more interested in the Gordon Castle conference then taking place between Salisbury, Cairns and Richmond, which brutally emphasized the full extent to which he was being ignored.[6]

That was so, but Northcote need not have assumed that Cairns, Richmond or anybody else was better placed. Salisbury's enunciations and various hints as to what was desirable or what attainable merit tabulation, not for their prismatic diversity (which has only antiquarian interest), but as proof that he saw the need to accommodate a spectrum of interests and opinions. Argyll was prompted by a passage in Salisbury's Sheffield speech of 22 July – that Redistribution was too important for settlement by one party – to suggest 'what used to be called in the Old India Board "P.C." = Previous communication'[7] between the leaders, with Argyll of course as chairman. The need to keep Moderate-Whig-Constitutionalists sweet was perhaps paramount, for Gladstone spared no effort to 'work down the majority & work up the minority in the H. of Lds'[8] and repeatedly declared his faith in the good sense of the Conservative party, if not of its leaders.

To the independent observer, settlement always seemed most likely to be reached not by Salisbury and Northcote, 'but by a

---

[1] Northcote to Salisbury, 21 Sept. 1884. Salisbury Mss., Series E.
[2] Northcote to Winn, 29 Sept. 1884. Nostell Mss., 2/8.
[3] Northcote to Salisbury, 7 Oct. 1884. Iddesleigh Mss., 50020 fol. 77.
[4] Northcote to Winn, 7 Oct. 1884. Nostell Mss., 2/12.
[5] Northcote to Salisbury, 10 Oct. 1884. Salisbury Mss., Series E.
[6] Clarke, *Life*, p. 224.
[7] Argyll to Salisbury, 24 July 1884. Salisbury Mss., Series E.
[8] Gladstone to Kimberley, 3 Oct. 1884. Gladstone Mss., 44547 fol. 119. Lyons in Paris and Lansdowne in Canada were both asked to journey home for the November division, and Dufferin to delay his departure for India.

section of their party who will break away'.[1] Under whom? – 'the question is whether some 30 will turn[;] if anything like a man of influence gave them a lead I have no doubt of it, but I do not see the man to head them.'[2] To Argyll, as at Gordon Castle to Richmond and Cairns, each of whom might cast himself in that role, Salisbury reported himself 'in no way opposed to some compromise being arranged'.[3] Indeed, he somewhat ungenerously let it be known that it was Northcote's hostility to the January 1886 date clause which had determined the course of action in July.[4] When bearded by Norton about the delegation of Redistribution to the 'righteous men', Salisbury avoided the snub[5] which might have cost him Carnarvon's backing. Suspicious, too, that the Queen might enjoy a conspiratorial role in the constitutional battle, Salisbury 'cheerfully compl[ied]' with her every suggestion;[6] even to the extent of appearing to welcome a confidential discussion between the party leaders on the basis of Hartington's Rawtenstall speech.

Salisbury always knew that the 'conceding temper' of his 'two wise counsellors in the north' and Cairns' weakness for the Grey clause would pose difficulties in the future.[7] Would not Lowther 'come 1,000 miles to vote against that proposal'?[8] On the other hand, since he knew he had to calm his *ultras* – Chaplin, Lowther, Winn and all who hoped to 'put off the evil day of extension of the Franchise a little and perhaps get something out of the scramble'[9] – he left the impression of wishing the Lords to defer the Franchise bill's Second Reading to 1 May 1885 as likely to 'checkmate the Government, & bring about a crisis.'[10] Winn urged that Conservative policy must be 'to force on a dissolution by every means in our power',[11] because 'say what you will, [the Government's] horror of a dissolution does not go down.'[12] Of course, Salisbury hoped for a

1 Bath to Weymouth, 22 Sept. 1884. Bath Mss.
2 Bath to Weymouth, 1 Oct. 1884. Bath Mss.
3 Richmond to the Queen, 9 Oct. 1884. Goodwood Mss., 872/P43.
4 Richmond to Cairns, 24 Sept. 1884. Cairns Mss., PRO. 30/51/4, fol. 193.
5 Hamilton Diary, 26 Oct. 1884. Hamilton Mss., 48638 fol. 18.
6 Carlingford to Gladstone, 5 Nov. 1884. Gladstone Mss., 44123 fol. 233.
7 Salisbury to his Wife, 12 Oct. 1884. Lady Gwendolen Cecil, *Salisbury*, Vol. III, p. 116; Salisbury to Manners, 8 Oct. 1884. Salisbury Mss., Series D.
8 Lowther, 11 July 1884. 3 *Hansard* ccxc. 861.
9 Kennaway to Harrowby, 15 Nov. 1884. Harrowby Mss., 2nd Ser., Vol. 53, fol. 93.
10 Salisbury to Winn, 4 Sept. 1884. Nostell Mss., 2/1.
11 Winn to Salisbury, 6 Oct. 1884. Salisbury Mss., Series E.
12 Salisbury to Northcote, 9 Oct. 1884. Iddesleigh Mss., 50020 fol. 86.

new and better Commons before a Redistribution bill was introduced, and he did not despair of the chances.[1] Well into the eleventh hour, Chaplin, under such encouragement from Salisbury, was taking bets 'round the dinner table' that Franchise would not find its way onto the Statute Book during the present Parliament.[2] Whether or not Salisbury's article, 'The Value of Redistribution', published in the *National Review* in October, was intended to act as a 'wet blanket' on this section of his followers (the Downing Street interpretation),[3] there was nothing here to commit the party. He proclaimed that the Conservatives need have no dread of enfranchisement provided it was coupled with a fair Seats bill which would recognize and accord due representation to all the interests in the country. He bound himself neither to minority representation nor to cumulative voting: he called for a responsible Boundary Commission and a fairer representation of urban and rural interests (which might involve single-member constituencies). At Pomona Gardens, in urging the electors of Lancashire not to rest until they obtained their 63 MPs, he had countenanced a pure population base, which was interpreted immediately as a sop to Churchill[4] and as heralding 'a sort of open competition [to see] which party can go furthest.'[5] It says much for his duplicity that while Salisbury was thought to be considering even 'an alliance with Chamberlain & electoral districts'[6] or 'some system of voting which shall disregard territorial divisions altogether',[7] he could reassure traditionalist Tories that the representation of interests and demarcation between urban and rural was '*the* thing to struggle for'.[8] It says much also that while Gladstonians feared a 'monstrous' coalition of Lubbock, Courtney, Fawcett, Grey, Goschen,[9] the Parnellites and the Tories[10] on the minority voting issue, Salisbury returned the most oblique of evasions to Smith's tabling of the disparity (to Conservative

---

[1] Salisbury to Winn, 13 Oct. 1884. Nostell Mss., 2/16.
[2] Hamilton Diary, 17 Nov. 1884. Hamilton Mss., 48638 fol. 53.
[3] Hamilton Diary, 30 Sept. 1884. Hamilton Mss., 48637 fol. 100.
[4] *Pall Mall Gazette*, 11 Aug. 1884, p. 1.
[5] Kimberley to Dilke, 2 Sept. 1884. Dilke Mss., 43891 fol. 264.
[6] Childers to Halifax, 12 Sept. 1884. Hickleton Mss., A4.90.
[7] *The Times*, 25 Sept. 1884, p. 9.
[8] Salisbury to Norton, 24 Oct. 1884. Childe-Pemberton, *Life of Norton*, p. 257.
[9] Lubbock clearly hoped for more positive, energetic involvement from Goschen during the autumn Session than he had hitherto offered in the Proportionalist game. Solicitations were, however, rebuffed. Goschen to Lubbock, 19 Oct. 1884. Avebury Mss., 49644 fol. 75.
[10] Reay to Hamilton, 27 Oct. 1884. Hamilton Mss., 48618; Reay to Rosebery, 27 Oct. 1884. Rosebery Mss., Box 34.

disadvantage) between votes cast and Members returned:[1] 'I understand that G.O.M. lays it down as a condition precedent to any agreement that there should be no legislation in favour of minorities. I wonder if this is true.'[2] Dilke took Salisbury to be 'only keeping his friends in good humour with minority representation'.[3] As in this particular, so in all respects, Salisbury was indeed 'keeping his friends in good humour'. What is wrong is to expect anything beyond this or to think it worthwhile to inquire for which of all these various courses a 'free' Salisbury would have settled. In historical evaluation, his self-effacement (which has no bearing upon strength or weakness of leadership) matters infinitely more than any suggestion that he had 'a leaning to proportional representation, especially for Ireland'.[4] Nothing that he said and no comfort that he proffered during the Recess impaired his ability – as Cabinet members recognized – to assail the Government '*for* [*its*] *moderation,* if [it was] moderate in [its] scheme of Redistribution; and for being revolutionary, if [it was] not.'[5] He settled for time, for what was attainable at any moment in time and, throughout all moments of time, for unity under his lead.

There remain two apparent obstacles to acceptance of this view of Salisbury's political brinkmanship. First, that on 12 November, at a meeting of Tory leaders, Salisbury, supported by Manners and Winn, advocated forcing a dissolution and found himself in a minority against Carnarvon, Cross, Northcote and Smith (to whom Cairns and Richmond would have been added had their train arrived earlier from Scotland). Secondly, there is what Lady Gwendolen Cecil calls 'an unquestionable note of regret – almost of apology' in Salisbury's later report to Cranbrook, that 'if we had taken the other course [i.e. continued to resist the Franchise bill] we should have gone to a dissolution very heavily weighted...a great many indications combined to prove that the ice was cracking all round us'.[6] Lady Gwendolen herself, however, unwittingly explained away the second objection in noting that Salisbury's account was for 'the most militant of his colleagues'. The right deduction is surely not that the tone was revealing because the

[1] Smith Memo., 6 Nov. 1884. Hambleden Mss., PS8/125.
[2] Salisbury to Smith, 9 Nov. 1884. Hambleden Mss., PS8/126.
[3] Dilke Memoir, 31 Oct. 1884. Dilke Mss., 43938 fol. 276.
[4] Hartington to Gladstone, 12 Nov. 1884. Gladstone Mss., 44147 fol. 175.
[5] Selborne to Argyll, 31 Oct. 1884. Selborne Mss., 1868 fol. 296.
[6] Lady Gwendolen Cecil, *Salisbury,* Vol. III, p. 121.

letter was confidential; it was resignedly apologetic because resigned apology seemed the surest way of soothing the 'most militant'.

In October 1884, Bath came to the conclusion that Salisbury had taken 'the chance of the Franchise Bill breaking down in the Commons under Irish and Conservative opposition, & of the Government falling to pieces through its foreign policy.'[1] On both counts, this is plausible. The Parnellites would vote on the Second Reading according to the answer they had to the question 'Whether Lord Salisbury means to cut down the Irish vote?'[2] They were already up for auction. As to the second consideration, an emotional outburst may carry weight. When Granville appeared 'much agitated' in insisting that the Lords' Second Reading be brought forward to Tuesday 18 November (the Thursday had already been agreed to), Salisbury volunteered a sinister motive: 'Mark my words, Khartoum has fallen.'[3] But Bath went beyond this, to the essential reasoning behind Salisbury's mask. 'If he has resisted throughout he thinks he will be in a better position when the Bill is before the Lords and most likely even if he approves a compromise he desires to avoid appearing to assent to one but to allow it to be carried as it were over his head.'[4]

[1] Bath to Weymouth, 19 Oct. 1884. Bath Mss.
[2] Northcote to Salisbury, 7 Nov. 1884. Salisbury Mss., Series E.
[3] Harrowby Memo., 11 Nov. 1884. Harrowby Mss., 2nd Ser., Vol. 55, fol. 194. The rumour was circulating yet again. According to Hartington's secretary, 'The F.O. believe the thing has been "got up" by the Paris Bourse, for some reason unknown.' Brett to Milner, 3 Nov. 1884. Milner Mss., Box 181.
[4] Bath to Weymouth, 19 Oct. 1884. Bath Mss.

7

'VERY QUEER SOLUTION'[1]

...portentous relations between the Ministry & Lord Salisbury. The latter seems to be taken into their councils, as if a Cabinet Minister.
Elliot Diary, 22 Nov. 1884. Diaries, Vol. 10.

Lord Salisbury is not at liberty to describe the negotiations between the Government & the Leaders of the Opposition, or to communicate the authorship of particular provisions...But he has no difficulty in contradicting the statement you quote, namely that 'Lord Salisbury & Sir Stafford Northcote were taken into a room, where the Cabinet were sitting, & the Government scheme was laid before them & they were told to accept it as it was, & they did so.'
R. T. Gunton (Salisbury's secretary) to W. J. Chalk, 5 May 1885.
Salisbury Mss., Series C.

THERE WAS never any doubt that the differences about Redistribution which divided Salisbury, Dilke, Churchill, Gladstone and Northcote were negotiable – if only because those who were not weak knew the value of flexibility. Nor were these the only leaders who engaged in negotiation. Even those whose normal positions were not encouraging played their part. It was, after all, Hartington and Hicks Beach who scythed through the undergrowth in three private business meetings – Hartington who has always been tagged 'the last great Whig', Beach who had denounced any 'moderate redistribution, based upon ancient lines' and called for 'electoral districts'.[2] It was, however, open to question whether either party, unaided or faced by inflexibility, could push its own Redistribution bill through the Commons. Neither Gladstone nor anyone else after the experience of 1866–7 would introduce a Seats bill as 'a target to be shot at'[3] by Tory Democrats, Whigs, Proportionalists, Radicals, University Members, the 'country Party', Parnellites, Ulstermen, or the unseated and otherwise afflicted.

As all knew, the Parliamentary game of Redistribution enjoyed

---

[1] Elliot Diary, 18 Nov. 1884. Diaries, Vol. 10.
[2] At Bristol. *The Times*, 8 Oct. 1884, p. 7.
[3] Selborne to Argyll, 4 Nov. 1884. Selborne Mss., 1865 fol. 300.

its own cynical rules: if the Government was defeated on, say, single-member constituencies, the Tories would 'come in and carry the same Bill.'[1] It was, then, no more than an odd pipe-dream of Gladstone's (appropriately furnished with that overture to political irrelevance, 'if the reason of the case were to prevail') that it was incumbent upon the Opposition to propose to the Cabinet a framework of Resolutions '& then be governed by the result.'[2] But Hamilton was wrong if he thought it a shade more realistic to proffer resolutions commanding ministerial adhesion once the Franchise bill was through the Commons.[3] Such a mode of procedure might have been fraught with greater danger even than the introduction of a bill. In an amendment to the latter, 'Minority Representation would...have to be put into shape, whereas in vague terms as an amendment to a Resolution it might be carried.'[4] Dilke, with every justification, objected to stating 'details which might stimulate combinations to defeat all Reform', and retorted sourly when asked what were the bases of Redistribution (bases which might be made the subject of bi-partisan settlement) that 'there are no tenable principles in our bill...our bill is the best we can carry'.[5] If there was to be prior agreement upon Hicks Beach's 'revolutionary' scheme, he was emphatic that the Tories should accept the odium of introducing it. It must 'come out' publicly and avowedly 'from them as theirs & not from us as ours',[6] for fear that, however loyal Conservative front-benchers might be to a front-bench pact, the House might reject the framework. It was an understandable fear when politicians as disparate as Bright, Cranbrook and Goschen united in revulsion against the Beach–Churchill provision whereby 'town and country [were] to be ripped asunder everywhere & to the uttermost';[7] yet Dilke himself agreed that a counter, 'moderate' scheme could never pass.[8]

The less blustering Conservatives confessed that they recognized Redistribution to be as tough a nut for their own party as for

---

[1] Dilke to E. R. Russell, n.d. Dilke Mss., 43913 fol. 28. See also Albert Grey to Halifax, 8 Nov. 1884. Hickleton Mss., A4.84 Part 4.
[2] Gladstone to Hartington, 13 Oct. 1884. Gladstone Mss., 44147 fol. 156.
[3] Dilke to Chamberlain, 26 Sept. 1884. Chamberlain Mss., JC5/24/59.
[4] Dilke to Gladstone, 10 Nov. 1884. Gladstone Mss., 44149 fol. 260.
[5] Dodson Cabinet Minutes, 22 Oct. 1884. Monk Bretton Mss., 62.
[6] Dilke to Hartington, 12 Nov. 1884. Devonshire Mss., 340.1571A.
[7] Gladstone to Derby, 7 Nov. 1884. Gladstone Mss., 44547 fol. 134; Gladstone to the Queen, 7 Nov. 1884. Cab. 41/18/49; Cranbrook to Salisbury, 21 Nov. 1884. Salisbury Mss., Series E.
[8] Dilke Memoir, 13 Nov. 1884. Dilke Mss., 43898 fol. 296.

Gladstone.[1] The accumulation of 'piddling points' – each with endless reverberations – was daunting to both parties. The spectre of Courtney, Fawcett, Grey and Lubbock was rather more than daunting: Salisbury's prior rejection of the 'cumulative vote' or 'some form of minority representation' was to be made a *sine qua non* even of agreement towards agreement and talks about talks.[2] This 'one point [was] everything.'[3]

Proportional Representation and the threat posed by its Parliamentary devotees again serve as the link and clue to political actions. Late in October, the Manchester branch Committee met to discuss 'the best means of prosecuting our crusade'. They decided to 'arrange for lectures during this winter in the local Clubs, and . . . to have a series of public meetings as soon as the Franchise Bill is sufficiently out of the way to allow of public attention being occupied by the Redistribution question.'[4] That the Proportionalists should 'miss out' was in the nature of things.[5] But for others, too, Franchise could never be allowed to pass 'sufficiently out of the way' for Redistribution (*pace* the *Standard*) to absorb public or Parliamentary attention. Gladstone could not allow it, because Franchise must appear threatened so as to be usable as a lever with which to prise the Liberal party towards a speedy settlement of the Redistribution question, and the likelihood of years in the wilderness if they were obstinate. Nor could the Conservatives, in view of

[1] Cairns to Richmond, 12 Nov. 1884. Goodwood Mss., 872/P75. Who would choose to disentangle South-East Scotland? If the combined county constituency of Selkirk and Peebles was not to be deprived of its Member (distasteful to both parties and as unpopular in the House as at grass-roots level), Selkirk town might be removed from the Hawick Burghs to boost county numbers. Hawick and Galashiels would surely cast off with gratitude an unwanted associate in imposed alliance, but then the addition of urban Selkirk to a rural electorate created 'swamping' difficulties. Minto to Elliot, 31 Oct. 1884. Elliot Mss., Bundle 32.

[2] Hartington Memo. of 2nd Conversation with Beach, 2 Nov. 1884. Devonshire Mss., 340.1565.

[3] Dilke to Hartington, 3 Nov. 1884. Devonshire Mss., 340.1566A. See also Dilke Diary, 4 Nov. 1884: 'Beach said that Salisbury thought the minority question shd. be left open like the other points to be discussed between representatives of the two sides. (We object.)' Dilke Mss., 43926 fol. 40.

[4] C. Corbett to Cromwell White, 24 Oct. 1884. P.R.S. Mss.

[5] Albert Grey to Halifax, 8 Nov. 1884: 'but what will you say when I tell you that I believe the compromise will be on the basis of an Ultra Democratic Redistribution. . . Up to yesterday I thought the best security against a Redistribution scheme on the American plan lay in the settlement of Redistribution by the same Parliament which passed Extension. . . . if the Radicals & the Conservatives agree that the equal electoral districts system is the best, then we may chuck up the sponge – Our only chance is in delay.' Hickleton Mss., A4.84 Part 4.

Salisbury's acceptance of Cairns' doctrine that the Lords could not tamper with the details of Redistribution,[1] which was the rightful, even prescriptive, concern of Members of the House of Commons. It was a contention of Salisbury's that 'if everybody rises in the morning with the belief that everything is arranged in the best of all possible worlds – it will give Gladstone a terrible advantage.'[2] This was, of course, plausible, but it was in the long term as necessary for Salisbury (should Redistribution fall into his lap) as for Gladstone that everybody should rise one morning to find that everything had already been arranged.

'Nothing can defeat a measure drawn up concurrently by the two great parties in the State';[3] Buckle was right, but it is almost impossible to identify the point of time at which the realization dawned upon front-rank politicians that a settlement behind the Commons' backs was the one way of obviating the 'curious results' which might be expected from a matter upon which 'local preferences and partialities' dwarfed any 'well defined principle'.[4] Certainly, as early as April, Goschen enjoyed the distinction of a Parliamentary pronouncement that Tories and Liberals must lay their heads together. Argyll, again, in July, had taken up the banner of 'Previous communication', and in September, Hartington chose to interpret a Gladstone 'offer' as meaning an attempt to reach accord with Salisbury on Redistribution.[5] If Harcourt was long disgusted by the idea of '*pourparlers*' and collaboration,[6] Churchill showed himself to be bound by no ordinary party conventions when he communicated to James his and Hicks Beach's views 'which are in favour of nearly equal districts and one member for each district.'[7] Beach suggested to Salisbury, and then to Northcote, the idea of a meeting with Hartington,[8] for which Churchill claimed the credit of authorship,[9] casting James as messenger-boy, with Wolff and

[1] Salisbury to Northcote, 11 Oct. 1884. Iddesleigh Mss., 50020 fol. 88.
[2] Salisbury to Northcote, 7 Nov. 1884. Iddesleigh Mss., 51120 fol. 93.
[3] The Times, 18 Nov. 1884, p. 9.
[4] Cowen to Francis Appleton (of the Newcastle Liberal Association), 7 Aug. 1884. Cowen Mss., F51.
[5] Hartington to Gladstone, 29 Sept. 1884. Holland, Devonshire, Vol. ii, pp. 53–4.
[6] Harcourt 2nd Minute, 13 Nov. 1884. Gladstone Mss., 44199 fol. 111.
[7] James to Hartington, 3 Oct. 1884. Devonshire Mss., 340.1541.
[8] Northcote to Salisbury, 24 Oct. 1884. Salisbury Mss., Series E. Salisbury and Northcote, naturally enough, gave no indication to Charles Peel (i.e., by political transposition, to Richmond) that they knew of the Hartington–Beach meetings. Carlingford to Gladstone, 5 Nov. 1884. Gladstone Mss., 44123 fol. 233. [9] Portarlington to Churchill, n.d. Churchill Mss., 4/486.

Hartington to exchange preliminary diplomatic civilities across Alfred Rothschild's dinner table.[1] The circle of involvement widened and indiscretions multiplied. Dilke, 'to clinch the matter', at once volunteered to draw up a scheme on the Beach lines,[2] contacted Churchill and told Sclater-Booth what Lambert had been doing at the Local Government Board.[3] Cross, hearing that the Government would accept all feasible terms to avoid a repetition of 1866–7, set himself up as representative of sober Conservatism, and declared his preferences to Dilke.[4]

There was, henceforward, a degree of inevitability about the way in which intermediaries or self-styled plenipotentiaries were reduced once more to the ranks by the leaders themselves. Dilke and Churchill were both babblers, to which Beach saw only one answer: 'if the fact of negotiations cannot be kept secret, would it not be better that it should be known that the leaders were conducting them?'[5] Certainly it was better for the Tory leaders. Wolff was already curbing Salisbury's freedom of action by assuring Hartington that there was no chance of the Lords inserting minority clauses into the bill.[6] And there was no knowing what Cross might give away, or quite how 'useful' Cairns and Richmond would try to make themselves to Gladstone.[7] Northcote, like the Queen, found Beach 'too Radical',[8] and himself stepped in to meet Gladstone at Algernon West's house – high midnight drama this (or opera bouffe), with West ushering a last obdurate dinner-guest, Mrs. Beerbohm Tree, into a back room before he opened the door to Northcote. The key to this scurrying in the maze was provided by Beach: his every move stemmed from the need, while pressing Gladstone 'to bring in a Redistribution Bill as soon as possible', to

[1] Wolff Memo., 13 Nov. 1884. Churchill Mss., 4/492.
[2] Dilke Memoir, 31 Oct. 1884. Dilke Mss., 43938 fol. 276.
[3] Hicks Beach to Hartington, 9 Nov. 1884. Devonshire Mss., 340.1569.
[4] Dilke Memoir, 7 Nov. 1884. Dilke Mss., 43938 fol. 286.
[5] Beach to Hartington, 9 Nov. 1884. Devonshire Mss., 340.1569. Compare Hartington's original statement to Beach of objections to a meeting of leaders: 'It could not be kept secret, and even if it were secret, such formal communications could scarcely be, as ours had been, without prejudice. Conditions which had been demanded, suggestions which had been made or rejected must almost necessarily, with the reasons of rejection become the subjects of debate, and a new element of complication and misunderstanding would be introduced into the debate.' Hartington to Gladstone, 4 Nov. 1884. Gladstone Mss., 44147 fol. 169.
[6] Wolff Memo., 13 Nov. 1884. Churchill Mss., 4/492.
[7] Granville to Gladstone, 17 Nov. 1884. *Correspondence*, Vol. II, p. 285.
[8] The Queen to Gladstone, 10 Nov. 1884. Guedalla, *Queen and Gladstone*, p. 313.

prevent him saying anything in the Commons that would commit the Government to bases which the Opposition could not publicly accept. Thus Gladstone's Second Reading speech of 7 November, which was infuriating or disappointing to others in its lack of detail, earned Beach's political commendation and acclaim: 'he was quite right *not* to be definite on redistribution in it.'[1]

In an historical sense, what matters above all is the sudden emphasis placed (in particular by Dilke, whose responsibility Redistribution was) upon the party benefits to be expected from franchise extension – almost to the point of seeming to believe that 'the horny-handed, manly, intelligent sons of toil were dying for votes for no other purpose than to lay them at [Gladstone's] feet.'[2] Thus it was that a Franchise bill which on introduction had been passed off by its sponsors as the essence of conservatism and was universally dismissed in debate, was now to be deemed the alpha and omega of Reform and hailed in retrospect as 'revolutionary'.[3] On Redistribution, Dilke told his back-benchers, 'we may be willing to yield our opinion... in view of the enormous advantage... from a large measure of enfranchisement.'[4] This extraordinary *bouleversement* of all established Reform teaching, that they might sacrifice the character of Redistribution in order to get an extension of the franchise, constituted the Liberal party's primary education in November 1884 – leading it from the premise learnt in 1866 that it would be 'absurd... to shipwreck their whole scheme of electoral reform only in order to let the Tories in to pass a more Radical one',[5] to the deduction of political petulance and despair: 'I hate grouping but I would group, extend boundaries, & generally do all they [the Opposition] might agree on.'[6]

If the Liberals were impelled towards a settlement by the cry

[1] Hicks Beach to Churchill, 7 Nov. 1884. St. Aldwyn Mss., PCC/20.
[2] J. S. Fletcher, *Memories of a Spectator* (1912), pp. 252–3.
[3] Dilke to Hill, 7 Nov. 1884. Dilke Mss., 43898 fol. 79; see also George Dixon to Chamberlain, 4 Nov. 1884. Chamberlain Mss., JC5/27/5.
[4] Dilke, 7 Nov. 1884. 3 *Hansard* ccxciii. 1240. This passed rapidly into the stream of orthodoxy and platitude. See, e.g., Bath to Weymouth, 22 Nov. 1884: 'Of course it is possible for negotiations to break down but you may rely with tolerable safety on their being carried through, for one if for no other reason that the extension of the Franchise is in itself such an enormous advantage to the liberal party that they can afford almost any concession in redistribution.' Bath Mss. But note that while Dilke devalued the measure, in the Conservative camp Redistribution was still 'the great question... on which our future depends'. Bartley to Northcote, 8 Nov. 1884. Salisbury Mss., Series E.   [5] Milner to Goschen, 6 Nov. 1884. Milner Mss., Box 182.
[6] Dilke to Hartington, 3 Nov. 1884. Devonshire Mss., 340.1566A.

that they must at all events secure the Franchise bill, Conservatives were impelled thither by the shrill cries from Protectionist quarters. With wheat on the London market in September 1884 at 35/– a quarter – the lowest figure quoted since the introduction of returns – the temptation to Tory politicians was apparent. And it was Protection which was judged to have won the South Warwickshire by-election of 8 November,[1] which followed immediately in the wake of the Franchise bill's Second Reading. But those Liberals, anxious for settlement, who saw the Second Reading majority of 140 as a 'glorious victory' and who were 'really *abattu*'[2] by the result in the country, were mistaken in now expecting 'a fearful agitation'.[3] It was the secondary reaction which was of primary significance, and this reaction served to 'moderate the transports of the Opposition'.[4] If a by-election success *per se* was welcome to the Conservative party, the manner in which victory had been secured in South Warwickshire was not welcome to Salisbury. He had always declined to lend even a conniving support to Fair Trade League activity,[5] and though he would tolerate any 'debunking' of the 'bigotry & doctrinaire folly' which pervaded liberal speeches, it was quite emphatically a question on which 'I cannot go with you.'[6] In a sense, this personal disinclination was less important than the fact that South Warwickshire provided a stick with which Salisbury could goad his party in a desired direction. To what extent Salisbury's lessons were learnt spontaneously and to what extent he had to press back-benchers to accept his views, it is impossible to determine. But the doctrine was imperative and immediate: it was 'all very well to play with', but if the Conservatives intended to go to the country on Fair Trade, they would split their party.[7] Asked whether he did not expect to carry the counties in the event of an election, Pell, long-recognized spokesman for the 'agricultural party',[8] said 'he doubted, & if they did at what a price going in for protection!!'[9]

---

[1] In the contest for the Liberal-held seat, Sampson Lloyd defeated Lord William Compton by 3095 votes to 1919. Dr Weston suggests that the Tory victory 'confirmed Salisbury in his firmer approach'. 'Royal Mediation', pp. 307–8. See Appendix II. [2] Trevelyan to Spencer, 8 Nov. 1884. Spencer Mss.
[3] Mundella to Leader, 12 Nov. 1884. Mundella–Leader Mss.
[4] *Pall Mall Gazette*, 11 Nov. 1884, p. 1.
[5] Winn to Salisbury, 1 Sept. 1884. Salisbury Mss., Series E.
[6] Salisbury to the Duke of Rutland, 19 Aug. 1884. Belvoir Mss.
[7] *Pall Mall Gazette*, 11 Nov. 1884, p. 1.
[8] T. E. Kebbel, *Lord Beaconsfield and Other Tory Memories* (1907), p. 118.
[9] Acland to Gladstone, 12 Nov. 1884. Gladstone Mss., 44092 fol. 316.

Childers talked of 'Manners' and Lowther's violence, backed by the majority of the squire County Conservative Members' as having produced 'a Cave in which Hicks Beach, W. H. Smith, & possibly Cross (when he is sober) are prominent'.[1] In asking what pressures would bring Salisbury to negotiate with Gladstone, Childers was right to dismiss the pressures of Cairns and Richmond. What he did not ask was what pressures would bring Gladstone to negotiate with Salisbury. A Scots 'outsider' who refused to term it a spirit of 'moderation' which had produced a 'compromise' gave judgment of impartial asperity and historical validity: both parties 'would have gone further if they had not been equally uncertain of the particular consequences which might have happened to themselves.'[2] In explaining the leaders' meeting, is it not as relevant that Henry Fowler told Raikes (who told Beach, who in turn passed it on to Salisbury) 'that the Radicals below the gangway wd. agree to postpone the coming into operation of Fr. Bill to a named date outside the *possible* duration of the present Parlt'?[3] Is it not as relevant that Acland warned Gladstone of '20 or 30 men on our side who are anxious for the Govt. to lay a [Redistribution] Bill on the table & think there is no risk in doing so'?[4] And were there not those on either side of the House who already put Ireland above all other matters and who doubted the possibility of renewing the Coercion bill in 1885 if an intermediate general election doubled Parnellite strength?[5]

[1] Childers to Halifax, 13 Nov. 1884. Hickleton Mss., A4.90. On the morning of 7 November, Cross communicated to Dilke the substance of his Commons' speech for that night. Mundella to Leader, 12 Nov. 1884. Mundella–Leader Mss. He was, according to Dilke, persuaded towards maintenance of Irish representation at its present total by Dilke's counter that in any reduction the seats for Trinity College, Dublin (held by Plunket and Gibson) must be amongst those sacrificed. Dilke Memoir, 7 Nov. 1884. Dilke Mss., 43938 fol. 286.

[2] Hugh Elliot to Gilbert Elliot, 29 Dec. 1884. Minto Mss., Box 172.

[3] Hicks Beach to Salisbury, 13 Nov. 1884. Salisbury Mss., Series E.

[4] Acland to Gladstone, 12 Nov. 1884. Gladstone Mss., 44092 fol. 316. The project had been fostered during the autumn Recess by Stead; see, e.g., *Pall Mall Gazette*, 25 Sept. 1884, p. 1, asking 'whether the Government would not do well to take whatever wind there may be in [Salisbury's] sails by laying its Redistribution Bill on the table of the House'.

[5] Kennaway to Churchill, 12 Nov. 1884. Churchill Mss., 4/491. MacColl saw no advantage to Salisbury in coming in only to dissolve, faced by an adverse Commons majority. 'He would then have to propound...his intention to renew or not to renew the Irish Coercion Act. If he renewed it, the Irish vote would go against him, and if he declined to renew it, he would disgust many of his own party.' MacColl to Bath, 25 Oct. 1884. Hardinge, *Carnarvon*, Vol. III, pp. 113–14. The Queen, in conversation with Trevelyan, said

On 17 November, Northcote was parading his obduracy and declaring loyalty in case of war.[1] Next morning, Salisbury was 'fishing' to find out what limits the Liberal party would impose on the application of the single-member principle, and asking Dilke for the divisions and boundaries of Lancashire, the West Riding and the Metropolitan constituencies.[2] One incident in this revolution deserves mention for its symbolic pathos. Blinds were pulled down at every window of the Carlton Club Library after a Member had noticed two figures across the road in the Reform Club spying with the aid of an opera glass on the Conservative gathering at which Salisbury and Northcote recommended acceptance of the Government offer.[3] For it was from that moment also that blinds were drawn down not so much between Liberals and Conservatives as between leaders and followers in both parties.

The settlement of Redistribution was effected to all intents and purposes by three men – Salisbury, Gladstone and Dilke. Three more attended: Hartington, Northcote, and Granville who was dropped by Gladstone after the preliminary gathering as 'threatened with emotional disturbance'.[4] If the two former were inevitable participants, neither intervened to any purpose during the constructive stages of negotiation.

Northcote did not know the art of horse-trading. He assured Gibson that 'as we have first to be satisfied of the character of the Redistribution bill, and it may take time in discussion, the absolute passing of the Franchise bill by the H. L. may possibly not be accomplished before the [Christmas] holy-days'.[5] In writing to Salisbury, he made of constitutional unfitness and reluctance a diplomatic subtlety: 'let our weakness be our defence...two *idiotai* against four experts armed with official statistics, we shall always be able to plead for time.'[6] Most probably, he foresaw his thankless Commons' role in the early months of 1885 as the butt of

'forcibly..."we must not have a dissolution." She was much convinced of the danger of having 70 Parnellite members *before* the Prevention of Crimes Act came to be considered'. Trevelyan to Gladstone, 29 Oct. 1884. Gladstone Mss., 44335 fol. 174. On altogether a different plane, Finch-Hatton offered Conservative support in renewal of the Crimes Act if the Government would protect against the possibility of an election on the bastard Register. 7 Nov. 1884. 3 *Hansard* ccxciii. 1274.

[1] Northcote to Salisbury, 17 Nov. 1884. Salisbury Mss., Series E.
[2] Salisbury to Dilke, 18 Nov. 1884. Dilke Mss., 43876 fol. 19.
[3] *Memoirs of Sir Wemyss Reid*, p. 365.
[4] Gladstone to Hartington, 19 Nov. 1884. Gladstone Mss., 44147 fol. 186.
[5] Northcote to Gibson, 18 Nov. 1884. Ashbourne Mss.
[6] Northcote to Salisbury, 18 Nov. 1884. Salisbury Mss., Series E.

Conservative (and perhaps Whig) ill-temper, as the man responsible for all imperfections and bias, as the defender of provisions settled in a few moments of 'give and take', and as the unhappy leader, lonely in a Government lobby, standing by a compact. Hence his desire to leave 'details to be settled in the House'.[1] In that respect and as to timing, he lost. The need to avoid 'any appearance of prolongation without progress' (which Gladstone, Dilke and Salisbury held most dear)[2] won hands down against the Northcote and Carnarvon insistence on knowing exactly what results any scheme of Redistribution would be likely to produce before it was accepted.[3]

At these meetings Hartington behaved much as in Cabinet, but what in Cabinet was a legitimate strategy became in bi-partisan conference what Dilke could only call ineptitude: 'He pressed the subject of grouping, wh. Sy did not intend to name at all, – because as he told me afterwards when I remonstrated "it might have come up next time"!!!' And, shades of 1883, 'Harty afterwards hankered after minorities.'[4] These were his sole contributions – not promising from the man designated by Gladstone to guide Redistribution through the House of Commons. Hartington was by nature as ill at ease as Northcote, disliking the makeshift character of these gatherings where there was no table nor any means of taking notes, and where maps were strewn about the floor.[5] It is, indeed, an engaging thought that the poor deal the Whigs got from this Redistribution may be traced to the casual arrangement of a sofa and arm-chairs in the Downing Street long room – with Hartington, opposite Salisbury and Dilke, able to secure only an upside-down view of all electoral arrangements.

What calls for emphasis is that the trio who 'survived' did so by dint of mental alacrity; more crudely, Salisbury, Gladstone and Dilke set a pace they knew to be beyond any but themselves. Their sense of relief in each other's company, after the wearisome past months, was overwhelming – and found expression. Gladstone was 'much struck with the quickness of Lord Salisbury, and evidently [enjoyed doing] business with so acute a man.'[6] Salisbury was enjoying the novelty of simple market exchange and, 'having now

1 Northcote to Salisbury, 17 Nov. 1884. Salisbury Mss., Series E.
2 Gladstone to Dilke, 23 Nov. 1884. Gladstone Mss., 44547 fol. 139.
3 *Mary Gladstone Diaries*, p. 334; Hardinge, *Carnarvon*, Vol. iii, pp. 118–19.
4 Dilke to Chamberlain, 22 Nov. 1884. Chamberlain Mss., JC5/24/76.
5 Hartington to Hamilton, 25 Nov. 1884. Hamilton Mss., 48618.
6 Hamilton Diary, 19 Nov. 1884. Hamilton Mss., 48638 fol. 57.

adopted it...[was] determined it shall succeed.'[1] And Dilke for his part enjoyed Salisbury's highest accolade: 'No other member of the Government would have been equally tricky....Dilke...ought to spell his name with a B.'[2] This was surely sweeter to Dilke's ears than the now customary acknowledgment of his technical mastery. But the testimony does at least give the lie to any notion of retirement from party view simply in order to ratify a consensus long acknowledged in all its elements, but suppressed for the season of autumn polemic. This was never less than hard business dealing. Granted euphoria in the moment of escape, granted satisfaction in the mode of escape and the prospect of politics cleared of Reform, there was no relaxation. It was indeed the key to Salisbury's ascendancy, as established during these first encounters, that he was the object of such awful mistrust. Nobody knew just what he might be up to. This applied to Liberal representatives who feared that 'having got from us the whole of our scheme & given us nothing in writing which was worth anything', he might yet 'mean to sell us'.[3] It applied equally to Northcote who saw fit, should Salisbury indeed entertain the possibility, to end a detailed listing of Commons' front-benchers' wants and aversions with a longing glance at the possibility of getting 'the whole thing in our hands'.[4]

Exchanges were exchanges in commodities of unknown quantity and variable or unsure value. A proposal to deprive boroughs between 15,000 and 20,000 population of separate representation might attract Conservatives as hitting Gladstonians painfully below the (raised) belt. Might it not appeal equally to Radicals who would thus 'submerge' the counties? or, for all its approach to doctrinaire symmetry, be made palatable to moderates of either party, on the principle that the higher the figure was, the greater was the chance of fixity and settlement? The glances were backward, the prices asked based upon an unshaken confidence in the continuance of old habits. There was no thought of Arch disturbing rural peace; there was acceptance of business-quarter and villa Toryism, and of terrace Radicalism, but little anticipation of an Old Tory Adam in the urban residuum. Some two million county householders were to be enfranchised. Rather over a million people in the merged boroughs were henceforward to be county voters,

[1] Hamilton Diary, 21 Nov. 1884. Hamilton Mss., 48638 fol. 60.
[2] Salisbury to Northcote, 9 Dec. 1884. Iddesleigh Mss., 50020 fol. 108; Salisbury to Northcote, 21 Dec. 1884. Iddesleigh Mss., 50020 fol. 110.
[3] Dilke Memoir, 23 Nov. 1884. Dilke Mss., 43938 fol. 313.
[4] Northcote to Salisbury, 20 Nov. 1884. Salisbury Mss., Series E.

while slightly more (400,000 by Dilke's extension of borough boundaries, and perhaps 800,000 by the creation of new boroughs) were transferred from county to borough.[1] If the two million increase was perhaps taken as read, barely a sound was heard about the impact of this equally dramatic enforced electoral migration beyond *The Times*' warning to the Tories that they might recognize, but owed it to themselves not to deepen, distinctions, between urban and rural interests, since the consequence for the 'rural element thus contra-distinguished will be... a position of permanent numerical inferiority.'[2]

But then, if the price is seen in hindsight necessarily to have taken no account of what actually happened in the future and to have been based to that extent on extrapolation from the past, the whole concept of a fair exchange, where fairness necessarily encompassed rationality and right prediction, *impedes* understanding. A *political* solution meant a solution that could be reached in a tolerably short time, shortness of time precluding sobriety of appraisal.

Redistribution, as settled, was the child of political reflex. The historian would do well to remember this. Bath was, of course, no more than a Tory 'outsider', but his befuddlement in the immediate wake of the agreement must cast doubt on the claim that there was great clarity of intention, or much understanding of consequences: 'single ward districts [in counties], this is the proposal I had favoured and am very glad I was not responsible [for,] for it works out much worse than I could have anticipated... but it is possible we may do better in the divisions or wards in the large towns.'[3] Moreover, one sees the force of this advice when one asks who put forward the suggestion that three-membered boroughs be divided into three wards? who countered with 'two plus one'? who went on to propose the creation of a two-membered business-premises nucleus in the cities which returned four Members or more?

---

[1] D. D. Cuthbert, 'The Origins, Enactment and Effects of the Redistribution of 1885' (Unpublished Ph.D. thesis, Monash University, 1968), p. 83.

[2] *The Times*, 24 Nov. 1884, p. 9.

[3] Bath to Weymouth, 16 Dec. 1884. Bath Mss. This, which is immediate, is for our purpose the more telling, but note also the record of Chamberlain's advice early in 1885 upon the relative merits of various constituencies with which Channing had been in communication: 'The London seat he thought best went Tory, the other London seat and a big borough division, which he put next, have been in and out ever since, while my own prize constituency [East Northants.], the steadiest in Great Britain, he had little faith in.' F. A. Channing, *Memories of Midland Politics, 1885–1910* (1918), pp. 4–5.

Respectively, in fact, Northcote, Salisbury and Gladstone; but the difficulty in attributing effective authorship stems from understanding that the talks were a conscious attempt to reach accord between parties by exchanging sops to satisfy interests within one's own party; or, when conducted in terms not of accommodation but of opposition were a conscious attempt to anticipate the demands of delegates opposite. In other words, all or any of the three might have promoted each of these projects, either positively or as a stymie.

Rather less than an hour on 19 November was needed to settle 'how far and in what terms the Ministry was to be bound to the prosecution of the Seats Bill in the two Houses'; to vow secrecy (Salisbury might communicate in strict confidence with Privy Councillors who sat in Disraeli's last Cabinet – a requirement Churchill could not fulfil); to understand that each spoke responsibly 'and, so far as might be, for the respective parties in the two Houses'; and to agree to expedite these conversations.[1] Such refinements must have met the objection of any who found the terms announced to Parliament on the 17th 'uncommonly loose',[2] if not of those who were appalled at the overthrow of party and Parliament.[3] Gladstone enumerated the Government proposals, copies of which were handed to Salisbury and Northcote. On just such a point the language of concession reveals its utter inadequacy. True, Gladstone had surrendered the notion that he might propose nothing, and simply answer those questions which Salisbury and Northcote remembered to put;[4] but he thereby put the onus upon others to declare specific objections, to state a workable alternative and to be articulate in a positive rather than a querulous manner.

The first meeting to discuss Redistribution *per se* was called for the afternoon of 22 November. In the intermediate days, Gladstone had assured himself that the proposed over-representation of Ireland and Wales as national entities did not involve over-representation constituency by constituency but was the quite defensible (if fortunate) product of a uniform rule of enfranchisement and disfranchisement throughout the United Kingdom; and

---

[1] Gladstone to the Queen, 19 Nov. 1884. Guedalla, *Queen and Gladstone*, pp. 315–16.
[2] J. B. Kinnear to R. P. Bruce, 19 Nov. 1884. Bruce Mss.
[3] Elliot Diary, 18 Nov. 1884. Diaries, Vol. 10.
[4] Gladstone Memo., 19 Nov. 1884. Gladstone Mss., 44768 fol. 157.

he had learnt his lines in case Salisbury pressed either for an Irish minority clause or for a reduction in the number of Irish seats.[1] Dilke, having heard more, at the Royal Commission on the Housing of the Working Classes, about Salisbury's desire 'to keep the urbans out',[2] had offered an extension of certain borough boundaries which might secure a clean, rural Conservatism in the surrounding counties, and, to test Salisbury's competence, had slipped into the list the extension of Portsmouth to Alverstoke and Gosport. Salisbury was indeed alive to the threat to two insecure Tory seats: he drew a red line through the proposal.[3] Northcote, meanwhile, had been inundated with detailed critiques, master plans and the memoranda of those who ventured to presume that, though of course 'general principles' would guide the Conservative leaders, 'an aggregate of local circumstances will influence you in the adoption of principles'.[4] He was told that a bold grouping of unrepresented Scottish towns gave 'the only chance' of winning seats there outside the Universities and the Wigtown burghs.[5] He was put on his guard against over-generosity to Wales and Ireland or any increase in the numbers of the House.[6] He was advised to cut the whole country into equal electoral districts of 150,000, allotting three Members and the minority vote to each district.[7] He owed it to his party, he was told, to expose Dilke's 'show of fairness' in adding 68 Members to 'what are called "counties"', while in fact county interests were to be swamped by the overflow from large towns.[8] He must stand firm against wards as lowering the class of Member, but could approve the division of counties, since the squires who threatened to retire might see in the compactness of a constituency some prospect of continuing to exercise their personal charm.[9] He should recognize the futility of quibbling over detail and seek salvation in Protection.[10]

Though some offerings may have confirmed a hesitant opinion, there is precious little to the conclusion that Salisbury allowed the

[1] Dilke Memoir, 21 Nov. 1884. Dilke Mss., 43938 fol. 310.
[2] Northcote to Salisbury, 20 Nov. 1884. Salisbury Mss., Series E.
[3] Cuthbert, 'Redistribution', pp. 61–2.
[4] Maxwell to Northcote, 20 Nov. 1884. Salisbury Mss., Series E.
[5] Reginald MacLeod to Northcote, 19 Nov. 1884. Salisbury Mss., Series E.
[6] Northcote to Salisbury, 20 Nov. 1884. Salisbury Mss., Series E.
[7] Manners to Salisbury, 23 Nov. 1884. Belvoir Mss.
[8] Hicks Beach to Northcote, 21 Nov. 1884. Iddesleigh Mss., 50021 fol. 240.
[9] Lowther to Northcote, 20 Nov. 1884. Salisbury Mss., Series E; Stanhope to Northcote, 21 Nov. 1884. Salisbury Mss., Series E.
[10] Winn to Lowther, 19 Nov. 1884. Salisbury Mss., Series E.

'weight' of this opinion (even were it ascertainable) to affect his course. His comments and proposals were, to say the least, idiosyncratic and unfamiliar if considered as Tory nostrums. 'He assumed that Ireland will not be reduced...He said we had been over-generous to some English agricl. counties, wh. is true!!!'[1] He raised the minority vote in a somewhat bizarre form – proposing to leave a three-membered core in Leeds, Liverpool and Manchester, while surrendering it in Birmingham and Glasgow, where the Liberal machine made nonsense of this Tory insurance, and to divide London into four-membered constituencies where each elector should be given only one vote. On his first proposal, he simply retired before the heavy artillery of Gladstone's offensive laughter. Met on the second with the anticipated 'No', he went straight for single-member constituencies in the Metropolis (where, so mandarins in both camps had it, without a Schnadhorst the Liberals would be lost), in the counties (where it might tend to secure variety of representation) and in the larger boroughs (which united Hartington and Chamberlain in alarm). Dilke was prepared to create a handful of further single-member boroughs in London, which he took to be all that Salisbury was after. So surprised were Gladstone and Dilke that Salisbury won outright on the counties, while the dividing of boroughs was left to another day. The Schedule A minimum of 15,000 remained untouched; in order to return two Members, a borough had now to have a population of 50,000.[2] Borough boundaries, as agreed privately with Dilke, were to be extended in numerous instances. The question of burgh grouping north of the Border was to be left open until there was agreement about Scotland's representation. This was enough for one Saturday afternoon: Salisbury requested and was granted an adjournment for three clear days.

There followed an episode in which Dilke, bamboozled into the belief that Salisbury did not know his subject, fell for two of the oldest tricks of the bazaar – that men declare most precious what they are ready to trade, and that they demand what is out of reach so as to be able grudgingly to accept what they really want. Salisbury drew up a memorandum proposing various groups of unrepresented industrial boroughs (Chesterfield, Worksop, Burton,

[1] Dilke to Chamberlain, 22 Nov. 1884. Chamberlain Mss., JC5/24/77.

[2] On present returns, the Liberals were spared some party embarrassment as against 20,000 for total merger in counties, but in the 10,000 rise of Schedule B sacrificed 11 of their own to the Conservatives' and Nationalists' 3 apiece.

Leek, Crewe, Congleton, Macclesfield, Wellingborough and Jarrow) which threatened the Conservatism of otherwise rural districts. Dilke was aghast at the jerrymandering involved[1] in this partial espousal of a cause which, when raised by Hartington at the Saturday conference, had found no support, and made it clear that it could not be accepted. He failed, as a consequence, to see through to Salisbury's real demand – a counterbalance to this Conservative surrender, though it was a surrender of the unattainable. In similar vein, he took Salisbury's demand to see Lambert's 'boundary work', upon which turned 'the whole of the matter in which we are so much interested – the adequate representation of the agricultural population',[2] as *prima facie* ludicrous, since a start upon 'boundary work' waited on the political decision how far to apply the single-member principle. Delay meant rupture, and for Dilke rupture was inconceivable. He immediately promised 'such a commission as you would consider fair, working under words strongly directing them...to separate as far as possible the urban from the rural'[3] and, in the boroughs, to have regard 'to the varying nature of the representation' – though nobody cared to distinguish between 'class, or sectional, or social pursuits'.[4] If Dilke still entertained the idea (plausible on the 22nd) that Salisbury meant to fight for single-member seats only in the Metropolis,[5] he was faced on 26 November with a proposal to apply them universally – Salisbury naming only one exception, the City, in deference to Smith. Dilke's report lacks conviction in its recital of Tory concessions. 'They make our agreement the condition of passing the Franchise, of giving up all forms of minority vote, & of giving up all grouping.'[6] To the bulk of Members, Franchise had long appeared settled, grouping (outside Scotland) unpopular to the point of impracticability and the minority vote anathema.

This process one Tory thought of as 'going down hill fast...to a red Republic'.[7] Dilke, Salisbury and Gladstone might, in the momentum of auction, have gone much further had not Salisbury resurrected the question of the minimum population necessary to escape merger, and proposed raising the figure to 20,000. It was

[1] Dilke Memoir, 25 Nov. 1884. Dilke Mss., 43938 fol. 315.
[2] Salisbury to Dilke, 25 Nov. 1884. Dilke Mss., 43876 fol. 23.
[3] Dilke to Salisbury, 26 Nov. 1884. Dilke Mss., 43876 fol. 38.
[4] Dilke–H. H. Fowler exchange, 4 Dec. 1884. 3 *Hansard* ccxciv. 655.
[5] Dilke to Chamberlain, 22 Nov. 1884. Chamberlain Mss., JC5/24/77.
[6] Dilke to Chamberlain, 26 Nov. 1884. Dilke Mss., 43886 fol. 272.
[7] R. N. Fowler Diary, [1 Dec. 1884]. Flynn, *Robert Fowler*, p. 297.

sufficient to stir Northcote who spoke of the heart-burning involved even in a 15,000 line, found no lasting comfort in the partisan bag (22 Liberals and 5 Nationalists to 9 Conservatives) and probably less, after the experience of 1867, in talk of the quest for a sure resting place. Salisbury faltered, the impetus was lost and Hartington intervened to raise the Whig bogey of an omnipresent caucus for the selection of candidates. Gladstone faltered too in searching for some arithmetical underpin to historic practice: perhaps they might allow 100 Members to be returned à deux, or alternatively one-third of the borough seats. In fact, he found the requisite number without recourse to mathematics, in saving from compulsory division those urban constituencies, outside the Metropolis, which now possessed and were to retain dual representation[1] – a suggestion which Salisbury had foreseen more than a week before as the treatment most likely to be meted out to them.[2]

Momentum in conference, once forfeit, was not recaptured. The rest is dribs and drabs, bar a final flurry of excitement over University seats, in which Lady Salisbury trespassed beyond the bounds of woman's rightful business to appeal personally to Gladstone 'by all the old Church and Oxford memories...and...her knowledge of her husband's character on the assurance' that abolition, upon which 'Ministers insisted...was a point upon which he would never yield.'[3] In fact, Gladstone did not insist, but University representation was no more than a test case with interpretation of silence the point at issue. What Hicks Beach, the sorest of Conservatives, called for, and was refused, was that he might still initiate amendments on points not directly connected with concessions made to Salisbury, and might attempt to persuade either House to adopt 'Conservative' views where the Government had refused to yield: in other words, that opposition responsibility must not extend beyond those concessions distinctly labelled 'Concession to Conservatism'.[4]

What Salisbury wanted was to tie Gladstone to the Government statement at the preliminary meeting on 19 November, and to the points then declared vital but never subsequently discussed. Further, he required of Gladstone and Dilke that they should introduce no new contentious matter and admit no changes in the

---

[1] Dilke to Chamberlain, 26 Nov. 1884. Dilke Mss., 43886 fol. 272.
[2] Salisbury to Dilke, 18 Nov. 1884. Dilke Mss., 43876 fol. 19.
[3] Lady Gwendolen Cecil, Salisbury, Vol. III, p. 124.
[4] Hicks Beach to Salisbury, 26 Nov. 1884. St. Aldwyn Mss., PCC/30.

Commons without Northcote's express prior approval.[1] What
Gladstone had 'all along . . . belie[ved]' was that in conference 'the
Opposition leaders were presenting to us points they deemed
vital' and that those which were not explicitly mentioned were not
included.[2] Hicks Beach's gay abandon was so obviously an extension of Salisbury's stringency that it provoked Gladstone's most
significant contribution. He saved the nine University seats from
the less than tender mercies of the House in order to wed Salisbury
(their champion) and Dilke (the abolitionist).

The acquiescence of the latter need excite little comment once
the question, customarily portrayed as threatening a renewal of
trouble, emerges as the means or excuse to tighten the last screws
upon Commons' liberty. The number of Members now allotted to
existing constituencies and the proportionate allotment to counties
were declared sacrosanct; the decisions of the Boundary Commissioners were to be in all cases binding unless both parties agreed
upon an alternative. The only freedom accorded Beach was that
'any one may walk out.'[3] Somebody remembered the harsh words
of July and supplied the requisite twist: 'the rope which was [now]
round their necks...was being pulled and tugged at by Lord
Salisbury and the Leader of the Opposition [in the Commons] in
conjunction with the Government'.[4]

The leaders retired 'to look cloudy till Monday',[5] each clutching
an Agreement 'not less strictly secret than the conversations by
which we have been enabled to frame it',[6] each aiming to educate
his party and needing, first, to secure the front benches.

Salisbury summoned his counsellors – 'or such of them as will
come' – to Arlington Street for the 26th,[7] perhaps without any
intention of taking advice[8] and certainly at too late a stage to allow
anything other than marginal amendments. His control of the
Conservative party was now recognized, with gratitude, by
political opponents;[9] the need to exercise his powers was probably
rather smaller than might have been expected. The Carlton Club

[1] Salisbury to Gladstone, 27 Nov. 1884. Gladstone Mss., 44488 fol. 150.
[2] Gladstone Memo., 28 Nov. 1884. Gladstone Mss., 44768 fol. 171.
[3] Salisbury to Hicks Beach, 29 Nov. 1884. St. Aldwyn Mss., PCC/69.
[4] Chaplin, 4 Dec. 1884. 3 *Hansard* ccxciv. 711.
[5] *Mary Gladstone Diaries*, p. 337.
[6] Gladstone to Salisbury, 28 Nov. 1884. Gladstone Mss., 44488 fol. 160.
[7] Salisbury to Richmond, 24 Nov. 1884. Goodwood Mss., 872/P98.
[8] Dilke to Chamberlain, 22 Nov. 1884. Chamberlain Mss., JC5/24/77.
[9] Hamilton to Ponsonby, 24 Nov. 1884. Ponsonby Mss., 45725 fol. 85.

THE POLITICS OF REFORM 1884

meeting had, indeed, invested him with an authority which was widely accepted as being the most realistic antidote to bitterness, jealousy and interminable wrangles.[1] And if, in the event, Smith for his part did not 'like the look' of the Metropolitan constituencies, to whose re-arrangement Salisbury had given his consent, he was as ready as Salisbury in negotiation to move to single-member districts.[2] Many ruled out the possibility of resistance – Winn, for the 'Old Guard', by a 'Cassandra-like' despondency which stifled all action;[3] Lord George Hamilton, for disquieted loyal Ulster, by recognizing that the battle, once lost over the Franchise bill in May, could not be re-fought on Redistribution;[4] Lowther, out of cost-consciousness and strictly financial relief that the smaller each constituency was likely to be, the smaller the demands faced by Members from 'every Village Cricket Football Bicycle &c &c Club'.[5] Manners, who had been ready with a vast and attractive scheme for 'natural' grouping, yet felt, out of copy-book loyalty, that 'your position [is] one of such exceptional difficulty and delicacy that whatever you and Northcote agree upon I shall accept'.[6] Stanhope debarred himself from resistance by the self-satisfaction he felt at what he mistook for recognition of his own weight.[7] Cairns, sulky and quite out-manoeuvred, retreated to Reigate and refused to come to London.[8] The Peers, by a sort of collective act, agreed to place any opinion they might entertain 'in abeyance in deference to any conclusion...colleagues...of the House of Commons may arrive at'.[9] 'Everyone', in short,

[1] Northcote to Salisbury, 18 Nov. 1884. Salisbury Mss., Series E.
[2] Northcote to Salisbury, 25 Nov. 1884. Salisbury Mss., Series E.
[3] Northcote to Salisbury, 20 Nov. 1884. Salisbury Mss., Series E; Winn to Lowther, 19 Nov. 1884. Salisbury Mss., Series E. Northcote directed Winn's attention to Winn's home surrounds: county districts in South-West Yorkshire 'will be greatly relieved of urban population by the extension of the boundaries of some of the boroughs, and they will be so arranged as to give a fair chance of several of them having mainly agricultural constituencies.' And a challenge to his energies: 'If you can't pick up a few members out of these 15, you must be in evil case indeed.' Northcote to Winn, 29 Nov. 1884. Nostell Mss., 2/22.
[4] Hamilton to Salisbury, 18 Dec. 1884. Salisbury Mss., Series E.
[5] Lowther to Northcote, 20 Nov. 1884. Salisbury Mss., Series E.
[6] Manners to Salisbury, 23 Nov. 1884. Belvoir Mss.
[7] *Manchester Guardian*, 25 Nov. 1884, p. 5: that Northcote and Salisbury had 'in the negotiations consulted with Mr. W. H. Smith and Mr. Edward Stanhope...upon the schedules of the Redistribution Bill. It is apparently the opinion of all experienced members of the House that if this had not been done there must have been differences and defeats in the House, whoever might have had charge of the bill.'
[8] Cairns to Salisbury, 25 Nov. 1884. Salisbury Mss., Series E.   [9] *Ibid.*

according to Carnarvon, thought 'it better not to break off the negotiations.'[1]

At the beginning of the negotiations, all this had been the subject of Cranbrook's sardonic prediction: 'No one seems to have thought out a system... your hands will be very free... Having no very definite views they [the majority] will catch at what seems *prima facie* reasonable.' Some *were* more committed than others. Cranbrook himself had 'very definite views', expressing disgust that Beach should advocate electoral districts;[2] but while now finding some aspects of the agreement 'perilously' akin to electoral districts, he felt 'for [his] own part... that [he] must support or at least not oppose what is arranged.'[3] More committed than any, of course, were Beach and Churchill. Churchill had, indeed, seen no reason to stop airing his Redistribution 'essentials' while the conference was in session. He would separate urban from rural, 'go on the basis of population', and make single-member constituencies 'the soul of the whole concern', for they afforded 'the only working system of minority representation.' But Churchill knew as well as anyone else that both parties were 'pledged too deeply to allow the negotiations to fail',[4] and, though he might list details 'directly & indirectly unfavourable to our interests', saw no future in active opposition. His reasoning calls for little comment. It is immediate, personal, explicit and shrewd:[5]

If the bill is upset on some side issue such as Sir J. Lubbock's the Govt. resign & Ld. S. & Sir S.N. come in, a contingency too terrible to contemplate; if the bill is enlarged Salisbury & Sir S.N. are more or less thrown over & the party divided, and in confusion on the eve of an election.

A combination to seriously alter the character of the bill will be of such a nature as to discredit any one at the head of it; Chaplinites Parnellites & Lawsonites, all more or less disreputable, agst. men whom the public (wrongly enough no doubt) credit with respectability.

I am of opinion that the Govt. having been placed in possession of your views & knowing as they must know the probability of your being able to give effect to them, might look with great composure & satisfaction upon any crisis which wd. enable them to resign & therefore have deliberately assisted Ld. S. & Sir S.N. to set aside those views.

There can also be no doubt that those views were greatly prejudiced in the eyes of our leaders by the supposition that they were shared by me.

[1] Carnarvon Journal, 26 Nov. 1884. Hardinge, *Carnarvon*, Vol. III, pp. 118–19.
[2] Cranbrook to Salisbury, 21 Nov. 1884. Salisbury Mss., Series E.
[3] Cranbrook Diary, 29 Nov. 1884. Cranbrook Mss., T501/299 fol. 285.
[4] *Pall Mall Gazette*, 27 Nov. 1884, p. 1.
[5] Churchill to Hicks Beach, 29 Nov. 1884. St. Aldwyn Mss., PCC/82.

I do not write more as I know you hate long letters. You will see from what I have said that I am disinclined to take any active part in this matter & to let things take their course.

Reports of Churchill's forthcoming journey to India were thought exciting only by the newspapers which reported them and, in doing so, left the impression that the Committee stage of the Redistribution bill would be very 'interesting'.[1] Beach knew better than Stead: Churchill 'could not have chosen a better time to be away – for I never remember a more complete lull'.[2] And again, when he returned in early April, Churchill did nothing to revive interest in Redistribution. He stopped only to ask a facetious question of James, to remind Northcote publicly that he was at his shoulder (*'which* Leaders of the Opposition' had Dilke consulted as to Westminster's representation?), and to reveal his own boredom.[3]

Ministers fared even worse, if that were possible, than their opposite numbers, even as regards confidence: a Cabinet before the conference of 26 November could only increase Dilke and Gladstone's difficulties,[4] so none was called. This cavalier treatment provoked little resentment; if the point in calling the Cabinet anyway was ceremonial rather than consultative, then Harcourt need not undertake the wearisome journey to Town, since he would ratify anything short of Women's Suffrage and Proportional Representation.[5] The Cabinet meeting, on the 27th, did not however pass off without incident. Childers threatened resignation if the merger line was fixed at 20,000 – ill-rewarded devotion this to Pontefract, whose electors promptly sent him scurrying to Edinburgh in search of a seat. And Grosvenor displayed a hostility which ill-became the party Whip with elections pending. The majority moved as normally they did, along the line from uninformed criticism and 'swearing at large' to (albeit grudging) acceptance.[6]

Those who made no sound provide the greater historical interest.

[1] *Pall Mall Gazette*, 20 Nov. 1884, p. 3.
[2] Hicks Beach to Churchill, 10 Jan. 1885. St. Aldwyn Mss., PCC/20.
[3] 16 Apr. 1885. 3 *Hansard* ccxcvi. 1862; 24 Apr. 1885. 3 *Hansard* ccxcvii. 644 (My italics); 29 Apr. 1885. 3 *Hansard* ccxcvii. 1051. Northcote rose belatedly to the occasion, in referring to the November conferences as 'entered into between the Representatives – he would not venture to call them Leaders in the presence of the noble Lord – of both sides'. 29 Apr. 1885. 3 *Hansard* ccxcvii. 1054.
[4] Dilke Memoir, 23 Nov. 1884. Dilke Mss., 43938 fol. 313.
[5] Lewis Harcourt Journal, 25 Nov. 1884. Harcourt Mss.
[6] Dilke Memoir, 27 Nov. 1884. Dilke Mss., 43938 fol. 323.

Northbrook remained silent – in a dangerous and foul temper, but reserving his violence for the serious business of Egyptian finance. Hartington remained silent, because he was privy to the negotiations and in large degree bound by them, however sorry his own performance. Chamberlain, also, remained silent. At an early stage in the negotiations, he had supposed that, in conference, Dilke would always satisfy all his wants, expecting him, if Gladstone or Hartington jibbed at any Radical proposal to 'take them out of the room & tell them you & I wont stand it.'[1] Chamberlain, of course, was far from certain that others accepted his indispensability or would pay attention to what he wanted: his instructions were as presumptuous in asserting identity of purpose as they were crude in their conception of conference manner. Dilke in any case was tired of tutelage. He left Chamberlain very much 'out of the room', bringing him in only to buy his acquiescence. He bought it cheaply, too, with a seventh Member for Birmingham (by the device of extended boundaries) and with a misleading prophecy: Redistribution, he claimed, would be 'wrecked by the House at large' (for the 'real Tories' hated single seats quite as much as Chamberlain), Liberals would enjoy the credit for extending the franchise, and on Redistribution 'we can get our own way in the next bill.'[2]

Redistribution was, in back-bench mythology, the back-benchers' happiest hunting ground; now they learnt that they might fire off only blank cartridges. The sense of grievance entertained by one essentially so loyal as Henry Fowler was acute. He had given his blessing to extra-Parliamentary talks on the understanding that the 'treaty, if agreed to, will require the absolute passing of a Franchise Bill, and the conditional passing of the Redistribution Bill, conditional I mean, as depending on contingencies, which [the] Government cannot control and from which the Franchise Bill is safe.' Two days later, he was aware that, if not actively misled, he had not been directed to a full understanding. With Salisbury's approval of the details of Redistribution being treated as a necessary condition, 'we below the gangway...are we not powerless?'[3] It was a situation with which Gladstone alone might cope. There could be no question of his delegating the introduction of the bill to Hartington: 'what the "Left" will accept from G, they wd. never

---

[1] Chamberlain–Dilke exchange of notes, n.d. Dilke Mss., 43886 fol. 262.
[2] Dilke to Chamberlain, 26 Nov. 1884. Dilke Mss., 43886 fol. 272.
[3] Fowler to Morley, 19 Nov. 1884. *Life of Henry Fowler*, p. 168.

stand from any one else.'[1] Hartington himself, Harcourt, Dilke and Hamilton were agreed.[2] This Cabinet concord was confirmed by Elliot, who could never be numbered amongst the 'Left'. He urged the House to look to its independence, was 'backed...up well' by Buchanan, but enjoyed only the 'limited support' of Illingworth, and, for the rest, though 'my line was what most people on our side were thinking...very few were willing to speak out; such is the authority of the G.O.M.'[3] If calm acceptance of powerlessness was too much to expect of Members during these dark days, their obsession with powerlessness was countered – by denial of that impotence, by directing attention or self-interest to Redistribution, by playing upon loyalty, by bluff and by procrastination. Within the week, the borderline between education and self-education became hopelessly blurred.

Tory Members had been given fair notice by Northcote that any product of bi-partisan deliberation would be larger by far than the *Standard* draft.[4] They were given no further indication or advice until the day after Gladstone's introduction of the measure. Some must have been satisfied with Salisbury's asseveration that they were 'as free as air'. Others must have reflected more soberly that 'our party gave the commission and the confidence & cannot throw over its trustees.' Still more, who laboured under the impression (a deduction naturally drawn from Northcote's prior statement) 'that our Chiefs made the measure more Radical', may have been calmed by Salisbury's bland refutation of the charge.[5] And when Gladstone leaked it to *The Times* that the Government had wanted to 'multiply ...the two-member constituencies',[6] or Dilke told Churchill that they were quite prepared for more grouping if Salisbury and Northcote had pressed for it,[7] Salisbury could reasonably counter with open letters: 'Heartily glad should I have been if it had been possible to maintain the 3 cornered system [in large boroughs].'[8]

Liberal Members assembled at the Foreign Office in the early afternoon of 1 December. Gladstone thanked the party for the confidence (which had not been misplaced) in their leaders and

---

[1] Hamilton Diary, 19 Nov. 1884. Hamilton Mss., 48638 fol. 57.
[2] Hartington and Harcourt Minutes, 24 Nov. 1884. Devonshire Mss., 340. 1584–5.
[3] Elliot Diary, 24 Nov. 1884. Diaries, Vol. 10.
[4] Speech at the Beaconsfield Club, 24 Nov. 1884. *Annual Register*, p. 252.
[5] Cranbrook Diary, 3 Dec. 1884. Cranbrook Mss., T501/299 fol. 287.
[6] *The Times*, 2 Dec. 1884, p. 9.
[7] Northcote to Salisbury, 4 Dec. 1884. Salisbury Mss., Series E.
[8] Salisbury to H. W. Freston, 3 Dec. 1884. Salisbury Mss., Series D.

representatives, portrayed the amicable spirit in which these exceptional conferences had been conducted (without pointing to the likelihood that they would be repeated), and detailed 'a few heads of the Bill *on their merits*' ('referring however *a.* to statement 2 hours hence *b.* to Bill which I hope will be circulated tomorrow'). This Redistribution would, he trusted, be found 'large[,] equitable[,] neither unduly regardful & not gratuitously regardless of ancient rights and arrangements'.[1] Labouchère supplied a plain party man's gloss, 'put[ting] everything that was good in it down to the Prime Minister, and everything that was bad in it to the Marquess of Salisbury.'[2] With the more peaceable thus lulled into contentment and the less peaceable given no indication of the 'vital' points to 'run at',[3] the meeting passed off true to Gladstonian form – 'somewhat flat'[4] and satisfactorily so. There was, quite literally, 'No discussion.'[5]

Gladstone, however, in directing back-benchers' attention to some future moment of enlightenment, disappointed only those who made an unwarrantable deduction and looked then to a full and free discussion of the bill 'on the merits'. They were disappointed '2 hours hence'. They were disappointed three days later, for 'debate', Gladstone then said, ought to be 'reserve[d]' upon the Redistribution bill because Members had had so little notice of its provisions and because it did not involve 'any great and broad matters...of Party contention'. The Committee stage, he added, would provide 'far better and less embarrassed means of discussing the whole subject'.[6] Did any suppose that their dreams would be realized in March? If they did, they should have reflected that Gladstone was quite capable, when it suited him, of interpreting silence on the Second Reading, for whatever reason, as a sign of total acquiescence. Elliot paid dearly for a Commons' question that gave 'considerable offence':[7] 'no objection', Gladstone countered, 'was made to these preliminary communications when the idea was announced – why then shd. they be discussed before their conclusion?'[8] Why, one might add, should they be discussed at all,

---

[1] Gladstone to Salisbury, 1 Dec. 1884. Gladstone Mss., 44547 fol. 142; Notes for F.O. speech, 1 Dec. 1884. Gladstone Mss., 44768 fol. 193.
[2] 24 Nov. 1884. 3 *Hansard* ccxciv. 302.
[3] Gladstone to Northcote, 4 Dec. 1884. Gladstone Mss., 44547 fol. 144.
[4] Hamilton Diary, 1 Dec. 1884. Hamilton Mss., 48638 fol. 73.
[5] Bright Diary, 1 Dec. 1884. *Bright Diaries*, p. 521.
[6] Gladstone, 1 Dec. 1884. 3 *Hansard* ccxciv. 383–4.
[7] Elliot Diary, 28 Nov. 1884. Diaries, Vol. 10.
[8] Gladstone to Elliot, 28 Nov. 1884. Gladstone Mss., 44547 fol. 139.

when the 'preliminary communications' were known to be an inviolable contract? Yet the casualties of conference (virtually every Member) made even less mark than the casualties of peace (a third of the House). Why? The answer lies in both the diversity and the deflection of interest. Reactions to the ward system epitomise the whole. Harrowby, after hearing Gladstone's introduction of the Redistribution bill from the Gallery, remained in the Commons' lobby to test Conservative opinion 'in the first flurry of the announcement.' His reward was to find 'Whitley and C. Hamilton breathing fire & sword about the degradation of Liverpool, & threatening ruin to the Bill.'[1] Mundella, in this same 'first flurry', was euphoric – 'five districts, and five Members...What a wonderful revolution... Gladstone will have crowned his life.' His euphoria may be traced directly to the unexpected increase in Sheffield's representation but he was light-headed also at the possibility of herding all Tories into one constituency. This mood did not survive the night; soberly, Mundella acknowledged that the 'West End, of course, will be Tory', and that the Liberals would probably have to fight for two other seats, whatever the boundary arrangement. By the following week, he was distinctly sore; grievances must be aired in the form of a remonstrance from the large boroughs, not as an idle protest, but in the knowledge that Chamberlain, who had 'been forced into a hateful arrangement [from] which he would be glad to escape', would use this as the base for his offensive. Mundella's commitment was near-binding by now, and even the minority scheme seemed preferable. 'I hate this sub-division and cannot reconcile myself to it at all. If I sat below the Gangway, I think I should fight it tooth and nail. *I may do so yet.*'[2]

Combinations even less likely than that of Chamberlain, Mundella and the Proportionalists had been thrown up by Redistribution – though only threats were heard from this conspiracy. Whitley, for his part, continued to entertain fears for the Parliamentary stature of a Liverpool of 'small petty interests and men to represent them', but in a matter of days came to admit that his 'strongest feeling [was] a personal one' against Forwood. Smith 'said to him [,] what will you substitute for the proposals of the Bill – which is within the range of practical politics, and... he did not seem...to see his way...[to anything that might]

---

[1] Harrowby to Salisbury, 1 Dec. 1884. Salisbury Mss., Series E.
[2] Mundella to Leader, 2, 3, 8, 11 and 13 Dec. 1884. Mundella–Leader Mss.

promise a better expression, on the whole of the views of the Conservatives.'[1] What matters politically is that there was no simultaneous uprising from both sides. When the Radicals had at an earlier stage displayed 'delightful savagery', with Lawson ready to dilate in the Commons upon a 'humiliating surrender, the old man grovelling on his knees before the Peers',[2] Salisbury had clamped down upon violent expression in the Commons and in the party press: '"The Prime Minister's Submission" grates on my ear as a little too strong: & wd not be good for us in our negotiation. "Advances" would be better.'[3] Now, such Conservative and Liberal hostility as was manifest in December at the proposal to divide large towns achieved no coincident climax. The one was an immediate and quickly spent anger, the other a lapse into disillusioned resentment. And to many a Member it must have seemed that his constituency was a 'dark horse' until the boundaries were struck. The injunction again was to wait and, when the commissioners had done their work, to pay attention to party organization in those wards which might 'fairly be fought'[4] – in Birmingham and Sheffield, as in Liverpool.

Journalists recognized 'a practical usurpation – carried out... with the utmost appearance of deference and for which an imaginary necessity will be made to bear the blame; yet still a usurpation of the office and powers of Parliament.'[5] Independent Members were told, what they already knew, that Redistribution had been 'fixed...by the few men...who constitute the real players in the game of politics.'[6] What is significant is that so many of those who had been cheated of their rightful inheritance were prepared to adopt the language of 'imaginary necessity' and to convince themselves of the miseries they would suffer if they united to upset the scheme over, say, Proportional Representation – six months' further agitation and the prospect, for their pains, that not Proportional Representation but something 'very much worse' would be adopted.[7] Grey went off with his ludicrous blackboard and chalk. Elliot turned his attention to Scottish redistribution and, as he ought to have expected, found himself bogged down in a 'good

---

[1] Smith to Harrowby, 6 Dec. 1884. Harrowby Mss., 2nd Ser., Vol. 54, fol. 228.
[2] Clarke to his Wife, 20 Nov. 1884. Clarke, *Life*, p. 230.
[3] Salisbury to Austin, 24 Nov. 1884. Austin Mss.
[4] Mundella to Leader, 3 Dec. 1884. Mundella–Leader Mss.
[5] *Manchester Guardian*, 3 Dec. 1884, p. 5.
[6] George Howell to Albert Grey, 2 Dec. 1884. Grey Mss.
[7] Balfour, 2 Mar. 1885. 3 *Hansard* ccxciv. 1840.

deal of rather vague talk' on that subject.[1] Buchanan and Sellar probably spoke for many Scots in promising 'very little trouble' on the issue of the independence of the House[2] if the Government would only declare that increased representation for Scotland was vital and the dozen extra 'an irreducible minimum'.[3] For his part, Forster defended the bill's provisions. Goschen was 'quite cast down', but neither elicited nor solicited sympathy: 'What has he done...to help to anything better?'[4] Both had, in fact, long veered away from the whole subject as unfit for their energies. Through O'Shea, Parnell received assurances from Chamberlain and Dilke that Ireland would be accorded 103 Members if the House agreed to add 12 to its number and not less than 100 if it did not, that there would be no 'manipulation' in favour of the Loyalists,[5] and that boundaries would not be left to the 'Mountjoy Barrack Staff' under the pernicious influence of Ball Greene.[6]

But once Redistribution was reduced to its component parts and seen by Members as it affected them, the 'independence of the House' collapsed to reveal disunity, a welter of irreconcilable nostrums and an unconcern which verged upon a *sauve qui peut* antipathy even within recognized blocs. Any Minister might count on the sympathy of the House in a speech of resignation: Courtney, who was 'strong...[on] the *method* of settling redistribution difficulties', forfeited even interest 'when he got on to his arithmetical puzzles.'[7] From the opposite direction, but with the same significance, Warton's side-swipe at Sellar was of more than personal interest: 'The hon. Member for the Haddington Burghs...had... got the start of those who waited until the Bill had been read a second time before they handed in their Amendments. It was a regrettable circumstance that, instead of having an important debate on the Bill in the first instance, the question was narrowed'.[8] The historian can but pass to the lapidary conclusion that there was no 'important debate' on Redistribution or its genesis.

[1] Elliot Diary, 6 Dec. 1884. Diaries, Vol. 10.
[2] 4 Dec. 1884. 3 *Hansard* ccxciv. 697.
[3] Buchanan to Elliot, 13 Dec. 1884. Elliot Mss., Bundle 32.
[4] Cranbrook Diary, 3 Dec. 1884. Cranbrook Mss., T501/299 fol. 287.
[5] 'Proposal from Parnell to Chamberlain and Dilke' in O'Shea's hand, 27 Nov. 1884, and Dilke's reply of the same date. Chamberlain Mss., JC8/8/1/28–9.
[6] Sexton to Dilke, 9 Dec. 1884. Spencer Mss.
[7] Elliot Diary, 29 Nov. 1884. Diaries, Vol. 10 (My italics); Hamilton Diary, 5 Dec. 1884. Hamilton Mss., 48638 fol. 82.
[8] 4 Mar. 1885. 3 *Hansard* ccxcv. 3.

8

SWANSONG[1]

This should be a slow, solemn, intelligent, deliberate procedure...
Warton, 10 Apr. 1885. 3 *Hansard* ccxcvi. 1381.

...this was, in more senses than one, an academical discussion...
Thorold Rogers (on Bryce's amendment to abolish University
representation), 6 Mar. 1885. 3 *Hansard* ccxcv. 373.

On 17 March 1885, a Liberal back-bencher asked whether,
before the Schedules came on for discussion, the Redistribution
bill might not be reprinted. Dilke demurred: 'hardly any Amendments had been made...and certainly none...that were of the
slightest importance. There would, therefore, be nothing to
reprint.'[2] It would not be extravagant to hail that retort as the
acme of Dilke's Parliamentary career. From the outset, he had
made it clear that his controlling course was determined by the
nature of the bill, and he abided by that declaration. The Redistribution measure was one which enjoyed 'the general concurrence of
all sections of the House', it was in many matters 'a compromise
between various opinions', and (which was a *non sequitur* though
the propositions appeared mutually determinant) 'we intend to
stand by its provisions.'[3]

In the baldness of such declarations, he was loyally echoed by
Northcote, who found an 'irrefutable argument' in 'the character
...of the Bill, and...of its introduction' against admitting anything which could 'jeopardize and break up the whole machinery'
of a measure in which 'one part hangs to another'. But Northcote could not quite sustain the dictatorial mask, and an idle
qualification – 'unless you are dissatisfied with the machinery as a
whole' – brought forth 'Ironical cheering from the Conservative
Benches'.[4] It was not a moment for the display of qualms. Parties
forgave ruthless obduracy only when finely executed, and while his

[1] Members 'sacked' under Redistribution provisions were tagged 'dying
swans' by Labouchère.
[2] 17 Mar. 1885. 3 *Hansard* ccxcv. 1557.
[3] Dilke, 6 Mar. 1885. 3 *Hansard* ccxcv. 338.
[4] 13 Mar. 1885. 3 *Hansard* ccxcv. 1163–4.

task was so much akin to Dilke's, Northcote sealed his own political fate during the spring of 1885. Nor did Dilke ease his path, playing fair only by his own ungenerous standards. One incident characterized the whole. Back-bench Tories uncovered in the swamping of Haverfordwest respectability by Pembroke dock-workers 'a case that smelt a good deal'.[1] Dilke, assuring them that Welsh grouping was an open question, did not scruple to turn the hounds on Northcote. 'It has not been directly provided for in the agreement, one way or the other. But it was one of the proposals submitted to the right hon. Gentleman and his Friends, and...no objection was taken.'[2] That came uncommonly close to breach of faith as regards secrecy.

A detailed look at Dilke's manner in the Commons provides the proper introduction to an understanding of the impotence of the Commons during these months. He was quite ready to congratulate any Member on a 'capital defence for the ancient borough' yet tersely to repeat that 'the limit of 15,000 was a vital principle', and so 'non possumus'.[3] He was quite ready to say that he had 'avoided discussing the question on its merits'.[4] He was quite ready even to admit that an opponent had a 'good case' which, in the absence of contrary information, Dilke would have found convincing; 'but he did not feel himself a free agent in this matter' for 'the Boundary Commissioners were more likely than [the opponent] to be right.'[5] And where the 'merits or demerits' were 'almost impossible' to determine in the House, he and Northcote were agreed that the appeal must be to an external authority – an authority which was to be accepted in all cases.[6] Members whose first article of political faith was that they 'should care for the opinion of no one but themselves'[7] were now reminded of the chaotic precedent of 1868 and heard their competence questioned 'to deal with a matter of this sort in a proper and satisfactory way'. Unless 'there was strong reason to think that the Commissioners had not had all the facts brought before them, or that by some unfortunate circumstance they had been in some way or other misled', back-benchers would do well to acquiesce in

[1] Lewis, 25 Mar. 1885. 3 *Hansard* ccxcvi. 544.
[2] 24 Mar. 1885. 3 *Hansard* ccxcvi. 515.
[3] 18 Mar. 1885. 3 *Hansard* ccxcv. 1597–8.
[4] 11 Mar. 1885. 3 *Hansard* ccxcv. 825.
[5] 15 Apr. 1885. 3 *Hansard* ccxcvi. 1798–9.
[6] 10 Apr. 1885. 3 *Hansard* ccxcvi. 1411–12.
[7] Warton, 10 Apr. 1885. 3 *Hansard* ccxcvi. 1381.

what was proposed and hold their tongues.[1] All this might have been one degree more palatable had not the Boundary Commissioners adopted the same line at grass-roots inquiry level over the Christmas Recess. Pelham, in 'taking note' of the suggestions of Sclater-Booth, Beach, the Secretary of the North Hampshire Conservative Association, the Mayor and Corporation of Andover, the Andover Liberals and the Town Clerk of Romsey, 'remarked that if everybody had a scheme to present, the only course the Commissioners could adopt would be to stick to their own.'[2] Sacrosanctity devolved, too, upon the Census of 1881. Dilke stood firm against endless complaints from ports and fishery-towns that their menfolk were at sea. He stood by the Census where calamity had reduced a population: Wigan, at 48,196 lost its second Member in 1885, because some 3,000 men had sought temporary employment elsewhere in the wake of a colliery strike – a case, it was urged in vain, 'strong[ly] analog[ous to that] of Granada during the recent earthquake.'[3] He stood by it against Gorst's allegation that the Government had engineered a night return to reduce the influence of the City of London – its population in Census terms being only the few poor who slept there. And he stood by it 'rather than going upon fancy as to the future', to the detriment of rapidly expanding cities and towns like Cardiff, which had a population of 82,761 in 1881, 109,067 in 1885 and seemed likely to reach 160,000 by the time of the next decennial Census.[4] The Census also served to bolster matters, like the 15,000 disfranchisement line, which had already been politically determined. Dilke challenged Arnold's amendment to raise the barrier to 20,000 on three counts: that boroughs under attack (he listed those in Liberal hands) were not all declining, that the proposal would work unduly to the advantage of Wales and Ireland (thus playing upon anti-Celtic prejudice) and that it would disturb the English county/borough ratio and balance (eminently satisfactory, with 234 County Members for a population of 12,506,000, and 226 Borough Members for 12,106,000).[5] Again and again, Members complained that only thus, and indirectly, did they learn what the compact meant or how vital was every detail. At least one Tory front-bencher withdrew, in embarrassment, an amendment which

[1] Northcote, 10 Apr. 1885. 3 *Hansard* ccxcvi. 1384.
[2] *The Times*, 31 Dec. 1884, p. 6.
[3] Egerton, 20 Mar. 1885. 3 *Hansard* ccxcvi. 168.
[4] Sir Edward Reed, 23 Mar. 1885. 3 *Hansard* ccxcvi. 298; Dilke, 23 Mar. 1885. 3 *Hansard* ccxcvi. 302.   [5] Dilke, 10 Mar. 1885. 3 *Hansard* ccxcv. 726–8.

he had put down 'in complete ignorance' of the fact that the representation of the City of London 'was part of the bargain which the Prime Minister had confirmed that evening.'[1] Dilke was not often caught short of plausibility. Anyone who follows the passage of the Redistribution bill will come to anticipate which response he will offer to any challenge out of the twenty or so variations he seemed to have available. His arguments were not unanswerable, but there was no effective political answer to implacability. He enjoyed the last word. If the Commissioners had cut across wards, as at Leeds, without equalizing populations, it was 'in consequence of the great difference in the character of the population in different parts of the same ward.'[2] If they had joined Redruth and Camborne because both were engaged in mining, they had 'strictly adhered to their Instructions', whatever the mutual sense of *mésalliance* and the experience that 'there were no two places in the kingdom which worked so badly together'.[3] Yet, on other occasions, he would reverse these priorities. Boundaries might not be extended to encompass an admittedly identic population, because there was 'a complete ring of Local Board districts all round the borough...strongly opposed to being absorbed.'[4] And each time he achieved such a *coup*, however blatant the inconsistency, he was consolidating his position. Empirical triumph established precedent: Dilke felt himself 'compelled to resist the Amendment, as he had already resisted Amendments...for which, at all events, a[n equally] strong case had been made out.'[5] Moreover, a Member complained, 'after he had used every argument which the circumstances of the case in any way justified, he always wound up as a clincher..."you have not told us where we are to get the seat."'[6] If Exeter (just below the 50,000 line) was to retain her second Member, the donor could hardly be a constituency which satisfied the population requirement; the seat would therefore 'have to be taken' from one of the 'great English borough constituencies like Wolverhampton and Sheffield'[7] – and the merest hint that this was so sufficed to enlist into active service and vocal support the Members for Wolver-

---

[1] Giffard, 13 Mar. 1885. 3 *Hansard* ccxcv. 1172.
[2] 10 Apr. 1885. 3 *Hansard* ccxcvi. 1411.
[3] 13 Apr. 1885. 3 *Hansard* ccxcvi. 1560.
[4] 20 Mar. 1885. 3 *Hansard* ccxcvi. 163.
[5] 15 Apr. 1885. 3 *Hansard* ccxcvi. 1799.
[6] Lewis, 25 Mar. 1885. 3 *Hansard* ccxcv. 545.
[7] Dilke, 20 Mar. 1885. 3 *Hansard* ccxcvi. 152.

hampton and Sheffield. Dilke, indeed, relied heavily upon Members to adopt the attitude of Kilkenny cats. He could count also upon ignorance, fatigue and boredom. All merit attention.

Healy gave support, as regards Antrim and Lisburn, Tyrone and Drogheda, to a grouping proposition from Crichton ('the charmer, the noble Viscount the Member for Fermanagh') – and was repudiated by Biggar and Sexton.[1] Giffard ostentatiously separated himself from R. N. Fowler on the representation of the City of London.[2] Even the 'faithful phalanx of Scotch Liberal Members' divided against itself 'when it came to the particular burghs.'[3] Elliot pressed Grant, the Member for the Leith Burghs, to withdraw an amendment whose result would be to 'separate Portobello and Musselburgh from Leith and throw them into the county, without giving a second Member to Mid Lothian'. Grant went forward: his proposal was the first step to securing a second Member for Midlothian. This duly alarmed C. S. Parker, whose constituents would feel 'much aggrieved if...it were arranged to give a second Member to Mid Lothian, with a smaller population than Perthshire, and to deprive Perthshire of the second Member already promised to it.'[4] When Bateson proposed to save for County Down (i.e. from engulfment in Belfast) the 'villa' residents of the parishes of Holywood and Knockbreda, he encountered the hostility of his fellow Orangeman, Corry. Lack of community of interest with the millworkers of Belfast mattered less than the borough's fourth seat; and, as sitting Member, Corry 'could not be a party' to a proposal for boundary adjustment which might undermine parity with Dublin.[5] The examples might be multiplied tenfold.

The level and matter of discussion were never of a sort to attract the interest of the disinterested. There was not infrequently a crescendo of boasting by the local boys – and nothing more. Henry Tollemache intervened in a wrangle between Dilke (omniscient) and Raikes (twelve years Chester's MP) about the naming of one Cheshire division, to remind both that 'he knew a great deal more about the neighbourhood covered by the Amendment than either of the right hon. Gentlemen'; Cross promptly capped this, for *he* knew 'as much of [this matter]...as anybody in the House.'[6] Those

[1] 10 Mar. 1885. 3 *Hansard* ccxcv. 739, 751 and 798.
[2] 13 Mar. 1885. 3 *Hansard* ccxcv. 1172.
[3] Trevelyan, 20 Mar. 1885. 3 *Hansard* ccxcvi. 79.
[4] 20 Mar. 1885. 3 *Hansard* ccxcvi. 111–12.
[5] 25 Mar. 1885. 3 *Hansard* ccxcvi. 579–80 and 585.
[6] 13 Apr. 1885. 3 *Hansard* ccxcvi. 1549–50.

outsiders who rushed in did so to their cost. Sexton, authoritative on County Sligo and much of Ireland beside, made an ass of himself in relying upon the greenery of place-names in the environs of Birmingham: all 'groves and hills and dales', the area must, he concluded, be 'practically rural'.[1] Certainly it was better to bore, assailing with an unassailable recital of home-town topography and knowledge of idiosyncratic pursuits, and better to dispute contiguity of boroughs[2] or to assert the affinity of those proposed for grouping in one's own county, than to trespass upon the preserve of others. Sir George Campbell, perversely silly, 'would not enter upon the [local] details' though they were 'very important', in proposing the addition of five towns to the Dumfries group. Rather, he chose to 'exhaust...the general argument', by reference to Ayr and Hawick, Dunfermline and Stirling, Peebles and Selkirk. Retribution was severe. So incensed were Members that they did not spare him the howled refrain of 'Question, question', and 'No, no', when, belatedly awakening to his error, he announced his intention very properly to 'refer for a moment to the Dumfries Burghs'.[3] If few remembered that this was indeed what was under consideration, hardly anyone cared.

Even where charges of jerrymandering were put with all the force of detail, it must have been all but impossible for the willing Member on first hearing to grasp and weigh the argument – to understand why it was (if it was) justifiable to jump across Lough Swilly in Donegal and join Innishowen to Kilmacrenan, but not, in the Downpatrick division, to straddle Strangford Lough so as to take in Lower Ards. Fiddle and counter-fiddle were not readily distinguished. Was it more significant that thirty miles of Lough Swilly's waters separated Innishowen and Kilmacrenan, or that the Lough was no more than three miles wide at the ferry? Was it more disconcerting to learn that Dilke did not know that the ferry existed, or that in County Down the Nationalists had themselves proposed a scheme which would have traversed Strangford Lough at a point much wider than in this case of Donegal?[4]

---

[1] 24 Mar. 1885. 3 *Hansard* ccxcvi. 404.

[2] 'The fare by hired carriage was never less than 2s. 6d., and very often the driver tried to get 3s.' Wilmot, 25 Mar. 1885. 3 *Hansard* ccxcvi. 566.

[3] Hay, 18 Mar. 1885. 3 *Hansard* ccxcv. 1641–2; Campbell, 18 Mar. 1885. 3 *Hansard* ccxcv. 1633–40 and 1644.

[4] Healy–Dilke–Sexton exchange, 4 Mar. 1885. 3 *Hansard* ccxcv. 14–23. This Lough Swilly battle was fought out in the Commons on more than one occasion; names appear under various guises, *viz.* Kilmacreenan and Kilnachrennan.

There is a further point. The Report of the Boundary Commissioners sold at 17s. 6d. It is a fair guess (and was Healy's grumble) that few Members took the trouble to invest and familiarize themselves with such geographical and parochial detail affecting others as was available there but not in the Redistribution bill itself. It was (Healy entered the complaint on the division of Waterford) 'monstrous that they should have in a Bill such words as these – "And the barony of Decies without Drum (except so much as is comprised in Division No. 2, as herein described)." '[1] They were lost and without a map. The House could never know the rights and wrongs of including in North Tyrone the villages of Ballynasollus, Cruckaclady, Glashygolgan, Glencoppogagh, Landahussy Lower, Landahussy Upper, Letterbrat, Meenagorp and Tullynadall. Consequently, it rarely troubled about the rights and wrongs: if Callan, Healy, Kenny and T. P. O'Connor assailed the scheme which Dilke and Plunket defended, then those few Britons who had been prevailed upon to remain in the House, knew what they had to do.[2]

Salisbury had predicted difficulty in Parliament. The more the Redistribution bill was studied, 'the more its faults [would] come to light – & the memory of what might have replaced it [would] fade away.'[3] But he was only half right. There came a point when exhaustion made the heavier mark, when faults were thought better than endless discussion about them and when an exhortation from Thorold Rogers was set in the right key: abandon these 'ludicrously irrelative and absolutely pitiable' discussions, and 'in an emphatic way, negative all this heap of rubbish.'[4] Tempers, and consequently speeches, shortened as the bill moved from Committee to Report. Those who wished to reiterate the protests of previous weeks did so in only summary fashion before begging leave to withdraw. Several were laughed, coughed or shouted down. O'Donnell exasperated Members by pressing amendments to 'pock-mark' the Irish electoral map with names of antiquarian interest, beyond humiliating divisions (97–16, 120–8, 91–3) to the point of historical inevitability at which 'no Member appearing to be a second Teller for the Noes, Mr. Speaker declared that the Ayes had it.'[5] William Redmond embarked upon an attack on those officials who threw

[1] 21 Apr. 1885. 3 *Hansard* ccxcvii. 376.
[2] 21 Apr. 1885. 3 *Hansard* ccxcvii. 367–76.
[3] Salisbury to Austin, 2 Dec. 1884. Austin Mss.
[4] 14 Apr. 1885. 3 *Hansard* ccxcvi. 1727.
[5] 8 May 1885. 3 *Hansard* ccxcviii. 78.

every obstacle in the way of the national, Nationalist, will: 'The great majority of the Returning Officers in Ireland were men –'. It was an ill-chosen moment to pause for breath before the indictment: the Commons responded, as would any Saturday night music hall audience, with wild applause.[1] The more sensitive knew that no attention was being paid to them, said so, and resumed their seats.[2] But if the House assembled only to 'register decrees of a cross between the two Front Benches',[3] and if Members, intolerant of the claims of others and fully recognizing that it was a 'farce' to move the Chairman in and out of the Chair,[4] endured such treatment 'only because they were so near the eve of the General Election',[5] the question remains: why did Redistribution drag on so long? Why? – if a Conservative Opposition was 'in honour debarred from any vexatious or dilatory opposition',[6] with independent revolt denounced by Salisbury in 'what some people called the "flagellation" at the Carlton' on 16 March.[7] Why? – if the Parnellites 'did not wish to play ducks and drakes with the Bill'[8] but wished only to be able to say now that they 'understood the game'[9] and at the next election to claim 'that they [the conjoint authors] had tried to be dishonest and failed'.[10] It is a simple question, too readily overlooked: why did Members speak?

Upon essentials, no-one pretended that he had any hope of success. Time and time again, Dilke gave that '*non possumus* answer which the hon. and gallant Member *appeared to anticipate*.'[11] Many entered the protest which they had postponed throughout 1884 when they had been met by 'the argument[,] "Oh, trust to the Redistribution Bill."'[12] Now they found no safeguard. What they found was numbers reinforcing numbers, and they 'repudiated numbers altogether in this matter'. Wilmot delivered the backhander he thought merited, moving to reduce the representation of Birmingham from 7 to 5, because Birmingham would not be able to

---

[1] 28 Apr. 1885. 3 *Hansard* ccxcvii. 1004.
[2] Wilmot, 20 Mar. 1885. 3 *Hansard* ccxcvi. 156.
[3] Bateson, 25 Mar. 1885. 3 *Hansard* ccxcvi. 589.
[4] Lewis, 11 Mar. 1885. 3 *Hansard* ccxcv. 802.
[5] Cotton, 13 Mar. 1885. 3 *Hansard* ccxcv. 1132.
[6] Northcote to Salisbury, 30 Nov. 1884. Salisbury Mss., Series E.
[7] Dalrymple Diary, 17 Mar. 1885.
[8] Healy, 10 Mar. 1885. 3 *Hansard* ccxcv. 739.
[9] T. D. Sullivan, 17 Apr. 1885. 3 *Hansard* ccxcvii. 101.
[10] Sexton, 17 Apr. 1885. 3 *Hansard* ccxcvii. 52.
[11] 18 Mar. 1885. 3 *Hansard* ccxcv. 1598 (My italics.)
[12] Crichton, 4 Dec. 1884. 3 *Hansard* ccxciv. 693.

find 'gentlemen' to fill the seats.[1] J. G. Hubbard found Bethnal Green's interests to be 'uniform and homogeneous', knew that Members represented interests and deduced that 'one Representative of the Bethnal Green [silk-]weavers would be as effective as half-a-dozen'.[2] Beresford told the long and sorry tale of Mr. Cox, the works-manager of an English company in Leitrim, who was shot at his bedside after a dispute with an Irish employee; 'whereupon the Company gave up the works and left the country...Let them compare that state of things with the manufacturing industries... at Lisburn, Lurgan, Portadown, and Armagh....was it wise to disfranchise such constituencies and reduce them to the same condition as the population in the South and West of Ireland?'[3]

The language used was that of checks and balance. Beresford Hope found no compensation in the 'undue preponderance' accorded to 'local feeling'; what was wanted, he thought, was the maintenance and extension of University representation as an intellectual counterweight to the 'hopelessly *reactionary* and deplorably Philistine' tendencies of this measure; even if 'among the non-residents might be found country squires, whose degree was a poll or a pass one, and whose talk was of bullocks and such things, was it not something to be able to talk of bullocks with that reasonable education which any degree indicated'?[4] Though the charge of betrayal levelled against their leaders was nearer the surface, this was in essence the language of Warton, who 'deplored very much that the Bill was based on the principle of population' but was grateful for 'the sake of public peace and public decency' for an agreement which 'must be honestly carried out.'[5] It was language no more threatening than that of Firth who 'would accept the Parliamentary Elections (Redistribution) Bill to-day, but...contest it to-morrow'.[6] It was the language of salved conscience and of 'respectful protest' against a 'suicidal' course.[7] It was a necessary public discharge of disappointment, real or feigned, and the price that had to be paid for the loud-mouthed advertisement of the previous autumn.

The purpose of back-benchers in these debates was not simply to

[1] Wilmot, 23 Mar. 1885. 3 *Hansard* ccxcvi. 295–7.
[2] 24 Mar. 1885. 3 *Hansard* ccxcvi. 455.
[3] 11 Mar. 1885. 3 *Hansard* ccxcv. 780–1.
[4] 6 Mar. 1885. 3 *Hansard* ccxcv. 362–3. (My italics.)
[5] 4 Mar. 1885. 3 *Hansard* ccxcv. 3–5.
[6] 13 Mar. 1885. 3 *Hansard* ccxcv. 1146.
[7] Lubbock, 17 Mar. 1885. 3 *Hansard* ccxcv. 1465.

air grievances or establish their consistency. Radicals found comfort in the failure of Bryce's amendment: they 'would remember and talk about the matter, and...would not fail to tell the country to whom it was they owed the retention' of University seats.[1] Some went several degrees further in establishing how far their interests had been compromised. The Lord Advocate agreed to confer with Scottish Members in February 'with a view if possible to the modification of the Government scheme, so far as this is practicable and within the limits that can be considered.'[2] But while the handful of Scottish Conservatives supported resolutions to insist on a representation of 72, Liberals themselves chafed at the formation of 'any thing like a Scotch party in the House'.[3] They were there as Liberals to draw from the Government the sort of Redistribution scheme which a Liberal Government would have proposed if it had not been compromised by negotiation with Salisbury. It was hardly surprising that when the Lord Advocate produced proposals to meet these feelings they should have been denounced by the Scottish Tories as 'a complete system of jerrymandering'.[4] To say that Scottish Members were practically unanimous (the minority numbered only eight)[5] on the need to amalgamate Bute and Argyll, for example, was simply to say that there was division on party lines.[6]

Though discussions of this sort continued – and continued to carry 'improvements' in the grouping system – Salisbury was bound to declare that they were all *ultra vires*. When he did so, Dilke seemed relieved. Scottish Tories were to 'get nothing out of the shuffle',[7] but 'very little change will be made in the Bill, & perhaps that is better than what the Ld. Advocate's proposals wd. have done to us.'[8] Scottish Liberals could forget their differences as to grouping and create a fuss at the triumph of three (poetic licence) over the will of fifty.[9] The Scottish example was, however, exceptional only in the degree of organization. Time after time, proposals from one side and counter-proposals from the other were

---

[1] Thorold Rogers, 6 Mar. 1885. 3 *Hansard* ccxcv. 375.
[2] *Scotsman*, 4 Dec. 1884, p. 5.
[3] Buchanan to Elliot, 25 Dec. 1884. Elliot Mss., Bundle 32.
[4] Dalrymple Diary, 3 Feb. 1885.
[5] Buchanan, 4 Mar. 1885. 3 *Hansard* ccxcv. 40.
[6] There might be a corollary drawn: would Liberals accept resolutions passed at a bloc meeting of English county Members, where the parties were in a comparable state of imbalance?
[7] Dalrymple Diary, 24 Mar. 1885.   [8] Dalrymple Diary, 5 Mar. 1885.
[9] Peddie, 20 Mar. 1885. 3 *Hansard* ccxcvi. 76.

essentially what Healy called them – 'a species of masked battery in order to hold the divisions already made'.[1] In all these months, virtually nothing is heard of those matters which students of electoral behaviour regard as fundamental. Did those who complained of the mixing of lawyers and costermongers in Holborn[2] progress from the conception that employment should form the basis of representation to a belief that class should? When it was suggested that the 'wealthy merchants' of Lime Street should be transferred to the Abercrombie ward so as to ensure the Irishness of Liverpool Exchange,[3] was it really being implied that an irreconcilable quarter – a 'Belleville' – should be established in every major industrial centre? Was this, indeed, anything more than comment on the incomplete realization of a given objective? The Boundary Commissioner for Derbyshire reminded his audience of the 'principal object' – 'to keep the different populations apart, the agricultural from the mining and the manufacturing population',[4] and found that such objections as were made to the proposals contained in the bill referred only to the names of districts. Another, in Cornwall, issued the stern rebuke that they should 'endeavour to make a good division, rather than fight about the name to be given to it.'[5] It was as much the response of those in the localities who were sufficiently concerned to attend public inquiries as of MPs. For the psephologist, it may be a disappointing response: he will find precious little to awaken him in *Hansard* or in press reports of the Commissioners' circuit. Yet this very silence is of immense political significance. Redistribution became for long weeks the game of the name. It was here that Members found the opportunity to challenge the dictates from above but even if the leaders' measures had been thought pernicious or the main bulk of the Commissioners' executive work faulty, no ice was likely to be cut by questions as trumpery as the ones they brought before the House of Commons.

Each Member stood by his constituents in whichever way he thought sufficient. He was performing 'a function which could scarcely be avoided'[6] and had visible proof of effort if compass-point nomenclature was overthrown. This might be a flimsy shield:

---

[1] Healy, 4 Mar. 1885. 3 *Hansard* ccxcv. 17.
[2] P. W. Clayden, *The Proposed Electoral Divisions of London: a Great Blot on a Great Measure* (1885), p. 17.
[3] T. P. O'Connor, 10 Apr. 1885. 3 *Hansard* ccxcvi. 1360–1.
[4] Major Tulloch. *The Times*, 13 Dec. 1884, p. 7.
[5] Pelham. *The Times*, 19 Dec. 1884, p. 7.
[6] Sexton, 25 Mar. 1885. 3 *Hansard* ccxcvi. 554.

233

'It was just possible that when some new democratic wave passed over the country, some great man might rise up and propose to do away with the divisions North and South, East and West, and that all Members for the county should thenceforth be chosen by the county at large.'[1] On the other hand, there was something to be said for simple geographical convenience:[2]

> Cockermouth is much the best,
> For it is neither East nor West;
> Nor can we call it North or South,
> For it is only Cockermouth.

More often, success in keeping a name, even when a seat was abolished, was sufficient in itself to satisfy constituents. Raikes' motion that the Abingdon division of Berkshire be re-named the 'Northern or Abingdon' division was immediately agreed to; but had Raikes proposed simple substitution and compass-point brevity, Cremer Clarke, Member and sometime Mayor, would 'have been compelled' to oppose him. He and his constituents had found their only morsel of solace in Gladstone's professed readiness to make disfranchised boroughs 'the head of county divisions'.[3] Indeed, for a Member not to speak on a matter of this sort was to expose himself to taunts: 'Possibly he had found another constituency, or had discovered, for some other reason, that he did not want to represent this constituency. . . .more likely. . .the proposed new constituency did not want him.'[4] But comment of such asperity was rare; the Commons enjoyed good humour in loosening tongues. Dilke took Raikes' challenge to the title of Buckrose for an East Riding division as 'part of a deep-laid design'[5] to provoke a speech from Christopher Sykes, whose only previous utterance in twenty years had been on amendment to the Fisheries (Oyster, Crab and Lobster) Act of 1877, and who was indeed never again to address the House.

Few needed prompting. Battle was joined. Boroughs were decried as 'sinks of iniquity'[6] or as 'ante-diluvian. . .and fossil-sleepy hollows of which the world knows nothing'.[7] Objection was taken to Eccles 'on the ground of its historic cakes',[8] to Caxton

---

[1] T. C. Thompson, 15 Apr. 1885. 3 *Hansard* ccxcvi. 1809–10.
[2] Warton, 14 Apr. 1885. 3 *Hansard* ccxcvi. 1645.
[3] 13 Apr. 1885. 3 *Hansard* ccxcvi. 1527; 4 Dec. 1884. 3 *Hansard* ccxciv. 650.
[4] Rose, 13 Apr. 1885. 3 *Hansard* ccxcvi. 1562.
[5] 15 Apr. 1885. 3 *Hansard* ccxcvi. 1833.
[6] Raikes, 20 Mar. 1885. 3 *Hansard* ccxcvi. 141.
[7] M. P. Barry to Richard Bourke, 9 Jan. 1885. Irish Boundary Commission Mss.
[8] *Manchester Guardian*, 24 Jan. 1885, p. 7.

('only known for its gibbet'),[1] to Sodbury as 'an unmusical and ill-omened name'[2] and to Youghal as 'unpronounceable on English lips'.[3] (But Raikes could say 'Ystrayfodwg' quite as well as Sir Hussey Vivian.)[4] Thornbury found an advocate, as a division of Gloucestershire: it had a mayor and corporation – 'a statement which seemed to amuse a large part of the audience and which, if truth must be told, was received with somewhat unkindly laughter.'[5] Picton sang the historic praises of the Leicester parish of Belgrave: 'The place was mentioned in the Doomsday Book', though 'under the name of Merdegrave';[6] perhaps as many savoured the felicitous change as were impressed by antiquity. Stanley Leighton pleaded that Williton should give its name to a Somerset division; after all, 'that great man, Reginald Fitzurse, one of the knights who killed Thomas A'Becket, was born there.' It was an irreverent, perverse history which failed to impress (or a parody of antiquarianism which alienated) the House: he secured eleven votes against ninety.[7] Another fared better. For R. H. Paget, 'sweetness and simplicity' demanded 'Bridgwater' as against the 'Mid' division of Somerset; and 'sweetness and simplicity', so interpreted, triumphed over the less than sweet memory of corruption – the unseating of two Members and disfranchisement of the borough in 1870.[8]

And so, to Slagg's celebrated amendment on the Seventh Schedule, page 63, line 9, to leave out the words 'Farnworth-cum-Radcliffe' and insert instead 'Radcliffe-cum-Farnworth'.[9] Henry Lucy comes into his own, for the matter was of no importance, and there are only trivia to record. Summoned from his soup by the division bell, Sir Charles Forster stood forlorn in the centre of the Chamber. No Government tellers were named to guide him aright; indeed, the Ministerial Whip, along with two of the Law Officers, was arrayed against Dilke, Northcote and Churchill. 'At length, Mr. Slagg coming to his assistance, led him out, and to-morrow, on looking down the division list, Sir Charles will find that he voted for Radcliffe-cum-Farnworth.'[10] That amendment might stand as an epitaph to the process by which political issues retreat into statute.

[1] *The Times*, 16 Dec. 1884, p. 6.   [2] *The Times*, 31 Dec. 1884, p. 6.
[3] Barry to Bourke, 9 Jan. 1885. Irish Boundary Commission Mss.
[4] 23 Mar. 1885. 3 *Hansard* ccxcvi. 311.   [5] *The Times*, 31 Dec. 1884, p. 6.
[6] 24 Mar. 1885. 3 *Hansard* ccxcvi. 501.
[7] 15 Apr. 1885. 3 *Hansard* ccxcvi. 1785–6.
[8] 15 Apr. 1885. 3 *Hansard* ccxcvi. 1783.
[9] 8 May 1885. 3 *Hansard* ccxcvii. 41.
[10] Lucy, *A Diary of Two Parliaments*, Vol. II, p. 424.

EPILOGUE: A NECESSARY
DISCHARGE

HISTORIANS whose sympathies lie with the inarticulate in their unknown graves, and who dismiss as an exercise in word-play the subtle exercise of power by 'an insolent aristocratical band', are those to whose academic predilections and moral outrage one cannot defer. There are yet others to whom one might be thought to make concessions. None has been made. There is in this work only a cursory account of the operation of the franchise in the United Kingdom before 1884, and no attempt to see it in relation to the bill as it was passed. It is neither a history of the passage of a measure nor a chronicle of electoral revolution and democratic triumph. If it passes critical scrutiny, it will do so by reason of a superficial consonance with a manner of writing which has been too readily labelled as coming from an earlier generation.

Of course, it is dangerous, in so far as it devalues the subject matter, for the historian or the reader ever to forget that with which he is concerned and that with which politicians concerned themselves – the bases of power for a generation. What one is asking is that a historical consciousness of further electoral reform in 1918 should not be allowed to obscure the more immediate political convulsion in 1886. This is a study of the months in which the Third Reform bill was the *major question* in British politics; it is worthy of attention precisely because the Third Reform bill was not the occasion of a *major crisis*. 1884 does not have the makings of a compelling narrative. The whole episode is of comparative unexcitement in a decade of extraordinary turbulence; the Government which introduced the measures saw them through in all essentials, parties did not realign themselves, and daring young men emerged in mid-1885 still on the make and unmade. What one is analysing is the functioning of the Parliamentary system of the 1880s at a point in the 1880s when the functioning was fairly normal. It is for others to determine whether the understanding which emerges justifies conclusions which apply not just to the period we have been discussing but to political decision-making as it occurs in Parliamentary systems.

A final word as to the structure of this book and the manner of its writing may not be amiss. There exists a near unanimity – aired by onlookers (who may be dismissed) as by revered practitioners (who seek to disarm their critics by honest confession) – that the reconstruction of high politics is an academic canter, and that between the archive and the monograph there lies only a simple manipulation of cards. There is truth in the charge but the fundamental truth is missed. It is true that what has been presented in this book reflects the substance of an ordered mass of transcription. The outcome, this is to say, is chronological narrative. What one is asking now is that the belief about politics which determines one to write what is dismissable as 'mere narrative' be understood. Though their words dominate the text, few of those who were involved in the events of 1884 were concerned to provide explanation either of their actions or of the actions of their rivals. Yet explanation is what historical thinking demands and this is what this book attempts to provide – not a dull reissue of the linguistic currency of past controversy, but a language which, while protagonists would understand it, simultaneously manipulates their words to portray their purposes. Furthermore, the belief registered in this book about the nature of political determination – the importance of political in-fighting, the significance of duplicity as a means of conciliation, and the overriding impact of ambition or frustrated ambition on the wills and actions of politicians – must antedate any interpretation that is offered of the evidence from which this book has been made. Indeed, it possibly determined the very field of research and is the justification for the paradox with which we close – that anyone who does not find reform an absolute attraction may still find attraction in the politics of reform.

APPENDIX I

PARNELLITE PARTY POLITICS: THE EVIDENCE

THE ABUNDANCE of primary material available for this study does not extend to Ireland; or, more specifically, it does not encompass Nationalist manoeuvre. This relative paucity is reflected in the 'apparent marginality' of Parnell in Hurst's *Joseph Chamberlain and Liberal Reunion*. Parnell figures so slightly as an 'active agent' because 'unlike the other participants in this little drama, the Irish Leader did not keep up a vast correspondence, so that his demands, opinions, and passing moods have gone unrecorded'.[1]

In the National Library of Ireland, there exists but a rat-gnawed, single bundle of Parnell's outward correspondence, for the years 1874–91. The large collection of John Redmond papers, though he was already a party Whip, contain little this early in his career. There is a fair amount relevant amongst the letters of Timothy Harrington, Secretary of the Irish National League, precious little in the T. D. Sullivan Mss. The O'Shea collection comprises, for the most part, copies of letters to Chamberlain and replies thereto – more accessible in Birmingham University Library. O'Shea's partner in the representation of County Clare, The O'Gorman Mahon, was wholly pre-occupied with domestic tragedy. O'Neill Daunt, who kept a full and valuable journal, Mitchell Henry, P. J. Smyth and Sir Charles Gavan Duffy pass waspish comment, but rank essentially as old-time Home Rulers and, increasingly after 1880, as uninformed outsiders. Their password marks, indeed betrays, the limit to their understanding of Parnell's political activity: 'Insanity, hereditary in his Family, tinges all he does.'[2] Constituency circulars, copies of resolutions, election addresses and so forth are to be found in the Richard Lalor collection: Lalor himself was excused regular attendance at Westminster in 1884 to concentrate efforts upon saving his Queen's County seat. J. F. X.

[1] G. R. Searle, *Victorian Studies* XIII (1969), p. 237.
[2] Mitchell Henry to Daunt, 11 Jan. 1880. Daunt Mss., 11446.

PARNELLITE PARTY POLITICS: THE EVIDENCE

O'Brien's correspondence, memoranda and account-books have been consulted, but he did not enter Parliament until 1885. A mere eighteen letters to or from the editor of the *Freeman's Journal*, Dwyer Gray, are to be found in the Library of Trinity College, Dublin. Michael Davitt's diaries, in the possession of Professor T. W. Moody, and the John Dillon Mss., still in family hands, were not at the time of research open for consultation.

There is, of course, a good deal to be gleaned from English and Ulster collections, from *Hansard*, memoirs and biographies. But reliance has been heavy upon the Nationalist press, the Harrington and Lalor Mss., and the minute book of a Dublin branch of the National League. There is potentially an imbalance, a weighting in favour of organization, in such evidence, and the interpretation offered may not have sufficiently corrected that imbalance. A word, too, needs to be said upon the position of the *Freeman's Journal* vis-à-vis the Parnellites. The revolutionary and Fenian elements always looked on the paper as prepared or attempting 'to do the Government work if & so far as it can.'[1] Such denunciation may be taken as read. It is of greater account that Grosvenor and Spencer fondled the idea of securing control of it as the most influential Parnellite organ. Approach could not be made through Gray (an untrustworthy drunkard) but perhaps to Parnell himself, whom Grosvenor had 'always found...amenable & honourable in my dealings with him.' The Chief Whip was prepared to provide up to £3,000 for two years, with an option for a third 'if we keep in', funds being handed over 'by one man, who should be the sole arbiter as to whether the paper...was doing its part of the bargain ...The business might be commenced by negotiating for a Leader ...by a good man who would begin a bit strong, & then get more Liberal by degrees.'[2] Nothing, so far as is known, came of the scheme; what might have been is illustrative of the paper's pre-eminence.

Primary evidence, then, is sketchy. What of scholarly analysis? Harrison states that Parnell 'wanted electoral reform – and wanted it urgently...for his strategy of affecting the balance between the principal British parties.' It was, so Harrison argues, 'to this end that his influence in "slowing down" the agitation' in the post-Kilmainham period was exercised.[3] O'Brien, in partial refutation,

---

[1] Patrick Egan to Quinn, 17 Aug. 1881. Harrington Mss., 8577.
[2] Grosvenor to Spencer, 7 Dec. 1883. Spencer Mss.
[3] Henry Harrison, *Parnell, Joseph Chamberlain, and Mr. Garvin* (1938), pp. 65 and 85–6.

traces the policy of moderation back to February 1881, at which time 'the question of electoral reform was not dominant in anybody's mind'. He follows Garvin's straight reading of Chamberlain, that Parnell's 'phalanx in the next House would be something over 80 with the franchise reform but of something under 80 without it'. And he warns against exaggeration with the unarguable fact that 'even the restricted franchise was already returning Parnellites steadily at by-elections' – before wrecking his handiwork with a pat on the back for Chamberlain, as appreciating 'the signs of the future' and the full Irish 'implications' of the Franchise Act.[1] Most recently has come Hurst's appraisal, but even in so sharp an essay there is ambiguity about the grant of a 'popular vote' to Ireland. If we accept that 'Parnell was no democrat', if we accept that after 1880 Parnell's aim was to create a 'highly disciplined force in parliament', and that 'Irish Nationalism had plenty of room for expanding its parliamentary representation at the next election, *whether or not the franchise had been widened*', then how are these to be reconciled with the subsequent contentions – that 'reform was always in Parnell's mind', that it was necessary 'to keep the Liberal party sweet on franchise', and that enactment brought not simply a 'crucial' change (which, in the event, it may have been), 'tighten[ing] rather than decreas[ing]...control over Nationalist M.P.s' (which it may, in the event, have done), but that expectation was thereby fulfilled in this 'long awaited' reform?[2]

[1] C. C. O'Brien, *Parnell and his Party, 1880–1890* (Oxford, 1957), pp. 87 and 91.
[2] Michael Hurst, *Parnell and Irish Nationalism* (1968), pp. 49, 70, 73 (my italics), 78–9 and 84.

APPENDIX II

'THE ROYAL MEDIATION IN 1884' BY C. C. WESTON, *ENGLISH HISTORICAL REVIEW* LXXXII (1967), pp. 296–322

Dr Weston's interest lies in the constitutional field, in the survival of the House of Lords as an effective power, and hence in Third Reform as a crisis episode for that institution. What is dangerous is the ease of transference for the reader into a belief that here is adequate portrayal of 'politics in the round' even for these November days. The historian who juxtaposes the more moderate demands of one pacific section of one party, and the more optimistic hopes of one belligerent section of the other, who finds the former met and declares this – as here – to be the effecting of the Liberal programme, is a political tiro. The historian who, in an appendage, labels as Salisbury's 'quiet revenge' his summary dismissal of her heroes when it came to the business of settling Redistribution, does not know what political battles are about.[1] If the point is made with a stridency which verges on hectoring offensiveness, it is because what is at stake is the manner of writing political history.

Dr Weston's scholarship, which is orderly and meticulous, reflects her sources, which are ill-chosen. She has lighted (in her inspection of Conservative archives) upon cracks in party unity, which is what political correspondence must always reveal. She has enlarged upon the misgivings of certain Conservatives, which matters little, but she has ignored the possibility (for she cites no Liberal collections) of Liberal troubles, which matters much. In relying so heavily on the Royal Archives, and the Goodwood and Cairns Mss., she has in fact created a crisis which had no reality, and brought the Queen, Ponsonby, Richmond, Charles Peel and Cairns to the forefront of the stage to solve this crisis. Dr Weston's failure may be one of political comprehension but it is an incomprehension which a wider reading of the primary material on both sides must have corrected. Where, at the first count, are

---

[1] Weston, p. 316.

241

Churchill, Dilke, Hartington and Hicks Beach? Where, wonder of wonders, is Gladstone?

But is Dr Weston asking the right questions? When a break is made in any established course or pattern of conduct (when, in this instance, the shouting had to stop), the historian will search for cause – first the build-up of long-term pressures and then adventitious, new and crucial change of circumstance. There can be no wholesale rejection of that order but there must be strong disinclination simply to view the events of November 1884 as comprising Conservative (or, for that matter, Liberal) surrender, for which we are to seek and assign cause. The exercise is historically unprofitable and academically undemanding. However neatly the intervention of the Queen coincided with peace, perverse artistry or naive reading alone can make cause of coincidence. Politicians leapt far ahead of the Queen to render superfluous and obsolescent her every move – witness that scene where Rowton, despatched from Sandringham, confronted Dilke: 'But we only sat and smiled at one another; he saying that he had come because he had been told to come, and I saying that I had nothing to tell him, for Lord Salisbury knew all we had to say.'[1] However attractive the notion of effective royal conspiracy and however romantic the sending of letters which bore no 'tell tale postmarks',[2] the problems are these: how did leaders convey to the led that if they had not obtained all that was demanded in the full flow of Recess oratory, they had gained all that they must now imagine themselves to have meant?[3] and again, how did leaders maintain their primacy over united parties? Harcourt may have been right in his sardonic analysis of the Government statement, that this was 'the apple woman spitting on her old apples and shining 'em up',[4] but even were the goods those refused before, a later acceptance calls as much for examination by the light of the imperatives of party management as for apportionment of those crude judgment labels, 'success' and 'failure'.

If there are neither certainties nor any answers, if there can be nothing more than rhetorical questioning, the historian must still set forth the imponderables. Dr Weston has betrayed no consciousness even of their plausible existence. If that is criticism beyond her chosen terms of reference, it is an indictment of a genre of flaccid political inquiry.

[1] Dilke Memoir, 17 Nov. 1884. Dilke Mss., 43938 fol. 301.
[2] Weston, p. 305.　　　　[3] *The Times*, 19 Nov. 1884, p. 9.
[4] Dilke Memoir, 15 Nov. 1884. Dilke Mss., 43938 fol. 297.

APPENDIX III

THE CABINET
(AS AT 1 JANUARY 1884)

First Lord of the Treasury | W. E. Gladstone
Lord Chancellor | Earl of Selborne
Lord President and Lord Privy Seal | Lord Carlingford
Chancellor of the Exchequer | H. C. E. Childers
Home Secretary | Sir W. V. Harcourt
Foreign Secretary | Earl Granville
Colonial Secretary | Earl of Derby
Secretary for War | Marquess of Hartington
Secretary for India | Earl of Kimberley
First Lord of the Admiralty | Earl of Northbrook
Lord Lieutenant of Ireland | Earl Spencer
Chancellor of the Duchy of Lancaster | J. G. Dodson
President of the Board of Trade | J. Chamberlain
President of the Local Government Board | Sir C. W. Dilke

APPENDIX IV

PORTRAIT GALLERY

THESE NOTES are no more than complement or supplement to the preceding narrative, where character has been integral. Age is that attained during 1884. Though the occasional later achievement is included, no attempt has been made to trace careers subsequent to that date.

ACLAND, Sir Thomas Dyke (75). His father, 37 years in Commons, close friend of Wilberforce. Ed. Harrow (head of school) and Christ Church (Double First and President of Union); Fellow of All Souls. Conservative/Peelite MP for West Somerset 1837–47; Liberal, North Devon, from 1865, sharing representation with Northcote. Educational reformer, 'scientific' farmer of 40,000 acres, and Lt-Col. 3rd Devonshire Volunteer Rifles. Declined a Peerage, accepted Privy Councillorship 1883. To Gladstone, 'a dear old friend'.

ACTON, First Lord (50). Born in Naples, son of Sir Ferdinand Acton, 7th Bt; Granville's stepson. Ed. Oscott, and under Döllinger. Liberal Catholic. Historian: his library totalled 59,000 volumes. MP 1859–66: graces just 2 columns of *Hansard*. Suggested for Berlin Embassy 1884. Morley labelled him a 'friendly, philosophic and observant onlooker': no positive evidence that his influence upon Gladstone *c.* 1884 was in any way decisive – though a frequent caller at No. 10.

ARGYLL, Eighth Duke of (61). Son of 7th Duke, who had been engaged in suppressing the Irish, 1798. Office under Aberdeen, Palmerston, Russell and Gladstone. At the Government's survival of his resignation 1881, *Punch* blessed him with Macbeth's lines, 'The time has been / That when the brains were out the man would die.' Whig, self-styled cross-bencher, but essentially for 1884 the Queen's man: his heir, Lorne, married to Princess Louise. In poor health (gouty since 1860s) and old beyond his years.

ARNOLD, Arthur (51). Wrote a *History of the Cotton Famine* after 3 years as Assistant Commissioner in 1860s. First Editor of the *Echo*. Radical MP for Salford since 1880. Advocate of enfranchisement of women, and of land nationalization.

AUSTIN, Alfred (49). Son of Leeds wool-stapler; his uncle an obscurantist Liberal MP. Ed. Stonyhurst and London University. Catholic. Short career at Bar. Poet. Stood unsuccessfully 1880 for Dewsbury as Conservative (the party of chivalry). Leader-writer for the *Standard* since 1866, and joint Editor of the new *National Review*.

PORTRAIT GALLERY

BALFOUR, Arthur (36). Son of J. M. Balfour (who died when A. J. B. was 7) and Blanche, daughter of 2nd Marquess of Salisbury. Ed. Eton (fag to Fitzmaurice) and Trinity, Cambridge. Sat for Salisbury pocket borough of Hertford from 1874. Author of *Defence of Philosophic Doubt.*

BARRINGTON, Seventh Viscount (60). Ed. Eton and Christ Church. Conservative MP for Eye 1866–80. Private secretary to 14th Earl of Derby when Prime Minister. Vice-Chamberlain of the Household 1874–80.

BARTLETT, E. Ashmead (35). Born in Brooklyn. Ed. privately in Torquay, and Christ Church (First; President of Union, Easter 1873, defeating Asquith). Fine platform speaker, campaigning strongly against Russia in late 1870s. 1880, founded *England*, a Conservative penny weekly, and elected MP for Eye. Wavered through 1883 between Northcote and Churchill; in 1884 plumped for Salisbury. Gorst was not generous: 'a very clever man, but without any power of influencing or even getting listened to in the H. of C.'

BATESON, Sir Thomas (65). Conservative, sat for Londonderry (which his father had represented) 1844–57; for Devizes from 1864. Deputy-Lieutenant for Down and Londonderry, and active in Orange politics.

BATH, Fourth Marquess of (53). Ed. Eton and Christ Church. Succeeded his father at age of 6, and thus never sat in Commons; his brother was Conservative MP for South Wiltshire from 1859. Magistrate for Co. Monaghan, where he owned 20,000 acres. Cranbrook found him unduly cynical. Gladstone, on being told of his final defection in 1884 (to bring forward his heir as Conservative candidate in Somerset) suggested that 'a cold Bath is better than a tepid Bath.'

BEACH, Sir Michael Hicks (47). Eldest son of 8th Bt, briefly MP for East Gloucestershire. Ed. Eton and Christ Church (First), after which 5 months' tour of Egypt. Office under Derby and Disraeli: Irish Secretary 1874–8, and (not particularly happily) Colonial Secretary 1878–80. Managed his properties without the aid of an agent, but devoted to politics and a thorough politician.

BORTHWICK, Sir Algernon (54). Ed. K.C.S., London. Succeeded his father as Editor of the *Morning Post* at 22, becoming owner 1876. Stood unsuccessfully 1880 as Conservative for Evesham, his father's former seat. Harcourt's brother-in-law – which might prove an important link if his papers are unearthed.

BOURKE, Robert (57). Younger son of 5th Earl of Mayo, and brother of celebrated Indian Governor-General. Married eldest daughter of 1st Marquess of Dalhousie (marriage ended in divorce, charges going back to 1875). Conservative MP for King's Lynn since 1868. Under-Secretary for Foreign Affairs from 1874, while his chiefs, Derby and Salisbury, were in Lords.

BRADLAUGH, Charles (51). Son of solicitor's clerk. Failed coal merchant, failed soldier; popular pamphleteer, booming lecturer – atheist, republican, and advocate of birth control (the 'creed of the cesspool'). Editor and proprietor of the *National Reformer*. Elected Radical MP for Northampton on Grosvenor's recommendation (4th attempt to enter Parliament) in 1880, though out of the House for all but a few moments, à la Wilkes.

BRETT, Reginald (32). Eldest son of Lord Justice of Appeal, and MP for Helston 1866–8. Ed. Eton and Trinity, Cambridge. Elected MP for Penryn 1880. Hartington's private secretary. His appeal, said Dilke, lay in the combination of 'advanced views with beauty & dress.'

BRIGHT, John (76). Somewhat ineffective now in Commons, but still, as Gladstone knew, an elder statesman to the country, and meet to be sounded. Had suggested in 1876 that extension of franchise to Ireland would kill Home Rule.

BROADHURST, Henry (44). Son of a journeyman stonemason, and so himself; at Christ Church – to fix new chimney pots. Rejected by army. 1873, elected Secretary of Labour Representation League, and 2 years later of T.U.C. Parliamentary Committee. Successful Liberal Caucus candidate at Stoke, 1880. Clothes made by his wife. Advocate of leasehold enfranchisement. On Royal Commission on Housing of Working Classes.

BRUCE, Robert Preston (33). Brother of 9th Earl of Elgin. Ed. Eton and Balliol. Liberal MP for Fifeshire since 1880.

BRUCE, T. C. (59). Son of 7th Earl of Elgin. Ed. Jesus, Cambridge. Director of London & North-Western Railway, and Chairman of Imperial Ottoman Bank. Perseverance rewarded at Portsmouth in 1874: 5th attempt to enter Parliament.

BRYCE, James (46). Born in Belfast. Ed. Glasgow High School, University of Glasgow, and Trinity, Oxford. Distinguished academic career as historian and jurist, culminating in appointment as Regius Professor of Civil Law at age of 32. Elected (2nd attempt) Liberal MP for Tower Hamlets, 1880. 1883–4, writing *American Commonwealth*.

BUCHANAN, T. R. (38). Son of Glasgow merchant. Ed. Glasgow High School, Sherborne and Balliol (Double First); Fellow of All Souls. Liberal MP for Edinburgh since 1881, having unsuccessfully contested Haddingtonshire at General Election.

BUXTON, Francis W. (37). Son of former Liberal MP for South Essex. Married daughter of 1st Lord Lawrence of the Punjab. Ed. Trinity, Cambridge. London banker, partner in Messrs. Prescott, Cave & Co. Liberal MP for Andover from 1880.

CAINE, W. S. (42). Mother a local leader of anti-slavery movement. Married Baptist minister's daughter. Took over his father's iron works; Director also of a Cumberland mine company. Elected as 'Advanced Liberal', Scarborough 1880, after two shots at Liverpool. Band of Hope, first President of National Temperance Federation. Appointed Civil Lord of Admiralty, November 1884, but Dilke found him though 'shrewd & first rate in his way', already 'too old to get on.'

CAIRNS, First Earl (65). Intended by his father, a retired Army captain, for the Church; but never progressed beyond Sunday-school teaching. Ed. Belfast Academy and T.C.D. (First in Classics). Called to the Bar

1844. Conservative MP for Belfast 1852–66. Solicitor-General, Attorney-General, and then Lord Chancellor 1868 and 1874–80. Party leader in Lords, 1869. Deaf and asthmatic. *D.N.B.* says of him: 'As a judge he did not explain the process by which his mind had been persuaded'. Salisbury said of him that his Irish relations had 'a great hold on his mind'.

CALLAN, Philip (49). Sat for Dundalk 1868–80 and (having been denounced by Parnell) for Louth from 1880. Drunken wit.

CAMERON, Charles (43). Ed. Madras College, at St Andrew's and T.C.D. Distinguished academic career (Medicine). Editor and co-proprietor of the *North British Daily Mail*. Radical MP for Glasgow since 1874.

CARLINGFORD, First Baron (61). Son of Lt-Col. Chichester Fortescue, member of the last Irish Parliament. Ed. privately and Christ Church (First). Family owned 23,000 acres in Ireland. MP for Co. Louth 1848–74; office under Aberdeen, Palmerston, Russell and Gladstone. Lord Privy Seal since 1881 and President of Council since 1883, but had served his purpose and was no longer consulted on Irish matters. Broken by the death in 1879 of his wife, the society hostess Countess Waldegrave: he was her fourth husband.

CARNARVON, Fourth Earl of (53). Succeeded to title at 17: Acland, his father's cousin, acted as a guardian. Ed. Eton and Christ Church (friend of Salisbury; First in Classics). Colonial Secretary 1866–7; resigned with Salisbury over Reform, and voted against his party on Irish Church Disestablishment. Resigned again as Colonial Secretary 1878. High Churchman. Lady St Helier thought him temperamentally ill-suited to the hurly-burly of political life; he thought there was 'a road open to me in either direction.'

CHAMBERLAIN, Joseph (48). One-time screw manufacturer, twice widowed, thrice Mayor of Birmingham – and ever after thought 'the universe only a "replica" of a provincial town'. Appointed President of Board of Trade 1880, after 4 years in Commons. Hartington and Harcourt in January 1885 met to consider the personnel of a Cabinet should Gladstone retire; they found 'no office sufficiently tempting for Chamberlain'.

CHAPLIN, Henry (44). Son of clergyman and lord of manor; succeeding also to his uncle's estates in Lincolnshire. Bankrupt nevertheless. Married daughter of 3rd Duke of Sutherland (she died 1881), after his former fiancée had eloped with rake. Ed. Harrow for 2 years, thereafter privately, and at Christ Church, where he was close to Prince of Wales; forsook Oxford in favour of expedition to Rockies. Won Derby 1867, keen sportsman, M.F.H. etc., but too easily mocked as 'the evangelist of an obsolete creed': independent, threatening, and aiming high (Cabinet or die). Conservative MP for Mid Lincolnshire from 1868.

CHILDERS, Hugh (57). Son of Yorkshire clergyman. Ed. Wadham (briefly), and Trinity, Cambridge. Served his political apprenticeship in Australia, holding seat as Auditor-General in Victorian Cabinet.

Gladstone's junior at Treasury 1865–6, and now Chancellor of Exchequer. Disturbed career in which he had suffered at least one breakdown, and had made way for Bright in Cabinet shuffle of 1873. Ineffectual in debate, thought little of by his officials; in Cabinet, Dilke numbered him amongst the 'clerks', when the highest accolade was 'naughty boy'.

CHURCHILL, Lord Randolph (35). Third, but second surviving, son of 7th Duke of Marlborough (his mother, daughter of 3rd Marquess of Londonderry). Ed. Eton and Merton; or self-educated on Gibbon. Conservative MP for Woodstock from 1874. 352 references to him in the Sessional Index to *Hansard* 1881; Northcote later called him the shrewdest member of 1885 Cabinet: latter is the greater monument. In Salisbury Mss., there is preserved no letter from Churchill between 26 July 1884 and 27 April 1885.

CLARKE, Edward (43). Product of the Crosby Hall Debating Society, and Lincoln's Inn (Q.C.). Conservative MP for Plymouth since July 1880, having been ousted in General Election at Southwark after a six week tenure. Busy politician (an 'undesirable' in Fourth party eyes), who never missed an opportunity to place a memo. before his leaders.

COLLINGS, Jesse (53). Son of bricklayer; always called himself of good yeoman stock. Prominent in Birmingham politics during 1870s, Mayor 1878, and a founder of Education League. Closely associated with Joseph Arch; known in the Commons (Radical MP for Ipswich since 1880) as 'Chamberlain's barometer'.

COLLINS, Thomas (59). Son of clergyman. Ed. Charterhouse and Wadham. Conservative, had first represented Knaresborough, where family had been settled for two centuries, in 1851: in and out ever since.

COOPER, Charles (55). Editor of *Scotsman* since 1876: Liberals were now taught to remember that the paper represented only itself – and not Scottish Liberalism. Said to be 'always with Rosebery'; heard things from Childers; not enamoured of Gladstone.

COTTON, W. J. R. (62). Elected Alderman of London 1866; subsequently Sheriff and Lord Mayor. Owner of Norwegian iron-ore mines. Conservative MP for the City since 1874.

COURTNEY, Leonard (52). Son of Cornish bank cashier. Rudimentary schooling to 13; *via* bank and private tutor to St John's, Cambridge: Prizeman and Fellow there. Elected Professor of Political Economy at London, 1872. Leader-writer to *The Times*: considered by Delane 'not the man' to succeed him as Editor. Liberal MP for Liskeard from 1876. Declined to work under Chamberlain at Board of Trade 1880; Financial Secretary to the Treasury since 1882. As Deputy-Speaker, his decisions were thought 'impartially unfair to both sides'. Married Kate Potter 1883, which may have *piqued* Chamberlain.

COWEN, Joseph (53). Jingo Radical and Home Ruler, stepping into his father's seat at Newcastle, 1874. Ed. Edinburgh University. Active in Reform League 1866–7, in management of coal-mines, and as editor/

PORTRAIT GALLERY

proprietor of local press. Disraeli complimented him on maiden speech; Gladstone censured his style as smelling of the lamp – and was not forgiven.

COWPER, Seventh Earl (50). Shaftesbury's nephew and related to virtually all great and good Whigs. Ed. Harrow (oversensitive, removed) and Christ Church (First). Pioneer with Wemyss of volunteer regiments. Never sat in Commons. Lord-Lieutenant of Ireland 1880–2: ill-equipped for the job.

CRANBROOK, First Earl of (70). Son of proprietor of Lowmoor Iron Works, barrister and MP. Ed. Shrewsbury (where he was bullied) and Oriel (where he was Lowe's pupil). Married 'an Irish girl with a pretty face'. Moderate/High Churchman. Cabinet office under Derby and Disraeli; Home Secretary 1867. Expected leadership of Commons 1876, but in disappointment immediately 'shook hands' with Northcote. Combative first, cogent second.

CRICHTON, Viscount (45). Son of 3rd Earl of Erne (mother a cousin to Marquess of Waterford). Married daughter of Earl of Enniskillen. Ed. Eton and Christ Church. Conservative, sat for Enniskillen, 1868–80, Fermanagh since 1880.

CROSS, Sir Richard (61). Ed. Rugby and Trinity, Cambridge. Barrister and Chairman of Quarter Sessions, turned banker. MP for South West Lancashire from 1868, having previously sat for Preston. Disraeli's Home Secretary 1874–80. In opposition would have passed unnoticed had not Churchill seized publicly upon his inadequacies, of which all were aware. Thereafter absolutely dependent upon Salisbury. Personal friend of Derby.

DALRYMPLE, Charles (45). Son of Sir Charles Dalrymple Ferguson, 5th Bt, assuming name of Dalrymple in accordance with will of Lord Hailes, to whose estates he succeeded. Ed. Harrow and Trinity, Cambridge. Conservative MP for Buteshire from 1868, with exception of a few months in 1880.

DERBY, Fifteenth Earl of (58). Ed. Eton (expelled), Rugby and Trinity Cambridge (Double First and an 'Apostle'). Protectionist MP for King's Lynn 1848–69. Refused throne of Greece 1863. Refused Colonial Secretaryship offered him by Palmerston, accepted it under his father, and now again, after a spell as Disraeli's Foreign Secretary, under Gladstone: family motto, 'Sans changer'. Salisbury (whose widowed step-mother he married) named him Titus Oates, and implied that Oates might with justice feel aggrieved.

DILKE, Sir Charles (41). Father, 1st Bt, sat as Liberal for Wallingford 1865–8. Ed. privately and Trinity Hall (Senior Legalist, Vice-President of Union, and able oarsman). Radical MP for Chelsea from 1868. Author of *Greater Britain*. Under-Secretary Foreign Office 1880–2, President of Local Government Board since then. If no longer saying republican things, yet his absence from Duke of Albany's funeral still raised press comment. Reay thought that whatever Dilke did, he would do 'on the sly'.

249

DODSON, J. G. (59). Son of judge, Tory MP, and Privy Councillor. Ed. Eton and Christ Church (First). Liberal MP for East Sussex 1858–74, Chester 1874–80, Scarborough 1880–4. President of Local Government Board 1880–2, Chancellor of Duchy of Lancaster to November 1884, when relegated to Lords. Regarded kindly by Queen. Once came late to a Cabinet: his absence, Dilke suggested, had escaped all notice.

DUNDAS, John C. (39). Grandson of 1st Earl of Zetland. Married younger daughter of 1st Viscount Halifax. Ed. Harrow and Trinity, Cambridge. Whig MP for Richmond (Yorks.) from 1873, but declined again to stand there, where his brother's 'legitimate influence' would be 'invoked to the aid of a Conservative candidate'.

EDWARDS, John Passmore (60). Son of Calvinist carpenter–publican–strawberry grower. Village school education. Early under spell of Cobden and Bright, in Manchester. Knew downs and ups of newspaper business: bankrupt 1853, bought the *Echo* 1876, sold it to Storey and Carnegie in 1884 for £50,000. Peace at any price Radical MP for Salisbury since 1880, but a Westminster failure; found the Commons a 'House of waste', and withdrew at dissolution of 1885 to build free libraries, erect drinking fountains and found an epileptic colony.

EGERTON, Algernon Fulke (59). Son of 1st Earl of Ellesmere (mother a daughter of Charles Greville). Married daughter of Lord George Cavendish. Conservative, 25 years in Commons for various Lancashire seats, Wigan from 1882.

ELLIOT, Arthur (38). Second son of 3rd Earl of Minto. Ed. privately (having had a leg amputated at age of 4), Edinburgh University and Trinity, Cambridge. Practising barrister. Since 1880, Liberal MP for Roxburghshire, which had first returned an Elliot to Westminster in 1708. Keen admirer of Forster and Goschen, *bien vu* by Selborne, and the apple of Selborne's daughter, Lady Sophia Palmer's, eye.

FAWCETT, Henry (51). Son of draper turned gentleman farmer, active in Anti-Corn Law League. Blinded in shooting accident 1858. Ed. K.C.S., London, and, migrating from Peterhouse, Trinity Hall 'where there appeared to be a better chance of obtaining a fellowship' (*D.N.B.*). Elected to Chair of Political Economy, Cambridge, 1863; as narrow in mind as Mill. Liberal MP for Brighton 1865–74, Hackney thereafter. Postmaster-General. Gladstone called him a '*periculosa haereditas* to the Liberal party'; mutual antipathy. Died suddenly November 1884.

FIRTH, J. F. B. (42). London LL.B. President of Chelsea Liberation Council. Author of *Municipal London; or, London Government as it is, and London Government as it ought to be.* Favoured shortening of period of residential qualification for voters, removal of registration from hands of party agents, etc. Dilke's partner for Chelsea from 1880.

FITZMAURICE, Edmond (38). Lansdowne's brother. Ed. Eton and Trinity, Cambridge (First). Enjoyed tenure of Lansdowne family seat at Calne from 1868. Under-Secretary Foreign Office since 1882.

PORTRAIT GALLERY

FOLJAMBE, F. J. S. (54). Ed. Eton and Christ Church. 'Attached to old Whig principles', which had suited East Retford for 27 years. Cousin of Sir Frederick Milner, Conservative MP for York.

FORSTER, W. E. (66). His father died on an anti-slavery mission in Tennessee. Ed. Quaker schools in Bristol and Tottenham, where a master warned, 'Beware of acrimony, William, lest while inveighing against an unchristian system thou shouldest be influenced by an unchristian spirit.' Married daughter of Arnold of Rugby. MP for Bradford, where he was a worsted manufacturer, continuously from 1861: remarkable achievement latterly, in defiance of local Liberal Association. Within an ace of leading the Commons party after Gladstone's 1874 withdrawal. Chief Secretary for Ireland 1880–2. Top-flight politician.

FORWOOD, A. B. (48). Merchant, ship-owner, Chairman and 'soul' of the Liverpool Conservative Association. Churchillian.

FOWLER, H. H. (54). Son of Wesleyan minister. Grammar school education. Admitted a solicitor 1852, with practices in Wolverhampton and London. Alderman, magistrate and sometime Mayor of Wolverhampton, where he was returned, too late in life, as Liberal 1880. Appointed Under-Secretary Home Office, December 1884. Felt that Gladstone never gave him 'full measure running over, but only a bare acknowledgment of indisputable claims'. Letters of inordinate length to Morley.

FOWLER, R. N. (56). Son of Quaker City banker, and himself a banker, though from the age of 33 'warmly attached to the Established Church'. Distinguished himself at University College, London. Alderman, Sheriff 1880–1, and Lord Mayor of London 1883–4. Conservative with an 'abhorrence of all demagogic ways', sat for Penryn 1868–74, London from 1880. Defender of Northcote in the *Standard*. Eleven children (ten surviving), nine daughters.

GIBSON, Edward (47). Son of Tipperary solicitor. Since 1875, Conservative MP for Dublin University (he had distinguished himself at T.C.D.). Attorney-General for Ireland 1877–80. Most effective Parliamentary orator. Gladstone spoke of him 'as altogether preeminent in H. of Commons among the Conservatives on Irish questions, but... off these thought nothing of him.'

GLADSTONE, Herbert (30). Youngest son of the Premier. Ed. Eton and University College, Oxford (First in Modern History, Third in Classics). Liberal MP for Leeds since 1880, having unsuccessfully contested Middlesex. Private secretary to his father 1880–1, a Whip since then. Declined to 'pledge himself as to the Home Rule question'.

GLADSTONE, W. E. (75). Said, 'all ideas ascribed to me are in truth other people's opinions of my opinions.'

GORST, J. E. (49). Ed. St John's, Cambridge, of which he became Fellow. Civil Commissioner in Waikato, New Zealand, 1861–5 (in danger of his life during Maori riot). Conservative, elected for Cambridge 1866, and expected office 1874 after tending party machinery.

251

MP for Chatham since 1875. Difficult, restive man; hurt and/or hurt by almost everyone.

GOSCHEN, G. J. (53). Son of City merchant and financier. Ed. in Saxe-Meiningen, at Rugby ('the best debater in the school, especially in reply'), and Oriel (Double First by effort). At 27 a Director of Bank of England; author of *The Theory of the Foreign Exchanges*. First returned for London 1863, and rapidly into Cabinet. MP for Ripon from 1880. Refused Vice-Royalty of India 1880, War Office 1882, Speakership 1883. Some said that he was on the road which led through Brooks's to a moderate coalition, others that his election to the *Officia preconsulum* of the Breakfast Club presaged re-entry into the Liberal Cabinet. But neither did any politician, nor should the political historian, forget him. To the latter, he bequeathed a warning against that dependence upon newspapers which might only stunt 'original constructive thought – the thought which creates its own materials.'

GRANVILLE, Second Earl (69). Hartington's cousin. Ed. Eton and Christ Church. Ten years in Commons. Foreign Secretary first in 1851, and Liberal leader in Lords from 1855; all but Premier 1859, and expected summons 1880. Motto, '*Frangas non flectes*', inappropriate. All but unique as a Cabinet Minister in belief that 'nothing should be so sacred as a threat of resignation'. Gouty, but his youngest child born as late as 1880. Said to have bequeathed to F.O. successors cupboards of papers with which he was ever disinclined to deal and increasingly unable to cope.

GREY, Albert (33). Eldest son of Gen. Charles Grey, private secretary to Queen; nephew of and heir to the octogenarian 3rd Earl who in 1884 made over to him the entire management of family estate. Ed. Harrow and Trinity, Cambridge (First). Married daughter of former Conservative MP for East Gloucestershire. Liberal MP for South Northumberland from 1880. Unpaid secretary to Childers 1884–5. Lady Minto shrewdly noted 'A. Grey has a *wandering eye*, wh. I don't think accompanies the highest ability.'

GROSVENOR, Lord Richard (47). Son of 2nd Marquess of Westminster. Ed. Westminster and Trinity, Cambridge. First returned for Flintshire 1861: voted against Russell's Reform bill. Chief Whip since 1880; *D.N.B.* records that his 'life work, however, was done in connection with the London and North Western Railway Company' – which is sufficient comment. Personal friend of Gladstone.

HALIFAX, First Viscount (84). Had pathetically been 'clamouring for office' in 1880 (motto, '*Perseverando*'); on the sidelines, but in receipt of news and views. Wife died 6 July 1884.

HAMILTON, Edward (37). Ed. Eton and Christ Church (never took degree). Secretary to Lowe before coming to No. 10. Everybody's friend, but most especially Rosebery's. Belief: 'The more one reads history, the more convinced does one become that, with certain mistakes inherent in human nature, the Liberals are right in the long run.'

HAMILTON, Lord George (39). Third son of 1st Duke of Abercorn, former Lord-Lieutenant of Ireland. Ed. Harrow. Coldstream Guards. Conservative MP for Middlesex since 1868. Under-Secretary for India (having declined post at F.O. on account of indifferent French), while Salisbury was in Lords, 1874–8, Education Office 1878–80. In opposition, intervened on all matters Irish. A less shrill and more effective politician than his elder brother Claud, MP for Liverpool. Both visited America, late summer/autumn 1884.

HARCOURT, Sir William (57). His father a canon, and grandfather Archbishop, of York. Ed. Trinity, Cambridge (First in Classics and an 'Apostle'). Whewell Professor of International Law. Had refused Disraeli's offer of a safe Welsh seat. Solicitor-General 1873–4, Home Secretary from 1880. Supposedly unpopular in the House. Fitzjames Stephen, who was no admirer, found in him 'many of the qualities which enable a man alternately to bully and to wriggle' – which Gladstone turned to good account, employing Harcourt as 'special Ambassador in cases of differences of opinion' between Cabinet members. His son Lewis (21) already enjoyed his every confidence; his elder brother, Conservative MP for Oxfordshire, did not.

HARROWBY, Third Earl of (53). Ed. Harrow and Christ Church, whence with Carnarvon on a tour of Asia Minor. Palmerstonian MP for Lichfield 1856–9, for Liverpool (gradually turning to orthodox Conservatism) 1868–82, when he succeeded to title. Education Office 1874–8, in Cabinet as President of Board of Trade 1878–80. Prominent Evangelical. Resolution for 1884: 'No more compliments to the Government or to any single member of it.'

HARTINGTON, Marquess of (51). Ed. by his father, 7th Duke of Devonshire, and at Trinity, Cambridge. Family owned extensive estates in Ireland. Brother of the assassinated Lord Frederick Cavendish. Entered Russell's Cabinet at 33. India Office 1880–2, War thereafter. Astute, *not* idle (though careless in matters of dress: remembered by one who knew him as always forgetting to do up his flies). Gladstone said he was possessed of 'a worldly standard much affected by the Newmarket kind of life.'

HAY, Admiral Sir John (63). Conservative MP for Wakefield 1862–5, Stamford 1866–80, Wigtown Burghs since 1880. Introduced his own Redistribution Bill.

HEALY, T. M. (29). Married daughter of his close friend T. D. Sullivan, MP for Co. Westmeath. Journalist. Nationalist MP for Wexford 1880–3, for Monaghan (famous victory) since 1883. Parnell later said that Healy had the only 'head' among his followers; but never his master's confidant. Reputedly able to recite the Bible and Shakespeare by heart.

HENEAGE, Edward (44). Son of MP for Lincoln, which he himself represented 1865–8. Liberal MP for Grimsby since 1880. Edward Hamilton thought him 'inclined to exaggerate the importance of himself & his actions'.

HERSCHELL, Sir Farrer (47). Ed. University College, London. Moved from Dissent to C. of E. Called to Bar 1860, Q.C. 1872. Liberal MP for Durham City from 1874. Solicitor-General; aspired to, and clearly thought in line for, the Chancellorship.

HILL, Frank (54). Editor of *Daily News* from 1869.

HOPE, A. J. Beresford (64). Son of author (mother the daughter of an Archbishop of Tuam). Married Salisbury's sister. Ed. Harrow and Trinity, Cambridge: distinguished academic career. Conservative MP for Maidstone and Stoke, before Cambridge University (from 1868). Favoured maintenance of Established Church 'both as a divine institution, and as an estate of the realm'. Ever remembered Disraeli with loathing.

HUBBARD, J. G. (79). Russia merchant, and Director of Bank of England; author of several tracts on income tax, commercial and financial policy. Conservative MP for Buckingham 1859–68, City of London since 1874. High Church.

JAMES, Sir Henry (56). Son of Hereford surgeon. Ed. Cheltenham, at its founding. Called to Bar 1852, Q.C. 1869 in which year he was first elected for Taunton. Solicitor-General 1873, Attorney-General 1873–4 and from 1880. Much praised for his guidance of Corrupt Practices Bill through Commons 1883. Never at a loss for words: later, before the Parnell Commission, spoke for 12 days. Probably came to know Churchill through Wolff. Cricket enthusiast. Unmarried. Granville wrote to him, ' I hear almost every day, little facts about you, which do not surprise me in the least, but which are very agreeable to know.'

JOHNSTON, William (55). The demagogue of Ballykilbeg, whose cell in Downpatrick Gaol became an Orange shrine. Embarrassingly, one of his daughters succumbed to the charms of Rome while a brother married a Papist.

KENNAWAY, Sir John (47). Ed. Harrow and Balliol (First). Conservative MP for East Devon from 1870. Gorst cruelly nominated him to write Northcote's biography.

KENNY, J. M. (23). Son of Co. Clare solicitor. Nationalist MP for Ennis from 1882.

KIMBERLEY, First Earl of (58). Ed. Eton and Christ Church (First). Never sat in Commons. Served under Aberdeen and Palmerston before Gladstone. Colonial Secretary 1870–4 and 1880–2, Indian Secretary thereafter. Lord Redesdale wrote of him, 'He knew his trade, but he had not the secret of treating business with charm.' Papers withheld.

LABOUCHÈRE, Henry (53). Son of banker, nephew of Lord Taunton. Ed. Eton; in 2 years at Trinity, Cambridge, ran up debts of £6,000, and was accused of cheating during examinations. Colourful wanderings in Latin America, living with Mexican circus artiste; later married Henrietta Hodson, actress. 10 years in diplomatic service: willingly dismissed. Brief spell in Parliament 1865–8. Successful proprietor and editor of *Truth*. Since 1880, the Radical and Christian Member for Northampton. No political reward beyond notoriety. Chain-smoker.

LALOR, Richard (61). Magistrate and farmer. Nationalist MP since 1880 for Queen's County, which his father had briefly represented. Persuaded in February 1884 to defer retirement by Healy.

LAMBERT, Sir John (69). That 'excellent old public servant' at the Local Government Board. His Radicalism was of a past generation, his ideas on Redistribution puny. In retirement continued to draw up statistical tables which might interest Gladstone. Forster called him, as Chairman of the Boundary Commission, 'the most powerful man in England'; this was idle exaggeration.

LANSDOWNE, Fifth Marquess of (39). Ed. Eton and Balliol (under Jowett). Said, 'The longer I live the more firmly do I believe in blood and breeding', and married daughter of 1st Duke of Abercorn. Never sat in Commons – his father died 1866. Governor-General of Canada from 1883. Disraeli said his resignation in the first year of the Liberal Ministry, as Under-Secretary for India, would be remembered when all the Government's errors had been forgotten: 'Many will think it is his grandfather.'

LAWSON, Sir Wilfrid (55). Son of 1st Bt, and nephew of Sir James Graham. Of the *Wealth of Nations* said, 'All I know I learned from it.' Bought John Peel's hounds. Director of Maryport & Carlisle Railway. Twenty years Radical MP for Carlisle: for Bradlaugh, Home Rule and peace; above all, against liquor traffic. Versifier and wit: as political coroner in summer 1885 said that the Government had 'Died by the visitation of God *under very suspicious circumstances.*'

LEATHAM, E. A. (56). Son of Wakefield banker, and himself a banker with a novel to his credit. Ed. University College, London. MP, 'Reformer', for Huddersfield 1859–65 and since 1868. Brother of Bright's second wife.

LEWIS, C. E. (59). Son of Oxford cleric. Grammar school education. Retired solicitor, author of several legal handbooks, and sometime election agent. Conservative MP for Londonderry City from 1872.

LOWTHER, James (44). Son of Bt. Ed. Westminster and Trinity, Cambridge. Called to Bar 1864. Chief Secretary for Ireland 1878–80, without the Cabinet seat which his predecessor, Hicks Beach, enjoyed. Strong Tory and Protectionist. Mundella called him the 'foolometer of his party', Cairns 'uniformly rash'.

LUBBOCK, Sir John (50). Withdrawn at 14 from Eton to enter father's bank, Robarts, Lubbock & Co., of which he became senior partner. Numerous scientific publications, and member of Council of Royal Society. Liberal MP for Maidstone 1870–80, for London University (of which he was former Vice-Chancellor) from 1880. A political dabbler whose monument is the Bank Holidays Act. Remarried, May 1884.

LYMINGTON, Viscount (28). Eldest son of Earl of Portsmouth, and Carnarvon's nephew. Ed. Balliol. Elected Liberal MP for Barnstaple, 1880.

MANNERS, Lord John (66). Ed. Eton and Trinity, Cambridge, gradually overcoming bad stammer. Conservative, 40 years in Commons, at one time sharing representation of Newark with Gladstone. Church and State mattered above all. Never progressed beyond the Post Office. Appears in *Coningsby* as Lord Henry Sydney who was shocked at the substitution of the word 'labourers' for 'peasantry'. His son Henry (32) was secretary to Salisbury.

MAXSE, F. A. (51). Bears responsibility for introducing Morley to Chamberlain at a meeting called to protest against Forster's Education Act. Against Woman Suffrage, against anything Irish: pamphleteer who never succeeded in entering Commons.

MAXWELL, Sir Herbert (39). Son of 6th Bt. Ed. Eton and Christ Church. MP for Wigtownshire since 1880. Declared himself for *Dod* 1884 as opposed to lowering of Franchise, and was nominated by Northcote to advise on Reform bill clauses as they affected Scotland.

MILNER, Alfred (30). Born in Germany, son of doctor (mother nearly 20 years older than her husband). Ed. Tübingen Gymnasium, King's College, London, and Balliol (*stupor mundi*); Fellow of New College. Assistant editor to Stead on *Pall Mall Gazette*, and from February 1884 private secretary to Goschen, who taught him the trick of making no mention of Gladstone in any political speech.

MORLEY, John (46). Son of Yorkshire surgeon. Ed. University College School (after Chamberlain), Cheltenham and Lincoln, Oxford: open scholar, but left with only pass degree after father had cut off his allowance. Journalist and historian. Declared himself in *Dod* a 'steadfast though not mechanical adherent' to the present administration. Personally as close to Goschen as to Frederic Harrison, and in growing conflict with Chamberlain once he chose to fight with word (Chamberlain's weapon) as well as pen (Chamberlain's choice of weapon for Morley). Wrote once of a Gladstonian argument, 'A poorer sophism was never coined even in that busy mint of logical counterfeits.' Returned for Newcastle, 1883.

MUNDELLA, A. J. (59). Son of Italian political refugee. Left school at 9. Made his fortune in stocking manufacture: President of Nottingham Chamber of Commerce. Keen interest in labour relations led him to politics – Liberal MP for Sheffield from 1868; on to factory legislation and compulsory education. Appointed to Education Office 1880.

NORTHBROOK, First Earl of (58). Son of 1st Baron. Ed. privately and Christ Church. Former private secretary to Sir George Grey, his uncle, at Home Office, and to Halifax at India Office and Admiralty. Whig MP for Penryn and Falmouth 1857–66. Junior posts under Palmerston and Russell. Governor-General of India 1872–6 (most unhappily after 1874), First Lord of Admiralty from 1880. Said that 'upon home questions he would gladly have seen a conservative Government remain in power'. Never forgave Gladstone the treatment accorded his reports on Egypt and her finances, 1884.

NORTHCOTE, Sir Stafford (66). Ed. Eton and Balliol (First in Classics, Third in Mathematics). Conservative MP for Dudley and Stamford, before North Devon (from 1866). Secretary to Gladstone at Board of

Trade. Chancellor of Exchequer 1874–80. Rested on Queen's promise at time of Disraeli's death, that 'She was ready to be of any use that She could, that She looked to me as the real leader, and should let it be known that She did so'; this was not enough. Heart trouble since 1851. His second son, Henry (38), elected MP for Exeter, 1880.

O'BRIEN, William (32). Son of Catholic solicitor's clerk, but himself Protestant. Ed. Cloyne Diocesan College, and Queen's College, Cork. Editor of *United Ireland* whose outrageous language ('All hail' to the Mahdi, that he might 'drive every whey-faced invader' into the Red Sea) daily exercised Members at Question Time. Nationalist MP for Mallow from 1883.

O'CONNOR, T. P. (36). Son of shopkeeper. Ed. College of Immaculate Conception, Athlone, and Queen's College, Galway. Journalist on *Daily Telegraph, Scotsman*, and *Pall Mall Gazette*. His biography of Disraeli appeared anonymously in serial form during 1876, as a book with authorship acknowledged, 1879. Came to love the House above all things, and for that reason enjoyed Parnell's confidence. Secured nomination, through Dilke's exertions, at Derry as Liberal 1880, but chose Galway City as Nationalist.

O'DONNELL, F. H. O'C. (36). Ed. Ignatius' College, Galway, and Queen's University. Author of *Mind education in Ireland*. MP for Dungarvan since 1877. Celebrated obstructionist, elected as Parnellite in 1880, but resigned ostentatiously from party in summer 1883, and now simply a flatulent bore.

O'SHEA, Captain W. H. (44). Ed. Oscott and Trinity, Dublin. MP for Co. Clare since 1880. 'Retired husband', playing a Mercurial role.

PARNELL, C. S. (38). Ed. privately, and Magdalene (rusticated after conviction for assault, and never returned). Butt, when Parnell offered his political services, said, 'the Saxon will find him an ugly customer, though he is a d–d good-looking fellow.'

PLUNKET, David (46). Third son of 3rd Baron Plunket. Ed. Trinity, Dublin, of which he was Conservative MP from 1870. Called to Irish Bar 1862, Q.C. 1868. Solicitor-General for Ireland 1875–7, and briefly Paymaster-General. Unparalleled oratorical dignity. Unmarried, but not inactive.

PONSONBY, Sir Henry (59). Private secretary to the Queen since 1870. Whig.

RAIKES, H. C. (46). Son of barrister, who twice stood for Derby. Ed. Shrewsbury (head of school) and Trinity, Cambridge (President of Union; failure to obtain First rankled all his life). Called to Bar 1863. Conservative MP for Chester 1868–80, Preston 1882, and Cambridge University from 1882. Chairman of Council of National Union 1870–4. Deputy-Speaker of Commons 1874–80. Ardent Churchman.

RAMSDEN, Sir John (53). Son of Malton MP (mother a Dundas). Married daughter of Duke of Somerset. Ed. Eton and Trinity, Cambridge. Whig, with unenviable record of travels from 1853:

Taunton, Hythe, Yorkshire West Riding, Monmouth, and West Riding Eastern Division. Heavy influence in Huddersfield.

RATHBONE, William (65). The 6th Wm Rathbone in direct succession, Liverpool merchants from 1730. At school in Everton (with Stansfeld), and at Heidelberg. After 12 years representing Liverpool as Liberal, had in 1880 perforce moved to Carnarvonshire. Philanthropist: founded nursing school. Said that in Commons he was 'often far more tempted to take a low and sordid view of human nature than he had ever been in the slums'. R. P. Bruce thought him 'hopeful, busy, benevolent but not very profound'.

REEVE, Henry (71). Chief leader-writer for *The Times* under Delane, who nicknamed him 'Il Pomposo'. Editor of *Edinburgh Review* from 1855. His incoming (published) correspondence reads as a Book of Lamentations.

RICHARDSON, J. N. (38). Son of Quaker who founded Bessbrook model village on temperance principles. Ed. Grove House, Tottenham. Mill owner. Returned as Liberal for Co. Armagh, 1880, on programme of extended Tenant Right and experiment in peasant proprietorship.

RICHMOND, Sixth Duke of (66). Ed. Westminster and Christ Church. Conservative MP for West Sussex 1841–60. President of Poor Law Board 1859, Board of Trade 1867–8, Lord President of Council 1874–80. Led the Conservative Peers, 1869–76. The Queen called him her 'Country neighbour': the journey from Gordon Castle to Balmoral took 7 hours.

RIPON, First Marquess of (57). His father, 'Prosperity Robinson' Goderich, traced descent from Cromwell, his mother from John Hampden. Golden-spoon birth at No. 10. Privately educated. Sat in Commons during 1850s. Minor office under Palmerston before admission to Cabinet, 1863. Received into Catholic Church 1874. Since 1880 Viceroy of India, where 'I get more Radical every day'. Christian Socialist.

RITCHIE, C. T. (46). Son of East India merchant. Ed. City of London School, and straight into his father's business. Became first Conservative MP for Tower Hamlets in 1874, sensibly tending to interests of dockers (extension to them of Bank Holiday provisions) and of sugar refiners (proposing, with historical irony, something akin to Protection).

ROGERS, J. E. Thorold (61). Professor of Political Economy at Oxford 1862–8, and indefatigable author. High Churchman, relinquishing Holy Orders to enter Parliament (foiled at Scarborough 1874). Won Southwark in 1880 as an advanced Liberal, and at cost of £8,000 for 9,500 votes. Employed hysterical language for the Commons.

ROSEBERY, Fifth Earl of (37). Ed. Eton and Christ Church (no degree). Married Hannah Rothschild who was worth £2m., and named his first child after Disraeli's heroine, Sybil. Never sat in Commons. Under-Secretary Home Office 1881–3 (resigned, *pour mieux sauter*). On a tour of Antipodes, September 1883 to March 1884, which for seven months relieved Gladstone of one worry. Owned vast pornographic library.

ROWTON, First Baron (45). Shaftesbury's grandson. The elevation of Disraeli's 'model of secretaries' to the peerage in 1880 provoked Lowe's celebrated *mot* that there was precedent in Caligula's creating his horse a consul. Gladstone thought that the Queen depended on his counsel.

RUSSELL, G. W. E. (31). Younger son of Lord Charles James Fox Russell, former MP for Bedfordshire. Ed. Harrow and University College, Oxford. Barrister. Liberal MP for Aylesbury since 1880. Dilke's Parliamentary Secretary since 1883.

RYLANDS, Peter (64). Ed. Warrington Grammar School. Early active in Anti-Corn Law League. Ex-Nonconformist, now C. of E., and author of *The pulpit and the people*. Director of iron and coal company, and of Manchester and Liverpool District Banking Co. Liberal MP for Warrington 1868–74, Burnley from 1876.

SALISBURY, Third Marquess of (54). Son of 2nd Marquess who died 1868. Ed. Eton and Christ Church (entered for pass degree after 2 years, and secured an 'honorary Fourth'); Fellow of All Souls. 15 years in Commons for Stamford, always returned unopposed. Secretary for India 1866–7 and 1874–8, Foreign Secretary 1878–80. Gladstone could remember him 'as a little fellow in a red frock rolling about on the ottoman.'

SCLATER-BOOTH, George (58). Ed. Winchester and Balliol. Conservative MP for North Hampshire from 1857. President of Local Government Board 1874–80, without Cabinet seat. Solid, stolid politician – 'not of the sort to fill the House at the dinner hour'.

SCOTT, C. P. (38). Appointed Editor in 1872 of *Manchester Guardian* by his cousin.

SELBORNE, First Earl of (72). Son of wealthy Rector of Mixbury, Oxon. High Churchman: brother seceded to Rome. Ed. Rugby, Winchester (where he and Lowe 'sharpened each other's wits'), and Trinity, Oxford; Fellow of Magdalen 1834–48. Peelite MP for Plymouth 1847–52 and 1853–7, Whig for Richmond 1861–72. Solicitor-General, Attorney-General, and finally Lord Chancellor 1872–4 and from 1880. T. P. O'Connor called him the 'Grand Old Woman' of the Ministry.

SELLAR, A. C. (49). Ed. Rugby and Balliol (First). Called to Scottish Bar 1862; subsequently legal secretary to Lord Advocate, and secretary to W. P. Adam. Active on Gladstone's behalf in Midlothian. Failed at Devonport 1880, elected Haddington Burghs 1882.

SEXTON, Thomas (36). On the editorial staff of the *Nation*. Carpet-bagging MP for Co. Sligo from 1880. One of the Parnellite 'inner circle', certainly on matters of party organization. Fine speaker.

SHAW-LEFEVRE, G. J. (52). Son of J. G. Shaw-Lefevre. Married daughter of Earl of Ducie. Ed. Eton and Trinity, Cambridge. Called to Bar 1856. Liberal MP for Reading since 1863. Secretary to Admiralty 1871–4 and 1880, First Commissioner of Works from 1880. Bustling politician, knew everybody, and related to quite a few. In receipt of political pension.

SHERBROOKE, First Viscount (73). Now practically forgotten and practically blind. Like 'some matron who had sown wild oats in her early days warning a young married woman against the same course', had advised Goschen to swallow county franchise.

SMITH, Samuel (48). Son of farmer. Ed. parish school, Kirkcudbright Academy and Edinburgh University. Merchant and cotton-broker; President of Liverpool Chamber of Commerce 1876–7. City Councillor, and Liberal MP for Liverpool from 1882 (defeating Forwood). Philanthropist, temperance advocate, and 'strong supporter' of Gladstone. Engaged in single-combat public debate with Henry George at National Liberal Club.

SMITH, W. H. (59). The 'bookstall man' who had started work at 16, and was to leave £1¾m. Wesleyan, received into C. of E. Conservative MP for Westminster since 1868; always concerned himself with party organization. Financial Secretary to Treasury 1874–7, First Lord of Admiralty 1877–80. *Punch* called him 'Old Morality', Gilbert immortalized him in *Pinafore*, but he was a politician of massive strength.

SPENCER, Fifth Earl (49). Ed. Harrow and Trinity, Cambridge. In Commons for less than a year, 1857. Lord Lieutenant of Ireland 1868–74 and again from 1882, having been Lord President of Council 1880–2. Chamberlain said that on Irish matters it was impossible to fly in his face. In mid-1884, 'turning his eyes towards the Vice-Royalty of India'. His brother-in-law, Horace Seymour (41) was one of Gladstone's secretaries.

STANHOPE, Edward (44). Brother of 6th Earl. Ed. Harrow and Christ Church; Fellow of All Souls. Called to Bar 1865. Conservative MP for Mid-Lincolnshire from 1874, and minor office. Succeeded Smith as Chairman of Central Committee, November 1882.

STANLEY, Edward Lyulph (45). Brother of 3rd Lord Stanley of Alderley; younger brother was a Catholic priest. Ed. Eton and Balliol, of which he became Fellow. Called to Bar 1865. Elected Liberal MP for Oldham 1880, at third attempt. Member of Royal Commission on Housing of Working Classes. Rendel said he represented 'political garlic. Put him in the ministerial dietary and the whole party would reek of him.'

STANLEY, Col. F. A. (43). Derby's brother. Married daughter of Earl of Clarendon. Ed. Eton. Conservative MP for Preston 1865–8, North Lancashire from 1868. Brought by Disraeli into Cabinet as War Secretary 1878 upon his brother's resignation, that Lancashire might not feel neglected.

STANSFELD, James (64). Only son (with 7 sisters) of Nonconformist County Court judge. Ed. University College, London. Brewer. Radical MP for Halifax from 1859. Minor office under Palmerston, first President of Local Government Board 1871–4. Commonly repeated that he threw over prospects of advancement in espousal of a cause (repeal of Contagious Diseases Act) 'too nasty to be touched'; but in 1880 indignant at offer of his old job without the Cabinet seat formerly

PORTRAIT GALLERY

his. Wrote of his 'growing feeling of resentment & distaste' towards Gladstone.

STEAD, W. T. (35). Editor of *Pall Mall Gazette* in succession to Morley, 1883. Did not like Chamberlain, distrusted Dilke.

STOREY, Samuel (44). Thrice Mayor of Sunderland, where he was returned as Radical, 1881. Proprietor with Carnegie (motto, 'Money no object as compared with *power*') of the *Echo*. Mundella thought him 'hand in glove with Cowen'; certainly not with Chamberlain.

TREVELYAN, G. O. (46). Son of Sir Charles Trevelyan, and nephew of Macaulay. Married eldest daughter of R. N. Philips, MP for Bury. Ed. Harrow (head of school) and Trinity, Cambridge; failed to obtain Fellowship. Liberal MP for Tynemouth 1865–8, Hawick Burghs from 1868. Secretary to Admiralty 1880–2, Chief Secretary for Ireland 1882–4 (without Cabinet seat, which he asked for), Chancellor of Duchy of Lancaster 1884–5 (in Cabinet). Anxious to please. Wrote from Phoenix Park, 'They go on year after year making official paper which *just* does not fit into the envelopes. It is exactly like everything else here.'

WEMYSS, Tenth Earl of (66). Of colourful ancestry. Ed. Edinburgh Academy, Eton and Christ Church. Conservative/Palmerstonian MP for East Gloucestershire 1841–6, Haddingtonshire 1847–83. *D.N.B.* describes him, in another context, as in 'persistent opposition to... each administration in its turn'. Married his second wife at age of 82, and 4 years later exhibited at the Royal Academy what was hailed in *The Times* as a 'remarkably good' statue of Venus.

WHITBREAD, Samuel (53). Ed. Rugby and Trinity, Cambridge (no degree). Married daughter of Earl of Chichester. Whig-inclined MP for Bedford from 1852. Refused Board of Trade and Cabinet seat, 1880: 'one of the most conspicuous and respected figures in the House'. Northbrook's confidant.

WILMOT, Sir J. E. Eardley (74). Ed. Rugby, Winchester and Balliol (Prizeman). Recorder of Warwick, and County Court judge. Conservative MP for South Warwickshire since 1874: thus first standing for Parliament at 64. Protectionist.

WINN, Rowland (64). Son of Charles Winn of Nostell Priory. Married niece of 5th Earl of Lanesborough. Ed. privately and Trinity, Cambridge (no degree). Opposition Chief Whip from 1880.

WOLFF, Sir Henry Drummond (54). Son of clergyman (mother a daughter of 2nd Earl of Oxford). Ed. Rugby, leaving at 16. Entered Foreign Office 1852; private secretary to Bulwer Lytton. Conservative MP for Christchurch 1874–80, Portsmouth from 1880. Had accompanied Goschen to Egypt in 1876, inquiring into finances on behalf of bondholders.

BIBLIOGRAPHY

THIS BOOK rests upon the collections of private correspondence detailed below. As will be apparent from the textual notes, some have proved indispensable throughout and most were critical at one juncture or another. Those archives which were found to contain nothing of importance for the period are not included. For anyone sufficiently interested, a full list of printed sources is to be found in my Ph.D. thesis, deposited in the Anderson Room of the University Library, Cambridge.

(a) PRIVATE PAPERS

Ashbourne Mss.: papers of Edward Gibson, in the possession of Lord Ashbourne, Liphook, Hampshire.

Austin Mss.: papers of Alfred Austin, in the Library of the National Liberal Club, London.

Avebury Mss.: papers of Sir John Lubbock, in the British Museum.

Balfour Mss.: papers of A. J. Balfour, in the British Museum.

Bath Mss.: letters of the Fourth Marquess of Bath to his Son, Lord Weymouth, at Longleat, Wiltshire, by permission of the Marquess of Bath.

Belvoir Mss.: papers of Lord John Manners, at Belvoir Castle, Leicestershire, by permission of the Duke of Rutland.

Brabourne Mss.: papers of the First Lord Brabourne, in the Kent County Record Office, Maidstone.

Broadhurst Mss.: papers of Henry Broadhurst, in the British Library of Political and Economic Science, London.

Bruce Mss.: papers of the Hon Robert Preston Bruce, in the possession of Lord Bruce (now Earl of Elgin), at Broomhall, Dunfermline.

Bryce Mss.: papers of James Bryce, in the Bodleian Library, Oxford.

Cairns Mss.: papers of the First Earl Cairns, in the Public Record Office, London, by permission of Rear-Admiral the Earl Cairns.

Carlingford Mss.: papers of the First Lord Carlingford, in the Somerset County Record Office, Taunton.

Chamberlain Mss.: papers of Joseph Chamberlain, in the Library of Birmingham University.

Chilston Mss.: papers of Aretas Akers-Douglas, in the Kent County Record Office, Maidstone.

BIBLIOGRAPHY

Churchill Mss.: papers of Lord Randolph Churchill, when in the possession of the late Randolph Churchill, at Stour, East Bergholt, Suffolk; now in the Library of Churchill College, Cambridge.

Courtney Mss.: papers of Leonard Courtney, in the British Library of Political and Economic Science, London.

Cowen Mss.: papers of Joseph Cowen, in the City Libraries, Newcastle-upon-Tyne.

Cranbrook Mss.: papers of the First Earl of Cranbrook, in the Ipswich and East Suffolk Record Office.

Cross Mss.: papers of Sir Richard Cross, in the British Museum.

Dalrymple Diary: transcript made by Mr A. B. Cooke of the diary for 1885 of Charles Dalrymple.

Daunt Mss.: papers of W. J. O'Neill Daunt, in the National Library of Ireland.

Derby Mss.: papers of the Fifteenth Earl of Derby, at Knowsley Hall, Prescot, Lancashire, by permission of the Earl of Derby.

Devonshire Mss.: papers of the Marquess of Hartington, at Chatsworth, Bakewell, Derbyshire, by permission of the Duke of Devonshire.

Dilke Mss.: papers of Sir Charles Dilke, in the British Museum.

Duffy Mss.: papers of Sir Charles Gavan Duffy, in the National Library of Ireland.

Elliot Mss.: papers of the Hon Arthur Elliot, in the National Library of Scotland.

Elliot Diaries: diaries of the Hon Arthur Elliot, in the possession of Mrs Hubert Elliot, Dalliotfield, Muthill, Perthshire.

Gladstone Mss.: papers of W. E. Gladstone, in the British Museum.

Viscount Gladstone Mss.: papers of Herbert Gladstone, in the British Museum.

Goodwood Mss.: papers of the Sixth Duke of Richmond, in the West Sussex County Record Office, Chichester, by permission of the Duke of Richmond and Gordon.

Granville Mss.: papers of the Second Earl Granville, in the Public Record Office, London.

Grey Mss.: papers of Albert Grey, in the Department of Palaeography and Diplomatic, University of Durham.

Hambleden Mss.: papers of W. H. Smith, in the possession of W. H. Smith & Son Ltd, Strand House, Portugal Street, London.

Hamilton Mss.: papers of Edward Hamilton, in the British Museum.

Harcourt Mss.: papers of Sir William Harcourt, and of Lewis Harcourt, in the possession of Viscount Harcourt, Stanton Harcourt, Oxford.

Harrington Mss.: papers of Timothy Harrington, in the National Library of Ireland.

Harrison Mss.: papers of Frederic Harrison, in the British Library of Political and Economic Science, London.

Harrowby Mss.: papers of the Third Earl of Harrowby, in the possession of the Earl of Harrowby, Sandon Hall, Stafford.

Hickleton Mss.: papers of the First Viscount Halifax, deposited in the City Library, York, by permission of the Earl of Halifax.

Iddesleigh Mss.: papers of Sir Stafford Northcote, in the British Museum.

James of Hereford Mss.: papers of Sir Henry James, in the offices of Gwynne James & Ealand, St Peter Street, Hereford, by permission of Philip Gwynne James Esq.

Johnston Mss.: diaries of William Johnston, in the Public Record Office of Northern Ireland.

Lalor Mss.: papers of Richard Lalor, in the National Library of Ireland.

Maxse Mss.: papers of F. A. Maxse, in the West Sussex County Record Office, Chichester.

Milner Mss.: papers of Alfred Milner, in the Bodleian Library, Oxford, by permission of Dr G. V. Bennett, Librarian of New College.

Minto Mss.: papers of the Third Earl of Minto, and of Gilbert Elliot, Viscount Melgund, in the National Library of Scotland.

Monk Bretton Mss.: papers of J. G. Dodson, First Lord Monk Bretton, in the Bodleian Library, Oxford.

Miskelly Mss.: papers of John Miskelly, in the Public Record Office of Northern Ireland.

Montgomery Mss.: papers of H. de F. Montgomery, in the Public Record Office of Northern Ireland.

Mundella–Leader Mss.: letters of A. J. Mundella to J. D. Leader, in the Library of Sheffield University.

Nostell Mss.: papers of Rowland Winn, at Nostell Priory, Wragby, Yorkshire, by permission of Lord St Oswald.

Passfield Mss.: typescript copy of the diary of Beatrice Webb, in the British Library of Political and Economic Science, London.

Pim Mss.: papers of Jonathan Pim and W. H. Pim, in the National Library of Ireland.

Ponsonby Mss.: papers of Sir Henry Ponsonby, in the British Museum.

Ramsden Mss.: papers of Sir John Ramsden, in the City Archives, Sheepscar Library, Leeds.

Rathbone Mss.: papers of William Rathbone, in the University Library, Liverpool.

Ripon Mss.: papers of the First Marquess of Ripon, in the British Museum.

Rosebery Mss.: papers of the Fifth Earl of Rosebery, in the National Library of Scotland.

St. Aldwyn Mss.: papers of Sir Michael Hicks Beach, in the possession of Earl St. Aldwyn, Williamstrip Park, Coln St. Aldwyns, Cirencester.

Salisbury Mss.: papers of the Third Marquess of Salisbury, in the Library of Christ Church, Oxford, by permission of the Marquess of Salisbury.

Selborne Mss.: papers of the First Earl of Selborne, in the Library of Lambeth Palace, London.

Smyth Mss.: papers of P. J. Smyth, in the National Library of Ireland.

BIBLIOGRAPHY

Spencer Mss.: papers of the Fifth Earl Spencer, in the possession of Earl Spencer, Althrop, Northampton.

Stanmore Mss.: papers of Sir Arthur Hamilton-Gordon, in the British Museum.

Stephen Mss.: papers of Sir James Fitzjames Stephen, in the University Library, Cambridge.

Wemyss Mss.: papers of the Tenth Earl of Wemyss; part thereof, covering the years 1881–3, deposited for microfilming in the Scottish Record Office.

Whitbread Mss.: papers of Samuel Whitbread, in the possession of Samuel Whitbread Esq, Southill Park, Biggleswade, Bedfordshire.

(b) CABINET PAPERS

Various Memoranda etc., some in manuscript, some printed, for the use of the Cabinet, seen on microfilm in the Seeley Library, Cambridge.

Gladstone's reports to the Queen of meetings of the Cabinet, in the Public Record Office, London.

(c) SOCIETY RECORDS, MINUTES, ETC.

Proportional Representation Society Mss.: correspondence and papers, in the offices of the Electoral Reform Society, 3 Whitehall Court, Westminster, by permission of Miss Enid Lakeman.

St James Branch, Dublin, of the Irish National League, Minute Book: in the National Library of Ireland.

Scottish Liberal Association Minute Book: in the University Library, Edinburgh, by permission of W. Mackenzie Esq, Administrative Secretary of the Scottish Liberal Party.

(d) RECORDS OF THE PARLIAMENTARY BOUNDARY COMMISSIONERS, 1884–5

Irish Boundary Commission Mss.: instructions to the Commissioners, minutes of proceedings, and general correspondence: in the Public Record Office of Ireland.

(No such records have survived for England, Wales and Scotland.)

INDEX

267

INDEX

Cambridge Studies in the History & Theory of Politics

TEXTS

LIBERTY, EQUALITY, FRATERNITY, *by James Fitzjames Stephen*. Edited, with an introduction and notes, by *R. J. White*

VLADIMIR AKIMOV ON THE DILEMMAS OF RUSSIAN MARXISM 1895–1903. An English edition of 'A Short History of the Social Democratic Movement in Russia' and 'The Second Congress of the Russian Social Democratic Labour Party', with an introduction and notes by *Jonathan Frankel*

TWO ENGLISH REPUBLICAN TRACTS, PLATO REDIVIVUS or, A DIALOGUE CONCERNING GOVERNMENT (*c*. 1681), *by Henry Neville* and AN ESSAY UPON THE CONSTITUTION OF THE ROMAN GOVERNMENT (*c*. 1699), *by Walter Moyle*. Edited by *Caroline Robbins*

J. G. HERDER ON SOCIAL AND POLITICAL CULTURE, translated, edited and with an introduction by *F. M. Barnard*

THE LIMITS OF STATE ACTION, *by Wilhelm von Humboldt*. Edited, with an introduction and notes, by *J. W. Burrow*

KANT'S POLITICAL WRITINGS, edited with an introduction and notes by *Hans Reiss*; translated by *H. B. Nisbet*

MARX'S CRITIQUE OF HEGEL'S 'PHILOSOPHY OF RIGHT', edited with an introduction and notes by *Joseph O'Malley*; translated by *Annette Jolin* and *Joseph O'Malley*

STUDIES

1867: DISRAELI, GLADSTONE AND REVOLUTION. THE PASSING OF THE SECOND REFORM BILL, *by Maurice Cowling*

THE CONSCIENCE OF THE STATE IN NORTH AMERICA, *by E. R. Norman*

THE SOCIAL AND POLITICAL THOUGHT OF KARL MARX, *by Shlomo Avineri*

MEN AND CITIZENS: ROUSSEAU'S SOCIAL THOUGHT, *by Judith Shklar*

IDEALISM, POLITICS AND HISTORY: SOURCES OF HEGELIAN THOUGHT, *by George Armstrong Kelly*

THE IMPACT OF LABOUR 1920–1924. THE BEGINNING OF MODERN BRITISH POLITICS, *by Maurice Cowling*

t